The geographical impact of migration

Edited by
Paul White and **Robert Woods**
Lecturers in Geography at the University of Sheffield

Longman
London and New York

For Elizabeth, Katherine, Alison and Rachel

Longman Group Limited London

*Associated companies, branches and representatives
throughout the world*

*Published in the United States of America
by Longman Inc., New York*

© Longman Group Limited 1980

First published 1980

British Library Cataloguing in Publication Data

The geographical impact of migration.
  ·1. Emigration and immigration – Social aspects
  I. White, Paul II. Woods, Robert
   301.32   JV6121   79-40463

ISBN 0-582-48941-5
ISBN 0-582-48942-3 Pbk

Printed in Great Britain by Richard Clay (the Chaucer Press), Ltd
Bungay, Suffolk

Contents

List of figures

List of contributors

Morag Bell is a Lecturer in Geography at the University of Loughborough. She has had considerable fieldwork experience in East Africa.

Paul Buksmann is a Visiting Professor at the National University of Brazil, Rio de Janeiro. He has carried out research in both Ecuador and Bolivia on population and agrarian systems.

Peter Cromar was formerly a Junior Research Fellow in Geography at the University of Sheffield. His main research interest is in the field of nineteenth-century British labour history on which he has contributed to *Economic Geography*.

David Grigg is Reader in Geography at the University of Sheffield. He is the author of *The Agricultural Systems of the World* and *Population Growth and Agrarian Change*.

Philip Ogden is a Lecturer in Geography at Queen Mary College, University of London. He is the author of articles on the population geography of France in both English and French journals.

Paul White is a Lecturer in Geography at the University of Sheffield. He has carried out research in Switzerland, Italy and France on rural social geography.

Robert Woods is a Lecturer in Geography at the University of Sheffield. He is the author of *Population Analysis in Geography* (Longman, 1979) and has contributed articles on population to several major journals.

Preface

By tradition geographers have made their most important contributions to the study of population in the analysis of, firstly, the relationship between man and the environment in which he lives and, secondly, the changing spatial pattern of population distribution. This particular volume seeks to divert the emphasis of geographical enquiry towards the examination of how particular changes in population distribution affect the organization of human society. It deals specifically with the economic, social, political and demographic impacts of migration on origin and destination areas; and with the attitudinal and behavioural influences that mobility can have on the migrants themselves. That is it seeks to establish answers to the following questions: (*a*) Who migrates and why? (*b*) What characteristics do migration streams display? (*c*) Chiefly, what are the geographical impacts of migration?

The first three chapters provide a general discussion of points arising from these questions. For example, the concept of human migration must be defined carefully and its various manifestations classified before its impact can be assessed. The behavioural perspective is given a central place in these chapters by the emphasis placed on the value of studying the links between individuals' perceptions, attitudes and patterns of behaviour in the context of the decision to migrate and the choice of destination. These chapters also give a framework for the evaluation of the impact of migration.

The second part of the book contains seven case-study chapters, together with a short introduction. These studies deal with specific ways in which migration has affected the organization of human activity. They illustrate the concepts and models discussed in Chapters 1 to 3, but they nonetheless also stand in their own right as contributions to the study of migration.

The geographical impact of migration has been written with three objectives in mind. Firstly, it aims to provide illustrations of the theoretical and substantive contributions that geographers can make to the understanding of how human society is organized by analysing the variety of social changes that are the outcome of the workings of but one dynamic phenomenon, in this case migration. In other words, given a human organization with a particular spatial manifestation then answers to the question, 'what are the effects of migration occurring?', will not only be revealing about migration, but will also shed light on the organization of that society. The second objective is to provide the reader with an extended introduction to the view that migration is a behavioural process and not merely an automatic consequence of spatial economic inequalities. The third objective is rather more basic – it is hoped that readers will gain some impressions of the methods of analysis and the sources available to students of migration and that they will, as a result, be stimulated to make their own researches.

Finally, the editors would like to express their thanks to the contributors – Morag Bell, Paul Buksmann, Peter Cromar, David Grigg and Philip Ogden – for their good-natured support. Thanks must also go to those who have laboured with manuscript or illustrations – Carole Elliss, Anita Fletcher, Wendy Mann, Elizabeth White, Stephen Frampton and Sheila Ottewell; and to colleagues and students at Sheffield for their valuable criticisms and guarded encouragement.

Paul White and Robert Woods
January 1979

Acknowledgements

We are grateful to the following for permission to reproduce copyright material: Editions Albin Michel for an extract translated by P. E. Ogden from *La Révolution Agricole* by Michel Angé-Laribé from *L'Evolution de L'Humanité* series; Institute of Geography, University of Clermont-Ferrand for an extract translated by P. E. Ogden p. 184 from *La Vie Rurale en Vivarais* by P. Bozon; Librairie Armand Colin for an extract translated by P. E. Ogden p. 96 from *Géographie Electorable de l'Ardèche* by Siegfried; Presses Universitaires de France for a Fig. from *La Mesure de la Mobilité* by Tugault and a Fig. from *L'Exode Rural* by Merlin; Taylor and Francis Ltd and the author, Dr A. J. Boyce for Fig. 4 p. 7 of a paper 'Population Structure and Movement Patterns' in *Biological Aspects of Demography* 1971 by Boyce *et al.*

Chapter 1

The foundations of migration study

P. E. White and R. I. Woods

Introduction

The study of population migration has been a rapidly developing branch of several academic disciplines. Economists, sociologists, historians, psychologists, demographers and geographers all find the residential movements of the human population to be of importance to their respective subjects, and for this reason the study of migration is both a multi-disciplinary and also, in its widest sense, an inter-disciplinary field. It is difficult to overestimate the importance of migration in creating and sustaining a wide range of patterns of human activity and the awareness of this fact is arguably increasing.

From whatever academic discipline population migration is examined there is basically only a limited range of questions to be asked concerning any particular migration phenomenon.
1. Why does migration occur?
2. Who migrates?
3. What are the patterns of origins and destinations and of the flows between them?
4. What are the effects of migration on the areas, communities or societies that the migrants come from?
5. What are the effects of migration on the areas, communities or societies of destination?

The economist may be particularly concerned with the first, fourth and fifth of these questions since the migration of labour is an important form of resource redistribution. The sociologist may concentrate on questions four and five since these may be interpreted to deal with the inter-relationships between the migrant and his own or other social groups. These questions are similarly important to the demographer, who must consider the role of the migrant in the general evolution of populations.

To the geographer, traditionally, the third question has been the most important since it is the one that is most concerned with spatial flows, with interaction between different places, and with areal differentiation between places of origin and destination. Yet the residential movements of the human population have spatial manifestations other than through the transitory nature of flows of migrants. Redistribution of population through migration can have profound effects on the whole spatial patterning of human activity, the repercussions of which may be felt long after the migration events themselves have taken place. A simple world map of population distribution is a reflection of the past migrations of mankind as well as of the patterns of natural population growth both past and present. Without massive migration from Europe the population density and distribution maps of North America or Australasia would certainly be vastly different today. And at a more detailed scale of analysis migration has played a vital role in the process of urbanization throughout the world and of rural depopulation in many industrially developed nations.

But migration is important not just because of the redistribution of population *per se*. Each migrant has certain attributes – for example age, sex, family status, occupation, intelligence, educational attainment, social and cultural attitudes, language and religious affiliation. Migration brings about much more than simple population redistribution; it also leads to a redistribution of such attributes, or of social, occupational or religious groups, and to a restructuring of the spatial patterns of a multiplicity of demographic variables. Such structural changes can be termed 'geographical impacts of migration'; they are those structural changes in the distribution and organization of human activities which are brought about by population migration.

It should be clear that the types of structural changes brought about by migration are very largely dependent upon the attributes of the migrants themselves, while the scale of the structural changes is, at least in part, dependent upon the scale or volume of migration. So the geographer, in seeking to account for the effects of migration, must be concerned with the answer to the second question posed above, that of 'who migrates?'.

It is important, however, to realize that the attributes of the migrants are not all fixed and immutable. Although sex is unchangeable, and what change there is in age follows a specific course, several of the other migrant attributes change because a person has undertaken a migratory move. Migration may lead to a change in an individual's occupation, or to a change in family status, for example where migration occurs at the time of marriage. The introduction of the migrant into a new social and cultural setting may lead to the alteration of certain of the migrant's attitudes towards social and cultural behaviour. The sheer fact of having made a migratory move can produce in the migrant a different attitude to future possibilities of migration. Analysis of these impacts of migration on the migrant is often fraught with difficulties, in particular in the allocation of causality between migration and attribute change. For example, it may be that a migratory move brings about a change in the occupation of the migrant, but it is equally possible that the migration occurred as a result of the offer of a new job in a distant place. Even with attitudinal change there can be complications, apart from the difficulties involved in the successful measurement of attitudes in the first place. The phenomenon has been described (for example by Galtung, 1971, p. 194, for Western Sicily) whereby the migrants undergo attitudinal change prior to migration and are socially lost to their communities of origin before actual migration occurs.

These considerations therefore dictate that account must be taken, in any detailed investigation of migration and its effects, of why migration occurs in the first place. What is it that prompts an individual to move? What aspirations do migrants have? Why do some people move whilst others stay? The answers to these questions help to provide the solution to the second of the general questions – 'who migrates?'. And from the answers to that question can flow the investigation of the fourth and fifth questions concerning the impacts of migration on sending and receiving areas.

This volume is largely concerned with the answers to questions four and five although, as Chapter 3 will demonstrate, the impacts of migration are wider than just the effects on places of migrant origin and destination. To the geographer one of the most important migration impacts occurs in the creation of migration flows with particular spatial patterns – the third of the general questions posed at the start of this chapter. This topic is discussed in Chapter 2.

The remainder of the present chapter is devoted to the discussion of why migration occurs and of who migrates. But before embarking upon such considerations it is necessary to define the term 'migration' and to outline the sources of information available for migration analysis. Chapter 1 concludes with a discussion of a variety of approaches to the classification of migration and of migrants.

Definitions and sources

In the form of a simple concept the definition of migration is straightforward: in operational terms any workable definition is likely to be both complex and only partial. The reason for the difference between the conceptual and the operational definitions lies in the nature of the sources available for the study of any migration phenomenon.

The dictionary definition of the verb 'to migrate' is to 'move from one place (country, town, house) to another'. The geographer's simple definition of migration is not very different from this general view: a migration is a change in the place of residence. Such a change of residence necessitates movement, although at a scale varying from a transfer between dwellings both in the same street to, at the other spatial extreme, inter-continental movements. Migrations, or changes of residence, form only a small part of all the movements across the surface of the globe undertaken by mankind, and a distinction is often made between migration (involving change of residence) and 'mobility' or 'circulation'. These terms encompass all movements, such as those for the purposes of journey-to-work, of recreation and tourism or of shopping excursions. Zelinsky (1971) has examined the general field of mobility and pointed out the difficulty of providing an overall measure of all such movements.

Nevertheless, the concept of mobility and its sub-set, migration, is of use in clarifying what is implied by a residential movement. The patterns of mobility or circulation followed by any particular individual must centre on his place of residence which provides a permanent reference point and base. Hägerstrand (1957, pp. 27–8), in his major study of Swedish migration fields, has defined migration as the change in the centre of gravity of an individual's mobility pattern. The destinations of the mobility flows need not, themselves, change as a result of the change in their centre of gravity: for example, in a local intra-urban move (between C and D in Fig. 1.1A) the termini of journey-to-work, recreational and shopping movements may remain the same, while in an inter-urban move (between two towns X and Y in Fig. 1.1B) they are likely to change. Roseman (1971) calls these two types of migration 'partial displacement' and 'total displacement' respectively.

These definitional suggestions are of great utility, yet there may be problematic cases where the application of such concepts is impossible. Nomads and vagrants are without a fixed residential base and are, in a sense, permanently migrating: as such they are often dealt with separately in distinction from

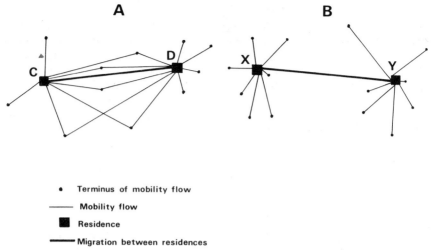

Fig. 1.1   Mobility and migration of an individual.

'normal' migrants. A second problem group is those owning two homes since they have two centres of gravity. An allied problem occurs with tourism since the holidaymaker takes up 'residence' in a resort and 'circulates' or tours from that base. The tourist is usually excluded from consideration as a migrant on the grounds that he retains his permanent residence elsewhere: as with nomadism, tourism can be dealt with as a separate sub-set of migration.

To overcome the problems of such phenomena as business journeys, holiday movements or pilgrimages the simple definition of migration is often extended to the form of 'residential changes of a permanent or semi-permanent nature' to eliminate transitory and immediately reversed flows. This definition makes the very important addition of a temporal dimension which becomes of particular importance in the consideration of data sources on migration. The introduction of the words 'permanent or semi-permanent nature', whilst drawing attention to the need to omit very short time-interval relocations from consideration, is in practice very difficult to operate. Consider two phenomena: the movement of students from parental home to university and back three or four times per year in each direction: and the seasonal flows of labour across international frontiers, such as for agricultural harvesting activities. These flows result in population redistribution which, although temporary, can be an essential structural element in the human activity of the affected areas; and although the migrants stay in their destinations for only a short time they are replaced by more of the same kind so that the phenomenon of migration is a permanent one. University students and labour migrants are both likely to have a permanent 'residence' to return to so that in a sense they differ from tourists only in the length of their stay outside that permanent 'residence'. What seems at first to be a simple conceptual definition of migration becomes, when it is applied in practice, either a matter of arbitrary distinctions, or of the total acceptance of all residential changes as migrations. Neither of these definitional procedures is entirely satisfactory.

In operating a definition of migration the concepts of time and of geographical scale become of vital significance. In general terms the definition of migration that is operated for the purposes of data collection is that migration is 'any residential movement which occurs between administrative units over a given period of time'. The scale of administrative unit used and the time period differ between different studies and according to the various sets of data utilized.

Migration data are basically of three kinds: continuous data, survey data and that derived from population censuses. The term 'continuous data' can be applied to those records where all residential moves are recorded. Certain European countries require their inhabitants to register an address with the police or other authority and to notify all changes of residence: The Netherlands and Switzerland both operate this system, while Italy had similar provisions in the inter-war period. Continuous data often exist for other purposes; for example health records or school records may provide data on all residential moves, although often such data sets are not readily available for consultation. Where continuous records are kept, in whatever form, the definition of migration used for them is the simple one of any change of residence. But where summary data from continuous registers are published they are often based on a different definition. For example, each year Switzerland publishes summary tables of migration into and out of each *gemeinde* or parish. Only migrations between the parish and the rest of the world are dealt with, moves within a parish being ignored, and the time-scale of a calendar year is imposed on the data, so that both administrative unit and time become important in the data available.

Survey data on migration are more commonly available than continuous data. The importance of survey data is that such sources often deal in great detail with the characteristics of migrations and migrants, usually in terms of individuals as opposed to groups. Questionnaire-based surveys are perhaps the only means by which the questions of the links between attitudes and behaviour in the migration process can be fully analysed. For example, the study reported by Johnson *et al.* (1974) on the association between labour migration and housing in England and Wales employed a questionnaire survey to derive the necessary information. Questionnaire surveys are important both when information is needed in addition to that provided by other sources and when nothing at all is known about migration flows or who migrates (see Ch. 6 and 7 for examples of attempts to overcome this particular problem in the African and Latin American contexts respectively). Other kinds of surveys can also provide valuable data on migration; for instance 'Who's Who' listings in local yearbooks have been used to show the pattern of élite migration (see Ch. 10).

Although continuous data and survey data are important sources of information most quantitative data on migration is derived from population censuses (see, for example, Lawton, 1978). Two sorts of migration data are commonly available in censuses: birthplace migration data and period migration data. In both cases the administrative unit framework of the society under consideration is of great importance, for in the vast majority of national censuses migration within an administrative area is not dealt with under either of these two headings.

Birthplace migration data usually consist of tables showing the present residence of the members of a population against their places of birth. The time-scale thus introduced is a variable one since the period within which migration may have occurred lengthens with the age of the individual concerned. The data say nothing about the number of residential moves that may have occurred between birthplace and present residence, nor is any information given about the length of stay at the origin, destination or places *en route*. Consequently birthplace migration data are very imperfect sources of migration information.

Nevertheless it was the examination of such data from the census of England and Wales that led to Ravenstein's (1885; 1889) work on the 'laws of migration' that has formed a cornerstone of geographical thought on migration ever since (Grigg, 1977; see also Ch. 2).

More useful are period migration data whereby census questions are asked on the respondent's place of residence at some previous date – usually one, five or ten years earlier – or at the time of the previous census. The last-mentioned is the case in France where recent censuses have been held at irregular intervals. Once again the administrative unit framework imposed upon the preparation of the data is important, but here, unlike the case with birthplace migration data, the time-period is a fixed one. Nevertheless, there are still the disadvantages of the lack of information on the total number of moves made between censuses, or on the extent of out-and-back movements by individuals who appear in the same administrative area at succeeding censuses but have lived elsewhere in the intermediate period.

In certain censuses, the British and Italian are examples, it is normal to distinguish between the *de facto* and the *de jure* populations of each area by including in the census forms questions on a respondent's usual place of residence. In Britain such information is only available at local authority area scale, while in Italy a more rigorous definition is used and the results are published for each *comune* or parish. In other countries presence in a particular place on census day means the counting of such individuals as resident. Under this latter convention the distinction between semi-permanent and temporary movements is abandoned by the rigid imposition of the 'present-on-census-day' rule. That this creates its own problems can be seen in the complications that arise over, for example, military personnel (Jackson, V. J., 1968).

The quality and coverage of national population censuses varies considerably, but most countries attempt to collect information on how many people migrate, whence and to where, in a specified period of time and within a defined framework of administrative areas. Furthermore, it is now commonplace in the censuses of the statistically advanced nations to elicit information on certain characteristics of the migrants. In general, however, complete disaggregations of the migrants according to their demographic, social and economic attributes are rare or only available at unsuitable spatial scales. Census information provides figures on gross and net flows, but often recourse must be made to survey methods to obtain a detailed picture of the migrant participants.

Migration between two places is always a two-way process, and in the study of migration impact information on these gross flows is desirable. Where such data are unobtainable information on net flows may be of some use. If data on the population totals at two different time periods (p^t and p^{t+n}) are available, and if the numbers of birth ($B^{t,t+n}$) and deaths ($D^{t,t+n}$) between t and t+n are also known, then net migration ($NM^{t,t+n}$) can be calculated from the formula for the 'basic demographic equation':

$$NM^{t,t+n} = p^{t+n} - p^t - B^{t,t+n} + D^{t,t+n}$$ 1.1)

Where p^t and p^{t+n} are available disaggregated by sex and age, and where the deaths are similarly known for this disaggregation, net migration can be calculated for smaller demographic groups (Woods, 1979) but even at this level such data are vastly inferior to information on gross flows in the analysis of migration impact.

The questions of migration definitions and migration data sources are inextricably tied up, to the extent that too often the type of data available dictates the kind of migration problems that can be examined. The simple definition of migration as all changes of residence is by no means easy to operate, and although that definition is at the root of virtually all work on migration individual data sets differ from each other in the two characteristics of the time-scale over which migration may occur and the spatial or administrative scale over which it must occur to be officially recorded.

Why does migration occur?

Migration occurs because migrants believe that they will be more satisfied in their needs and desires in the place that they move to than in the place from which they come. An important emphasis must be placed on the word 'believe'. Migration occurs as a result of decisions made by individuals in the light of what they perceive the objective world to be like: it does not matter if the migrant holds an erroneous view – it is that erroneous view that is acted upon rather than the objective real-world situation. Thus there may be cases where migration occurs despite the lack of an objective reason for it, and other cases where an objective appraisal of the world, were it possible, might suggest that migration should occur where it is, in fact, absent. For this reason normative explanations of migration, for example as a response to economic wage-rate fluctuations, are only partial explanations in that they neglect consideration of the perceptions prevalent among the potential migrants, although attempts have recently been made to incorporate the subjective appraisals of migrants in cost-benefit models of migration flows (Bogue, 1977).

Important within the analysis of why migration occurs is the perception of spatial differentiation of opportunities – the idea that different geographical locations offer different levels of potential well-being to various sections of the human population. It is these perceived differences between places that are important rather than any simple 'push' or 'pull' mechanism. On an isotropic plain the amount of migration would arguably be relatively small, but in a spatially differentiated economy and society migration is likely to be of greater volume and significance, as long as the population perceives differentiation to be present. Historically the volume of migration has increased as technological development has occurred. In an agrarian society the spatial differentiation of opportunities may extend only to the difference between villages and market centres. As industrialization and urbanization take place a greater variety of spatial differences become manifest and increase in intensity, the process being accentuated, as in all unplanned economic development, where investment in, and labour demand for, the growing industries is unevenly spread in space. Ravenstein (1885) recognized the importance of economic development in stimulating migration, and this realization is a basis of Zelinsky's (1971) work on changes in mobility and migration over time.

If migration occurs as a result of the perception by individuals of differences between places in the opportunities offered for the fulfilling of wants and needs, then in more detailed explanations of why migration occurs consideration must be given to the processes of decision-making whereby individuals decide to migrate and decide where to move to. This field of study owes much to behavioural psychology, and to the work of Julian Wolpert who introduced certain behavioural concepts to a wider geographical audience (1965; 1966).

Common to most behavioural work on migration is the notion of 'place utility' which can be defined as an individual's degree of satisfaction or dissatisfaction with a place (Wolpert, 1965). Were this to be measurable it would be found that the place utility for any specific locality would differ markedly between different individuals for two reasons. Firstly, different individuals would consider different attributes of a place in their scale of satisfaction or dissatisfaction. Secondly, different individuals evaluate the objective world in varying ways as a result of the differential availability of more or less biased information about places. An individual's place utility for the place he lives in has a strong element of certainty about it, for the individual has actually experienced at first-hand the advantages and disadvantages of life in that place. For other places the individual's evaluation can only be of anticipated utility or disutility, based on whatever information he has available to him. Such information may take the form of recollections of personal visits; letters from past migrants; conversations with friends who have visited other places; or books, newspapers and broadcasts. This 'information flow' is vitally important in enabling the potential migrant to develop a place utility idea for a range of competing places, and it is divergences between the information flow and objective reality that will in large measure provide the differences between the individual's perception of that reality and the actual facts of other places. Information flow must generally make up for the lack of past residential experience.

It is possible to use the notion of place utility to provide a model of why an individual may migrate. Figure 1.2 shows the framework of part of a matrix which illustrates for one individual the information he has about various places organised according to the attributes of those places that are important to him. The attributes, or variables, V_1 to V_m, constitute the rows of the matrix, while the places for which information is available, P_1 to P_n, constitute the columns. Not all variables are likely to have equal importance so provision is made for each to have a different maximum score. These maximum scores are used to weight the importance of the m variables. Positive or negative figures can be inserted in the

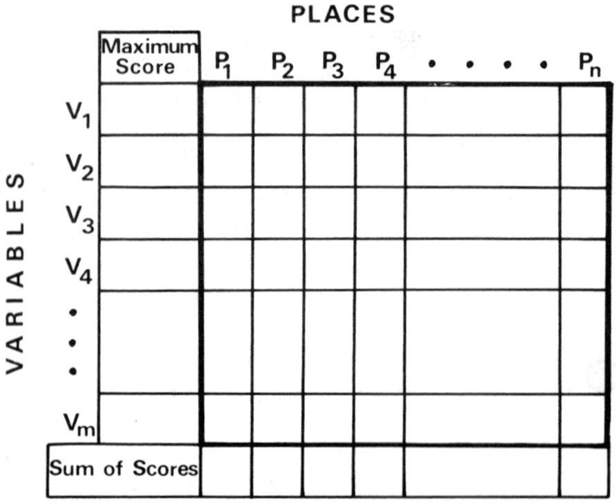

Fig. 1.2   An individual's place utility matrix.

individual cells of the matrix according to the degree of satisfaction or dissatisfaction that the individual feels would be his for each variable at each place considered, and these scores can be summed to give a final place utility figure at the foot of each column.

One further point needs to be made about the variables: their exact delineation will vary according to the geographical scale being considered. If an individual is weighing up his present residence against alternative locations within the same city or neighbourhood the variables will differ from those considered if the evaluation is between present residence and distant alternatives. In the first case, that of 'partial displacement' (see Fig. 1.1A), the actual residence and its immediate environs count almost exclusively – the wider context remains unchanged and employment, shops, schools or social activity considerations remain the same. In the second case, 'total displacement' (Fig. 1.1B), all these contextual variables must be taken into account and may be more important than those of house type or immediate neighbourhood. One variable that is included for all places except the potential migrant's present residence is that of the cost of moving to alternative new locations. Once again the individual's perception is more influential on his migration decision than is objective reality. The cost of moving, however, is a once and for all feature of migration while the other place variables have a long-term relevance: the importance, or weighting, of movement cost is thus likely to vary according to the length of time over which the migrant is prepared to allow positive advantages in his potential destinations to discount that cost (Speare, 1971).

In the use of the concept of the place utility matrix to explain why migration occurs it is possible to produce two specific answers. Migration occurs either because of a change in the delineation of the variables, or because of a change in the information about places. It is likely that the first of these is more important.

It has already been pointed out that the full list of variables considered is likely to differ from person to person, and that different individuals are also likely to put different weights on similar variables. Through a person's life the variables under consideration are likely to alter such that new variables are occasionally added, old variables are discarded and others change their importance. Changes in the delineation of variables are particularly likely to be associated with stages in an individual's 'life-cycle', an important concept in migration analysis (Rossi, 1955; Robson, 1973, p. 229). The number of life-cycle stages recognized varies from author to author, but Speare's (1970) use of six stages is fairly typical.

1. Young unmarried, up to 45 years of age.
2. Year of marriage. This is not a 'stage' in the normal sense but plays a vitally important role in migration since marriage normally involves a change of residence for at least one of the two involved and often for both when a new household is set up.
3. Young married, with children of below school age.
4. Married with school-age children (sometimes known as the child-rearing stage).
5. Older married without dependent children. A separate 'child-launching' stage is sometimes identified.
6. Older unmarried plus widows, widowers and the older divorced or separated.

To these six a seventh preliminary stage could be added – that of the dependent child, encompassing the first 15 or so years of life in which the child takes no active role in migration decision-making. The disaggregation of the fifth and sixth stages into 'pre-' and 'post-retirement' stages might also be useful.

At the point of changeover between each of these life-cycle stages the place utility matrix variables are likely to alter in some way. For example, between the third and fourth stages considerations of school type and quality first enter the variable list; such considerations then disappear in the fifth stage. Employment considerations disappear on retirement and in the final stage proximity to caring relations may become important. The suggestion may thus be made that according to their stage in the life-cycle people migrate for different reasons as a result of the consideration of different attributes of the various places for which information is available. And although each individual probably has a unique perception of place utilities there are likely to be certain broad similarities between groups of people who consider the same variables to be important.

Hence, in many developed countries there has been a long-continued migratory flow of young adults in the first of Speare's life-cycle categories from rural areas to towns, the accepted explanations (Rambaud, 1969) being that these flows are in response to the lack of employment in the countryside in comparison to the towns, the attraction of urban shops, entertainment and other amenities, and of a faster urban pace of life. In the reverse direction, from town to country, has been a flow of the retired in response to a reverse perception of benefits and disbenefits, the country being more attractive because of its lack of industry and its slower way of life.

Migratory flows of specific groups may, however, occur not just according to life-cycle stages. A distinct group of individuals may value a particular variable highly and in consequence migration may occur across the spectrum of age and life-cycle stage. The availability of unused land and freedom from interference were important variables in taking the Mormons to Utah in the nineteenth century (Meinig, 1965), and similar considerations influenced the Great Trek of the Boers from the Cape to the High Veldt in South Africa (Pollock and Agnew, 1963). In both cases the perception of opportunities elsewhere acted across a culturally distinct group of individuals.

From Fig. 1.2 it can be seen that the alteration of the delineation of the variables in an individual's place utility matrix leads to a new calculation of the scores at the foot of the columns. It is assumed in behavioural investigations that man is rational to the extent of moving to the place where he will derive the greatest utility from residence. Thus if the recalculation of place utility scores yields a higher score for a potential destination than the individual obtains where he is at present it is felt that migration is likely to result. Attempts to demonstrate the link between attitudes to places, expectation of migration and actual migration, although few in number, have generally been successful. Schulze *et al.* (1963) demonstrated that among high school students in central Michigan there was a strong negative association between individuals' satisfaction with their local community and their desire to migrate. Hannan (1970), in Eire, showed that although there were certain differences between expectations of migration and actual migration performance among a group of young adults, particularly in terms of migration differentials, the underlying similarities were strong. The most important reasons for expecting to migrate were frustrations with local employment and income opportunities in comparison with opportunities elsewhere.

Apart from changes in the delineation of variables the other cause of migration identifiable from the concept of the place utility matrix is a change in information availability. This is most likely to take the form of a re-evaluation of the attributes of particular places in the light of new or different information. The character of places is constantly changing, but there is inevitably a time-lag in the dissemination of knowledge of such changes. Nevertheless, an individual may be regularly receiving updated reports on particular places which may lead him to alter his view of their desirability as places of residence. One important source of such reports is often contact with other migrants who have made the journey already. Tannous (1942) provides a particularly interesting set of letters written from the New World to friends and relatives in their villages of origin in the Lebanon by migrants who left between 1900 and 1930. Many of these letters exhort others to follow the original migrants, thus setting up the familiar pattern of a chain migration flow, where each migration event leads to another after a time-lag for information to be sent back by the previous migrant. Any change in information about places may result in new totals for the columns in the place utility matrix which, if the assumption of rationality in man is valid, will lead to a migratory move to the place of greatest utility for the individual concerned.

The place utility matrix is thus a useful concept in demonstrating how an individual makes decisions on which place is the best for residence. However, the matrix is a tool for explanation rather than an operational model, and attempts to produce working and testable hypotheses from it encounter considerable problems.

One of the greatest difficulties lies in the amount of survey work that would be needed even to specify the variable list with its correct weights, or maximum scores, for a group of potential migrants. One of the few studies to attempt this is that by Lieber (1978) which used questionnaire analysis. Rather than carry out laborious research of this kind most students of the behavioural approach to migration explanation have utilized ecological correlations instead. By this method a comparison between different places can be made on the basis of any number of non-migration variables such as housing types, accessibility, socio-economic composition or environmental quality, with scores on these variables being compared to data on actual migratory movements (Brown and Longbrake, 1970, p. 372; Willis, 1974, p. 59). If there is net migratory flow from place A to place B then place B is deemed to be more attractive – to have a generally higher place utility for migrants – and the elements of that attractiveness can be identified from the relative scores of the two areas on the other variables. In view of earlier comments to the effect that different groups move for different reasons, and the fact that any net migration is the balance between two gross flows, this technique of ecological correlation in the elucidation of comparative gross place utilities is of doubtful validity, since the results can only apply to a non-existent 'net' migrant and not to any of the specific migrant groups or individuals involved. As long ago as 1962 Sjaastad pointed out that to relate net migration flows to various inter-regional differentials is fruitless where the net flows mask much larger gross flows (Sjaastad, 1962).

Another problem that occurs in the use of behaviouralist ideas in the explanation of migration decision-making is over the sequence of events. Brown *et al.* (1970, p. 176) believe that a decision to move precedes the search for a place to move to. The argument is that once a 'threshold reference point' (Wolpert, 1965) has been breached for the individual's place utility from his present residence he will start to look elsewhere (Brown and Moore, 1970, p. 1) in an effort to reduce the 'stress' induced by the insufficiences of the present residence

(Wolpert, 1966). It could, however, be argued that such a 'threshold reference point' can only exist in relation to perceived opportunities elsewhere, since such a reference point is only a measure of relative deprivation for the individual rather than an absolute quantity. It may similarly be suggested that it is increased knowledge of other places, and the consequent reappraisal of place utilities that this entails, that leads to the actual decision to move. In practice both sequences of timing may occur in reality, and may be linked with the scale of movement envisaged. In 'partial displacement' migrations (Fig. 1.1A), where much of the mobility pattern remains the same, the decision to move may precede the search for a destination and this 'search procedure' is well documented for intra-urban migrations (Michelson, 1977). In 'total displacement' migrations (Fig. 1.1B) the decision to move is probably the result of a preceding period of information flow.

Wolpert (1965) suggests that competing migration destinations are considered sequentially rather than simultaneously, and this may certainly be the case if there is a threshold of high utility which a place must possess for an individual if he is to choose to go there. The general applicability of this concept is, however, more open to question, particularly for 'total displacement' migrations where it is the knowledge of the relative merits of competing places that brings about the decision to migrate in the first place.

The behaviouralist approach to the explanation of why migration occurs has provided a useful set of concepts, but it has not yet provided a satisfactory set of predictive models. In some ways it is unlikely that it will be able to produce such models for some time to come, for behaviouralist ideas are only fully applicable at the level of the individual decision-maker, while prediction is only possible in the social sciences at the level of aggregates. Nevertheless, the examination of the importance of the individual decision-maker in migration provides a satisfactory background to the understanding of the selectivity of migration (sometimes known as the study of migration differentials); of why migration may occur in specific spatial patterns of common origin and destination linked by similar migrant participants; and of why migration cannot be in any sense an optimizing process in a situation of imperfect information availability. All of these considerations are of importance in the evaluation of migration impact.

The migrants – who migrates?

As has already been noted in the introduction, a prime determinant of the impacts of migration on both the areas of origin and destination is the character of the migrants – their personal and attitudinal attributes. In this context two generalizations concerning the migrant may be put forward.
1. Migrants are not a random selection from the population of the place of origin.
2. Migrants do not form a random cross-section addition to the population of the place of destination.

Migrants are thus always in some way differentiated from the mass of the populations with which they come into any form of contact, and from this fact flows much of the explanation for the specific impacts of the migration phenomenon.

These two generalizations are typical of others in the social sciences; they are not completely watertight, but they do affect the vast majority of cases. Certain specialized migration events can occur without this element of differentiation, for example forced migrations which remove a complete population from its place of origin as occurred in several areas of Eastern Europe during and immediately after the Second World War. Similarly, in areas of new land colonization the in-migrating population forms the only population so that there is no element of differentiation from an existing stock.

Despite these exceptions, in the vast majority of migrations an element of migrant selectivity or differentiation is present. Why selectivity should operate from the origin of the migration flow has largely been explained in the previous section. Specific groups of people are likely to react in distinct ways to the differentiation of places: they are likely to value different attributes of places, to have different information available to them, and therefore to react in different ways. It has been suggested that movement between stages in the life-cycle is an important cause of migration, and it can be argued that within each stage there may be less migration since fewer alterations are likely to take place to the composition of the list of variables considered. Other causes of differential migration will be dealt with shortly. In general, however, it may be said that selectivity occurs in out-migration from a place because there are always distinct differences between the place utility matrices of the individuals composing various groups within the population, and consequently those attitudinal differences between groups are manifested in their behavioural differences with respect to staying in or leaving the community.

It is less easy to produce a general explanation of why in-migrants do not form a random cross-section addition to the populations they move into, although this observation is empirically valid in most cases. Several partial explanations can be suggested. Firstly, according to the tenets of behaviouralism, in-migrants must come from an area, community or place which is in some way perceived as being different from their destination: as such they may bring with them the attitudes and beliefs which characterized their origin and which differ from the corporate outlook of the communities to which they move. A second explanation is that past migrants who arrived some time ago may, at the time of their migration, have had similar attributes to the present migrants, but that those attributes have now changed among the less recent arrivals. The past migrants will have aged and perhaps moved into a different life-cycle stage: they might also have changed their attitudinal and behavioural characteristics and become integrated with the communities or populations that they have moved into. Thus, although even over a long period of time the attributes of the actual migrants in a migration flow to a particular place do not change they never make up a random addition to the population already living there. A third explanation can be found in behavioural concepts of place utilities. A counter-flow of migration must always consist of people with different attributes than those of migrants who make up the flow in the opposite direction: they must be people who consider a different set of variables, or who have the opposite evaluation of a common set of variables. Among those arriving at a place there will therefore not be a significant number of people who are similar to those already resident in that place who are actively considering emigration from it. Ravenstein's 'law' that every migration flow has a counter-flow in the opposite direction has been shown to have empirical value (Grigg, 1977), but to it must be added a clause pointing out that the counter-flow will be composed differently from the flow. For a combination of these reasons, therefore, the migrants arriving at a place will rarely form a random addition to the existing inhabitants of that place, a fact of profound significance in any consideration of the effects of migration on the communities of destination.

Having dealt with these two generalizations concerning the migrants and their relationship to the areas they leave and the areas they go to, it will now be useful to outline the chief characteristics that are normally regarded as being important in differentiating migrants from non-migrants or in characterizing different migration streams.

Age

One of the commonest conclusions to emerge from studies of migrant selectivity is that age is of particular importance in explaining the likelihood of migration occurring. Customarily the propensity to migrate is greatest in the young adult age-groups, particularly between school-leaving and the age of 30 in economically advanced societies (see Ch. 11). Such migration is generally associated with the search for a job, and with job changes occurring at the lower rungs of a career ladder. Also of importance is migration at the time of marriage (see Ch. 9). After the age of 30 migration is generally reduced and residential stability becomes the norm. At the ages of 60 to 65 a further peak of migration may occur involving a change of residence at retirement.

Life-cycle stages

There is a close correlation, but not a direct one, between migration and age; it may be suggested that the direct association is between migration and life-cycle stages. Each stage in the life-cycle is associated with a particular age-group and this gives the link to age. Certainly, as has been suggested earlier, migration may be particularly prevalent among those moving between two stages of the life-cycle, and it may be that life-cycle is more important than age. Speare (1970) has compared the annual probability of migrating by age and by life-cycle stage and has concluded, for his case-study data on Rhode Island, that both age and life-cycle have some independent importance and that ideally both should be considered as significant factors of migrant selection. Leslie and Richardson (1961, p. 902) have called for the integration of life-cycle stages with career pattern in the analysis of migration selectivity.

Sex

Ravenstein noted that there were certain sex differences in migration. He wrote in 1885 (p. 196) that 'woman is a greater migrant than man', although he elaborated this conclusion by adding that men were more migratory over long distances and especially in international migration. It is arguable that Ravenstein's statement was a product of his time and place. Grigg (1977) has reviewed the work on nineteenth-century migration in England and Wales and suggested that there were important divergences from this 'law' even for Ravenstein's own period, and certainly since then the sex differentials in migration in the United Kingdom have been further reduced. In other societies sex differentiation in migration may operate in the reverse direction with males being, in general, more migratory than females. This is certainly true in many of the seasonal labour migrations of the African continent, or in much migration within the Mediterranean basin. Sex may, therefore, be a basis for selectivity in migration, but it does not operate in all cases, nor need it operate always in the same way (Peters, 1976).

Education

Several studies have suggested the importance of migrant selectivity on the grounds of intelligence or of educational attainment, although in practice it is only the latter that has normally been dealt with (and then only by the use of years of schooling or of school-leaving age) because of the operational difficulties in obtaining intelligence measures for suitable numbers of people. It has generally been found that those who spend a longer time in education are more migratory than those who spent fewer years in school. Those who went on to higher education are even more migratory, although there are problems because in many cases individuals wishing to obtain higher education must first make a residential move from their home. In Western Sicily, Galtung (1971, p. 198) found that among farmers 54 per cent of the illiterates were likely to be 'stayers' while only 30 per cent of those who had over five years educational training were in that category. In rural Eire, Hannan (1969, p. 206) found that while only 12 per cent of the secondary-school-educated young adults interviewed intended to remain at home the figure rose to 38 per cent among those whose education had only been at primary school level. Both of these are studies of attitudes to migration rather than of actual migration differentials, but both provide evidence of the importance of education in influencing attitudes (see also Ch. 6). Education may change the variables that an individual considers in his place utility matrix, for example by restricting job choice and location to a limited set of places (this is particularly so for university graduates), and it may also make the appraisal of available information more efficient, especially where to be educated means to be literate in a generally illiterate society. Two specific studies which, by the use of intelligence tests, have shown that rural school-leavers who have migrated to the city were more intelligent than those who stayed at home are those by Gist and Clark (1938) and by Rieger (1972).

Occupation, economic status and social status

Migrant selectivity according to occupation has often been shown to be present among migratory flows. In general, as Pryor (1969, p. 74) has pointed out, the conclusion in developed countries has been that selectivity operates in favour of the professional or white-collar element in the employed population and in consequence these sectors are over-represented among migrants, while in developing countries migration is more common among those of low economic status. Nevertheless there are distinct exceptions to this generalization, and the inter-linking roles of education, occupation and social status have not been fully researched. For inter-war Greece, for example, Friedl (1976) has shown that rural-urban migration to Athens first involved the children of the better-off families who could afford to support the migrant during his early period of training in the city, so here wealth and educational aspirations were linked. It has been suggested (Hart, 1973) that some apparent occupational differentiation in migration may be caused by the fact that different socio-economic groups migrate in response to different stimuli, with manual and unskilled workers moving for higher wages and the professional classes moving in anticipation of future promotion opportunities which carry with them higher social status as well as higher remuneration. The link between economic and social status is, in any case, likely to be a more complex one than is admitted in the single index of socio-economic status utilized in the British census. An intermediate variable may be housing tenure status, since economic status is likely, in many societies, to limit the possibilities of ownership of property while such patterns of ownership are influential in social status considerations. In Britain the restricted transferability of council house (public sector) tenancies between local authority areas means that inter-urban migration is often associated with the professional, managerial and other higher social status groups and with owner-occupation, while intra-urban moves also include the migration of those with local authority tenancies (Herbert, 1973, p. 105). It has been suggested (Bird, 1976, p. 32) that in the public housing sector, and thus, by implication, among certain economic and social status groups, a sizeable volume of desired migration is prevented from being realized because of the inflexibilities of the tenancy system.

Where the rented sector is virtually entirely privately rather than publicly operated, as in the United States, migration among renters is commonly found to be greater than among owners since the private rental system is more flexible in operation. Speare (1970) has analysed the difference between the rented and owned sectors and has suggested that owners of property form an economic bond to their residence at the time of its purchase and that this bond changes little as time passes. Hence, migration rates for owners of property are virtually constant with increasing duration of residence. By contrast the bonds tying renters to their areas of residence are social rather than economic and take time to form: for renters, therefore, the likelihood of migration falls as residence time increases. It is likely that this conclusion, applicable to the large privately rented sector of the United States' housing market, may also be applicable to private rented accommodation in other countries.

In certain studies of migration differentials an attempt has been made to isolate economic and social status from each other. Using attitudes to migration rather than actual migration performance as his indicator of selectivity Galtung (1971, p. 205) concludes that

> with low economic standing staying becomes difficult because the necessities of life are not met – with low social standing moving becomes difficult because of the decrease in perspective, the lack of initiative and connections.

While it may be argued that in the Sicilian society that Galtung was writing about economic and social status are unusually distinct, there is probably a wider general applicability for this statement. Certainly Pryor's (1969, p. 74) conclusion that in developing societies it is the poor who move may be explained in terms of the impossibility of life in the home community and the aspiration for something better elsewhere, even if that aspiration has little chance of being fulfilled. This would certainly appear to be the explanation for the gathering of the rural destitute in India's cities, or in the growth of squatter settlements around the capitals of the nations of Latin America (see also Ch. 5 and 7).

In general, therefore, it can be said that migration is often selective of potential movers according to a wide range of economic and social attributes of the population, but that those attributes which appear to produce the over-representation of certain population groups differ from place to place and from migration flow to migration flow. The occupational and social status of the potential migrant both play a major role in determining the place utility matrix variables that might be considered by the individual, and may also be of significance in determining the type and amount of information available on which the migration decision can be based. It is therefore not surprising that as a result of the occupational and social cleavages which exist in human populations migrants are not randomly selected from all population strata.

Cultural attributes

The distinction between social and cultural attributes is a difficult one to make with any clarity, but it has been found in certain studies that such factors as religion or language use may single out migrant groups from non-migrants. Toney (1973) has clearly identified differential residential mobility between Catholics and Protestants in Rhode Island, USA, while White (1974, p. 23) has suggested that in an area of notable linguistic minorities in Eastern Switzerland one linguistic group may have a greater number of local ties restraining them from migration than is the case for other groups. In general, however, the cultural attributes of a population appear to have been more important in the past than at the present time. History provides many examples of religious migrations involving such groups as the Mormons, the Huguenots, the Jews, or Hindus and Moslems in the great transfers of population that accompanied the termination of British rule in the Indian sub-continent.

Innovators versus traditionalists

Migration always involves an element of uncertainty since all migration is based on expectations of the future quality of life elsewhere rather than on past experience. To certain individuals this element of uncertainty is more important than to others, and some individuals have very high thresholds of certainty which must be exceeded before they will make a residential move. Others will respond much earlier and will not be put off by the relative lack of precision in their knowledge of opportunities elsewhere. Several researchers have produced evidence showing that the innovative elements in a population are over-represented among migrants, while others have noted the effect of this in removing social leadership and drive from the remaining population. The later migrants reduce uncertainty about destinations by waiting until they have the experiences of the early innovative migrants to add to their stock of available information. Hägerstrand (1957) has called these two groups 'active' and 'passive' migrants. Thus while migration in the first place may be innovative it may in the long run become a traditional aspect of society: such was the case with migration from Southern Italy to the Americas before the First World War. Petersen (1958, p. 265) has provided a reminder that in some cases migration involves the traditionalists while the innovators stay at home: the traditionalists are moving in order to be able to maintain an old way of life away from the changes occurring in their historic places of residence – such was the case with the migrations of several fundamentalist religious groups such as the Amish and the Hutterites to the United States.

These are only some of the more important aspects of migrant selectivity that have been isolated and discussed in the literature. There are other aspects that may be locally of some significance, but the general conclusion from any study of the characteristics of migrants is that they are not selected by any random process. This fact is of the greatest significance in explaining the impact of migration both in the sending and in the receiving areas, and an important part of the study of such impacts must necessarily be taken up with an investigation of the exact characteristics of the migrants and of how those characteristics differ from the attributes of the rest of the populations at the origins and destinations of the migratory flows.

Approaches to a typology of migration

Having proposed a definition of migration, discussed some of the sources of information available for the analysis of the phenomenon and outlined a number of important points to be considered in answering such questions as 'why does migration occur?' and 'who migrates?', attention may now be given to the consideration of a number of approaches to the problem of classifying migrations.

> Classifications of modern migrations appear to derive from the statistics that are collected, whether or not these have any relevance to theoretical questions (Petersen, 1958, p. 264).

It has already been seen that the operational definition of migration varies from study to study according to the type of data available, and it might be argued that there is little utility to be derived from any attempt at providing a typology of migration. Nevertheless, the consideration of methods of classifying migration provides a useful reminder that migration is a multi-dimensional phenomenon and that each dimension may be of importance.

First of all it is possible to classify migrations according to the distance travelled. The availability of information on this is extremely variable for, as has been pointed out earlier, migrations occurring within one administrative area are rarely dealt with in official figures, while the collection of distance data is often haphazard and may relate to the difference between residences at the time of two successive censuses, ignoring intermediate moves. There is some doubt about the significance of geographical distance on its own: in terms of migration impact the social or cultural distance moved (unmeasurable though these may be in practice) are arguably of greater importance. Similarly, the division of migration into internal and international can be a somewhat artificial distinction which appears to be significant only because it is a distinction that is made in virtually every country of the globe. The internal migrant within India may cross many more social and cultural frontiers than the international migrant between Northern Belgium and the southern part of The Netherlands.

A second means of classifying migration is concerned with the time-period over which migration is effective. At one extreme are short-term labour migrations on a seasonal basis: at the other are permanent moves from which the migrant never returns. In between are various forms of return migration occurring over periods ranging from a few months to a number of years. The role of the returning migrant in producing change in his home community is highly significant for the migrant brings back information gathered about other places, and may have adopted new attitudes and aspirations which he communicates to his stay-at-home compatriots. Temporary migration often paves the way for permanent migration in succeeding years: this was certainly the case in nineteenth-century France (Carron, 1965; Corbin, 1971). There are, nevertheless, disadvantages in the classification of migration on the basis of a time-scale. Firstly, the identification of return migrants in any migration stream is generally extremely difficult. Secondly, as has been pointed out earlier in this chapter, classification at one extreme of the time-scale cannot be achieved until the migrant dies. Several studies (for example Pourcher, 1964) have shown that migrants often intend to return to their place of origin, but that the intention is not always made a reality. Certainly in such countries as France and Italy retirement migration from urban areas to the countryside, to the villages from which the urban population originated, is relatively common (Cribier, 1975), but many more migrations that were originally intended as being temporary become permanent because death intervenes or other circumstances prevent the return move.

A third, and very common, method of classification of migrations is on the basis of the environments of origin and destination or, occasionally, of destination alone. The terms 'rural–urban', 'inter–urban', 'suburban' and 'frontierward' migration are all well established in the literature (Zelinsky, 1971) and provide a convenient set of generalized terms which can be applied to most migration flows with some profit in terms of description. The drawback of these terms is that they ignore the fact that migration is virtually always a two-way process, and that while the migration flow is moving in the direction described there is usually a counter-flow in the opposite direction.

Classification of migration on the basis of the reasons behind it has been commonly adopted and the terms 'economic migration', 'retirement migration' or 'educational migration' are familiar ones. Yet the most usual route to the adoption of the first of these terms lies through the process of ecological correlation analysis, considering the attributes of the places left behind and comparing these with the destinations. As has been pointed out, this practice is fraught with difficulties and ignores the great variety of considerations that may actually play a part in the decision of an individual to make a migratory move. Nevertheless, the terms mentioned, and also those dealing with environmental classifications, are in such common use and general acceptance that they are used in the remainder of this volume.

The final method of classification in common use deals with the migrants themselves. A complex classification system can be derived from even a few attributes of the migrants, but such a classification system would itself be multidimensional and would lose sight of the aim of classification – the provision of a useful shorthand description of the significant differences between specific migration flows.

In terms of the understanding of the impact of migration the last-named classification scheme has obvious advantages because migration impact derives in part from the characteristics of the migrants themselves in relation to their subtraction from one area and their addition to another. Nevertheless the consideration of alternative, and simpler, typologies is a useful exercise in identifying the many facets of migration and the many ways in which it impinges upon the continuation of human activities in specific localities. Any attempt to put into operation a general theoretical classification of migration, such as one based on the characteristics of the migrants, is rendered very difficult by the paucity and non-comparability of the available data, which must often be derived from small-scale local study. In practice an element of the *ad hoc* is almost inevitable.

In the consideration of the geographical impact of migration an under-standing of the reasons for migration and of the attributes of the migrants is of the greatest importance. Almost all human beings, certainly in the developed countries of the world, make at least one residential move during their lifetime, but the motivations for such moves are almost infinitely variable although certain groups of reasons can be identified. The motivations for migration are an integral part of the understanding of migrant selectivity which, in turn, is the single most important factor in the explanation of migration impact. At present our understanding of motivations and selection processes is only partial, and the development of behavioural concepts, although undeniably useful in the genesis of hypothetical models, has not yet resulted in the creation of an accepted set of 'laws' dealing with motivation and selection.

Chapter 2

Spatial patterns of migration flows

P. E. White and R. I. Woods

The introduction to Chapter 1 asked five important questions which the student of migration must seek to answer. The questions 'why does migration occur?' and 'who migrates?' have already been tackled. This chapter will be devoted to a consideration of the patterns created by migration flows: their shape, volume, length and direction. These patterns are at one and the same time indicative of the process of migration and also of its impacts. They are indicative of the migration process, for all residential changes among the human population must take on certain characteristics of distance travelled, or of direction or volume of movement. These patterns of migration may also be regarded as an impact of migration in that they represent the effects of migration in the intervening space between origin and destination (see Ch. 3). In addition, analysis of the spatial patterns of movement is important in showing the functional links within the migration system between areas of origin and destination. Thus the analysis of migration flows complements the understanding of migration selectivity (Ch. 1) to produce the background for a complete view of the multiple effects of any migration phenomenon.

It is important to distinguish between two methodologies that may be adopted in the analysis of migration flow. The inductive approach seeks to identify, describe or even model, process and pattern as a preliminary to enquiries of a more explanatory nature, taking as its starting point information on actual migrations. In the deductive approach it is usual to begin the sequence of analysis by formulating logical and internally consistent theories which may then be tested empirically against data drawn from actual observations. Clearly, these two approaches are not mutually exclusive; neither is the correct one to use and both make important contributions to social scientific enquiries. In terms of the study of migration the inductive method is epitomized by Ravenstein's 'laws of migration' while the deductive method can be exemplified by the use of theories derived from analogue models, both physical and biological, such as the gravity model.

The distinction between these two methodologies is maintained in this chapter. The first four sections employ the inductive and the fifth the deductive approach. The first section outlines the characteristic shapes which migration flows or streams take on. The second section attempts to impose order on these characteristic shapes by referring to the earliest exposition of migration laws, that of E. G. Ravenstein in the 1870s and 1880s. Developing from these 'law-like' generalizations, section three considers step and chain migration, and section four pays attention to streams and counter-streams in migration. The fifth section is concerned with the use of deductive methodology and the analogous relationship between migration and the force of gravity.

The shape of migration flows in time and space

Representation

Migration flows can be represented in a variety of ways. By convention it is usual to link origin and destination by a straight line in two-dimensional space. These lines have length and direction, and their width can be made proportional to the volume of movement. However, the drawing of such lines does require that the precise locations of origins and destinations are known, such that they are lines connecting points rather than areas. In fact it is rare to have precise information on the addresses of migrants unless they are derived from special surveys or individual census enumerations, but when they are available patterns similar to those shown in Fig. 2.1 can be identified (see also Fig. 9.8). Figure 2.1A deals with

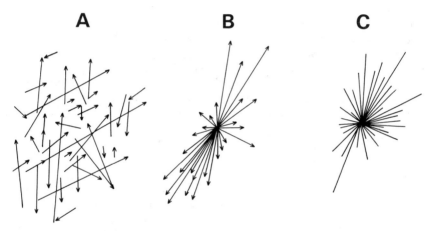

Fig. 2.1   Patterns of migration flow.

the case where movement occurs between a series of addresses – that is between points which may themselves be clustered, uniform or random in distribution according to the settlement pattern or population distribution itself. Figure 2.1B shows the case of out-migration from a single point while Fig. 2.1C shows in-migration to that same point. As is often the case, the spatial pattern of origins and destinations differs.

By a change of scale it is also possible to represent areas as though they are points. For instance, inter-urban migration is actually the movement between a number of areas, although for the purposes of analysing migration streams within a system of cities those urban areas are regarded as points. Such patterns can therefore be represented in the same sort of way that they are in Fig. 2.1.

It has already been made clear in the discussion of migration definitions and sources of data that an areal framework is normally specified and it is within this framework that migration is deemed to occur. Migration between the areal units provides a means of collecting data and it is this method that is generally employed by census organizations. In consequence, migration flows are usually recorded and represented as moves between areas rather than between points. In the United Kingdom the areal framework used in the census enumeration of previous place of residence is made up of local authority administrative areas so that analyses of the pattern of British migration flows are largely concerned with migration between local authority areas. It is much more difficult to obtain information on flows within such areas.

It is possible to consider migration flows between areas in a variety of ways, of which four will be discussed here. Firstly, the net interaction between each pair in a set of areas can be calculated simply by taking the difference between the numbers of movers in each direction to give net migration. For any area net migration is the difference between the number of immigrants (IM) and the number of emigrants (EM) and this can be calculated for either interaction with one other area or with all other areas ($NM^{t,t+n} = IM^{t,t+n} - EM^{t,t+n}$ as a development of Eqn (1.1)). An alternative approach is to calculate the gross migration flow (GM) between each pair of areas. This is found by adding the numbers of movers in each direction. As with net migration this can also be done for any single area: $GM^{t,t+n} = IM^{t,t+n} - EM^{t,t+n}$. Both the measures of net and gross migration are useful because they identify distinctive elements in the movement pattern; figures on net migration indicate the likelihood of population growth in the area receiving a positive balance and decline in the area of net out-migration, while gross migration figures convey an impression of the level of total interaction between pairs of areas. Both of these measures have been used in studies of inter-regional migration in Britain. Oliver (1964) used the net migration flows between regions, whereas Hart's (1970) study made use of the gross flows, although both researchers linked migration to various measures of economic well-being in the regions, such as unemployment rates. Migration flows have been combined in a single ratio by Lee (1966) to derive an index of migration efficiency whereby the flow in one direction is divided by its counter-flow. A ratio of 1.0 indicates a balance of flow and counter-flow cancelling each other out although, as Chapter 1 indicated, the counter-flow is likely to be composed of migrants with different attributes to those making up the flow, so that there is still likely to be an impact on both sending and receiving communities. Lee has provided a set of hypotheses which seek to explain how certain levels of migration efficiency ratio may come about, in part using behavioural ideas, but these remain largely untested, an exception being Grandstaff's (1975) work on migration in the Soviet Union which suggested their validity.

A second way of considering migration between areas is to deal with immigration and emigration flows separately. That is, to study separately the characteristics of those entering and leaving an area together with their origins or destinations. Such an approach adds greatly to the level of detail which can be identified in the pattern of migration and heightens the sophistication of potential analysis, but it can lead to data-handling problems, especially when immigration and emigration figures are cross-classified with information on age, sex, marital status and occupation. However, data of this nature are essential to any comprehensive study of migration and its impact.

By using immigration and emigration statistics it is possible to derive in-migration and out-migration rates. These rates express the number of persons entering or leaving an area during a specific period as a ratio of the average population of that area in that period, although occasionally the population at the start of the period may be used (Courgeau, 1976, p. 262). Such rates can be mapped by areas to give a visual demonstration of the places where immigration and emigration are most important. An amended form of this third method of representation has to be used when only birthplace data are available. In this instance the proportion of persons enumerated in one area and having their place of birth in another area is calculated: The location of the areas of origin can also be mapped in the manner shown in Figs 2.3 and 8.3.

A fourth method of representing migration between areas is provided by matrix analysis. Table 2.1 shows a 10×10 matrix of migration flows between the ten standard regions of Great Britain in the period 1966–71. The off-diagonal elements of the matrix give inter-regional migrations while the elements in the principal diagonal represent the population that has remained in each region during the five-year period and therefore includes those who have moved within each region but who have not crossed a regional boundary.

Matrices of this form can be used in a variety of ways. The patterns of immigrant, emigrant and net migration flows can be considered in the ways discussed above. Nodal flows may be identified (Nystuen and Dacey, 1961; Holmes and Haggett, 1977). Taking the matrix shown in Table 2.1 as an example; the largest emigration flows from each region (shown in the columns) were to the South East Region (7), apart from that region's emigration flow to the South West Region (8). Reading across the rows, eight of the regions also received their largest immigration flow from the South East Region, the exceptions being the Northern Region and the South East Region itself. Isolating the most important nodal flows, that is first-order flows, in an inter-regional migration system such as that of Great Britain, 1966–71, tells one very little other than that one region was very much larger than any of the others and was therefore of necessity both the destination and the origin of many of the migration streams. However, in other data sets such analysis can prove extremely valuable in identifying hierarchies of migration destinations and in assessing the existence or importance of sub-systems and regional peculiarities (see Ch. 6).

Another possible approach to the analysis of Table 2.1 involves the concept of impact flows. Although 47,530 persons moved from the Northern Region to the South East Region while 33,720 moved from the latter to the former region in 1966–71 the impact of the smaller number of migrants to the North on their receiving region was probably greater than that of the migrants to the South East simply because the population of the South East Region was so much larger than that of the Northern Region. By dividing the elements in each row of the matrix in Table 2.1 by the elements in the principle diagonal one gains an impression of the numerical impact of each migration flow on each particular destination region. The recently arrived immigrants are therefore compared to the population of their destination region who have not made an inter-regional move. The higher the resulting figure the greater the 'impact' of the arrivals is likely to be in terms of their addition to the immobile group. For example, the impact of the migration flow from the Northern Region to the South East (1–7) on the destination is 0.0030 (i.e. 47,530/15,982,720), while the impact of the reverse flow (7–1) on the destination region would be 0.0109 (i.e. 33,720/3,098,990). Similarly, one can consider the impacts on the origin regions of these migration flows. To do this the elements in the columns of Table 2.1 are divided by the relevant figure from the principal diagonal. The higher the resulting figure the more significant is that particular migration flow in depleting the region of population. Thus the 'origin impact' of migration between the Northern Region and the South East is 0.0153

Table 2.1 Inter-regional migration in Great Britain, 1966–1971 (10 per cent sample)

Regions	1966									
	1	2	3	4	5	6	7	8	9	10
1971 1	(309,899)	3,630	1,874	957	1,023	339	3,372	801	361	1,611
2	3,246	(442,442)	3,485	3,501	1,523	782	4,760	1,025	559	1,360
3	2,188	4,022	(634,479)	1,628	3,211	522	6,489	1,493	1,779	2,164
4	1,446	4,046	1,906	(306,822)	3,566	1,282	7,343	1,224	674	1,415
5	1,325	1,876	2,958	2,585	(466,071)	551	6,275	2,284	1,845	1,382
6	648	1,081	854	1,618	854	(143,466)	10,992	917	347	587
7	4,753	6,257	8,427	5,737	7,635	5,337	(1,598,272)	13,395	4,279	6,415
8	1,066	1,736	2,710	1,932	4,072	1,002	19,399	(332,345)	2,040	1,326
9	385	703	3,362	604	2,112	312	3,654	1,429	(253,926)	399
10	1,482	1,127	1,471	845	978	403	4,614	1,080	434	(500,171)

1 Northern; 2 Yorkshire and Humberside; 3 North West; 4 East Midlands; 5 West Midlands; 6 East Anglia; 7 South East; 8 South West; 9 Wales; 10 Scotland.

Data source: Population Census of England and Wales, 1971 (Migration Tables Pt. 1, Table 1B).

(i.e. 47,530/3,098,990) on the North but 0.0021 (i.e. 33,720/15,982,720) on the South East. This illustration demonstrates that both the loss to and gain from the Northern Region have relatively little numerical impact on the South East Region, but that loss to and gain from the South East Region have a substantial impact on the Northern Region.

Relative numerical impacts can be computed for all ten regions in Table 2.1, both in terms of the impact on destinations (row elements/diagonal element) and the impact on origins (column elements/diagonal element). Table 2.2 shows the results of both of these operations. Table 2.2(a) gives the impact on destination regions and Table 2.2(b) the impact on origin regions. However, it is possible to consider each of these matrices in two different ways. First, the columns of Table 2.2(a) show the relative impacts of the nine out-migration flows on each of the destination regions. For example, of the out-migration flows from Scotland (10) the one with the greatest relative numerical impact on a destination region was the one to the Northern Region (10–1). Second, the rows of Table 2.2(a) give the impacts of in-migration flows on each destination region. That in-migration flow with the greatest impact on the West Midlands Region (5) comes from the South East Region (7) – indeed eight of the possible nine regions receive their numerically most influential in-migration flow from the South East.

The columns and rows of Table 2.2(b) can be treated in the same way. There the columns give the relative magnitudes of the out-migration impact flows on the origin regions. Apart from the South East Region itself the out-migration flows with the greatest impacts on origin regions were all directed towards the South East. The rows of Table 2.2(b) may be used to answer the question 'for any destination region, which in-migration flow was responsible for the greatest numerical impact on an origin region?' Thus, of the migrants arriving in Wales (9) it is those from the North West (3) who have the greatest impact on their area of origin.

The impact flows described above can be represented in map form. Figure 2.2 provides two examples based on Table 2.2(a). Figure 2.2A shows, for each region, those out-migrations that had the greatest (first-order) and second greatest (second-order) numerical impacts on the nine potential destination regions, from the figures given in the columns of Table 2.2(a). Each region is the source of two flow lines in Fig. 2.2A, but in Fig. 2.2B each region is the focus for two lines. The ten regions are taken in turn and the origins of the in-migration flows with the greatest and second greatest impacts at destination are shown, reading from the rows of Table 2.2(a). Figure 2.2A demonstrates that from most regions the out-migration flows with the greatest impact on destinations were to a region adjacent to and usually immediately to the south of the origin region, and therefore shows the gradual shift to the south and south-east that occurred in the 1960s. It is clear from Fig. 2.2B that all regions of Great Britain received either their first- or second-order impact flows from the South East Region in 1966–71 – a reflection of the dominance of that region. The figures in the matrix of Table 2.2(b) could be mapped in a comparable fashion to illustrate the most important out-migration and in-migration flows on origin regions.

Four different ways of representing migration streams have been considered – as net and gross flows, as separate immigration and emigration flows, as rates by origin and destination and as the elements of a matrix – as preliminaries to an examination of the characteristics of migration streams: their direction, distance, volume and general shape.

Table 2.2 Relative numerical impact flows between regions of Great Britain, 1966–1971

(a) Impacts on destination regions

1971	1966									
	1	2	3	4	5	6	7	8	9	10
1	–	0.0117	0.0060	0.0031	0.0033	0.0011	0.0109	0.0026	0.0012	0.0052
2	0.0073	–	0.0079	0.0079	0.0034	0.0018	0.0108	0.0023	0.0013	0.0031
3	0.0034	0.0063	–	0.0026	0.0051	0.0008	0.0102	0.0024	0.0028	0.0034
4	0.0047	0.0132	0.0062	–	0.0116	0.0042	0.0239	0.0040	0.0022	0.0046
5	0.0028	0.0040	0.0063	0.0055	–	0.0012	0.0135	0.0049	0.0040	0.0030
6	0.0045	0.0075	0.0060	0.0113	0.0060	–	0.0766	0.0064	0.0024	0.0041
7	0.0030	0.0039	0.0053	0.0036	0.0048	0.0033	–	0.0084	0.0027	0.0040
8	0.0032	0.0052	0.0082	0.0058	0.0123	0.0030	0.0584	–	0.0061	0.0040
9	0.0015	0.0028	0.0132	0.0024	0.0083	0.0012	0.0144	0.0056	–	0.0016
10	0.0030	0.0023	0.0029	0.0017	0.0020	0.0008	0.0092	0.0022	0.0009	–

(b) Impacts on origin regions

1971	1966									
	1	2	3	4	5	6	7	8	9	10
1	–	0.0082	0.0030	0.0031	0.0022	0.0024	0.0021	0.0024	0.0014	0.0032
2	0.0105	–	0.0055	0.0114	0.0033	0.0055	0.0030	0.0031	0.0022	0.0027
3	0.0071	0.0091	–	0.0053	0.0069	0.0036	0.0041	0.0045	0.0070	0.0043
4	0.0047	0.0091	0.0030	–	0.0077	0.0089	0.0046	0.0037	0.0027	0.0028
5	0.0043	0.0042	0.0047	0.0084	–	0.0038	0.0039	0.0069	0.0073	0.0028
6	0.0021	0.0024	0.0013	0.0053	0.0018	–	0.0069	0.0028	0.0014	0.0012
7	0.0153	0.0141	0.0133	0.0187	0.0164	0.0372	–	0.0403	0.0169	0.0128
8	0.0034	0.0039	0.0043	0.0063	0.0087	0.0070	0.0121	–	0.0080	0.0027
9	0.0012	0.0016	0.0053	0.0020	0.0045	0.0022	0.0023	0.0043	–	0.0008
10	0.0048	0.0025	0.0023	0.0028	0.0021	0.0028	0.0029	0.0032	0.0017	–

For key to regions see Table 2.1.
Data source: see Table 2.1.

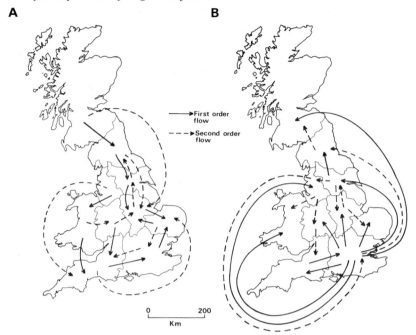

A

B

First order flow

Second order flow

0   200
Km

Fig. 2.2   Inter-regional impact flows, Great Britain, 1966–71.
A – impacts of out-migration flows on destination regions;
B – impacts of in-migration flows on destination regions.
Data source: Population Census of England and Wales, 1971 (Migration Tables Pt. 1, Table 1B).

Characteristics

Direction

Just as the meteorologist usually finds that there are prevailing wind directions at his recording stations so the geographer can identify directional bias in migration streams. Clearly, this phenomenon can be seen at a number of scales. At the global level there has certainly been a major movement of population to the Western Hemisphere from Europe, Africa and Asia (Thomas, B., 1954; Klein, 1978). These particular migration streams had a most important impact on the destination area, but they also led to the reduction of overpopulation in many European countries (see Ch. 5). At the scale of movement between towns Wolpert (1967) found a distinct south-westward bias in the movement between metropolitan areas in the United States – a pattern which both reflected and was a cause of the considerable shift in the spatial distribution of the American population. A great deal of research has been undertaken on the nature of intra-urban residential migration, much of which has identified the tendency for directional bias to occur. The places (P_1, P_2, P_3 . . . , P_n) shown in the matrix in Fig. 1.2, are potential destinations for migration, but they may be clustered within the urban environment; a person's 'action space' can represent only a particular part of the city within which he will assess the varying place utilities of different residences. A spatially biased action space usually leads to sectoral bias in the movement patterns of intra-urban migrants: a person living to the south of a city centre will tend to make short-distance moves within the southerly sector of the city (see Ch. 10).

Although it is possible to recognize directional bias in migration streams at a number of scales it is important to consider the simple geometry of the potential origins and destinations. To return to the American example, the population distribution of the United States is largely concentrated in the north-east: in consequence most long-distance internal migration is to the south, south-west or west (Schwind, 1971). The direction of migration flows is constrained by the geometry of population distribution within a fixed area (Getis and Boots, 1978, pp. 86–120).

As a final point on direction it must always be borne in mind that a net migration system which displays distinct directional bias (as in the southward movement of population in Britain discussed in connection with Table 2.1) is the product of gross flows in opposite directions: the existence of counter-streams must not be forgotten.

Distance

There is a strong tendency for the number of migrations to fall with increasing distance, whether distance is measured in kilometres – the prime concern of geographers – or in social or economic terms. The 'friction of distance' effect has often been observed in geographical studies – indeed the principle of least effort with which it is associated has been raised to the status of a fundamental axiom in human geography. In terms of its application to migration the principle of least effort may be interpreted to say that in choosing between two competing migration destinations of equal merit the migrant will opt for the one which will involve him in less cost of movement, in other words the nearer. In Chapter 1 it was suggested that this cost of movement could be regarded as one of the V variables in an individual's place utility matrix such that the movement costs of distance are evaluated along with the other attributes of place that are important to the migrant. An additional reason for the 'friction of distance' effect on migration lies in the related fact that distance restricts many forms of information flow such that potential migrants are likely to know less about distant than about nearby places (Miller, 1972, p. 475). Certainly most migration streams contain a relatively larger number of short-distance moves and a smaller number of long-distance moves; in other words, the frequency distribution of migration distances is positively skewed. A considerable number of empirical studies have been devoted to the precise measurement of this particular frequency distribution (Kulldorff, 1955). Three of the most valuable functions are the negative exponential; the double-log or Pareto; and the square-root exponential. Using I to stand for the number of migrations or interactions, and D to represent distance these three functions can be expressed in terms of regression equations as follows:

negative exponential $\qquad$ $I = a\, e^{-bD}$, $\hfill$ (2.1)

or $\qquad$ $\log I = \log a - bD$,

double-log *(Pareto)* $\qquad$ $I = aD^{-b}$ $\hfill$ (2.2)

or $\qquad$ $\log I = \log a - b \log D$

square-root exponential $\qquad$ $I = a\, e^{-b/\sqrt{D}}$ $\hfill$ (2.3)

or $\qquad$ $\log I = \log a^{-b/\sqrt{D}}$

where a and b are regression coefficients (b measures the slope-gradient of the least-squares regression line through the scatter diagram of points when I is plotted against D) and e is the base of natural logarithms.

Hägerstrand (1957), in his study of the migration pattern to and from the village of Asby in Central Sweden, employed the double-log (Pareto) function to describe the relationship between migration and distance. In that case I was expressed as the relative density of migrations per unit area and D was taken to be the mid-point of successive distance bands drawn round the village. By adopting this convention Hägerstrand was able to show that emigrants perceived distance as though it were logarithmically transformed – a place 100 km away from the origin seemed to be only twice as far away from the origin as a place 10 km distant. Hence the marginal effect on movement from each increase in distance is steadily reduced in scale for each extra unit of distance. Hägerstrand also demonstrated how Asby's migration field expanded over time by comparing the declining b regression coefficients. These findings – the logarithmic transformation of distance and the expansion of the migration field over time – appear to be general associations which are appropriate to the functional relationship between migration and distance.

In the years since Hägerstrand's (1957) important study was published a number of students of migration have considered the precise nature of the statement that interaction is a function of distance (I = fD). Cavalli-Sforza (1962) and Morrill (1963) have both outlined a series of general models which account for the effect of distance on the volume of movement, the former from the geneticist's point of view and the latter from the geographer's. Furthermore, Taylor (1971; 1975) has suggested that the double-log Pareto regression equation is not the best means of summarizing the migration distance pattern of Asby, rather that the square-root exponential equation provides a better least-squares fit with a lower standard error. Even this view has been criticized by Haynes (1974) who favours the negative exponential form of the regression equation on the grounds that it can be theoretically derived and that it has general applicability to animal movements and commuter trips as well as to human migrations (see Haynes, 1974, p. 100).

The debate over the measurement of the friction of distance effect by the use of least-squares regression analysis has taken on new vigour recently (Curry, 1972; Johnston, 1973; 1976; Cliff *et al.*, 1974). However, it is valuable to keep in mind the reasons for fitting regression equations to data on the I = fD statement. The first reason is the need to describe the particular and unique relationship in precise terms. Prediction is the second reason, the estimation of I given knowledge of the regression coefficients, a and b, and distance, D. When either of these two reasons are paramount then that equation, and transformation of I and D, must be chosen which maximizes the coefficient of determination and minimizes the standard error of the estimate. In this way residual error will be reduced to a minimum. The third reason for fitting a regression equation to I = fD is to allow comparison over time and through space. In this respect it would seem appropriate to fit a general model of the negative exponential or double-log variety rather than one of the more obscure forms outlined by Taylor (1971). In this way the regression coefficients may be compared between time-periods and between places in the knowledge that the differing sets of data are being expressed against the same general model.

Volume

It has already been suggested above that the number of migratory movements is reduced with distance and that the nodal flows in any migration system often tend to have a directional bias, but what of the overall volumes of migration flow; do these volumes vary over time and through space? Zelinsky's (1971) concept of the migration transition, which was mentioned in Chapter 1, argues that mobility, the rate of population movement, has increased over time and that it is higher in the economically advanced than the developing countries. Although Zelinsky deals with the broad sweep of population change, modernization and industrialization, it is important to re-examine some of his fundamental premises.

It should not be thought that the populations of pre-industrial societies were or are immobile. Two examples can be used to illustrate this point. The first comes from a study by P. Clark (1972). Using ecclesiastical court records for the period 1580–1640 he was able to show that as much as 75 per cent of the sample populations of three Kentish towns – Canterbury, Maidstone and Faversham – had not been born in those towns. In the case of Maidstone, some 18 per cent had been born outside Kent. Figure 2.3 shows the percentage of immigrants to the three Kentish towns who were born in each English county. Nearly every county contributed more than one person although, as one would expect, most of the migrants were born in the south-east of England. Clark's study also revealed the existence of long-distance 'subsistence' migration as well as short-distance 'betterment' migration. The former tended to be generated by poor conditions at the place of origin while the latter was part of the well-established flow between country and nearby town which was associated with trade, apprenticeship and the employment of servants.

The second example is drawn from geographical studies of the population structure of Africa (on East Africa – Claeson, 1974; Masser and Gould, 1975; and see also Chapter 6: on West Africa – Caldwell, 1968; Riddell, 1970a). These studies show that there is a high degree of short-distance rural–rural migration together with age and sex selective longer-distance movement to the towns of Tanzania, Uganda, Ghana and Sierra Leone. High migration rates are a fundamental characteristic of these societies and are both a cause and an effect of the modernization and industrialization process.

Although Zelinsky (1971) is in danger of undervaluing the role of migration in pre-industrial societies it must be emphasized that residential mobility, particularly in its long-distance form, did increase during the period of industrialization and now stands at a high level in the countries with advanced economies. During the five-year period between 1966 and 1971 17,444,170 people changed their place of residence between local administrative areas in Great Britain. This represents an annual average turnover rate of about 7 per cent. Even this figure conceals the fact that a large number of those who moved did so more than once – the census migration statistics are based on 'previous place of residence' questions and therefore fail to elicit the total number of migrations in a given period. For this reason it is probable that more than 10 per cent of the British population changes its place of permanent residence each year, a volume of movement not untypical of Western Europe, lower than the 20 per cent figure found in North America, but higher than the 5 per cent of the Soviet Union.

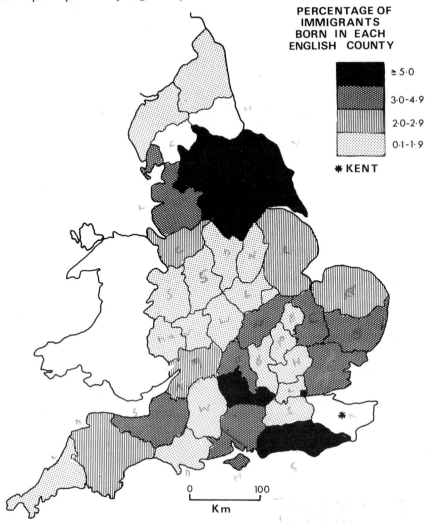

PERCENTAGE OF
IMMIGRANTS
BORN IN EACH
ENGLISH COUNTY

≥ 5·0

3·0-4·9

2·0-2·9

0·1-1·9

＊ KENT

Fig. 2.3 Percentage of immigrants to three Kentish towns born in each English county, 1580–1640.
Data source: P. Clark, 1972.

General shape

It is common in studies of the friction of distance to treat the $I = fD$ statement as though it were a simple bivariate relationship, whereas the frequency distribution from which it derives is truly three dimensional – it has volume, length and direction. Most models of the migration field contain the implicit assumption that it has a conical, or, at best, an inverted saucer-like structure. In other words they take the fitted regression equation and assume that it operates equally well for all distances in whatever direction. For example, extensive use has been made of the concept of the mean information field (M.I.F.) by Hägerstrand (1967), Marble and Nystuen (1963) and Morrill and Pitts (1967), among others. A mean information field consists of a network of cells each of which contains a number to represent the probability of a person in the central cell of the network moving to, or simply having contact with, each individual surrounding cell. The probability of migration is estimated from a regression equation fitted to a set of observed data so that a cell 5 kilometres to the north of the central cell has the same probability of being migrated to as a cell 5 kilometres to the south, east or west. Morrill (1965), in particular, has made extensive use of M.I.F.s in the simulation of spatio-temporal patterns of migration and the growth of urban settlement in Central Sweden.

The M.I.F. is a normative concept which assumes that both information flow and potential migrants' distance perceptions are equal in all directions, assumptions which are unlikely to be tenable in the real-world situation of distorted and biased opinions of places. The true amoeba-like nature of contact fields has been revealed by geneticists in their studies of marriage distance (the distance between the usual residence of bride and groom immediately before their marriage). Figure 2.4 shows an example from a study of the parish registers for the village of Charlton-on-Otmoor, Oxfordshire, over the last 360 years. The isarithms enclose places that contributed 0, 1, 2, . . . , 8 per cent of the exogamous marriages contracted in the central village. Clearly the contact field is by no means circular, conical or saucer-like; rather it shows a pattern of ridges, plateaux and indentations with a north-east to south-west orientation (Boyce *et al.*, 1971). The three-dimensional pattern of contact shown in Fig. 2.4 is probably also typical of the pattern of most short-distance migration fields (see

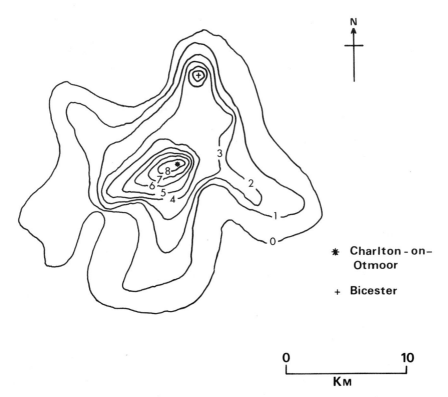

Fig. 2.4 The exogamous marriage contact field of Charlton-on-Otmoor, Oxfordshire, over the last 360 years.
Source: Boyce *et al.*, 1971.

Ch. 9). On average, the volume of migration does decline with distance, but there are often particular directional biases associated with prevailing economic, social, political and environmental conditions (Johnston and Perry, 1972) together with the pre-determined geometry of potential origins and destinations (Brown and Neuberger, 1977, provide additional examples of these patterns).

Laws of migration flow

Thomas Robert Malthus (1766–1834), William Farr (1807–83) and Ernest George Ravenstein (1834–1913) were three eminent nineteenth-century students of population. Each one made important contributions to population theory and analysis and, although their work was the subject of criticism both in their own lifetimes and since, their ideas have proved stimulating to social scientists and demographers even in the twentieth century. Malthus was the grand theorist on a large scale; Farr the statistical demographer and public health reformer; and Ravenstein the inductive empiricist. The justification for including Ravenstein in this distinguished list is that he made a number of statements about the nature of the migration process and, like the other scholars mentioned, he was not averse to calling his findings 'laws'.

Ravenstein's 'laws of migration' are broad generalizations on the characteristics of migrants and their origins and destinations, but chiefly on the characteristics of the migration streams. These 'laws' have been discussed at length by a number of more recent scholars – for example Porter (1956), Lee (1966) and Grigg (1977) – so that they need not be considered in detail here. The most important of Ravenstein's statements with relevance to the present discussion are as follows:

1. Most migrants move only a short distance.
2. The volume of migration increases with the development of industry and commerce.
3. The direction of migration is mainly from agricultural to industrial areas (rural–urban).
4. Most long-distance migration is to the major industrial and commercial centres.
5. Migration proceeds step by step.
6. Each migration stream or flow has a counter-stream.
7. Migrants are generally adults – families rarely migrate over long distances.
8. A majority of migrants are females, but males comprise a majority of international migrants.
9. Migrants are more likely to have rural than urban origins.
10. The major causes of migration are economic.

Several of these 'laws' have been discussed in Chapter 1 or in the previous section of this chapter.

It is important to appreciate the context in which the original statements were made, and to examine their universality. Ravenstein's 'law-like' statements first appeared in three papers published in the 1870s and 1880s (Ravenstein, 1876; 1885; 1889). The first was in the *Geographical Magazine* and seems to be a response to Farr's contention that migration appeared to lack any definite law; the other two papers were published in the *Journal of the Statistical Society*, of which Ravenstein was a Fellow. The statements were made at a time of growing interest, among the numerate bourgeoisie, in social conditions, education, public health and the developing science of economic and social statistics. The government and local authorities were taking greater responsibility for the regulation, if not the provision, of housing, water, gas, street lighting and other aspects of material well-being which had formerly been left to the individual, to local councils or to the Poor Law Guardians. There was a clear need for 'facts' on the effects of these new interventionist activities and to show areas where further intervention was needed. Ravenstein provided the 'facts' on migration, as Farr had done on mortality, by using the demographic statistics published by the Registrar-General. In particular he used the data on place of birth from the decennial population censuses which meant that only county of origin and current place of residence could be identified. This important point needs to be borne in mind in any evaluation of Ravenstein's 'laws'.

The universality of Ravenstein's statements varies from 'law' to 'law'. Most migrations do tend to be over short distances. Evidence on this point, and reasons for it, have already been presented in this chapter and more discussion will be found in certain later chapters. The length of the average migration tended to increase in most technologically advanced societies with the introduction of the train, omnibus, motor car, passenger ship and aeroplane simply because the number of very long-distance moves has markedly increased. The volume of migration does increase, therefore, with the development of industry and commerce, but the relationship is not a simple linear one, rather it takes the form of an attenuated S-shaped curve over time, as Zelinsky (1971) has suggested. Such increases in migration are also partly attributable to the increased importance, and general awareness, of spatial differentiation of opportunities as a result of economic development (Ch. 1). Ravenstein's emphasis on rural–urban migration is clearly specific to a period and place of rapid urbanization. Once two-thirds to three-quarters of a country's population can be classified as urban then migration is bound to be predominantly urban–rural or urban–urban. Similarly, the 'laws' dealing with the greater mobility of females and single persons, as opposed to males and families, must be seen in the context of the late nineteenth century when many young women were 'in service'. The social and economic conditions of Victorian England make these statements particular rather than universal.

In suggesting that the major causes of migration were economic Ravenstein was echoing the eighteenth-century political economists. Adam Smith (1723–90) in his *The Wealth of Nations* (1776) maintained that 'The demand for men, like that for any other commodity, necessarily regulates the production of men', and Arthur Young (1741–1820), in a more pithy vein, claimed that 'Employment is the soul of population', in his *Political Arithmetic* (1774). It is certain that economic reasons do play an important role in causing migration, particularly of the long-distance kind, but the argument presented in Chapter 1 for considering migration in a behavioural sense via the place-utility matrix (Fig. 1.2) has even greater value because it is capable of incorporating a whole series of potential variables which might explain the reasons for migrations and the choice of destinations. Economic factors may simply be included in the list of important variables.

Ravenstein's 'laws of migration' have proved of considerable stimulus to subsequent researchers because they are simple and, on the face of it, eminently reasonable statements about migration streams, who migrates, where they come from and go to. However, it must be remembered that Ravenstein's statements are inductive in origin – they stem from an analysis of birthplace data for one society in one time-period and they therefore have an applicability which is circumscribed by the context in which they are made. In short they are not statements of the same abstract universality as those of von Thünen or Christaller who based their deductive theories on the behaviour of economic man living on an isotropic plain. Nevertheless the general validity of certain of Ravenstein's observations can be demonstrated from a consideration of why migration occurs at all and other empirical studies continue to demonstrate the applicability of the 'laws' for societies as different as the Soviet Union and Malaysia (Grandstaff, 1975; Pryor, 1969).

Two additional aspects of Ravenstein's 'laws' will be discussed in more detail in the following sections – step and chain migration; and migration streams and counter-streams.

Step and chain migration

Ravenstein maintained that migration takes place in steps; that the population living in areas surrounding economically expanding urban centres migrate to those centres and that their place is taken by other migrants from further afield. Thus a migration system is comprised of a series of moves, which may be rural–rural, rural to small town, small town to large city or large city to metropolis, although the overall effect is to create a flow from the rural area to the metropolis. None of the census material that Ravenstein had at his disposal was capable of being interpreted in this manner because only lifetime migration could be measured. His statement is a surmise rather than a law, but it is one that has been reiterated by others. Redford (1926), for instance, treats short-distance movement by stages as though these are a permanent feature of labour migration.

It is possible to use the concept of information flow to provide a cause for step migration, if indeed it exists. As the migrant moves from place to place through the hierarchy at each new destination he first becomes exposed to information about opportunities occurring at the next level in the hierarchy: if such a process occurred it would imply that any step migration should take place in one direction, with the migrant moving from village to metropolis through other places which intervene both in size and in space and with the outer limit of information from the metropolis not reaching so far through that space as to affect the distant village. Villagers living near the metropolis and within its area of information supply would be likely to move direct to the large centre without steps on the way.

Alternatively, step migration could come about through a process whereby the migrant moves to the nearest larger place and, as a result of that move, changes his place utility requirements (for example by obtaining further education or job skills) which then leads to a further move.

The only way in which this issue can be resolved is by reference to longitudinal studies that trace all the movements of individual migrants. Such studies are rare, but a number have been completed in America. Taeuber (1961; 1966) and Taeuber *et al.* (1961) have investigated the migration patterns of rural-farm, rural-non-farm, small town, large town and large city populations using survey data on individuals. Taeuber *et al.* (1961) found that the categories of moves from rural-farm to metropolis (defined as a town of over 500,000 inhabitants) and from rural-farm to large town (50,000–499,999) were under-represented, and they therefore suggested that such classes of moves may involve more than one generation of migrants. Even these conclusions are tentative for, as the authors acknowledged, their survey data are not capable of being used to test with suitable rigour notions of stage and step-wise migration. Even the longitudinal data reviewed by Shryock and Larmon (1965), and the American census statistics of 1960 which recorded place of residence in 1955 and place of birth (analysed by Eldridge, 1965), proved inadequate in substantiating the 'law' that migration occurs in stages. Further comments on this particular aspect must wait until more research has been completed using longitudinal surveys or the continuous registration statistics which are available in some European countries (see, for instance, Goldstein's, 1964, study of Danish migrants).

The notion of chain migration implies that there are primary and secondary migrants who are active and passive, leaders and followers, pioneers and colonists. The primary group is comprised of the initial innovators who make the first moves from the origin area, and they are then followed by members of the secondary group. The primary group is often dominated by young adult males in search of employment or a better standard of living while the secondary group contains dependents – wives, children, parents – and also siblings, cousins, neighbours and fellow members of the origin community. Obviously this concept of chain migration is particularly important for long-distance moves and especially for international migration where information availability is poor other than through the experiences of those who have gone before.

Numerous studies have identified the pattern of chain migration and related it to the flow of information about potential places of destination ($P_1, P_2, P_3 \ldots, P_n$ in Fig. 1.2). It appears that knowledge of a relative or friend already living in a place of potential destination can establish a crucial link in the migration process which will ultimately lead to movement and even to the establishment of a system of organized migration. That existing contact may be important in two ways: firstly as a source of information on opportunities at that destination; and secondly as a place utility advantage of that place, especially in cases where the secondary or passive migrant moves in order to re-unite the family.

Two examples will suffice to illustrate these points (see also Ch. 7). Desai (1963) has shown the importance of chain migration for Indian immigrants to Britain: in particular he has looked at the origins, social networks and employment structure of Gujaratis living in Birmingham. The majority of immigrants from this particular region of Western India were helped to migrate by an initial group of active migrants who found them employment and accommodation and generally assisted them to make the transition to an alien culture and environment. The network of communication, in terms of the flow of information and the sending of remittances from Birmingham to India, was of great importance in establishing a clearly defined migration stream.

The second example is taken from a study by Ogden and Winchester (1975) of migration in late nineteenth- and early twentieth-century France. They were able to show a close association between the departmental origins of internal migrants and the *arrondissements* in which they resided in Paris in 1911. Migrants from the west of France were over-represented in the western *arrondissements*; those from the north appeared in the northern *arrondissements*; and those from the south-east were prominent in a particular *arrondissement* in the south-east of Paris. Such a pattern of segregation as an outcome of the complex process of provincial migration suggests that chain migration was significant in channelling migrants into certain parts of the city where they would be more likely to find other people from their own region. This impression is also supported by Eugen Weber's (1977, p. 281) wide-ranging examination of the social modernization process in nineteenth-century France.

Chain migration is the most natural means by which a migration stream can develop for those migrants who are not the innovators. The place utility matrix (Fig. 1.2) is again of value in analysing such streams because those who initially stay at home share vicariously in the experiences of the migrants, such that the number of potential destinations for these later migrants is restricted to those for which favourable information is available from the primary group (Greenwood, 1970).

Migration streams and counter-streams

Migration streams are not simply one-way; most involve flow and counter-flow. Table 2.1 shows the pattern of inter-regional movement in Great Britain in 1966–71. Each of the ten regions was both an origin and a destination for migrants and each region was connected with every other region by flows in both directions. Table 2.1 does not, however, give any indication of the numbers of return migrants within these flows – those who, for instance, left Scotland for the South East Region in 1961–66 only to return to Scotland in 1966–71. Subsequent re-migration to the South East Region would make such a group repeat migrants. Data on such topics are extremely difficult to obtain. But the numerical importance and the impact of return and repeat migration streams have been emphasized by King (1978). Olsson (1965) quotes a figure of 21.6 per cent of observed migrations in a Swedish sample as return migrations.

The characteristics of those in the initial migration stream and in the return stream are likely to be dissimilar (Ch. 1). Very often the return migrants will have spent a considerable time at their original destination and will therefore be older than those composing the migration stream in the opposite direction, although it must be remembered that not everyone in a counter-stream originally moved from the place to which they are now going: return migrants are only a sub-group within the flow of population from place to place in opposition to a dominant flow in the opposite direction. Not all of this sub-group of return migrants are likely to be old. Richmond (1968) has shown in a study of the migration flows between Britain and Canada that many of the return migrants to Britain were young, unmarried and in professional occupations, that many of these 'transients' wished to return to Canada in the future, and that some 85 per cent of those returning from Canada to Britain were generally quite satisfied with their lives in Canada.

The notion of repeat migration requires careful handling in practice if one wishes to avoid the inclusion of seasonal labour migrants. Should those nineteenth-century Irish workers who arrived in England each year in time for the harvest and then departed again (Johnson, 1967) be counted as repeat migrants? The general answer to this question depends upon the temporal criteria used to define 'permanent place of residence', although in this particular case the situation is complicated because seasonal migration did often lead to permanent emigration, as was also the case in France (Carron, 1965).

Migration and gravity

Earlier sections of this chapter have discussed the nature of migration streams from the empirical point of view and with general reference to an inductive methodology, although notice has also been paid to the possibilities of behaviouralist ideas providing more general explanations for observed patterns. The remainder of the chapter will be devoted to an outline of a particular deductive approach to migration that lies through the use of physical analogue models.

The laws of gravity put forward by Sir Isaac Newton (1642–1727) are intended to account for the attraction between two particles: the force of gravitational attraction is directly related to the product of the masses of the two particles and inversely related to the square of the distance between them. Thus:

$$F_{12} = G \cdot \frac{M_1 \cdot M_2}{D_{12}^2} , \qquad (2.4)$$

where F_{12} = the gravitational force between two particles, 1 and 2,
M_1 and M_2 = the masses of particles 1 and 2 respectively,
D_{12} = the distance between particles 1 and 2,
G = the universal gravitational constant (6.670×10^{-11} newton-square metre per square kilogram).

Such a physical law might have important implications for the social sciences. The interaction, or movement, between two places could be directly related to the product of the masses, or populations, of those two places and inversely related to the square of the distance between them. The analogy has been made between force and interaction, and mass and population size. Equation (2.4) would therefore become:

$$I_{ij} = a \cdot \frac{P_i \cdot P_j}{D_{ij}^b} , \qquad (2.5)$$

where I_{ij} = interaction, or movement, between places i and j,
P_i and P_j = the populations of places i and j respectively,
D_{ij} = the distance between places i and j,
a and b = constants.

However, the next consideration must be the nature of the constants used in Eqns (2.4) and (2.5). In Eqn (2.4) the universal gravitational constant (G) takes on a fixed value and distance is squared (raised to the power of a constant equal to 2). But in Eqn (2.5) the constants a and b must be estimated empirically and they will vary from interaction to interaction. Variation in the b coefficient is particularly significant. It is this value that represents the friction of distance discussed earlier in the chapter. The human space separating two interacting populations is of a different nature to the physical space of the Newtonian laws, and can be regarded as expanding or contracting according to such things as the transportation technology available and population density. The b coefficient measures this expansion and contraction of space, a low value indicating a low friction of distance. Empirically, many estimates of the b coefficient have lain between 1.5

and 2.5, reflecting the Newtonian value of 2. The procedure of estimating the values of the constants is normally accomplished by least-squares regression analysis on the following basis:

$$\log \left(\frac{I_{ij}}{P_i \cdot P_j} \right) = \log a - b \log D_{ij} \qquad (2.6)$$

which is a double-log equation of the form used in Eqn (2.2). These procedures – the use of analogies and the empirical fitting of constants by means of regression analysis – take the social scientist's gravity model several steps away from Newton's original specification of the physical law of gravity. Nonetheless, the fundamental analogies still hold good.

Olsson (1970), Gale (1973) and Willis (1975) have all discussed the value of physical analogue models in the study of migration flows. They have taken the function:

$$I_{ij} = f(P_i, P_j, D_{ij}) \qquad (2.7)$$

and expressed it in a multivariate form:

$$I_{ij} = a \cdot \frac{P_i^{b_1} \cdot P_j^{b_2}}{D_{ij}^{b_3}}, \qquad (2.8)$$

that is:

$$\log I_{ij} = \log a + b_1 \log P_i + b_2 \log P_j - b_3 \log D_{ij} \qquad (2.9)$$

where a, b_1, b_2, b_3 are multiple regression coefficients. This development means that the populations of i and j can be weighted separately and those weights derived empirically by using multiple regression analysis (see Johnston, 1978, p. 83).

By this stage in the examination of migration streams the simple bivariate relationship between interaction and distance has been extended to include the attributes of the two interacting places. But this particular line of argument has not ended there. Stouffer (1940; 1960) has insisted that the attributes of intervening distance must also be taken into account: he does not regard distance as being important in its own right, but only as an indicator of the number of intervening opportunities that a migrant may be exposed to in movement between two places (Miller, 1972, p. 476). Stouffer's 1960 paper suggested that interaction between two places, i and j, was directly related to the product of the populations of i and j and inversely related to the product of the number of intervening opportunities and the number of the competing migrants. Stouffer's version of the gravity model can be represented as follows:

$$P_{ij} = a \cdot \frac{(P_i \cdot P_j)^{b_1}}{(O_{ij})^{b_2} \cdot (C_{ij})^{b_3}}, \qquad (2.10)$$

that is:

$$\log I_{ij} = \log a + b_1 \log (P_i \cdot P_j) - b_2 \log O_{ij} - b_3 \log C_{ij} \qquad (2.11)$$

where O_{ij} = the number of intervening opportunities, measured by the total number of out-migrants in the circle centred mid-way between i and j and passing through i and j,

C_{ij} = the number of competing migrants, measured by the total number of in-migrants in the circle centred on j and passing through i.

There is still a glimmer of Newton's original concept in Stouffer's model, but the trappings of social science have accumulated so that even the simplicity of Eqn (2.5) has been obscured.

The idea that the stream of migration between two places is directly related to the sizes of those two places and inversely related to the distance between them is a fundamental one of universal applicability. However, the basic notion has been modified and adapted to fit particular cases in the hope that it will prove to be a means of predicting the level of interaction or the volume of migration (Wilson, 1970; Yannopoulos, 1971; Klaassen and Drewe, 1973). The gravity-model approach to the examination of migration patterns is a normative approach which assumes such things as perfect information availability, equal movement cost in all directions and the same processes of opportunity appraisal by all potential migrants. As such, this approach ignores the real-life behavioural context of all migration decisions, and yet in dealing with aggregate flows the gravity model is often successful in providing a general model of migratory movement: Wolpert's (1965) rejection of it is too extreme. In interpreting the results, however, the problem remains that this approach is one developed on an analogy with the physical sciences, and there is no general agreement on the basic social science axioms that could be used to justify the general form of Eqn (2.5) or to understand the differential weightings of populations that occur in the application of Eqn (2.9) to real-world data. Thus, although the gravity model is generally accepted as a tool for migration analysis it is by no means fully understood. Behaviouralist arguments presented in Chapter 1 suggest that distance is only one of many factors considered by a potential migrant, and that therefore the elevation of distance to the role of a prime determinant of spatial movement may anyway be unjustified. Nevertheless, as Stouffer's work demonstrates, distance of movement is likely to be related to population density, and to the distribution of settlements and opportunities. It may be suggested that experimentation with the incorporation of migrants' perceived distance instead of geographical distance might prove of interest and might thus help to provide a bridge between the behaviouralist discussion of individuals and the aggregate level of normal social science 'laws' and generalizations, especially as these are needed in the analysis of migration streams.

The analysis of migration patterns and flows has been approached in a variety of ways. It has been shown that generalizations are possible about such flows, and that useful information can be obtained from the examination of migration patterns to enable detailed study of the effects of migration on places of origin and destination to be carried out.

Chapter 3

The geographical impact of migration

P. E. White and R. I. Woods

In Chapter 1 it was argued that population migration is a field of study of importance to several different disciplines – to sociology, economics, psychology, demography and history as well as to geography. It is possible to go further and to suggest that the analysis of migration is fundamental to the understanding of many aspects of man and society. One of the tasks of all social sciences is to explain diversity, whether it be in economic well-being, in social or cultural structures, in patterns of historical evolution between nations, or in the spatial distribution of various forms of human organization or activity. The movement of people across the earth's surface has been, and is still, a major force in both creating and perpetuating diversity, particularly in the spatial manifestations of diversity which are of interest to the geographer. International or regional patterns of cultural affiliation, inter-regional variations in the rates of population growth, intra-urban variations in the spatial patterns of social segregation: these must all, in part, be explained in terms of past or present migration patterns. Migration has an impact at many different scales and on many aspects of human activity.

But migration is not just a creator of diversity: it is also a response to diversity itself or, at least, to individuals' perception of that diversity (Ch. 1). Consequently, migration systems often tend to operate as self-fuelling processes whereby once migration has started further population movement becomes almost inevitable for a variety of structural reasons relating to the societies affected and individual reasons relating to the migrants. Many migrations can be regarded not just as particularist 'events' but, in a larger context, as 'structures' themselves – as continuous phenomena which are embedded in the social and economic framework of human organization. Migration as a 'structure' is both an 'effect' of patterns of human diversity and a 'cause' of further diversity in the future. The full study of migration must inevitably take into account this long time-scale within which a migration structure develops and has its repercussions.

Jean Gottmann (1952, p. 1) has suggested that even if the earth had a uniform surface, like a billiard-ball, latitudinal location would be associated with climatological variations which would thus cause unequal distributions of plants, animals and of mankind which depends on these for food. Human spatial diversity is a basic fact of our planet made all the more acute by the great physical and resource variations that exist on our non-uniform globe. It has been demonstrated in Chapter 1 that the perceived variations between places are the root causes of migration, and it can therefore be argued that as long as these variations are realized or perceived by man there will be residential movement. The realization or perception of variation is, itself, likely to depend on other forms of movement, whether of people themselves or of information, by a circular process linking past with future mobility.

It is necessary to add to this concept of the environmental inevitability of migration the recognition of the importance of the original patterns of population movement which led mankind to spread the limits of the 'oecumene' or inhabited world. Since the late Upper Pleistocene major movements of population have been instrumental in distributing mankind across the globe from the centres of evolution of primitive hominids in East Africa and South-West Asia (Spencer and Thomas, 1978, pp. 33–44). The occurrence of population migration is therefore not only environmentally inevitable: it has been inherent in the evolutionary history of modern man.

If the importance of migration in influencing all aspects of human organization and activity is accepted, it becomes desirable that in the consideration of the impact of migration some sort of framework is adopted which will enable the inter-relationships between the different influences of migration to be drawn out. It is to the construction of such a framework that attention must now be given.

A framework for migration impact study

At the start of Chapter 1 five questions concerning the general study of migration were set out. The fourth and fifth questions were those of the effects of migration on the areas that the migrants come from, and on the areas that they go to. In Chapter 1 it was suggested that the single most important control on these effects was the nature of migrant selectivity and the way in which the migrants are differentiated from the rest of the population at both origin and destination. Chapter 2 has added to that picture by indicating the importance of migration volume, particularly in connection with the analysis of the inter-regional migration flows shown in Table 2.1.

Any migration event may be considered as having effects in five specific contexts. Firstly, there is the effect on the migrant in changing his way of life, his knowledge and experience of other places and his attitudes and beliefs. Secondly, there is the effect on the community that the migrant leaves, and thirdly, the effect on the community that the migrant goes to. Fourthly, the migration event produces a spatial pattern – a flow from origin to destination – which can be regarded as the effect of migration on the intervening space through which the migration occurs. Fifthly, migration takes place within a given structural context and can affect that structure in various ways which may, in certain cases, lead to the perpetuation of migration as a structure itself. Figure 3.1 presents a simple framework for migration impact study which enables these five aspects to be identified as part of an inter-connected system.

The migrants

At the centre of the framework are the migrants who can also be regarded separately as emigrants from their places of origin and as immigrants to their places of destination. The effect of migration on the migrants can take many different forms, and the motivations of the migrants are of obvious significance in evaluating the relative scale of changes in social outlook, in economic well-being,

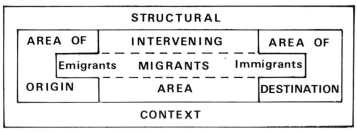

Fig. 3.1   A framework for the analysis of migration impact.

in education level or in levels of awareness of opportunities elsewhere. The effects of migration on the migrant result from the change of environment that is undergone, whether physical, social, cultural or economic, or a combination of all of these. Where some element of the human environment is altered the migrant may have to adapt to a new set of behavioural norms, but even where the migrant moves within a group of similar human environments the change in physical surroundings may have some psychological effect on the migrant, not least in providing him with information about new places.

Many of these effects of migration on the migrants have been the concern of psychologists and sociologists who have studied attitudinal changes that occur as a result of migration (for example see Levine, 1973, on rural migrants in Ankara, Turkey; or Duocastella, 1970, on Andalusian migrants in Catalonia, Spain). Certain aspects of the effects of migration on migrants are, however, of major importance to the geographer. One of these is the fact that migration may add new information to the migrant's place utility matrix (Fig. 1.2) and may also, through the social and cultural changes that the migrant undergoes, lead to changed aspirations and changes in the nature of the variables or attributes of places considered. The result of both of these processes may be that the migrant decides to make a further residential move and, as a further effect of these changes in information availability and in the place variables considered, such future migration may be restricted to a limited number of distinctive directional flows (see Ch. 6). For any individual, past migration behaviour and pattern (including the distance and direction of movement) may be a key to present or future migration activity and to the geographical character of such activity. It has been a general research finding that when an individual has moved once his propensity for future migratory moves is increased. Thus the self-fuelling aspect of the effect of migration upon the migrant may be understood.

Migration can also be self-perpetuating as a general system as a result of its effects on the migrants. If the migrants are satisfied with their move and communicate that satisfaction back to their friends and relatives in the communities of origin it is likely that a chain migration process will be set up (Ch. 2).

One final point concerning the effect of migration on the migrants is that migration itself – the physical act of moving from one place to another – is of much less importance than the environmental transfer that migration implies. In particular it is the change of community, with accompanying changes in attitudes manifesting themselves in new behaviour patterns, which provides the basis for the investigation of a whole range of repercussions for the migration system as a whole.

The areas of origin and destination

It has already been stated that in the consideration of the effects of migration on the areas that the migrants leave and on those that they go to detailed attention must be given to the nature of the selectivity of the migrants. In Chapter 1 it was noted that migrants are never randomly selected from the populations of the areas of origin, and that they do not form a random cross-section addition to the populations at the areas of destination. The migrant forms a loss to his community of origin of an individual with certain characteristics of age, sex, social attitudes and so on; and he similarly forms an addition to the destination community, bringing to it a further strengthening of those attributes. The analyses of the effects of migration on origin and destination are therefore intimately linked and can be dealt with together here in terms of the framework shown in Fig. 3.1

In this context it is useful to identify the attributes of migrants which may be of particular significance: in part these are the characteristics of selectivity discussed in Chapter 1. As a first group of characteristics, those concerned with demographic factors may be isolated. The numbers moving are obviously of great significance, but attributes of individual migrants such as age, sex, marital status and family size are also extremely important. One topic of particular concern in the demographic aspects of migration study is the working of the connection between migration and the natural growth of population. Where migrants are young married couples, for example, the demographic effects of the migration may include a reduction of the crude birth rates in the areas of migrant origin and an increase in crude birth rates in the areas of destination, brought about by the redistribution of a significantly large sector of the reproductively active population. Where a migration stream consists of the retired, crude death rates in the origin areas may fall while mortality in the destination areas rises. Migration may be a response to a particular pattern of natural change, and it may also create new patterns. Merlin (1971) has demonstrated the positive correlation between the rate of natural increase and the rate of emigration for rural France in the later years of the nineteenth century, and has therefore suggested the dependence of migration upon natural increases in population which reduced local rural opportunities. In the twentieth century, in many areas continued rural emigration has reduced natural increase rates considerably through the selective loss of the young adult age-group.

A second group of migrant attributes which gave rise to specific impact patterns is formed of social factor characteristics – intelligence or education, social status, race or ethnicity, or cultural background, including such questions as language or religion. The origin and destination communities are modified in some way if migration is at all selective in terms of any of these social factors.

The third group of attributes is a little more difficult to deal with – occupation, income levels and economic class. These are more problematic because in these respects the migrant is quite likely to represent different things to the sending and to the receiving communities. Certainly with some of the demographic variables, such as marital status, the migrant may 'change' his classification in the course of his move, but this is even more likely with occupational and income variables. The farm labourer who moves to the city for industrial employment is not only changing residence but also changing occupation and, probably, income level.

A final group of attributes is a development of those that have already been dealt with – the attributes of political allegiance and of attitudes to society in general, including elements of innovativeness or traditionalism. Although we have Petersen's (1958, p. 265) reminder that traditionalist migration does exist it is generally true that migration involves the more innovative elements in the origin communities and may deprive those communities of social leadership. It is harder, however, to generalize on the reception of innovative elements in the migration destinations: Galtung (1971, p. 191) has suggested that innovators can only be identified as such in terms of their origin communities – they may be strikingly conservative in the context of their destination societies. Nevertheless the selectivity of migrants in terms of attitudes and political ideas can lead to an altered political balance in the receiving areas if the volume of migration is large enough and if certain specific migration streams dominate (Mannucci, 1970, p. 261).

To the geographer the impacts of migration in the sending and receiving areas are most interesting in terms of their spatial manifestations. Any migration is a redistribution of population, and it has now been shown that redistribution also affects various demographic, social, economic and political attributes of that population, many of which have important spatial implications. Migration has played a vital role in many diverse fields. Patterns of spatial segregation of social groups in cities throughout the world have been created largely through differential migration between specific neighbourhood areas. Population distribution in much of North America or Australasia is inexplicable without consideration of migration from Europe. Within Europe the present-day distribution of languages in the continent as a whole is dependent upon migration over the last 2,000 years, especially in the Alpine realm (Rougier, 1977). In each of these examples migration has had effects at both origin and destination. Urban social segregation through migration has created distinct and homogeneous social areas for the population at both ends of the social spectrum (Ch. 10). European overseas migration led in part to a reduction of Europe's rate of population increase as well as to the peopling of new lands elsewhere (Ch. 5). The migrations of specific cultural groups within Europe have spread certain cultures at the expense of others.

In all of these considerations of the impact of migration on origins and destinations it is migrant selectivity that is of the greatest importance. It is because selectivity operates that it is possible to talk of 'redistributions' of populations with specific attributes. And it is through those redistributions – population growth in one area, decline in another, the reduction in a social group in one place, its strengthening in another – that migration has its strongest geographical impacts by modifying existing spatial patterns of human organization and by creating new ones.

The intervening area

In moving through geographical space between their origins and their destinations migrants set up distinct spatial patterns, the analysis of which has been a major concern of geographers over the last 50 years. These spatial patterns of movement have been the subject of major discussion in Chapter 2. In the present context two points about the effect of migration on the intervening area need to be made. Firstly, migrant selectivity is probably of lesser importance in this topic than in others. Certainly it can be suggested that for lower status groups intervening opportunities are more likely to limit migration distance than for high status groups for whom opportunities are fewer; but in general the majority of selectivity variables are of more significance in determining who migrates than in influencing the spatial patterns of movement once it occurs, except in the form of constraints upon direction imposed by the spatial distribution of perceived high place utility areas for particular groups of migrants.

Secondly, the effects of migration on the intervening space are largely intangible, only involving transitory groups who have no interaction with the area other than by passing through it. Intervening society is not directly affected by this migration. For these reasons geographers, with their interest in spatial patterns, have been the main group to look closely at this aspect of the migration system.

The structural context

All migrations take place within an economic, social or political context which in some way links the area of origin of the migrant with his area of destination. At the most basic level there must be a certain process of information flow operating whereby knowledge about potential destinations is built up among potential migrants: possibly the migration phenomenon itself forms part of this structural context if it is past migrants who provide the information link in the chain migration process encouraging future movement.

But the structural context is broader than this, and its inter-relationships with the migration process are two-way. Firstly, the economic and social context conditions to a large extent the type of migration that occurs by producing the particular context of spatial differentiation to which migrants respond. Secondly, migration itself can either alter or reinforce that context. Two examples can be given of these two-way inter-relationships: both are dealt with in greater detail later in this volume.

The process of rural-to-urban migration in nineteenth-century England and Wales occurred against a background of increasing urban labour demand as a result of capitalist industrial development (Ch. 8) and high rates of rural population growth leading towards rural overpopulation (Ch. 5). In many parts of the country the economic and social structures were based on fragmented small-scale production, often for a local rather than national market. The migration streams which left the countryside for the towns brought profound changes to the rates and types of urban development and also altered the pattern of rural population growth leading, in the long term, to the present-day phenomenon of rural depopulation (Saville, 1957; Thomas, J. G., 1972). In addition, however, this migration was one of several factors increasing rural–urban contact, thereby helping towards the creation of a 'national' social system which, in interaction with the old 'local' systems, has led to the transformation of the social significance of the village and the reduction in local parochialism in traditionally independent regions (Pahl, 1966). By reducing rural populations from the middle of the nineteenth century and thereby reducing the market for the production of local craft industries migration from rural areas also aided in the invasion of local rural markets by mass-produced industrial goods, while the growth of urban industrialization itself was in part fuelled by the absorption of more people into the urban consumer economy as a result of migration. Rural–urban migration in nineteenth-century England and Wales was brought into being by the existing structural features of the economy and society; but migration also contributed to a profound alteration of that social and economic structure on a national level.

A second example of the inter-relationships between migration and the structural context within which it operates is afforded by intra-urban movement in many Western societies. One of the important factors in much intra-urban movement (Ch. 10) is the desire of individuals at particular levels in the perceived hierarchy of social status to group together with others of a similar level, and to avoid contact with those of other levels. Within the city, therefore, migration takes place to put into effect these desires which are themselves a reflection of structural attitudes inherent in modern society. These structural social attitudes have a much wider relevance than simply their role in engendering migration (Halsey, 1978), but migration, by perpetuating social segregation in geographical space, helps also to perpetuate the underlying social structure by limiting contact between social groups and by militating against the creation of a residential social mix.

Many of the effects of migration on the structural context within which it occurs may appear to be of no direct geographical significance, yet in practice these impacts are just as important as the more small-scale effects on the sending and receiving communities. It is likely that if migration acts to maintain a particular social or economic structure the system will be self-perpetuating such that the need for further migration in the future is created. If migration acts to alter the underlying structural features movement may, in the longer term, diminish; however, it is possible that the new social and economic structures brought about in part by migration will have spatial manifestations of great significance. Thus, in the example already quoted, rural–urban migration in nineteenth-century England and Wales played a part in the creation of a new social and economic system at the national scale, the analysis of which is an essential task for all social scientists.

Systems analysis of migration

It should be clear by now that the impacts of migration occur at many different scales and affect many different phenomena. Indeed it has been shown that any migration event may have repercussions which manifest themselves in further migration, while all migration takes place within some structural framework and acts in some way either to alter or to reinforce that structure. When a migration event is repeated by many others in a particular migration stream these inter-related effects of migration on individuals, places of origin and destination, and on the structural context become of great importance. The study of migration impact is not simply a descriptive study: it must necessarily be analytical in terms of causes and effects in order that a fuller understanding be gained of how particular impacts of migration are brought about. But in the analysis of migration the cause-and-effect relationships do not operate only in one direction: there are feed-back links between different aspects of the migration system such that 'effects' can, themselves, become 'causes'. For example, the changes brought about in the life-style of an individual who has undertaken a residential move will condition the information that he may send back to his original community, and such information will control the extent of chain migration set off which, in turn, will affect the origin community as a whole.

Therefore the most complete analysis of migration can only be undertaken by adopting a systems framework in which the inter-relationships between the various phenomena involved in migration can be modelled, tested and more fully understood. Inevitably, however, there are severe problems with this approach. Firstly, there is the question of data collection: many of the inter-relationships between phenomena are unquantifiable and difficult to evaluate even at a qualitative level – such is the case, for example, with the information flow that sets up chain migration. Additionally, as pointed out in Chapter 1, the data needed for migration analysis must often be collected by survey methods which are time consuming and preclude a macro-scale approach. Secondly, there is the problem of disentangling the effects of migration from the effects of other changes in social and economic structures which occur in part independently of migration. Thus in the previous section rural–urban migration was said to have been important in giving a more 'national' aspect to the economy and society of England and Wales, yet such 'modernization' was also fostered by increasing literacy, by changes in agricultural organization at local, national and international levels, and by technological developments in transportation, as well as by many other factors. The chapter headings in Eugen Weber's book (1977) on the modernization of rural France provide an excellent list of the factors at work and show that migration was only one among many important and inter-connected processes of change.

The vast majority of published studies of migration have been concerned with only a limited number of aspects of migration impact, and few have dealt with the feed-back aspects of migration systems: the broader scale of migration analysis has not been attempted by many. Briggs (1978) has considered Italian migration to three cities in the USA and has looked at the sending and receiving areas and at the migrants themselves. Rudé (1978), in the course of a volume on the transportation of convicts from England to the colonies in the nineteenth century, has provided an interesting case study of the effects of forced migration. Other studies on a broader scale include Caldwell (1969) on rural–urban migration in Ghana, Redford (1926) on labour migration in early nineteenth-century England, Demko (1969) on land colonization in Russian Kazakhstan, and Paine (1974) on Turkish migrants in post-war Europe. Most of such studies have been written by economic historians, demographers or sociologists rather than by geographers.

Mabogunje (1970) has provided the major geographical contribution to the creation of a suitable detailed framework for the complete analysis of the migration process, both for its own sake and for its impacts. His model adopts a systems analytical structure which should enable the full implications of rural–urban migration to be considered as a series of inter-connected cause-and-effect loops. It shows that impacts in one area or in one sector of society bring reflexive changes in other areas or sectors through processes of mutual adjustment and readjustment.

An example of a systems framework: European labour migration

International labour migration to the industrialized countries of North-West

Europe provides an interesting case which can be used to illustrate the utility of an integrated systems approach to migration analysis. During the period from the end of the Second World War to the onset of general economic recession in 1974 massive population flows took place – the extensive and important repercussions of which can be analysed using a modification of the general framework of Fig. 3.1, recognizing the inter-relationships between migration impacts in different sectors. In the following discussion it is not the intention to explain in detail the full effects of European labour migration, but to demonstrate how a systems approach to migration analysis can provide a basis for dealing with questions of impact. Even in such a general outline it is necessary to limit the scope of the discussion by omitting detailed consideration of the counter-flows of return migration which are, themselves, of considerable importance in perpetuating the system as a whole (King, 1978). The field of European labour migration has been one in which researchers from many different disciplines have taken an interest but, with the partial exceptions of works by Böhning (1972) and Paine (1974), no coherent large-scale frameworks for analysis have been put forward.

The structural context – I   POST WAR MIGN IN EUROPE

The structural context of post-war labour migration can be dealt with in three parts: the receiving economies and societies as a whole; the sending economies and societies as a whole; and the structural inter-relationships between them. The receiving economies have been the European nations of Switzerland, Austria, West Germany, France, the Benelux countries, the United Kingdom and, although to a lesser extent, the Scandinavian group. The sending countries have been in the Mediterranean area – Portugal, Spain, Italy, Yugoslavia, Greece and Turkey – along with the new nations of the Caribbean, North Africa, the Indian sub-continent and the East Indies which were once part of European colonial empires.

The important structural features of the receiving economies and societies appear to be four-fold (Böhning, 1970; 1972). Firstly, these economies have experienced rapid industrial and economic growth over the past century or more, such growth taking place in a capitalist framework of unequal spatial development which allowed urban industrial expansion to be fuelled by migration from the rural areas. Secondly, the rural labour pool started to dry up in most developed European countries some time after the 1930s as rural population fertility began to fall and natural increase declined: local rural labour to aid urban industrial development was no longer available in large quantities. Thirdly, the indigenous birth cohorts coming on to the labour market after about 1945 tended to be roughly the same size each year, while retirement cohorts were in some cases larger than the school-leaver group (McDonald, 1969, p. 118): this was the result of the general overall fertility decline in most Northern European populations from the latter half of the nineteenth century. Fourthly, in consequence, post-war economic growth occurred at a rate faster than that at which the indigenous populations could supply labour: in such a situation full employment was the rule, and the job-seeker very often had a choice of employment whereby he could avoid those jobs that were seen as socially undesirable through low pay, employment conditions, unsocial hours or low status (Böhning, 1972, pp. 55–6; Castles and Castles, 1971, pp. 308–13). Such jobs varied from country to country – unskilled factory jobs were shunned in many societies, construction in virtually all, mining in Belgium, transport and nursing in the United Kingdom, agriculture in West Germany and the tourist industry in Switzerland (Castles and Kosack, 1973).

The structural features of the receiving economies and societies therefore created the demand and opportunities for labour from elsewhere: the structural features of the sending societies were such as to make labour available through the dearth of local opportunities in comparison. The sending societies were basically all affected by one major factor – rural overpopulation. These countries had either not experienced major industrial growth or, as in the cases of Spain and Italy, had not yet produced sufficient growth to absorb the rural surplus. All still had relatively high rates of natural increase of their populations.

The structural links between the sending and receiving economies were, in part, colonial or semi-colonial, involving not only administrative connections (of parent–offspring after the dissolution of the colonial empires) but also of embryonic and partial socialization and acculturation brought about by the colonial imposition of alien education and value-systems (Edmond-Smith, 1972). For the non-colonial countries of Southern Europe (with the exception of Yugoslavia) the links to the receiving countries were through the co-existence of free market capitalist economies of unrestricted labour movement.

This, then, is an outline of the structural context within which labour migration occurred. Already it is possible to pose questions about the effects of the operation of labour migration on these long-term structural factors. Has rural overpopulation in the sending societies been reduced? Has migration affected population fertility levels there? Has migration altered in any way the colonial or semi-colonial bonds between certain sending and receiving countries? What effect has migration had on fertility in the receiving societies, or on economic growth there?

The migrants

The structural context outlined above provided the reasons for migration through the unequal national pattern of employment opportunities. It also showed the links through which deliberate information dissemination on the part of the labour-demanding economies created in the populations of the labour-rich countries the perception of those opportunities elsewhere. However, as with all migrations, this labour migration was highly selective, the selectivity controls being of two kinds. Firstly, there was selection within the sending societies according to age, sex, occupation, innovativeness, education and so on – the various migrant characteristics discussed earlier in this chapter. Secondly, there was further selectivity operated by the receiving societies in terms of whom they wanted. Males were required for certain jobs, females for others, and nowhere were whole families welcomed until the 1960s when competition became intense between the receiving societies desiring to obtain migrants (Castles and Kosack, 1973, p. 38). In many cases the selection processes operated by the receiving societies were extremely restrictive and tended to intensify the process of age and educational selectivity already operating (Böhning, 1974, p. 14) so that migrants came from a particularly narrow segment of the total population of the sending society, although the extent and nature of selectivity changed over time as more and more dependents moved. An understanding of both kinds of selectivity control is vital in the analysis of the effects of the migration.

The labour migrants have followed specific migration paths and the matching of origins and destinations has been by no means random. This topic, the investigation of the spatial flows of migrants, may be regarded as the impact of migration on intervening space. While almost all receiving countries have accepted significant numbers of Italians and Spaniards the migrants from outside Europe have been largely confined to the lands of their ex-colonial powers. Thus North Africans have gone to France (Bourgeois-Pichat, 1974, pp. 585–6), Surinamers and Indonesians to the Netherlands (Bagley, 1971) and Jamaicans, Indians and Pakistanis to the United Kingdom (Peach, 1968). The spatial migration patterns, which have in the past been a major concern of geographers, result therefore from various factors – the locations of labour demand in the receiving countries (Rabut, 1973), the locations of labour supply in the sending countries (Álvarez and Antolín, 1973), the structural connections between the two, and the actual attributes of the migrants which may determine who goes where at a detailed level, particularly where strong selectivity controls operate (Selke, 1974).

It can be argued that the impact of European labour migration on the migrants is limited by the fact that many migrants have been held in a strong legal–administrative network of entry permits and residence documents which has been a development of the selectivity policies operated by the receiving countries. In such a situation the migrant has had little chance of upward social or educational mobility within the country he has moved to. This has certainly been the case in Switzerland and West Germany. In the latter country it was officially believed for many years that the labour shortage was likely to be only a short-term feature: as a result policies for migrant integration were not put forward until 1970 (Böhning, 1972, pp. 36–7; Puls, 1975). Even within a country such as the United Kingdom where migrants, once arrived, were largely free of special legal control, social and economic advancement has been to a large extent blocked by the existence of structural social antipathy towards an immigrant group, largely of distinct racial origins, performing socially undesirable, although essential, work and, partly as a result of such antipathy, suffering the problems of deprivation common to the lowest social and economic strata. Whether through either legal control or informal societal control large-scale upward mobility has not been possible for the European labour migrant.

However, one effect of migration on the migrant, even despite his usually low economic status within his host country, has been a higher income level than he enjoyed at home. Consequently, a distinctive feature of the labour migration system has been the creation of both remittance and of information flows back to the migrants' origin communities which has had the effect there of raising aspirations and of encouraging further movement.

The areas of destination

The effects of migration in the receiving society are likely to be many and only those of distinct spatial implication are mentioned here. European labour migrants, in whatever country they go to, are generally a distinctive group, set aside from the local indigenous population by several traits: the migrant group is usually predominantly young, has a markedly imbalanced sex structure and is of a distinctive cultural and ethnic origin. In addition, certain attributes of the host society are of importance in conditioning the local spatial implications of the migration flow – the detailed workings of the local housing market, for example, particularly as these operate for the relatively underprivileged and transient groups in society.

Such migrant and societal attributes together create patterns of both social and spatial segregation of migrant groups. The weak position of migrants in the housing market may force them into the poorest multi-occupied accommodation which is shunned by the host population, while chain migration processes and the desire among migrants for the maintenance of a socially and culturally familiar base (Schnapper, 1976) add further arrivals to such areas to create distinctive migrant districts of cities or suburbs (Geiger, 1975; Schenk, 1975). In some countries, such as France, Switzerland and West Germany, migrant workers have been housed in purpose-built hostels, thereby institutionally creating segregation from the indigenous populations (Castles and Castles, 1971, p. 309). It is, perhaps, in the general creation of new patterns of social and spatial residential segregation that labour migration has had its greatest impact in the receiving areas of Northern Europe – notably in the larger cities. But questions of migration impact here can only be understood through a recognition of the controls of migrant selectivity, and of the existence of distinct social attitudes and prejudices among both the migrants and their hosts – attitudes which, when played out as discriminatory behaviour, result in segregation of all kinds. It is, however, important to note that this labour migration has only added a further, and important, type of segregation to the spatial patterning of European cities (Pahl, 1970b). The existence of distinctive social areas certainly predates recent labour migration and results, in part, from other forms of migration continually in operation.

The areas of origin

Much of the labour migration has taken place from rural areas and has involved either a surplus or an under-employed agricultural labour force. According to the numbers involved and the exact people moving, agriculture may be either benefited (Álvarez and Antolín, 1973, p. 133) or disadvantaged by its loss of labour. If too many males leave, agriculture becomes a female employment sector on a part-time basis such that productivity declines: in any case migration is likely to involve the more innovative elements so that agricultural improvement is hampered. The impact of migration on agriculture is a major field and one that has not yet been fully explored.

Remittance and information flows from departed migrants to their areas of origin are likely to be of significance in two ways. Firstly, as already mentioned, they are likely to foster the creation of further migration in the future. Secondly, increased income in the areas sending the migrants may bring about a higher standard of living with emphasis being particularly placed upon the purchase of consumer goods (Leloup, 1972, p. 73): aspirations rise towards the local luxury commodities that are regarded as essential for daily life by the populations of the countries that receive the migrants.

The structural context – II

Finally, examination must be made of the impact of the whole migration system on the structural variables which created the system in the first place. The receiving countries undergo few major structural changes. Economic growth continues and creates further labour shortages which in turn encourage further migration. In those countries where legal controls force the migrants to return home after a year or two, long-term recruitment problems can build up such that attempts are made to attract migrants from further afield (Böhning, 1972, p. 29). As the movement of immigrants into socially undesirable jobs continues the margin of social undesirability tends to rise as upward social mobility of the native-born continues (Böhning, 1972, pp. 54–8). Similarly, as immigrants move into certain residential areas these become undesirable for the indigenous population so that social and occupational segregation intensify and new forms of spatial segregation are added as structural features. Declining population fertility may, to a certain extent, be arrested by labour migration where the migrants bring their families, as in the case of the United Kingdom (Immigrant Statistics Unit, 1978) or the Netherlands, but in countries where single-sex migration has dominated (such as West Germany) the total pattern of natural population change may be hardly affected, even though immigrant fertility levels may be relatively high (Ho, 1972, p. 312).

The structural features of the sending society are also affected by the migration system. The continued existence of rural overpopulation depends to a large extent upon the nature of the effects of migration upon agriculture and upon the selectivity of emigration. The effect of migration on population fertility levels will depend, as in the receiving countries, upon the actual age and sex structures of the migrants. For countries such as Turkey or Greece, from which most migrants have been males leaving their wives behind, the effect of migration in reducing fertility has been negligible.

In both receiving and sending countries economic growth and development depends largely on factors which are not directly linked to the migration system. However, even here migration does make a contribution. Remittances sent home by migratory workers have a deflationary effect on the economy of the labour-receiving countries, while having an inflationary effect on the economy of the labour-sending countries where more money is put into circulation without a corresponding increase in production. The purchase of consumer goods in such societies may even increase the exports of the labour-deficient countries, thereby fuelling further economic growth and producing greater demands for labour there (Böhning, 1974, pp. 11–14).

In total, therefore, the structural effect of European labour migration in the period of rapid economic growth from 1945 to 1974 was to perpetuate a pattern of unequal economic growth between different countries, and to foster migration as a semi-permanent, long-term social and economic feature.

The purpose of this discussion of post-war European labour migration has been to illustrate the inter-relationships between the many features of any migration flow and to outline a suitable framework within which individual aspects of migration impact can be investigated. It is clear that the effects of migration are of great significance, not only to geographers but also to economists, sociologists, political scientists and psychologists. The geographer may be basically interested in the spatial manifestations of migration impact, yet he must be aware, in producing his explanations of these spatial patterns, of the totality of human experience and organization and of the manifold indirect effects and feedback loops that operate in any migration system.

It is, of course, not correct to suggest that the only logical method of investigating migration impact is by means of a systems framework. As can be seen from the example presented, the effects of migration, the causes of the migration and the long-term structural correlates of migration are in combination almost inevitably too numerous for satisfactory investigation at anything other than a cursory level. Accordingly the majority of detailed studies of migration impact will continue to deal with only a part of the total migration system. It is essential, however, to realize the complexity of migration as a human activity, to recognize both the direct and indirect effects accruing from that activity, and thereby to accept the piecemeal nature of more detailed and limited studies.

Conclusions

To the geographer the basic impacts of migration are transformations in certain spatial patterns brought about by population movement. Those spatial patterns are of population distribution itself, along with detailed attributes of population, such as age, sex, employment characteristics, social attributes and the spatial manifestations of social class, and patterns of culture, attitude and political affiliation. Also of importance must be the impacts of migration, not just in terms of population distribution and patterns, but in terms of the location, genesis or collapse of economic activities and of wider social and political structures. It is inevitable that migration can rarely be studied as a whole because of the inexhaustible ramifications of any migration system, and it is consequently desirable to limit the study of migration impacts to manageable problems while accepting the wider importance of the field.

The study of the whole range of migration impacts by geographers is relatively novel. Until recent years more attention has been paid to the spatial flows of migrants than to other forms of migration effects, and it can still be argued that the effects of migration on the sending societies have been too little studied (Lowenthal and Comitas, 1962).

In producing a framework for the discussion of any questions concerned with migration impact it is essential to progress through various stages of analysis in a logical sequence. In the first place it is necessary to look at the inter-related questions of why a particular migration occurs at all and who is involved. The character of the migrant is of overwhelming importance in migration impact study for he is the agent of change – the actor and the reactor (Douglass, 1970) – reacting to structural diversity within the spatial social and economic system and acting either to reinforce that diversity or to alter it in some way. The full examination of why migration occurs must consider such spatial diversity and must attempt to do so through the eyes of the potential migrant as a way of understanding individual migration motivations. Neither the consideration of migration genesis nor of migrant selectivity may appear of themselves to be of direct geographical relevance, but in practice without such considerations there can be no full understanding of migration as a human process nor of the impact of that process in creating its own spatial patterns or altering others.

The creation of spatial patterns in migration is brought about by migration flows and by the common groups of origins and destinations found among migrants in any particular migration system. Migration is a purposive move in response to perceived spatial diversity, and therefore the basis for an explanation of the spatial patterns of movement must lie in those patterns of diversity that gave rise to it.

The investigation of the patterns of migratory flow, coupled with examinations of the effects of migration on origin and destination areas, must be the geographer's chief concern in the analysis of migration impact, for it is in these fields that migration has the most obvious repercussions on the spatial organization of human activities. It is in these fields that the relevance of the consideration of migrant selectivity becomes clear through the role that such selection processes play in explaining migration impacts.

Despite the obvious concern of geographers with the analysis of migration in this way, it is necessary to bear in mind the more large-scale and widespread repercussions of migration on other aspects of human activity, many of which, through the creation or alteration of underlying patterns of human economic, social, cultural or political diversity, will almost inevitably in the long term lead to further movements of population.

It is the intention of the latter half of this volume to provide a series of individual studies of various aspects of the impact of migration at various scales and for various time-periods. As each chapter is necessarily of a limited length the discussions are understandably partial: it is possible, however, to see how each chapter fits into the framework of migration impact study presented in Fig. 3.1. Indeed, a conceptual framework of this type must be an essential part of any investigation of the topic of migration since it provides a means of answering the basic questions about migration with which Chapter 1 commenced, and of leading towards a more detailed analysis of the whole set of impacts from any one migration system.

Chapter 4

Studies of the geographical impact of migration

P. E. White and R. I. Woods

An attempt has been made in the foregoing three chapters to provide frameworks with which to analyse the five questions posed at the start of Chapter 1. The tenets of behaviouralist theory can be applied to an individual's decision to migrate, and can thus provide an understanding of why migration occurs and why selectivity operates within any migration system. Chapter 2 outlined both inductive and deductive approaches to the study of the spatial patterning of migratory activities and showed that valid generalizations can be made about the flows of migrants between origins and destinations. In the third chapter the utility of general systems models was suggested for the full investigation of migration impacts of various kinds.

In the course of the following seven chapters illustrations are provided of the ways in which these suggested frameworks can be utilized in geographical studies of migration, paying particular attention to the question of migration impact. The case-study chapters can be read on their own as a series of contributions to the study of migration within their respective fields, but when read in conjunction with the three previous chapters they take up and discuss the applicability of the various migration themes in specific contexts.

In Chapter 3 it was suggested that migration impacts occur on five specific phenomena – on the migrants, on the areas of destination, on the areas of origin, on the intervening space and on the socio-economic structure within which migration occurs. It was also suggested, in looking at the spatial patterns of human organization in the origin and destination areas, that migrant attributes of four kinds were particularly important, those attributes being respectively demographic, social, economic and political or attitudinal. It is possible to build up a simple classificatory system for detailed migration impact studies, taking into account both the phenomena studied and the important migrant attributes of the relevant flow such that the inter-relationships between migrant variables and effects can be brought out.

Chapter 5 examines the important association between overpopulation and migration. Rural–rural, rural–urban and overseas migration are all seen as means by which overpopulation has been relieved in the societies of pre-industrial Western Europe. Migration had the effect of reducing population growth in the areas of origin, and in the destinations produced impacts in the expanding towns. The structural background to this type of migration is shown in Figs 5.2 and 5.3, and it is possible to see migration as one of a series of alternative responses to overpopulation. In Europe in the 'Age of Industrialization' migration succeeded, to a certain extent, as a means of demographic regulation. In the present-day Third World, in contrast, the scope for migration, particularly of the rural–rural or overseas varieties, is much smaller so that population movement is not capable of alleviating the problems of too rapid a rate of population increase. The impacts examined in Chapter 5 are structural and demographic in type and it is shown that present-day Third World migration affects the structure of overpopulation in ways differing from those of past migration in or from Europe.

Chapters 6 and 7 deal in different ways with the specific impacts of migration in the Third World. Chapter 6 uses behaviouralist concepts to explore the influence of past migration on the future migration preferences of university students and professional groups in Uganda. Figure 6.1 sets the framework in terms of the discussion of Chapter 1, and in the later analysis of questionnaire responses use is made of various methods of measuring directional bias in spatial flows. The case study highlights the value of the micro-level approach in elucidating the effects of migration on the migrants and shows that the future stream of inter-regional élite migration in Uganda is likely to perpetuate imbalances in economic development because the educated élite wish to move to the more advanced areas unless more opportunities are created for them in their home regions.

Rural Bolivia provides the context for the study reported in Chapter 7. The migration system under investigation is a rural–rural flow encouraged by land colonization and land reform measures. An initial set of reform legislation appeared to pave the way for a great improvement in rural living standards to be brought about by population redistribution, but it is shown in this chapter that neither the highland out-migration area nor the lowland in-migration zone have benefited from a migratory flow which has served to reinforce the pre-existing social and economic structures, especially those surrounding land tenure in the destination areas. Chapter 7 examines the effects of this rural–rural migration on the migrants themselves in terms of their economic well-being, and also on the sending and destination areas.

The case studies reported in the remaining four chapters deal with migrations occurring in the developed world over the last century and a half. Labour migration to Sheffield in the mid-nineteenth century is studied in Chapter 8 in which it is shown that the distinctive economic system and spatial distribution of opportunities of the period must be understood before the analysis of contrasting migration flows can be satisfactorily carried out. The chapter considers some of the problems of studying nineteenth-century migration flows and outlines procedures for handling data extracted from the enumerators' books of the census on individuals appearing in those books. Using this source a detailed picture is built up of the populations involved in migration to two suburban developments, and shows the inter-relationships between migrants and the social and economic structural context of their movement in a period of industrial growth.

In late nineteenth-century rural France economic stagnation was, by contrast, the main feature. From the middle of that century rural communities became less isolated and developed more contacts with the rest of the country. Those contacts were particularly fostered by migration which thus played a major role in what has been called the 'modernization' of rural France. Chapter 9 examines this role of migration, and especially the role of migration for marriage, in breaking down rural isolation in the department of Ardèche, on the eastern edge of the Massif Central, in the period from 1860 to 1970. Changes in marriage migration distance are examined, and the effects of long-term migration are shown in the demographic and social fragmentation of traditional peasant communities.

The case study reported in Chapter 10 deals with the movement of certain social groups in the English Midlands in recent decades. Intra–urban and intra-regional migration are shown to have perpetuated and even strengthened spatial patterns of social class segregation at various scales. Migration of an élite group is shown to have a distinct directional bias which contradicts the flow of other social groups in the opposite direction so that substantial inter-area class differences are reinforced. Chapter 10 examines questions of migrant selectivity by social status, and considers the effects of this selective migration in the spatial social structure of origin and destination areas.

The final chapter is a study of the demographic impact of migration loss in rural Normandy in the period 1962–75. The selectivity of migration is discussed in detail and a simulation process is used to examine how population structures might have evolved if migration had not occurred. Migration appears to be more important than natural change in the continuing development of small rural populations in the area studied, and the micro-level approach to migration investigation is shown to be valuable in examining the effects of migrant selectivity, according to demographic and economic variables, on the areas that the migrants leave behind.

Within the case-study chapters a wide range of migration impacts is studied, and consideration is given to several theoretical and technical problems commonly encountered in such work. The strengths and weaknesses of official data sources are discussed in Chapters 8 to 11, while Chapters 6 and 7 convey the particular difficulties involved in the analysis of Third World population migrations where adequate data do not exist.

The following chapters by no means cover all aspects of the geographical impact of migration, but they do serve to illustrate the general points raised in the first three chapters. Each study can also be fitted to at least part of the general framework for migration impact study of Fig. 3.1. Taken together the case studies show for particular periods and places just how important migration has been, and still is, in influencing the structure, distribution and organization of human activities.

Chapter 5

Migration and overpopulation

D. B. Grigg

In the last 30 years the population of Afro-Asia and Latin America has grown at a remarkable rate and this has had adverse effects upon economic development; much of what little can be saved in these low-income countries has to be diverted to maintaining existing capital equipment, and little is available for new industrial investment. The combination of constant or rising fertility and sharply declining mortality produces an unfavourable age structure, with a lower proportion of the population in working ages than in developed countries (Zaidan, 1969). But the most undesirable consequences are to be found in the rural areas which still contain the great majority of the population of the Third World. Farms have to be subdivided, and their fields are increasingly scattered; the number of holdings too small to provide a living has increased; the numbers without any land have risen; and real wages have fallen. Unemployment and, on family farms, underemployment are endemic. The price of land and its rent have risen. In some regions the cultivation of marginal land and the reduction of fallow have led to falling yields and often to soil erosion; grazing lands encroached upon by cultivation have been overstocked and overgrazed. In many areas farmers have turned from the preferred food crop to higher yielding but less palatable and less nutritionally valuable crops (Grigg, 1976).

Such problems of rural overpopulation are not found in many parts of the developed world today, but have certainly occurred in the past. European population history in the last millennium is often described as consisting of two phases; one of almost imperceptible growth from A.D. 1000 to 1750, followed by another of rapid growth to the present. But a closer examination reveals three periods of comparatively rapid growth separated by two of stagnation (Helleiner, 1967). From A.D. 1000 to 1300 was a period of increase throughout Western Europe; the population of England tripled between 1086 and 1340, and that of France doubled between 1100 and 1328. The pandemic of bubonic plague in 1348–50 – the Black Death – probably reduced numbers by a third, and there was no widespread recovery until the middle of the fifteenth century. But in many parts of Europe population doubled between 1450 and 1550; recovery began a little later in Northern Europe but was rapid in the sixteenth century. The population of Holland grew at 0.8 per cent per annum between 1514 and 1620, that of England by at least 0.62 per cent between 1528 and 1603 (de Vries, 1974, pp. 84–7; Cornwall, 1970). The seventeenth century, however, was one of decline or stagnation in all but England, The Netherlands and parts of Scandinavia. Between 1650 and 1750 there was a pause in growth: then from 1750 there was continued growth until the 1920s. Except in the British Isles, the rate of increase between 1750 and 1820 was no greater than it had been in the sixteenth century, and indeed by the middle of the nineteenth century Ireland's population was in decline and France's rate of increase was negligible. But in the rest of Western Europe high rates of growth were maintained until the First World War (Tranter, 1973, p. 43).

During these periods of rapid population growth many parts of Europe exhibited the same symptoms of population pressure that are found today in the Third World: to overcome these difficulties rural societies adopted a variety of strategies, one of which was migration. It may be useful, then, to inquire to what extent migration helps relieve population pressure; secondly to assess its role both in Western Europe before the age of industrialization – that is to say before 1750 – and in the early stages of European industrialization between 1750 and 1900; and thirdly to compare these periods with the situation in the Third World since 1950. Before doing this some note must be taken of the definition of overpopulation and the possible responses to population pressure in a pre-industrial society.

Overpopulation and optimum theory

Overpopulation has long been a matter of comment, but it was the work of Malthus that made it a matter of discussion among economists (Malthus, 1798, p. 826). Malthus believed that an increase in income *per capita* would lead to both earlier marriage and a fall in mortality, resulting in population growth. But because of the law of diminishing returns, which he hinted at rather than stated, population growth would outrun food output. As income *per capita* fell, so population growth would be halted by a combination of deferred marriage – which curtailed fertility – and rising mortality, which he envisaged to be due to a variety of factors: modern interpretations of his work have stressed war, famine and disease. Thus although population could increase, income *per capita* constantly tended to return to a level just above that necessary to maintain the means of subsistence. There are several modern restatements of this theory, most of which incorporate optimum theory (Minami, 1961; Moes, 1958), which was developed in the later nineteenth century, and which attempted to define the best population for a country to have (Sauvy, 1969; United Nations, 1973, pp. 40–56). Optimum theory has been subject to many criticisms (Hicks, 1971, pp. 297–9; Robinson, 1964) and the attempts to measure overpopulation in agrarian societies – which presumes a measurement of the optimum density – have not been entirely successful (Sen Gupta, 1970). Optimum theory, however, does have some expository value, in spite of the many justifiable criticisms which have been made of the concept. It is a static concept. At any given moment, assuming that resources, capital and technology are unchanging, the optimum population for a country is that which maximizes average output or income *per capita* (see Fig. 5.1).

With a population less than JK the country is underpopulated. As population increases from J to K – without any corresponding change in capital, technology or resources – total output increases, and so does the marginal and average product *per capita* for, with a larger population, increasing returns *per capita* are made possible by specialization, the division of labour and the spreading of the costs of social overheads (van de Walle, 1972). At PK output *per capita* is maximized, and marginal product equals average product *per capita*. Thereafter

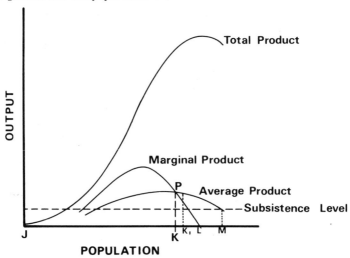

Fig. 5.1   Optimum population and types of overpopulation.

any further increase in population leads to a fall in the average product, and marginal product falls below average product, as diminishing returns to labour begin to operate. It would serve no practical purpose to mention the many criticisms made of this concept; suffice to say that no one has ever succeeded in establishing the optimum population density of any country. However, it does distinguish three different concepts of overpopulation (Sinha, 1976). Any increase in numbers beyond JK means that output *per capita* is less than the maximum output per head attained with the optimum population. Thus at any population above JK, however small (for example JK₁), overpopulation exists in terms of optimum theory. However, at JL the marginal productivity of labour becomes zero; any further addition to labour inputs adds nothing to output. At this point there is underemployment or disguised unemployment, and output *per capita* would increase if population was reduced. Many economists appear to recognize this as the point where overpopulation occurs (Mathur, 1964) and there have been many attempts to measure the degree of underemployment in Third World countries (for example by Rizvi, 1973; Robinson, 1969). However, at population JM average output *per capita* reaches the subsistence level, and beyond this mortality will rise to halt any further population growth. This may be called Malthusian overpopulation.

In practice it has not proved possible to find any acceptable means of establishing the optimum density of even a simple agrarian society (Bićanić, 1964), and some authorities have argued instead that population growth without any change in technology, capital or resources will give rise to a number of symptoms which can be easily recognized, such as the subdivision of farms, the increase in the number of landless, rising prices and falling real wages, soil erosion, a poorer diet and many other features (Robertson, 1939; Hance, 1970, pp. 384–417; Grigg, 1976). Some of these symptoms are depicted in Fig. 5.2.

In the long run, if there are no changes in technology or resources, these symptoms will multiply, income *per capita* will decline, and eventually output *per capita* will fall below the means of subsistence; mortality will then rise and population growth will be halted. In practice few societies are likely to let such a

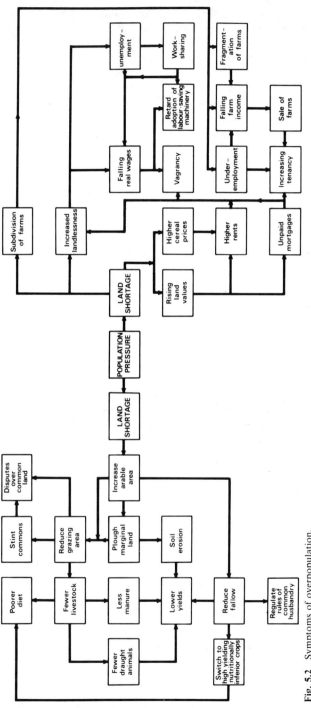

Fig. 5.2 Symptoms of overpopulation.

situation arise. Even the simplest peasant societies have ways of increasing their output or adjusting numbers so that such an extreme event does not occur, although they may not be able to avoid long periods of poverty.

It seems likely, then, that at some point to the right of the optimum density falling income *per capita* will trigger off a response. Four broad categories may be recognized (see Fig. 5.3). In the first place (A) agricultural output may be increased by expanding the area under cultivation, intensifying land use and farming practices, or by specializing in those crops for which the area has a comparative advantage. Second (B), farmers and labourers may undertake industrial activities in their homes – spinning and weaving most commonly – or they may undertake tasks such as carpentry or blacksmithing, work on other people's farms, or migrating seasonally to other areas – town or country – to supplement their farm income. Third (C), they may attempt to control the increase in the number of births, by not marrying, marrying later or limiting the number of births within marriage. This leaves one final possibility (D) – permanent migration, which is the subject of this chapter. One may distinguish between the movement to settle new agricultural lands – rural–rural migration; migration to the towns, which requires a change of occupation; and leaving for new lands overseas, which may be either rural–rural or rural–urban.

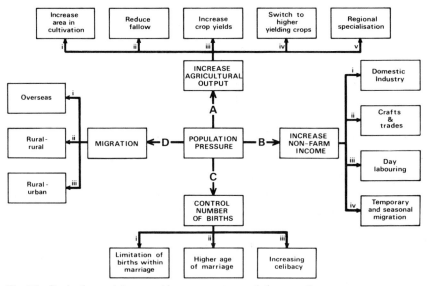

Fig. 5.3 Production and demographic responses to population growth.

A peasant society may of course choose – or have forced upon it – any number of combinations of these strategies (Davis, K., 1963; Friedlander, 1969). If we consider demographic responses alone, then in the nineteenth century the French peasants chose to limit their numbers by controlling births within marriage from the 1770s, and only very much later by emigrating to the towns. The Norwegians emigrated in large numbers, but did not reduce their fertility until after 1900, while in England the major demographic response was rural–urban migration. It is often difficult to estimate the relative importance of these different strategies. We will concentrate upon the changing importance of the three different types of migration at the three periods under discussion; the evidence that population pressure existed in parts of Western Europe in the thirteenth, sixteenth and early seventeenth centuries, and finally in the first half of the nineteenth century would require documentation beyond the scope of this study, but which is presented in detail in a forthcoming book (Grigg, in press).

Migration in pre-industrial societies, A.D. 1000–1750

Until the nineteenth century there is no comprehensive evidence on migration; even then information from the census and vital registration provides only indirect evidence on the nature of migration. Before the age of the census the only information comes from literary sources and unrepresentative lists of migrants such as freemen or paupers (Patten, 1973; Hollingsworth, 1970). It was once thought that there was little migration in pre-industrial societies, on the grounds that transport was slow, costly and often dangerous; and that institutions such as serfdom, or in England after the sixteenth century the laws of settlement, hindered mobility. Some evidence would support this view. In 1841 when four-fifths of Sweden's population lived in rural areas, 92.8 per cent of the population were still in the county in which they had been born (Alström and Lindelius, 1966 p. 11); in one Danish village in the second half of the eighteenth century 85 per cent of those born there were buried there (Frederiksen, 1976, p. 101). Research on parish registers shows that most women married men from their own or a nearby village; until after 1750 four-fifths of all French women married men from places within 5 kilometres of their village (Le Roy Ladurie *et al.*, 1975, p. 281). Similar studies of marriage registers in England show that English grooms were equally unadventurous (Constant, 1948) and that it was not until the 1830s and 1840s that marriage mobility began to increase (Küchemann *et al.*, 1967). But it does not follow from this that pre-industrial communities were completely isolated and lacked any mobility. Studies of English villages in Tudor and Stuart times suggest a remarkable turnover in inhabitants' names that can only be explained by migration, albeit short-distance (Laslett and Harrison, 1964). A study of ten parishes near York shows that of the inhabitants at the end of the eighteenth century, only 40 per cent had ancestors there in 1700 (Holderness, 1970).

Rural–rural migration

The relative importance of rural–rural, overseas and rural–urban migration in reducing rural population pressure undoubtedly changed between the eleventh and the eighteenth centuries, although of course this change cannot be measured. By the eleventh century some parts of Western Europe were already densely populated, particularly Northern France, the southern Low Countries and Northern Italy, but there were still large unoccupied areas. The population growth of the twelfth and thirteenth centuries saw much colonization of unoccupied areas. Before A.D. 1000 villages were the basic unit of rural settlement; in the following centuries people moved into the woodland between the primary settlements and established hamlets and isolated farmhouses (Beech, 1964, pp. 26–9); by the middle of the thirteenth century there was little good farmland left, and there was a movement on to marginal land. Many of the upland areas of Europe were settled for the first time – in Norway, in the French

Alps, on the Pennines and on Dartmoor, in the Vosges and the Pyrenees (Pounds, 1974, p. 174). By 1300 nearly all the villages of Western Europe had been founded.

Long-distance movement was more dramatic between 1050 and 1340; there was a movement of Germans east of the Elbe into sparsely populated Slav areas; in the twelfth and thirteenth centuries some 400,000 moved into this region (Duby, 1962, p. 79, p. 121). In Southern Europe the principal movement was by the Spanish southwards into the Muslim-occupied areas of Iberia (Koebner, 1966). But while these two movements have received much attention from historians, they were numerically less important than the innumerable short-distance moves that completed the rural settlement of Western Europe. In the late fourteenth and fifteenth centuries many of the settlements in the more marginal areas were abandoned as population declined after the Black Death. In the sixteenth century, as population again pressed upon resources, short-distance rural movement began again (Bennassar and Jacquart, 1972, p. 2) as did the eastward movement in Germany (Helleiner, 1967, p. 26; Abel, 1973, p. 143). But the great age of rural–rural migration was by then over in the West. In Hungary the great Alföld was settled after the withdrawal of the Turks in the early eighteenth century (den Hollander, 1960), and further east the Russians began the settlement of the dry steppes in the late eighteenth century. But in Western Europe the only significant later migratory movements to new lands were in Scandinavia in the nineteenth century.

Rural–urban migration

The importance of rural–urban migration in Europe before the age of industrialization is difficult to estimate; even in the eighteenth century the overwhelming majority of Europe's population lived in villages, hamlets and small market towns, except in the Low Countries and England. Until the nineteenth century rural birth rates generally exceeded urban birth rates, and urban death rates exceeded rural death rates, while in most towns, and particularly the large ones, death rates exceeded birth rates (Weber A. F., 1963, pp. 231–241; Herlihy, 1970, p. 57, pp. 90–1). In a study of German towns and villages in the mid-eighteenth century Süssmilch estimated the crude death rate in villages to be 26 per thousand, in small towns 30 per thousand, and in the large cities 40 per thousand (de Vries, 1976, p. 156). More reliable data from Sweden in the early nineteenth century confirm this differential (Thomas, D. S., 1941, pp. 23–5), and there is no doubting the very high death rates in London and Amsterdam in the seventeenth century (Wrigley, 1967; de Vries, 1974, p. 115). Thus it is generally assumed that, before the nineteenth century, towns could only grow by immigration from the countryside and this, it is thought, was often a response to rural population pressure; the towns provided a safety valve to the fertile and relatively healthy countryside (Russell, 1972; Duby 1962, p. 128; Dyer, 1973, p. 26).

In A.D. 1000 Europe had no more than 100 places that could be called towns and half of these were in Italy; by 1300 there were 4,000 or 5,000 such places (Pounds, 1974, pp. 100–1). The twelfth and thirteenth centuries were an undoubted period of urban growth, standing in marked contrast to the preceding centuries. By 1300 Venice, Milan and Paris probably had 100,000 people each; London 50,000. More important was the proliferation of small towns; in the sixteenth century there were 500 market towns in England and Wales and most of these had been founded in the twelfth and thirteenth centuries (Everitt, 1967, p. 467). But although there was urban growth in the later Middle Ages it is far more questionable if there was urbanization. Pounds believes that only 4 per cent of Europe's population lived in towns of more than 2,000 people in 1300 and only in the Low Countries and Northern Italy was a significant proportion of the total population urban (Pounds, 1973, p. 358).

The sixteenth century saw not only a renewed growth of population but also rapid urban growth. The most striking feature of this period was the emergence of a number of very large cities. London grew from some 60,000 in 1520 to 250,000 in 1600 and had exceeded 500,000 by the end of the seventeenth century (Emery, 1973, p. 293). Paris, the largest city in medieval Western Europe, grew from 250,000 in 1600 to 500,000 in 1700 (Bernard, 1970, p. 284), while Amsterdam, which had only 31,000 people in 1585, had reached 200,000 by 1650 (Kossman, 1970, p. 366). But whether this led to an increase in the proportion living in towns is a moot point; there was certainly no dramatic increase in urbanization in the period between 1500 and 1750; thus in Saxony 31 per cent of the population lived in towns in 1550, in 1750 36 per cent; in Northern Italy 12 per cent of the population lived in towns of more than 20,000 in 1600, only 10 per cent in 1750 (de Vries, 1976, p. 149). In France the population of the 20 largest towns formed 5.7 per cent of the total population in 1500, but still only 6.7 per cent in 1700 (Chandler and Fox, 1974, pp. 108–23). England, in contrast, did undergo some urbanization. At the beginning of the sixteenth century no more than 6 per cent of the population lived in places of 5,000 or more, but by 1700 this had reached 15 per cent (Hoskins, 1976, p. 89; Chalklin, 1974, pp. 3–14) with dramatic consequences for the economy of Southern England, and indeed the British Isles as a whole (Wrigley, 1967). Much of this growth was accounted for by London, which in 1520 made up two-fifths of the urban population of England, but by 1700 two-thirds. But England then was not the most urbanized society in Europe. In 1514 Holland was already highly urbanized, with 20 per cent of its population living in places of more than 10,000. The urban population increased nearly six times in the following century so that by 1622 half the population was living in such places (de Vries, 1974, p. 87).

As has been noted, urban growth depended upon immigration from the countryside, for death rates consistently exceeded birth rates in the towns. Much of the high death rate was made up by catastrophic mortality at times of epidemics. Thus in Paris in 1580 30,000 died from typhus; in London 33,000 died from plague in 1603, 41,000 in 1625 and in 1665–66 69,000 (Bennassar and Jacquart, 1972, p. 32; Coleman, D. C., 1977, p. 93). Most of the migrants into the towns came from only comparatively short distances away. Thus in fifteenth-century Frankfurt three-quarters of the immigrants came from places within 72 kilometres of the town (Kamen, 1971, p. 49); studies of four fourteenth-century towns in France show that 50 per cent of the migrants came from within 25 kilometres (Pounds, 1973. p. 339) whilst in Stratford-upon-Avon in the thirteenth century nearly two-thirds came from within 13 kilometres of the town (Carus-Wilson, 1965). In seventeenth-century Kent three-quarters of the migrants in Canterbury had come from within 24 kilometres, in Faversham 70 per cent and in Maidstone 84 per cent (Clark, P., 1972). Only the great cities recruited a significant proportion of their population outside the immediate locality. In the twelfth and thirteenth centuries London was attracting many migrants from outside the south-east (Russell, 1959) and in the sixteenth and seventeenth centuries half the apprentices in a number of guilds came from more than 120 kilometres away (McKenzie, 1958).

Where towns existed they provided an important outlet for the surplus population of the neighbourhood. Thus at Crulai in Normandy the annual rate of natural increase between 1675 and 1750 was 0.5 per cent per annum, yet the population hardly changed; each year young people left for Paris (Gautier and Henry, 1958, p. 227). In England Colchester suffered from eight outbreaks of plague between 1579 and 1666; in the latter year half the population died, but yet by the 1670s the town had recovered its numbers. Yet many nearby rural parishes hardly increased their population at all as the natural increase moved into the town (Doolittle, 1975). A similar circumstance has been noted at Nantes; both the town and the neighbouring parishes increased their populations between 1500 and 1580, but after 1580 rural natural increase was diverted to the port and the countryside stagnated (Croix, 1974, p. 164). A more dramatic instance relates London to the rest of England. Between 1650 and 1750 London's crude death rate probably exceeded the birth rate by 10 per thousand yet the population grew from 400,000 to 575,000. This required an immigration of about 8,000 per year towards 1750, rather more than in 1650. London was thus absorbing the natural surplus of about 2.5 million people, or half the population of England (Wrigley, 1967). It may be that urbanization not only reduced the rate of increase in the countryside but also, by exposing an increasing proportion of the total population to higher death rates, slowed the pace of total increase (de Vries, 1974, pp. 115–17).

Rural–urban migration thus played an important role in reducing the rate of increase in the rural areas of pre-industrial Europe. In most parts of Europe there was little increase in urbanization before the eighteenth century, but the difference in rates of natural increase between town and country – it was negative in the former – ensured that some of the rural surplus was absorbed. This was even more true of Holland and England in the sixteenth and seventeenth centuries, when the towns grew much faster than the country, and thus absorbed more of the rural surplus.

The periods of rapid population growth – the thirteenth and the sixteenth centuries – were also periods of overpopulation in the countryside; farms were subdivided, landlessness and vagrancy increased and marginal lands were cultivated (Duby, 1962). It is likely that the rapid urban growth of this period was partly a function of the 'push' from the countryside (Miller, 1964). But not only was the 'pull' of the towns also important, but the seventeenth century, not a period of rapid population growth, saw the continued growth of the big cities. London's growth between 1650 and 1750, a period of very little national natural increase, exemplifies this point.

Overseas emigration

It has been said that emigration overseas had no significant impact upon the countries of Western Europe in the medieval and early modern periods (Davis, R., 1973, p. 96). This may be true of the former time, for Scandinavian expeditions to Iceland were the only such movements, but once the Americas were discovered considerable numbers did move; some 100,000 Spaniards left for the New World in the sixteenth century (Braudel, 1972, p. 417). Such emigration from England was of little importance until the 1620s, but between then and 1640 80,000 left for Ireland, the West Indies and the North American colonies, between 1 and 2 per cent of the total population and the equivalent of approximately 15 per cent of the natural increase during the period (Bridenbaugh, 1968, p. 395). By 1700 500,000 people of English extraction were living outside England compared with just over 5 million in England (North and Thomas, 1973, p. 149). Movements within Europe may also have had some effect in reducing population pressure, notably in Switzerland. The movement of the Swiss abroad to act as mercenaries, the *reislaufen*, involved 50,000 to 100,000 in the fifteenth century, and possibly 250,000 in both the sixteenth and seventeenth centuries (Helleiner, 1967, p. 27). One may conclude from this that emigration, particularly from England, had a greater impact upon the rate of population growth than is usually admitted.

Migration and other adjustments

The relative importance of the three different types of migration varied between A.D. 1000 and 1750. Between A.D. 1000 and 1350 rural–rural migration was possibly the most important form of migration, but it declined thereafter. Rural–urban migration probably increased in volume during the sixteenth and seventeenth centuries, and certainly provided more of a safety valve than overseas migration or rural–rural migration. But during this long period there were other means of relieving population pressure. Population growth itself stimulated an increase in the area under cultivation, which was the principal means of increasing agricultural output. From the thirteenth century the replacement of the two-field system by the three-field increased the area under crops, and between the thirteenth and the late seventeenth century the improvement of farming methods may have allowed some increase in yields (Grigg, in press).

The control of numbers is far more difficult to ascertain; there is reasonable evidence to suggest that fertility was lower in the seventeenth than the sixteenth century, and that this was probably due to an increase in the age of marriage. There may also have been some limitation of births within marriage (Wrigley, 1966). In the medieval period little is known of fertility or mortality; it is often assumed that marriage was more widespread and took place at an earlier age than in the seventeenth century. If this was so, and bearing in mind the relatively backward agricultural technology of the period, it is likely that migration was one of the earliest responses made to population growth in the medieval period. By the seventeenth and eighteenth centuries a wider range of responses was being adopted.

Migration in the age of industrialization

Between 1650 and 1750 there was little growth in population anywhere in Europe. But after 1750 every country experienced a pronounced increase, so that by 1850 the population of most had doubled, and continued, except in the case of Ireland and France, to increase rapidly for the rest of the century. In England the century after 1750 saw the beginnings, and indeed the maturity, of industrialization. But in the rest of Europe industrialization did not get under way until later and, although there was urban growth, rural population increase was almost as rapid (see Table 5.1), so that by the middle of the nineteenth century the proportion living in rural areas had declined very little; indeed in The Netherlands the rural population increased slightly faster than the urban population in the first half of the nineteenth century. As a consequence the countryside of rural Europe had to absorb a great increase in numbers before

Table 5.1 Rural population as percentage of total population, nineteenth-century Europe*

	c. 1800	c. 1850	c. 1900
Belgium	n.a.	67.4	47.6
Denmark	79.1	76.4	66.1
England and Wales	66.6	45.9	21.9
France	85.6	82.2	68.1
Ireland	n.a.	80.0	72.0
Netherlands	70.5	71.1	57.1
Norway	91.3	87.9	72.0
Prussia	71.8	71.5	59.3
Sweden	90.2	89.9	78.5

n.a. Not available.
*The definition of 'rural' varies between countries but not from year to year within any country. Census dates are the nearest available to 1800, 1850 and 1900.

Sources: Weber, A. F., 1963, pp. 82–113, p. 114; Kennedy, 1973, p. 82; Derry, 1973, pp. 97–8, p. 114; Thomas, D. S., 1941, p. 42; Dupeux, 1974, p. 183.

industrialization had made any progress, and before the inputs of modern agricultural technology – reapers, the steam thresher, iron ploughs, chemical fertilizers, drainage machines and drainage tiles, steam pumps for marsh and polder, imported oilcakes and improved crop varieties – became generally available. In consequence many parts of Western Europe were suffering from rural overpopulation by the 1830s, and this was apparent in the growth of landlessness, the subdivision of farms, underemployment and falling real wages. In many regions – particularly in Ireland, Norway, the Low Countries and the Rhineland – food supplies were only sustained by the rapid adoption of the potato, and thus the potato blight that spread through Europe in the 1840s had a terrible effect, although nowhere were its consequences so disastrous as in Ireland (Woodham-Smith, 1962).

The responses to this population pressure were numerous. Improvements in agricultural methods were slow, and involved, until the 1840s, only the more general adoption of methods long known to some farmers. Increases in yields were small, and the reclamation of new land was possibly the major source of additional output, while the rapid expansion of the potato acreage in every country in Western Europe after 1810 – it had been widely adopted earlier in Ireland – helped increase food supplies (Langer, 1975). In the long run the problems of population pressure were to be resolved by the movement of an increasing proportion of the agricultural population into more productive sectors of the economy (Grigg, 1974a; 1975). After 1850 real income *per capita* rose in most countries in Europe. But in the mid-nineteenth century manufacturing industry had made little progress outside Britain, Belgium and Northern France.

Rural–urban migration in Britain

It was thus only in England that migration to the towns could help reduce the problems of the countryside before 1850, for it was only in England that industrial growth was rapid enough to absorb the rural surplus. Unfortunately there are no reliable figures before 1837 on births and deaths in England, and it was not until 1841 that the census included information on place of birth. Thus the great age of rural–urban migration in England is still little explored. It is normally assumed that migration was the major component of urban growth before 1851; indeed it is sometimes argued that urban death rates exceeded urban birth rates until well into the nineteenth century. Unfortunately, urban and rural demographic differentials are still little known. There is no doubt that the urban population of England and Wales increased rapidly in the later eighteenth century although estimates before 1801 are perhaps not entirely reliable (Table 5.2). Between 1751 and 1851 the rural population of England and Wales did not quite double, but the urban population of 1851 was six and a half times that of 1751. In the mid-eighteenth century three-quarters of the population of England and Wales lived in places of less than 5,000 inhabitants, by 1851 only 46 per cent did so.

Unfortunately, it is difficult to estimate the relative roles of natural increase and migration causing urban growth in this period. Migration can only be calculated by comparing the population of a town between two census dates, calculating the surplus of births over deaths within the town between the two dates, and subtracting it from intercensal increase to obtain a migration residual. But before civil registration was introduced in 1837 the only sources of information on births and deaths were the parish registers of baptisms and burials, and they are thought to be unreliable. Furthermore, some of the natural increase between census years must be due to births to immigrants, so that this method understates the role of migration. However, it is worth noting that the growth of cities in this period was not entirely due to migration, as is sometimes implied, for, in a number of towns which have been studied, there was growth due to natural increase after 1750, although before 1841 migration was always the larger component (Lawton, 1953; Chambers, 1960). But after the middle of the nineteenth century natural increase became increasingly important, migration less so. Between 1841 and 1911 three-quarters of London's growth was due to natural increase (Lawton, 1972), while after 1861 Bristol's growth was largely due to natural increase (Shannon and Grebenik, 1943). In Hull natural increase accounted for only 14 per cent of the growth of the city between 1750 and 1830, but 73 per cent between 1851 and 1911 (Brown, L. M., 1969).

The role of the migrant in urban growth can be illustrated by the use of the place of birth statistics in the 1851 census, which gave a measure of lifetime flows of migration and the relative importance of migrants and natives in the city. In 61 English towns in 1851 48 per cent of the population were migrants, in 10 Scottish towns 52 per cent and in London 38.8 per cent. However, there was considerable variation from town to town, from Gloucester where 71.6 per cent were migrants, to Coventry where only 31.5 per cent had not been born there.

There is no doubt that the movement from country to the town between 1751 and 1851 provided an important safety valve for the English rural areas. If it had not occurred, England in 1841 would have had a greater rural density than Ireland had before the famine. In the event the rural population of England and

Table 5.2 Rural and urban populations, England and Wales, 1751–1911

	Rural population (in places of less than 2,500)		Urban population (in places of more than 2,500)		Total population	
	Thousands	Percentage annual rate of increase	Thousands	Percentage annual rate of increase	Thousands	Percentage annual rate of increase
1751	4,661	–	1,478	–	6,140	–
1775	5,474	0.7	1,875	1.0	7,350	0.8
1801	5,820	0.3	3,009	1.8	8,829	0.7
1811	6,442	0.9	3,722	2.1	10,164	1.4
1821	7,195	1.1	4,804	2.6	12,000	1.7
1831	7,743	0.7	6,153	2.5	13,896	1.5
1841	8,221	0.6	7,693	2.3	15,914	1.4
1851	8,239	0.02	9,687	2.3	17,927	1.2
1861	8,282	0.05	11,784	2.0	20,066	1.1
1871	7,910	–0.5	14,802	2.3	22,712	1.2
1881	7,744	–0.1	18,180	2.1	25,924	1.3
1891	7,401	–0.5	21,601	1.7	29,002	1.1
1901	7,155	–0.3	25,371	1.6	32,527	1.2
1911	7,603	0.6	28,467	1.2	36,070	1.0

Data source: Law, 1967.

Wales increased very little after 1841, and declined after 1861 (see Table 5.2).

Such a sequence of events occurred in other parts of Western Europe but generally at a much later date, for industrial growth did not become important in most countries until the second half of the nineteenth century. In 1870, for example, manufacturing and mining occupied no more than 15 per cent of the work force of Norway and Sweden (Jörberg, 1973, p. 392); in 1801 Britain already had 30 per cent of its population employed in this category (Deane and Cole, 1962, p. 142). Yet Norway's population doubled between 1800 and 1865, and Sweden's between 1750 and 1850 (Drake, 1969, p. 165; Thomas, D. S., 1941, p. 32). Ireland also experienced a remarkable rate of growth between 1780 and 1841 (Connell, 1950, p. 25) without any significant industrialization. There was undoubtedly stress in the rural areas of these countries by mid-century; and while there was some rural–migration, the surplus rural population could not be absorbed in the towns. Fortunately there was an alternative open to the population – emigration to North America.

Emigration overseas from Europe in the nineteenth century

Modern writers have tended to emphasize the pull of North America as the major reason for the mass migrations of the nineteenth century, but until the 1870s the 'push' element in the rural areas of Western Europe must have been at least as important. 'Those who argue that the pull from the United States was the main force governing migration', Milward and Saul (1973, p. 145) have written, 'seem to have little understanding of the basic forces in European history.' Brinley Thomas, who has seen European emigration as a response to capital flows in the Atlantic economy, with alternating investment cycles in Europe and the United States, has nonetheless seen emigration before the 1860s as a response to overpopulation (Thomas, B., 1954, pp. 94–5). Not all countries were hit by emigration fever – there was little from France or the Low Countries; and it was only at the very end of the century that Eastern and Southern Europe achieved high rates (see Table 5.3). In Germany emigration rates, which in the 1850s were

Table 5.3 Annual overseas emigration rates per 100,000 population, selected European countries

	1861–70	1871–80	1881–90	1891–1900	1901–08
Austria–Hungary	11	31	108	155	450
Britain	284	401	566	358	526
Denmark	108	205	391	224	282
Germany	167	154	289	101	48
Ireland	1,465	1,024	1,492	1,010	1,108
Italy	n.a.	99	323	491	n.a.
Norway	581	470	963	454	855
Russia	1	7	33	51	157
Sweden	228	234	701	415	426

n.a. Not available.
Source: Hvidt, 1975, p. 14.

only exceeded by Ireland, faded as industrialization got under way and absorbed the rural surplus. Between 1841 and 1870 2.37 million left Germany; but between 1871 and 1910 the proportion living in places of 5,000 and more rose from 23.7 to 48.8 per cent, and as industry developed so emigration faded (Köllman, 1969). In England, in contrast, emigration rates were much lower than from Ireland, Scotland or Wales, but were nonetheless higher in 1901–11 than they had been in any preceding decade except 1881–90 (Thomas, B., 1962). By then most of the emigrants were not the rural poor but the ambitious urban artisans.

In many parts of Europe emigration was the only solution to rapid population growth. In Norway, for example, population doubled between 1800 and 1865 (Drake, 1969, p. 165). Nearly all this increase had to be absorbed in the rural sector. In 1801 91 per cent of the population lived in rural districts, and in 1865 only 15 per cent were living in towns (Hodne, 1976, p. 167). Opinions are divided on the progress of Norwegian farming in the first part of the nineteenth century, but there seems to have been little increase in crop yields, and only the rapid adoption of the potato maintained food supplies. Fishing and the merchant marine provided additional income for the peasants near the coasts, but even so times were hard (Smout, 1974). The first emigrants left in 1825, but they were few until the 1860s when a crop failure prompted the first mass migration in 1868–69. By then crossing the Atlantic was much cheaper, and the early emigrants had sent home news and money. Three peaks of emigration occurred – 1866–73, 1879–83 and 1900–10. The loss in these periods was the equivalent of 63, 66 and 60 per cent respectively of natural increase. A total of 754,000 left the country between 1840 and 1914, the equivalent of 40 per cent of total natural increase (Semmingsen, 1960). In Sweden urbanization and industrial growth were more rapid after 1870 than in Norway and the towns took more of the rural surplus (Lindberg, 1930, p. 125). Nonetheless 1,105,000 emigrated between 1840 and 1914, the equivalent of 25 per cent of the natural increase of this period. It has been estimated that Sweden's population of 6.1 million in 1930 would have been 8.5 million if there had been no emigration (Hofsten and Lundström, 1976, p. 76). In the event neither rural–urban migration nor emigration were sufficient to halt the increase of the rural population in either Norway or Sweden; but after 1880 the increase was very slow, and the rural economy was more able to absorb the extra numbers until the rapid growth of industry led to a decline in the rural populations in the inter-war period.

Irish emigration is often thought of as beginning with the famine, but it was already running at a high rate before 1845 (Connell, 1950, p. 25). The population doubled between 1754 and 1821, and in the next 30 years there was acute subdivision of farms, an increase in landlessness, falling real wages and an ever-increasing dependence upon the potato. There was little industrial growth – the Union with Britain had exposed Irish industries to factory competition – and little migration to the towns; and the country remained overwhelmingly rural. At the beginning of the eighteenth century only 6 per cent of the population lived in places of 5,000 or more, and in 1841 it was no more than 10 per cent; indeed between 1821 and 1841 the rural population had grown more rapidly than the urban (Cullen, 1972, p. 121).

In the absence of any internal outlet for the excess population emigration was the only solution, and between 1780 and 1845 1,700,000 left Ireland, one-third to Britain, the rest to North America (Connell, 1950, p. 28). Between 1840 and 1845 250,000 emigrated. The famine then merely accelerated the trend; between 1845 and 1851 about 1 million left, and in the following decade another million. Thereafter the absolute numbers emigrating steadily declined, as did the total population, a situation without parallel in Western Europe (Kennedy, 1973, p. 27).

It is difficult not to see emigration from Ireland before the 1850s as a response to population pressure; yet a closer study of Irish emigration does reveal some inconsistencies. Before the famine the poorest parts of the island were the western coastal districts; these were also the areas which had the highest rates of population increase between 1821 and 1841 and, together with parts of Ulster, the highest densities. But before the famine the highest emigration rates were found in Ulster, where religious differences between the Presbyterians and both the Catholics and the Church of Ireland prompted emigration. The existence of tenant right provided a capital sum that could pay the cost of travel. The western districts were remoter from Belfast and Dublin, and Irish was still spoken and thus less was known of prospects elsewhere. During the famine disaster was greatest in the west, but emigration rates were not as high in the west as they were in many parts of the east; part of the reason was the extreme poverty of the west. In Ireland, as in Norway and Sweden at later dates, it was not the very poor who emigrated, but those who had enough to pay their passage (Cousens, 1960).

Migration, industrialization and fertility control

The role of migration in the nineteenth century in helping relieve the numbers in the countryside is best seen in long-term perspective. In the two earlier cycles overseas migration had played a very limited role, for neither the size of ships nor the cost of travel permitted more than a small-scale migration and the resources of America west of the Appalachians were little known. Migration to the towns locally played an important role, and indeed without it towns would not have grown. But before the Industrial Revolution the towns did not have the capacity to absorb large numbers from the countryside. Agricultural techniques were, until the early nineteenth century, comparatively backward. The average yield of wheat in England in the thirteenth century was possibly 10 bushels per acre, in 1800 little more than 20 bushels. Thus, in the intervening centuries there was only limited opportunity for output to outrun population growth.

The critical breach through the Malthusian barrier is often put in the century after 1750 when in England agricultural techniques are supposed to have been revolutionized, and the growth of industry provided an outlet for the rural surplus. But it is important to remember that outside Britain the increase in population in the century after 1750 took place without any fundamental change in employment structure, and it was the rural areas that had to absorb the increased numbers. By 1850, when industrial growth was quickening in France, Belgium and parts of Germany, rural–urban migration was possible on the scale that it had been in England in the previous 100 years; yet it is not surprising that overseas migration took place in the many parts of Europe where industrialization was not under way. But migration was not the only response. It is normal to date the decline in fertility in Europe from the 1870s, and to attribute this to rising expectations, the more open discussion of birth control and the increasing availability of physical methods. However, in the two earlier great population cycles there is some evidence of attempts to curtail numbers both by marrying later and in limiting births within marriage. It seems possible, therefore, to argue that the decline in fertility in the last third of the nineteenth century was an attempt to limit numbers after a century of rapid growth as much as an attempt to do better in a period of rising incomes. Indeed, fertility in France may have been in decline since 1770 (Bourgeois-Pichat, 1965); in Ireland the deferment of marriage had been common from the 1820s, and after 1851 celibacy and later marriage were combined with emigration to reduce population pressure

(Kennedy, 1973). Some have argued that English fertility was in decline from the 1820s (Krause, 1958), while in Sweden there are signs of a decline from the 1850s.

The Third World since 1950: population growth and migration

We turn now to consider the role of migration in the rural areas of the Third World today. It is clear that there are a number of important differences between Third World countries at the present and Europe in the past. In the first place the rate of population increase between 1950 and 1973 was not only well above that in the developed countries but well above that achieved in the developed countries in the nineteenth century (see Table 5.4). Second, the ratio of agricultural land to rural population is lower than it was in nineteenth-century Europe (Hoselitz, 1957). Third, the high rate of increase is due to a very rapid fall in mortality which has been a result of the introduction of preventive medicine by outside agencies. Fourth, while mortality levels have fallen in 30 years so that they are little above those in developed countries, birth rates in the less developed countries are well above those found in Western Europe in the mid-nineteenth century.

Table 5.4   Regional rates of population increase, 1950–1973

	Population, in millions		Average percentage rate of increase, per annum, 1950–73
	1950	1973	
Africa	227	374	2.4
Latin America	162	309	2.8
Asia	1,355	2,204	2.1
North America	166	236	1.5
Europe	392	472	0.8
USSR	180	250	1.4
Australasia	10	16	2.1

Source: United Nations, 1974.

There is no denying that population growth has caused serious problems in Afro-Asia and Latin America, and particularly in the rural areas. But there is little agreement on the solution to these problems: the arguments of Malthus and Godwin are being repeated. There are those who believe, like Godwin, that poverty is caused by inequable institutions, and that a fairer distribution of income and the wider application of planning and science will solve the problem without the need for the control of population growth. An equally vociferous school believes that the limitation of births is a pre-condition for economic growth (Teitelbaum, 1974). Our concern here is not to enter this controversy, but to outline the role of migration in relieving rural overpopulation.

Overseas migration from the Third World

It will be apparent that overseas migration is unlikely to solve the problems of rural congestion. European migration in the nineteenth century took up the remaining areas of unoccupied land, and by the 1920s the flow from Europe had greatly diminished. Since 1950 there has been movement out of Third World countries but on a very small scale. Thus by the 1950s annual migration of Latin Americans into the United States exceeded that of Europeans (United Nations, 1973, p. 229), and there has been a considerable flow of migrants from North Africa, South-Eastern Europe and the Near East into North-Western Europe, but not on a scale sufficient to reduce population pressure at home (Kindelberger, 1965). The scale of movement which would be needed is well illustrated by the case of Java. It has been argued that the Javanese could migrate to the sparsely populated island of Sumatra. But it has been shown that to get zero growth in Java 57 per cent of the 1 million female children born each year would have to be moved. Yet the highest-ever annual total movement from the island was 60,000 – in the 1930s (Keyfitz, 1971). In the nineteenth century it was possible for some 40 per cent of Norway's natural increase to be removed over 50 years, a total of 750,000 (Semmingsen, 1960). A movement of a comparable proportion of India's natural increase between 1950 and 1970 would have involved over 70 millions, approximately equal to the total number of emigrants from Europe since 1800. Although international migration may have helped relieve population problems in some West Indian islands, and may have in the future similar localized effects elsewhere, there seems no prospect of overseas migration affording a solution to the population problem of Afro-Asia or Latin America.

Rural–rural migration in the Third World

Although much attention has been paid to rural–urban migration in the Third World it is often forgotten that there has been very considerable rural–rural movement. Since 1950 there has been a great increase in the area under cultivation and this has involved the movement of millions. Between 1950 and 1970 the area under the major crops in the world increased by one-fifth, and four-fifths of this increase took place in Afro-Asia and Latin America (Grigg, 1974b). Some of this has involved the spontaneous movement from congested rural areas to frontier regions – the migration of some 1.5 million from Luzon to Mindanao in the Philippines between 1948 and 1960 is a good example of this (Ng, 1975) – but, increasingly, government-sponsored land-settlement schemes have become more important. Migration has taken place in many regions. In Latin America there has been a move from the densely populated upland areas to the lowlands of the Pacific coast, and also to the humid tropical lowlands on the Caribbean coast and east of the Andes (Butland, 1966; Dozier, 1969). In India the main centres of colonization have been in Rajasthan, Assam, the Dandakanya and in the *terai* zone where the eradication of malaria has allowed colonization (Farmer, 1974), while in Sri Lanka the dry zone has been the main area of colonization (Farmer, 1957). Africa has seen numerous land-settlement schemes, many involving the extension of irrigation (Hance, 1967).

   Indeed, in spite of the greater attention paid to rural–urban migration, in some countries rural–rural migrants have been the more numerous. In India in 1961 73.7 per cent of all moves recorded were rural–rural, compared with only 14.6 per cent between country and town; much of the rural migration was of women on marriage, but if only males are considered rural–rural moves still accounted for 56.7 per cent of all moves (Gosal and Krishnan, 1975). In the Philippines much migration has been to Mindanao and rural–urban movement has been comparatively small (Simkins, 1970). In Ghana, in 1960, rural–rural migration formed 60 per cent of all moves (Ewusi, 1974).

Table 5.5 Rural and urban population growth, 1920–1970, in millions

	Rural population					Urban population				
	1920*	1940*	1960*	1960†	1970†	1920*	1940*	1960*	1960†	1970†
Africa	136.0	177.7	239.3	221.1	267.8	6.9	13.8	36.4	48.5	76.6
Latin America	76.6	104.7	144.6	110.2	124.1	12.9	25.2	67.8	103.3	159.2
Asia	957.1	1,113.5	1,375.4	1,313.1	1,547.8	66.1	132.1	276.6	332.2	508.0
North America	72.2	80.0	86.2	60.3	58.5	43.5	64.3	112.5	138.4	169.1
Europe	220.1	238.7	250.7	177.2	168.4	104.4	140.1	173.8	247.4	293.7
USSR	193.3	148.0	136.4	108.2	104.0	16.0	47.0	78.0	106.0	138.6
Australasia	6.0	7.3	8.4	n.a.	n.a.	3.1	4.5	8.3	n.a.	n.a.
World	1,607.3	1,869.9	2,241.0	1,995.5	227.0	252.9	427.0	753.4	986.2	1,358.3

n.a. Not available.
*Urban population defined as those in places of over 20,000.
†Urban population from local definitions.
Source: United Nations, 1968, pp. 11–12; 1971, pp. xxiv–xxxiii.

Even when rural–rural and rural–urban movements are combined, mobility is still fairly low in Afro-Asia and Latin America, although contemporary accounts give the impression of great activity. Thus in Thailand in 1960 87 per cent of the population still lived in the province in which they had been born, in the Philippines 84 per cent. But there are indications that mobility is increasing, for by 1970 only 75 per cent of the population of the Philippines were living in the province of their birth (Cummings, 1975), while in India the proportion living outside the district of their birth was 9.8 per cent in 1921, but 12.1 per cent in 1961 (Gosal and Krishnan, 1975).

Rural–urban migration in the Third World

In the last 30 years one of the most distinctive features of the Third World has been the rapid growth of the urban population. In 1920 only 87 million people lived in places of more than 20,000 in Afro-Asia and Latin America compared with 170 million in Europe, Russia and North America (Table 5.5). By 1960 the urban population of the developing countries was 390 million, some 18 million more than in the developed countries. As urban population has grown more rapidly than the rural population urbanization has increased, although the proportion living in towns is still much lower than it is in the developed world (Table 5.6).

Table 5.6 Urban population as percentage of total population, 1920–1960

	1920	1940	1960
Africa	4.8	7.2	13.2
Latin America	14.4	19.4	31.9
Asia	6.5	10.6	16.7
North America	37.6	44.6	56.6
Europe	32.2	37.0	40.9
USSR	10.3	24.1	36.4
Australasia	34.1	38.1	49.7
World	13.6	18.6	25.2

Source: United Nations, 1968, pp. 10–12.

The rates of urban increase have been well above those in the developed world over the last three decades, although the Soviet Union and Australasia had rapid urban growth in the 1950s (see Table 5.7). Rates of increase of 4.5 per cent per annum are much higher than the rate of urban growth in Europe in the nineteenth century, when the fastest rates achieved were about 2.1 per cent per annum (Davis, K., 1965). In nineteenth-century Europe urban growth absorbed large numbers from the countryside, and the rural populations grew slowly in the second half of the nineteenth century – indeed they were declining in the British Isles and France – and in this century they have universally stagnated or declined in Western Europe, although the tendency of urban employed people to live in the country and commute to work has often concealed this trend. But in the present-day Third World rural populations have continued to increase at very high rates (Table 5.7).

Why have the towns grown so rapidly? It is commonly argued that rural population pressure has 'pushed' migrants to the towns, even though there is considerable unemployment in the cities. Certainly before 1950 migration seems to have been the major component in urban growth. Thus between 1940 and 1950 the eight major towns of Brazil owed 71 per cent of their increase to migration

Table 5.7   Average annual percentage rate of growth of rural and urban populations, 1920–1970

	Rural population			Urban population		
	1920–40*	1940–60*	1960–70†	1920–40*	1940–60*	1960–70†
Africa	1.4	1.5	1.9	3.6	5.0	4.6
Latin America	1.6	1.6	1.2	3.4	5.1	4.4
Asia	0.8	1.1	1.8	3.6	3.8	4.3
North America	0.5	0.4	-1.0	2.0	2.9	2.0
Europe	0.5	0.3	-0.5	1.5	1.1	1.7
USSR	0.5	-0.4	-0.3	5.1	2.1	2.7
Australasia	1.0	0.7	n.a.	1.9	3.1	n.a.
World	0.8	1.0	1.3	2.7	2.9	3.3

n.a. Not available.
*Urban population defined as those in places of over 20,000.
†Urban population from local definitions.

Source: United Nations, 1968, pp. 11–12; 1971, pp. xxiv–xxxiii.

(Beaujeu-Garnier, 1970). In Colombia 74 per cent of urban growth was due to migration between 1938 and 1951. In the Moroccan city of Casablanca in the 1920s 80 per cent of urban growth was due to migration, in the 1930s 67 per cent. But Casablanca illustrates what appears to be a worldwide trend. By 1950 natural increase accounted for half the growth, by 1960 two-thirds (Potrykowska, 1975). Similar changes have been noted in Latin America, where in Colombia between 1951 and 1964 35 per cent of urban increase was due to natural increase. By the 1960s natural increase was accounting for more than the urban increase in many countries in Latin America, in Egypt and in Thailand (Arriaga, 1968; Goldstein, 1973).

Before 1950 high death rates in the towns of Afro-Asia and Latin America meant that there was comparatively little natural increase, and migration was the major cause of urban growth. But since 1950 death rates have fallen rapidly in town and country in the Third World without any commensurate fall in fertility. Although information on urban/rural differentials in the Third World is fragmentary, it seems that urban mortality has fallen more than rural mortality. Some United Nations estimates suggest that the rate of natural increase in country and town is now approximately equal (Table 5.8). Thus towns in the Third World would be growing rapidly, even without migration.

Table 5.8 Rural–urban demographic differentrials, 1970

	Developed countries, rates per thousand per annum		Developing countries, rates per thousand per annum	
	Urban	Rural	Urban	Rural
Crude birth rate	19.8	23.1	38.0	44.0
Crude death rate	9.0	9.5	15.3	21.6
Rate of natural increase	10.8	13.6	22.7	22.5

Source: United Nations, 1973, p. 197.

Although natural increase is now contributing a considerable share of urban growth this does not mean that rural–urban migration is unimportant. Between 1950 and 1960 alone there was a net migration of 14.6 million from the rural areas to the towns in Latin America (United Nations, 1973, p. 178). Most authorities on the subject have attributed rural–urban migration to the 'push' of rural population pressure (McGee, 1971, p. 115; Schultz, 1971; Kosiński and Prothero, 1970) rather than the pull of the towns, for while industrial wages are higher than incomes in agriculture only a comparatively small proportion of the population is employed in manufacturing industry. Not only is there insufficient capital to create industrial employment, but modern industry is capital intensive, compared with industries in much of the nineteenth century which were still labour intensive (Moir, 1976). In many underdeveloped countries a small proportion of the population is engaged in manufacturing industries, but a comparatively high proportion lives in cities. This, it has been argued, is because rural poverty drives man to the city, and gives rise to over-urbanization (Davis and Golden, 1954). The lack of industrial employment means they become either unemployed or engaged in the traditional urban economies of petty trading, domestic service, household crafts and many other marginal activities (Friedman and Sullivan, 1974).

The characteristics of migrants are in many ways similar to those of nineteenth-century Europe. They move comparatively short distances; in

Bangkok in 1960, for example, half of all immigrants came from within 80 kilometres of the city; in Djakarta one-fifth had lived within half an hour's distance of the city (McGee, 1971, p. 106). Most migrants are young adults, preponderantly between 15 and 30 years old (Martine, 1975). In Africa a high proportion are school-leavers (Byerlee 1974). But it is not the poorest people who leave the rural areas: migrants come from families with above-average incomes (United Nations, 1968, p. 48); furthermore, they often have somewhat more education than the average of the community they leave (Speare, 1974). But modern migration does differ in one important way from nineteenth-century movement, for there tend to be more males involved in migration than females (Byerlee, 1974; de Graft-Johnson 1974).

Rural–urban migration does, of course, help to reduce rural population growth. In the 1960s natural increase in the rural areas of the developing world as a whole was of the order of 2.25 per cent per annum (Table 5.8); net rural population growth, however, varied by major regions, between 0.8 per cent and 1.9 per cent, with the exception of South Asia where it reached 2.3 per cent per annum (Table 5.7). Thus the rate of increase of the rural populations is not greatly in excess of European total population increase in the nineteenth century. But, in contrast to the nineteenth century, the towns of the Third World are failing to provide adequate employment so that for many migrants underemployment in the rural world is exchanged for unemployment in the city.

Conclusions

Migration can be seen as one possible response to rural population pressure. Over the last 1,000 years its relative importance has varied, as have the three types of migration. Until 1340 rural–rural migration was probably the most important form of migration, and indeed may have been the overall most important adjustment to population pressure, for there is little evidence of attempts to limit numbers, agricultural technology was limited, and the towns held such a small fraction of the total population that they could have offered only a few of the rural surplus an outlet.

In the second period of population growth, in the sixteenth and seventeenth centuries, stress occurred once again in rural Europe. However, by 1600 a wider range of opportunities was open; changes in economic organization had seen the growth of industry in the countryside, a greater division of labour absorbed the landless in crafts, trades and transport. Agricultural technology, however, made little progress until after 1650. The rapid growth of great cities did provide an outlet for some of the rural population while overseas emigration may have had some impact on growth in England. But in the middle of the seventeenth century there is also some evidence of attempts to limit numbers both by raising the age of marriage and possibly by limiting births within marriage.

The last great cycle of growth began in the 1740s and affected the whole of Western Europe; but it was only in Britain that industrialization occurred at the same time. Until the middle of the nineteenth century most of Europe remained primarily agrarian and rural, and much of the poverty and discontent of the first half of the nineteenth century can be attributed to population pressure. But Europe now had a wider range of possible responses; improvements in oceanic transport meant that overseas emigration was a major outlet for much of the continent. Some 60 million – and possibly more – left between 1800 and 1940 (United Nations, 1973, p. 226). Within Europe, however, it was mainly rural–urban migration that absorbed the rural surplus and led eventually to an absolute decline in the rural and agricultural populations. The beginning of rural and agricultural decline may be said to mark the end of the traditional way of life; it began in Britain in the 1850s and reached Eastern Europe after the Second World War. In the 1960s the difference between countries with increasing agricultural populations and declining agricultural populations was the best measure of whether a country was developed or less developed (Grigg, 1974a). But of course the major change that occurred in the nineteenth century was the improvement of organization and technology in industry that provided employment, created greater wealth and provided the inputs that allowed greater agricultural output with fewer agricultural workers. Thus the Malthusian barrier was breached. Even so it is possible to see a final response. The decline in fertility in the late nineteenth century may have been a reaction to rising expectations. It is probably equally justifiable to see it as a delayed reaction to population pressure.

How far can the Third World repeat the experience of nineteenth-century Europe? First, it seems that overseas emigration cannot resolve the problems of these countries. Second, the towns have to absorb not only rural–urban migration but natural increase at a rate above anything experienced in nineteenth-century Europe. Third, although rural–urban migration reduces the pace at which the rural populations are increased, it seems unlikely that this will eventually lead to rural decline. Fourth, both the lack of capital and the nature of modern industry make it improbable that the cities of the Third World will be able to provide employment for all their populations. Not surprisingly, many authorities now advocate the provision of labour-absorptive industries in rural areas. Thus it seems that migration will not provide the solution to rural overpopulation as it did in nineteenth-century Europe. The viable responses are reduced to either technological change or fertility reduction. It is beyond the scope of this chapter to discuss the prospects of these responses as a solution to the problem.

Acknowledgments

The author wishes to thank the Syndics of the Cambridge University Press for permission to reproduce three figures from his forthcoming volume entitled *Population Growth and Agrarian Change.*

Chapter 6

Past mobility and spatial preferences for migration in East Africa

M. Bell

The traditional fields of enquiry into African migration

Within the African context one of the most significant implications of socio-economic development has been the evolution of new behaviour patterns, in particular new forms of population mobility (Riddell, 1970b; Southall, 1971). As Claeson and Egero (1972a, p. 1) point out,

> a knowledge of population movement, representing as it does both a cause and effect of societal processes, remains of fundamental importance to a complete understanding of social change, economic development and political organization.

Clearly, migration must be interpreted as a two-way process. It is not only a response to new social, economic and political circumstances, but equally important it is a major catalyst to change at both origin and destination. Studies focusing on the implications of population movement in the African continent are widespread (for example Clarke, 1965; Ominde, 1968; Claeson and Egero, 1972b). However, any assessment of its impact requires at the outset an appreciation of the significant features distinguishing modern migrations: reference is usually made to three in particular. Firstly, a change in the character of the migrant; there is a greater importance of individual as opposed to group movements and, in response to labour needs in specific locations, there is the emergence of the wage labourer (Mitchell, 1961). Second, there is the greater significance of economically motivated movement associated with the modern sector of developing economies, thereby replacing traditional tribal moves stimulated by famine and/or warfare (Prothero, 1968). In a review and analysis of tribal census data within East Africa, Hirst (1970) emphasizes the difficulties involved in assessing tribal movement within rapidly changing societies. Third, there is a change in the direction of flows away from rural locations to the growing urban centres of economic activity (Beals *et al.*, 1967; Caldwell, 1969).

The diversity and complexity of the processes operating to influence population movement have stimulated much research into the patterns and processes involved at a variety of scales over varying time periods. With Uganda, for example, widespread disparities in social facilities, income levels and opportunities for economic advance have encouraged much male-dominated labour movement since the turn of the century which is well documented in the literature (Richards, 1954; Middleton, 1960). Southall (1954) discusses the adverse effects of this out-movement on the Alur society within Northern Uganda. He points out that traditional social customs such as marriage by contract gradually break down since the few young males remaining are unable to pay bride-wealth. The agricultural economy also suffers as the initial clearance of undergrowth is no longer efficiently organized with the result that the total crop area is reduced in quantity and quality.

Individual studies of the major labour-supplying tribes have been supplemented by more comprehensive national surveys of labour movement within East Africa (Southall, 1961; Dak, 1968; Ominde, 1968; Claeson, 1974). The spatial pattern to emerge within many of these studies has shown considerable consistency; namely long-distance, highly directional movement from the relatively underdeveloped periphery to the economically advanced core, explanations being sought in the demographic, cultural and ecological conditions at origin and destination within a push–pull framework. In Uganda the dominant receiving area since the turn of the century has been Buganda, the fertile south-central zone on the shores of Lake Victoria focused on the capital city, Kampala. Richards (1954) discusses the social and economic consequences of large-scale immigration to this region as reflected in the relationships formed between relatively poor labourers from peripheral districts and the wealthy native Baganda people. The assimilation of migrant groups in Kampala itself has been analysed by Hirst (1975) in terms of their spatial segregation within discrete parts of the city. A multi-nucleated residential pattern emerged distinguished on the basis of the geographical origin of the migrants, emphasizing the importance of pre-migration social contacts in residential choice. The impact of population movement to urban areas is a theme also considered by Claeson and Egero (1972b) in Tanzania. Using 1967 place-of-birth data they illustrate the effects of selective migration on the demographic structure of the country's major towns, emphasizing in particular the overall excess of adult males and the marked imbalance in the sexes within the adult age ranges.

· While the geographical impact of migration represents an important field of enquiry in its own right, within developing societies analysis of this kind has wider implications. In the absence of direct migration data research workers in tropical Africa have used their knowledge of the consequences of migration to infer movement patterns. In view of the sex imbalances at both origin and destination resulting from labour movement this characteristic has been used to define areas of net in- and out-migration in such countries as Ghana (Hunter, 1965), Zambia (Kay, 1967) and Kenya (Ominde, 1968). More recently Hirst (1972a) has extended this work in a multivariate approach to net migration by incorporating the two additional variables of ethnic and age imbalances. Using 1957 and 1962 census data for Tanzania and Kenya respectively, principal components analysis was employed to isolate a net migration dimension on the first component. Mapping of component scores produced a spatial pattern corresponding closely to that predicted.

⌐ As a result of the interest generated in population mobility and the quantity of literature which has emerged attempts have been made to summarize and review the various findings within the continent as a whole (Prothero, 1964; Gugler, 1968; 1969). Furthermore, some concern has been given to classifying the various types of mobility within a qualitative framework (Prothero, 1968; Hance, 1970), including the formulation of a typology by Gould and Prothero (1975) combining spatial/temporal dimensions with the associated economic/non-economic variables. In addition to comprehensive classification studies of this kind, since the 1960s an improvement in the quantity and quality of migration information available has permitted more rigorous analysis of the process itself. The inclusion of place-of-birth data in the national population censuses of many

African countries has encouraged the application of sophisticated models and techniques in order to improve levels of explanation. Interaction models are widely used (for example by Goddard *et al.*, 1975) while Markovian principles have been employed by Hirst (1976).

The role of education

Despite this co-ordinated research work, there are two questions concerning population mobility which require greater study. The first concerns the precise focus of enquiry; the traditional interest in tribal and wage labour movement presents a somewhat restricted view of the total flow process and must be supplemented by analysis of the many short-term circulatory movements, unrecorded in census enumerations, which have become a feature of African mobility (Gould and Prothero, 1975). The demographic and socio-economic selectivity of these various movements must be analysed and explained. The second question concerns the scale and methodology of analysis; the results and insights gained into the processes operating are ultimately dependent upon the researcher's initial frame of reference and the scale of enquiry. Dependence upon any one scale provides an incomplete and biased view. Aggregate level studies focus essentially on the structural characteristics of movement, that is, the volume, distance, direction and timing. They are therefore ill-equipped to assume the motivations of migrants where detailed information concerning the individuals, their characteristics and precise behaviour is not available. Only through analysis at the so-called 'micro' level, that is at the level of the individual and small group, will the true effects of modern development on traditional society be identified. Study is therefore necessary at both the aggregate and small group levels. The approaches are complementary rather than in conflict, each with its appropriate theoretical and methodological framework.

With a view to fulfilling these needs this chapter brings together the closely related elements of modernization through educational development and population mobility by considering the implications of education for the student community as reflected in the patterns of movement generated. Focus is therefore placed upon a single category of migrants – the educated minority who form a small group within the youthful sector of the population, and whose patterns of movement remain unrecorded in decennial censuses. Among the key factors behind present-day movement the influence of aspirations is of considerable importance, and it is within this context that education plays a vital role. Hutton (1973, p. 97) suggests that movement comes about not only because of absolute poverty, but because 'aspirations reach a level at which they cannot be satisfied by local opportunities'. A major catalyst to the rise in aspirations is education and contact with the outside world. Castle (1966, p. 18) emphasizes the widespread faith in education as the route to socio-economic status:

> This is evident not only in the desires of parents that their children should have a
> better chance in life, but in the ambitions of young people themselves who see in
> education the highway to material success.

Mobility among young people has become, in many instances, a necessary prerequisite both for access to education and to employment afterwards.

It is reasonable to assume that a student's migration history, including the periodic long-distance movement between home and educational institution, has some bearing upon his future employment and migration decisions. This chapter seeks to identify the spatial implications of the residential preferences made by selected groups of the educated population, the aim being to uncover and explain the underlying regularities in the preference pattern. One developing country, Uganda, is selected as a case study for two main reasons. First, it is an area within which a hierarchical education tradition was quickly developed under British colonial administration from the early part of the twentieth century, and within which rapid expansion has taken place since independence. Second, as a result of educational development the two distinctive types of pre- and post-educational mobility mentioned above have become well established. In this analysis particular emphasis is placed upon the impact of past mobility in conditioning future likely migration patterns. In the course of the study due regard is taken of the important methodological issues which arise in spatial preference work of this kind. In particular, reference is made to the quality of the data sources and the techniques of analysis appropriate to the scale of enquiry.

Movement associated with education represents only a numerically small segment within the context of Ugandan population movement; nevertheless as education continues to expand the role of such movement will become increasingly important. Furthermore, in view of the implications of educational growth for socio-economic development, identification and explanation of the movement patterns generated by the system represent vitally important fields of enquiry.

Migration selectivity and education in Uganda

In the early years of independence the education system in Uganda assumed a position of considerable importance as a symbol of progress and the institutional basis of societal advance (Chesswass, 1966). The central government adopted overall responsibility for the education sector and, in line with most newly independent African administrations, made educational expansion an integral part of development planning. In formulating policy, while universal education was a desirable long-term aim, economic necessity confined investment within the limits of 'Uganda's financial position and future manpower requirements' (Castle *et al.*, 1963, p. ii). The demand for high-level manpower in particular led to considerable expansion of secondary and higher education in order to fulfil this need. The spatial diffusion of new secondary institutions to locations throughout the country formed an important element in political decision-making to satisfy widespread popular demand, and to fulfil the needs of hitherto under-provided areas (Gould, W. T. S., 1971; 1973a). However, despite the increase in educational opportunity across the national area it remains both a socio-economic and a sex selective process necessitating a high level of mobility among young people.

Educational attendance indicates parental acceptance of its value and also an ability to overcome the financial burden of fees unless the student is fortunate enough to obtain one of the few government bursaries.[1] Thus, while it may be suggested that proximity to an educational institution encourages favourable attitudes to education (Gould, W. T. S., 1973b), at the same time economic, social and cultural constraints prevent many young people from leaving the home environment even if an educational institution is easily accessible. Within the family group further sorting takes place, higher priority being given to male than female education when resources are scarce and competition for places intense (Castle, 1966). Socio-economic and sex selectivity is further compounded by political policy governing access to specific institutions. Since the 1950s a system of national catchments at the secondary level has been adopted by the central government as a means by which to promote national integration. All secondary candidates are required to indicate six institutions of their choice in order of priority (Chesswass, 1966). Students are under no obligation to attend their nearest school and indeed W. T. S. Gould (1973a) has found in many instances the first choice to be an old-established school of national reputation some distance from the home area. Having reviewed personal preferences School Boards and the Department of Education then distribute students to institutions across the national area in a deliberate attempt to promote inter-district movement, thereby encouraging ethnic mixing and the reduction of social barriers between disparate ethnic groups. At the level of higher education social contact among the educational 'élite' reaches a maximum within a single institution, Makerere University (Goldthorpe, 1965).

The movement of students from home area to be educated represents for many the first significant break with the extended family and may be regarded as perhaps the initial stage in their life-cycle of migration (Caldwell, 1969). The implications of this process are particularly important in view of the social, cultural and economic mixing which may result. Mitchell (1956) suggests that this break from home in a culturally heterogeneous community is a necessary basis, though not automatically a sufficient condition, for detribalization. Although definition and measurement of this latter process is the subject of considerable debate (Hirst, 1972b), there is some agreement that the separation from home environment brought about by migration encourages a change in social relationships and cultural values. Traditional codes of behaviour, customs and the disciplines of tribal authority are more easily modified or rejected (Molohan, 1957).

Given that some change in outlook is to be expected, an important question arises of relevance in development planning – namely what effect does separation from home have upon the subsequent migration possibilities and preferences of young people in search of employment? Inevitably it increases a student's awareness of the range of alternatives outside his area of origin and may act as a catalyst to further movement. Castle (1966) suggests that the influence of parental discipline is weakened and the student's role within the family altered in such a way as to encourage freedom and independence. The high migration propensity of educated young people has been widely discussed within Africa and numerous examples cited of their subsequent directional movement from rural to urban areas as evidence of a rise in socio-economic aspirations stimulated by formal training (Callaway, 1963; Roussel, 1970). Indeed Caldwell (1969, p. 60) suggests that the wide-ranging impact of education is 'possibly the most important matter to be considered . . . in inducing rural–urban migration'.

However, despite the broadening experience of education, evidence from within Uganda suggests that it does not automatically lead young people to regard village life as inferior. The volume of rural–urban movement following education is less than predicted (Currie and Maas, 1974), while traditional explanations couched in terms of the 'bright lights' theory of urban attraction are inadequate. Of greater importance is the 'push' effect of rural areas – their inability to supply young people with the required living standards. Hutton's (1973) study of unemployed school-leavers in Kampala emphasized that perceived opportunity for a higher income in towns, rather than a basic contempt for agriculture, was the key factor involved. While the search for employment inevitably plays a major role in migration movement, this factor alone is insufficient as an explanation of such movement. The decision to move is a highly complex process involving a variety of personal constraints conditioned by cultural values and personal motivation. Thus while manipulation of the education system to encourage student mobility may be regarded as a possible route to social cohesion and political integration, at the same time the ultimate success of such a policy demands that due consideration be given to the aspirations and preferences of the young people involved. The spatial implications of occupational preferences are therefore of considerable relevance within the framework of development planning, given that at least the partial satisfaction of personal aspirations is a necessary prerequisite for social well-being and economic progress. While rapid urban growth represents an increasingly alarming phenomenon within tropical Africa, rural–urban movement is not necessarily a natural, nor indeed an inevitable, consequence of educational development.

In explaining the factors behind movement greater insight is required into the influence of personal characteristics on the volume, distance and direction of observed flow. This enquiry analyses the spatial implications of occupational preferences from the migrant viewpoint by concentrating on the decision prior to movement. While in reality the opportunities open to the individual at various alternative destinations, and the patterns of movement resulting, are largely determined by external constraints such as job availability, examination of the migration decision introduces a wider set of constraints. Wolpert (1965) has incorporated the concept of preference within a behavioural model of migration, movement being a function of three factors, namely the attractiveness of place, the information known about it and the characteristics of the migrant. Clearly the background of the potential mover influences the motives for the decision and the way in which alternative destinations are assessed.

This study considers specifically the structure and spatial implications of preferred movement among groups of the educated minority where the external constraints operating on the decision are minimized. The objectives are two-fold. Firstly, it is intended to identify the influence of certain personal factors on the migration decision; the second objective is to consider the impact of preferred movement on regional development within Uganda. Figure 6.1 provides a framework for the study. Each potential migrant has a particular tribal and cultural background together with a distinctive personality which influence his propensity to move. His range of past experiences, in particular through exposure to the education system and, more generally, associated with previous migration, has two effects upon the decision. Motivation for movement becomes associated with rising job aspirations brought about by formal training in school and/or university. Furthermore, a past history of personal mobility in addition to that associated with educational attendance extends the individual's knowledge of various alternative destinations which influence in turn his desire to move. The most preferred destination finally selected is dependent upon his attitude to these various alternatives formulated in the light of personal motivation on the basis of an assessment of their relative attraction. Ultimately,

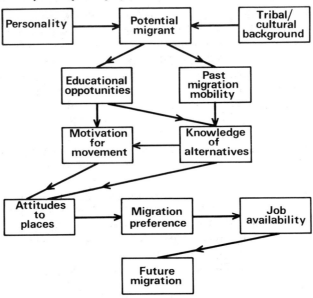

Fig. 6.1   Factors influencing the decision to migrate.

of course, external forces such as job availability may modify the preferred solution by controlling the precise spatial pattern of observed migration. In order to concentrate on the decision-making process a micro-level analysis is adopted, information being collected by means of a personal interview.

The survey

In the latter part of 1972 a questionnaire survey was carried out on students within Makerere University and selected secondary schools to examine their preferences for the various parts of Uganda as destinations for employment and residence. In designing the survey attention was focused on the role of four characteristics – area of origin, past mobility, age and education level – in explaining variations in the choice pattern. It was hypothesized that knowledge gained by personal experience of the country acquired through past migration and also through periodic movement between home and educational institution was of fundamental importance in the choices made. This knowledge would increase with age and length of education as mobility rose and extended a student's awareness of the potentials offered by a greater range of locations throughout the national area.

Variations in the quantity and quality of information concerning alternative destinations, together with a differential evaluation of their relative desirability, it was suggested, would influence the decision pattern in two ways. Firstly, given that students were from diverse spatial origins, while perceived employment opportunities might be the major criterion in the selection of a destination, the choices made would be biased by the student's particular social and cultural environment. This bias would be manifest in a preference for familiar locations within, or contiguous to, the home area. Social distance studies conducted among

African students illustrate the way in which ethnicity acquires a particular significance in situations where social relationships are of necessity transitory and superficial such as the school environment (Mitchell, 1956; 1969). It was proposed that a sense of cultural identity and social distance between ethnically diverse groups would be reflected in the imposition of a distance constraint upon the preference pattern. Secondly, in view of the sharp spatial variations in the distribution of economic activity within Uganda, in particular the strong contrast between the relatively prosperous southern core and the less developed periphery, it was considered that certain notable areas of the country would receive universally high or low ratings. Information flow of a markedly positive/negative nature emanating from these locations would reduce the discriminatory effect of physical and social distance, thereby producing a common view reflected in a sharp polarization of the country. The questionnaire survey was carried out in order to test these hypotheses.

Problems have arisen in preference studies of this kind concerning the respondents selected, the questionnaire design and the techniques of analysis. A restricted range of respondents, usually from only one sector of the student population, and a small sample size, typically under 100 respondents, have been characteristic of such studies hitherto (Saarinen, 1966; Gould, P., 1969). Here a broad cross-section of individuals drawn from different strata within Uganda's educated population was selected for questioning. A lower limit was set at sixth-form secondary schooling (equivalent to upper sixth level in the English education system) and those groups sampled had reached or proceeded beyond this educational level. Particular emphasis was placed upon students within Makerere University for whom employment opportunities are confined to a limited range of locations. By a stratified random procedure students were sampled from various faculties and year-groups within the undergraduate level. It was considered that greater insight might be gained into the underlying structure of student spatial preferences through comparison with different age and culture groups. Thus a random sample of responses was obtained from African professional people and from expatriate European professionals who had proceeded beyond formal education to high-level employment.[2] In addition, information was obtained from three senior secondary schools: Old Kampala, a government-founded mixed urban day school in the capital; Gayaza, a girls' boarding school of Church Missionary Society foundation 11 kilometres north of Kampala; and Namagunga, a Roman Catholic founded girls' school 37 kilometres east of Kampala. All three were old established and the latter two had come under government supervision before independence. In the opening section of the questionnaire certain background characteristics of the respondents were recorded – the individual's home district, nearest town and school district if born in Uganda; the respondent's age, sex, occupation and nationality (see Table 6.1).

In questionnaire design, problems arise over the nature of the stimulus presented, the precise motivational context for the decision and the method of scaling preferences. While it is desirable that all three be subscribed to ensure consistency of response, their precise specification determines and controls the nature of the results obtained. It is therefore conceivable that concentration on any one procedure produces a certain bias. For this reason information was collected by means of two approaches – ordinal scaling and free responses. The rank order analysis in which the motivational context for the decision is stated subsumed the individual's evaluation of his environment for employment and

Table 6.1 Respondents' characteristics

	Total number	Sex		Nationality*					Home region (Ugandans only)			
		M	F	U	K	T	S	E	South	East	West	North
University students and professionals												
Arts Yr I	77	56	21	77	–	–	–	–	25	9	31	12
Arts Yr II	94	83	11	94	–	–	–	–	21	27	27	19
Arts Yr III	30	27	3	30	–	–	–	–	8	8	4	10
Science Yr II	27	27	0	27	–	–	–	–	5	8	10	4
Science Yr III	20	17	3	20	–	–	–	–	2	6	7	5
Arts–Science Yrs I–III	39	34	5	–	28	7	4	–	–	–	–	–
Professionals	19	13	6	19	–	–	–	–	10	1	8	–
Professionals	36	30	6	–	–	–	–	36	–	–	–	–
Total	342	287	55	267	28	7	4	36	71	59	87	50
School students: Standard 6												
Namagunga	40	–	40	40	–	–	–	–	10	11	17	2
Gayaza	68	–	68	68	–	–	–	–	30	7	23	8
Old Kampala	30	30	–	30	–	–	–	–	21	1	5	3
Total	138	30	108	138	0	0	0	0	61	19	45	13
Grand Total	480	317	163	405	28	7	4	36	132	78	132	63

*U – Ugandan; K – Kenyan; T – Tanzanian; S – Sudanese; E – European.

residence. By contrast, open questioning elicited the factors influencing the decision to move independent of any environmental constraints. Each approach provided a valuable independent source of information and also a basis for evaluating the consistency of response (Downs, 1969).

Data collection

Respondents were asked to indicate the role of five different characteristics in influencing their choice of residence independent of any spatial consideration. This they did by placing each feature in rank order on the basis of its relative importance in their decision (Table 6.2). In selecting the characteristics to be

Table 6.2 Mean rank of characteristics influencing residential choice

Characteristics: 1. Possibility of employment   2. Friendly neighbours   3. Nearness to Kampala
4. Attractive landscape   5. Possibility of cultivating land

Sample group	Characteristics				
	1	2	3	4	5
Arts Yr I	1.90	2.43	3.36	3.52	3.77
Arts Yr II	3.12	2.66	2.96	3.11	2.87
Arts Yr III	2.81	2.56	3.28	3.03	3.12
Science Yr II	2.48	3.22	2.85	3.25	3.14
Science Yr III	2.85	2.85	3.19	3.28	2.66
Alien students	3.02	2.92	2.89	2.97	3.18
African professionals	3.63	2.84	2.10	2.94	3.47
European professionals	2.91	3.69	2.41	2.66	3.30
Namagunga	1.45	2.90	3.66	3.66	3.27
Gayaza	1.98	2.97	3.56	3.91	4.80
Old Kampala	1.86	2.53	3.26	3.70	3.63
Mean rank	2.54	2.87	3.05	3.27	3.38

ranked by respondents the results of recent migration studies within Uganda were considered and in particular the significance of social and environmental considerations in addition to economic forces (Hutton, 1973). While motivation for movement is a highly complex multi-dimensional process the results of this simple analysis proved valuable. Two characteristics were particularly important, namely employment opportunities and social cohesion, thereby confirming findings conducted elsewhere in the developing world (Gould, P., 1969), while in addition reinforcing the suitability of the motivational context for the decision prescribed in the later rank order analysis.

Ordinal information was collected by the following procedure. Respondents were presented with a map of Uganda containing the 18 district boundaries and their respective administrative headquarters (Fig. 6.2). They were requested to rank each district from 1 to 18 on the basis of preference for employment and residence, to name a specific location within the first five choices as a more precise indication of their preference, and finally to indicate those districts and towns previously visited.

Some justification of this approach is required. Within developing countries studies of this kind have adopted employment opportunities as the most important decision-context owing to the particular significance of such opportunities in stimulating movement (Gould, P., 1969; Gould and White, 1974). In this study, however, a combined index of employment and residence was considered the most appropriate means by which to produce a stable and

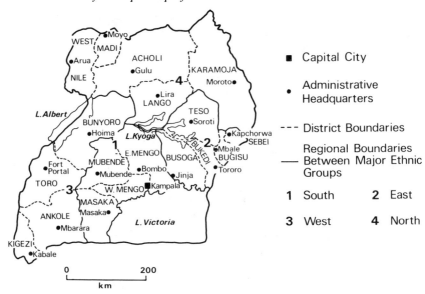

Fig. 6.2 Uganda: administrative headquarters, district boundaries and major ethnic regions. *Source:* after Richards, 1969, p. 38.

reliable response. The choice would not be specifically directed to the motive of expected economic return although this influence might appear of significance in the results. It is suggested that an individual's image of a region comprises physical, social and cultural elements in addition to economic ones. Although these components may be separated in an academic sense they are less likely to be distinguished by an individual unless requested to do so. In addition, it is conceivable that the economic well-being of an area changes more rapidly than the general image. By using a combined index the individual's personal undirected preference would be elicited more easily.

With respect to the environmental stimuli used, the 18 administrative districts were specified as type areas within which respondents applied their decision. While precise specification reduced ambiguity the areal units selected may be criticized for their artificiality and instability. Indeed, minor boundary changes have taken place with successive censuses. Nevertheless, in many instances the districts correspond fairly closely to tribal boundaries (Goldthorpe and Wilson, 1960) and it is reasonable to suggest that they each retain a degree of social and cultural identity among Ugandans. Johnston's (1971) work indicates that the rating by an urban population of a wider area such as a state or region is probably based on the nature of the main town. This assumption may be less valid in Uganda with a low level of urbanization. (If the 1969 census definition of urban as all settlements of 2,000 persons or more is accepted, then only 7 per cent of Uganda's population were urban.) In this survey the relative importance of urban and rural locations could be tested precisely over the first five choices.

Finally, with regard to the scaling method, both technical and practical problems arising from the use of an ordinal scaling procedure were considered. The relative value of nominal, ordinal and interval scaling has been discussed (Gould, P., 1969). While interval is the most precise measurement it has been suggested that for any group over 20 consistent results emerge with both ordinal and interval methods. Furthermore, while it is reasonable to assign a precise numerical value to a preference, assessing the relative attractiveness of locations on an ordinal basis is simpler and more realistic.

A major problem concerns the cognitive task involved in ranking 18 items in a significant order. Clearly the smaller the number of rank decisions to be made the more accurate are the decisions. Several studies have used over 50 ranks, a range which considerably reduces the value of the results (Gould, P., 1969; Gould and White, 1968). Even with 18 rank choices it was occasionally reported by students that many districts lay in their indifference zone, presenting difficulties in decision-making. Indifference may reflect a lack of knowledge and hence an arbitrary decision. Thus, an individual's rank of a specific district must be treated with caution. Repeated ranking by many respondents would provide valuable information concerning the district in question while no consistent ranking would add only a small component to the randomness in the analysis (Tinkler, 1970).

Methods of analysis

Clearly the analytical techniques used are influenced by the aims of the study. In space perception research hitherto these have been limited to isolating the main structural elements in sets of decisions for which purpose principal components analysis has proved valuable (Downs, 1969; Goodey, 1971). The basic premise in the use of this technique is that some portion of an individual's decision pattern is similar to that of another and that a common viewpoint can therefore be extracted from the total variation. Peter Gould (1967, p. 260) identifies it 'as a filter to extract, with least error, the major pieces of the variance not ascribable to unique preferences'. While the technique has proved useful in the early exploratory stages of this research field, conceptual and technical problems have arisen (Gould, P., 1967; Peterson, 1967). Gould indicates that the technique imposes a rigid orthogonal component structure upon the information when it may not exist and cannot be justified on theoretical grounds. Furthermore, while in theory total variance in a data set can be partitioned between common, specific and error terms, in practice they cannot be distinguished easily due to the influence of indifference on some of the choices made. This random element blurs the relationships between individuals and reduces the ability to extract the general preference pattern of a particular group. Peter Gould (1967) has found that the greater the indifference range the more difficult it becomes to extract the overall view. In most instances the major components extracted which define the common view have accounted for a relatively small percentage of the total variation among respondents (under 50 per cent), thereby emphasizing the problem involved (Gould and White, 1968; Johnston, 1971). The inadequacy of the results hitherto obtained has pointed to the need for greater methodological research (Wood, 1970; Jackson and Johnston, 1974).

In the light of these comments an alternative approach was adopted in this study. The initial formulation of a set of hypotheses concerning the migration decisions of a wide range of respondents permitted the application of precise statistical tests appropriate to the problem in hand. The analysis was in three parts. Firstly, the overall relationship between the respondents' past experiences of Uganda and the preference pattern was considered. This was followed by a more detailed study of the influence of cultural background on the choices made and, related to this, the patterns of future internal movement to be expected on the basis of preference only. Finally, the influence of cultural background and personal experience was extended further in an attempt to identify the distinction, if any, between the choices of native and non-native respondents.

Past mobility and spatial preferences

The role of information acquired directly through past migration and indirectly through inter-personal communication and the media has been widely discussed (Goodey, 1968; Jackson and Johnston, 1974). Goodey emphasizes the particular importance of direct personal experience in creating a distinct image, in this instance either a strong preference or dislike. In the present study, in view of the variations in the home districts of individuals within each sample and their resulting diversity of knowledge concerning Uganda, it was suggested on a general level that a significant relationship existed between areas visited most often and those chosen first.

For each respondent within each sample a Spearman's rank correlation was conducted between the two sets of variables. In most cases over 30 per cent of each sample's choice pattern did appear to be influenced by direct experience of Uganda. Table 6.3 summarizes the number of positive correlations within each sample together with the significance level of the coefficients. Some variation did, however, occur both within and between groups. The respondents within each sample exhibiting the lowest degree of correlation were those whose direct experience of the country was restricted largely to less developed northern and western regions. In these instances personal knowledge produced a negative image which was reflected in low rankings for such areas.

With regard to the 'between-sample' differences, levels of correlation tended to be somewhat stronger among younger students, that is those in the sixth form of secondary school and the first year of university, than among older students and those of non-Ugandan origin. In explanation it may be suggested that the decisions made by the latter were constrained less by the security attached to familiar areas than by greater knowledge of economically attractive alternatives.

The suggestion that older students had a wider range of experience and information on which to base their decisions could be assessed by considering levels of mobility among the student population as indicated in the mean number of districts visited (see Table 6.4 and Fig. 6.3). A strong overall relationship emerged. It was clear that a progressive increase in mobility occurred as students moved from school to university, which confirms similar findings elsewhere (Jackson and Johnston, 1974). In the present study any within-sample deviation from the summary mean value was made explicit by the coefficient of variation. This index emphasized that greatest deviations occurred among the youngest students due to the fact that, despite low mobility in general, a small minority had travelled fairly extensively.

The overall relationship between age and experience was confounded by two samples only – the African professionals and the alien students. Contrary to the hypothesis suggested, African professionals were not the most mobile group. Their knowledge of Uganda through past experience was exceeded by Year III Arts Faculty students, suggesting that a high level of internal mobility even

Table 6.3 Relationship between districts visited and districts chosen first

Sample group	Sample size*	Significant correlations		Levels of significance			
		Total	Per cent	0.05	0.01	0.005	0.001
Arts Yr I	71	32	45	12	9	7	4
Arts Yr II	90	34	38	19	15	0	0
Arts Yr III	28	4	14	3	1	0	0
Science Yr II	26	9	35	5	4	0	0
Science Yr III	20	6	30	3	3	0	0
Alien students	39	11	28	10	1	0	0
African professionals	18	8	44	3	5	0	0
European professionals	35	13	42	11	2	0	0
Namagunga	38	18	56	9	5	3	1
Gayaza	68	26	41	9	16	1	0
Old Kampala	30	8	27	5	3	0	0

*This figure excludes respondents who failed to record the districts which they had visited most frequently.

Table 6.4 Mean number of districts visited by each sample

Sample group	Mean districts visited, to nearest whole number	Standard deviation	Coefficient of variation (per cent)
Arts Yr I	9	3.59	40
Arts Yr II	10	3.27	33
Arts Yr III	12	2.43	20
Science Yr II	9	2.93	32
Science Yr III	11	3.12	28
Alien students	6	3.16	53
African professionals	11	3.69	33
European professionals	13	2.97	23
Namagunga	8	1.95	24
Gayaza	7	2.92	42
Old Kampala	7	2.88	41

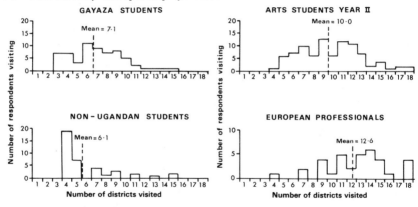

Fig. 6.3   Frequency distributions of districts visited.

among the educated population is a recent phenomenon. Alien students were the least familiar with Uganda of all samples. For many of them termly attendance at Makerere University restricted their experience of the country to the route from Kenya through Bukedi, Busoga and East Mengo to Kampala. However, despite the low average number of districts visited by this sample, the coefficient of variation was the highest recorded, indicating that a small proportion had travelled fairly extensively.

Having indicated a general correspondence between age and experience the influence of these variables on the choice pattern was considered in more detail. The suggestion that personal experience produces a distinct image of an area, either positive or negative (Goodey, 1968; Jackson and Johnston, 1974), was confirmed by this study. In general, as levels of mobility rose among older respondents the relationship between direct experience and preference declined. Two reasons for this may be suggested. First, among these older students the prospect of imminent employment dominated the decision. For them rising mobility was associated with a greater knowledge of less developed northern and western regions which evoked a negative image. This was reflected in an unfavourable response, so much so that the correspondence between choice preference and experience was obscured. Second, some importance must be attached to the role of indirect experience in influencing their decision. The information and advice concerning opportunities available on which the choices were based were acquired not only through personal experience but also, at this stage in their careers, indirectly through contacts at home and within educational institutions. Certain southern and eastern districts not visited, for example, but where employment opportunities were perceived, received favourable ratings emphasizing the influence of indirect experience on the decision.

Reference should be made to two non-conforming samples – Old Kampala school students and African professionals. Respondents from the mixed urban day school revealed an anomalously low correlation coefficient due to the fact that districts adjacent to the capital city were more favoured than those of which they had direct experience. The particular educational background of these students may help to explain this situation. An urban day school requires that students from some distance away find accommodation either in hostels or with relatives near the school. The transition between home and school, and the level of adaptation necessary for integration into an alien urban environment, is greater than that required by students entering the relatively secure campus existence of a boarding school. The importance attached to areas adjacent to their school district suggested that among Old Kampala students integration had been achieved. The pull of familiar areas was less significant than expected. The anomalously high correlation among African professionals reflects two conditions. First, the majority originated from, and only had direct experience of, the south and east. Second, their choice pattern was largely restricted to this area due to the concentration of employment opportunities. As a result the conformity between choice and personal experience was higher than predicted.

By this analysis the relationships between age, experience and the choice pattern were made apparent. Older students had a greater knowledge of Uganda and a wider range of information on which to base their decision. Thus, although in all cases the resultant choice pattern was constrained to some extent by direct contact with familiar areas, an important contrast arose between younger and older students. Among the latter the knowledge acquired indirectly concerning the opportunities available in districts not visited was also of considerable importance.

The influence of cultural background

An individual's evaluation of acquired information is in part determined by the attitudes and values engendered by his particular cultural environment. An extension of the above findings involved analysing the influence of this factor on the choices made. Cultural background was distinguished on two levels within the samples selected. First, the Ugandan respondents were treated separately and reference made to the role of their diverse spatial origins and, by implication, their varied socio-cultural environments, on the choices made. In this way the theme linking past mobility with future preferred movement was extended. Second, on a more general level, focus was placed upon the influence of the native/non-native division on the preference pattern.

In view of the culturally diverse nature of the Ugandan respondents it was suggested that within each sample an important sub-structure existed, cutting across the general preference pattern, which was influenced by the respondents' home location. By testing this hypothesis the extent of any bias and its spatial implications could be ascertained.

The analysis concentrated solely upon the early choices, that is, the three most preferred districts, to which respondents found no difficulty in assigning a rank. For each sample these three early choices of each individual were combined to form a single matrix comprising home district by district selected for employment and residence. This matrix was then combined across samples of similar age and education level to produce three composite matrices, one for each of the following groups: school students, Makerere Arts students and Makerere Science students, (an example is shown in Table 6.5). Information therefore existed in tabular form on the frequency of preference for districts throughout the national area.

The diagonal elements in each matrix recorded the volume of students preferring employment in their home district and indeed within all three groups it was given primary importance by over 50 per cent of respondents. The most notable exceptions were students from Mubende and Karamoja who retained no

Table 6.5 District choice preference of Makerere University Arts students, Years I to III. (Nodal flows are in bold)

Home district	District preference																	
	1	2	3	4	5	6	7	8	9	10	11	12	13	14	15	16	17	18
1	**18**	13	2	10	4	–	4	–	–	–	4	1	1	1	–	–	–	2
2	13	**11**	2	6	6	–	3	–	–	–	1	1	–	–	–	1	–	1
3	3	2	1	1	1	–	–	–	–	–	2	2	–	–	–	–	–	1
4	**11**	7	3	11	9	6	**8**	–	–	1	1	1	–	–	–	3	1	3
5	6	4	–	1	**14**	7	4	4	1	–	5	1	–	1	–	–	–	2
6	2	–	–	–	**5**	2	7	–	–	1	2	–	–	–	–	–	–	–
7	3	1	–	–	4	5	**6**	6	–	–	2	–	2	–	–	–	–	–
8	2	–	–	3	4	2	7	–	–	1	1	–	–	1	–	–	–	2
9	–	–	–	–	1	5	**3**	–	–	–	–	–	–	–	–	–	–	–
10	**5**	2	2	4	2	–	4	–	–	1	2	1	1	–	–	–	–	–
11	**4**	–	–	2	1	–	4	–	–	2	**6**	3	5	1	–	–	–	1
12	**12**	2	–	–	1	–	3	2	–	–	5	**18**	22	–	–	–	–	1
13	12	3	–	–	3	1	1	–	–	3	20	**27**	3	8	–	–	1	–
14	3	1	–	–	1	–	3	7	–	5	6	2	–	–	1	–	–	–
15	3	1	–	–	–	–	3	3	–	–	1	1	1	–	**1**	–	–	1
16	5	1	–	–	–	–	–	–	–	2	4	1	–	–	–	**13**	6	–
17	2	1	–	–	–	–	–	–	–	2	**5**	2	–	–	–	4	9	–
18	–	–	–	–	–	–	–	–	–	–	–	–	–	–	–	**2**	1	1

1. West Mengo ⎫
2. East Mengo ⎬ South
3. Mubende ⎪
4. Masaka ⎭

5. Busoga ⎫
6. Bukedi ⎪
7. Bugisu ⎬ East
8. Teso ⎪
9. Sebei ⎭

10. Bunyoro ⎫
11. Toro ⎪
12. Ankole ⎬ West
13. Kigezi ⎭

14. West Nile ⎫
15. Madi ⎪
16. Acholi ⎬ North
17. Lango ⎪
18. Karamoja ⎭

strong home tie: in both cases less than 10 per cent chose their home area, no doubt a response to the particular physical, social and economic conditions pertaining there. While Mubende forms part of the prosperous Southern region it is sparsely populated and relatively underdeveloped; Karamoja is regarded in social and economic terms as the most backward area of Uganda. Evidence suggests that having enjoyed the freedom and benefits of economically advanced areas young people from these two districts indicate no desire to return home (Castle *et al.*, 1963).

The remaining cells in the matrices recorded the frequency of preference for additional districts and therefore formed the basis for analysing patterns of preferred movement. Identification of these patterns would indicate the structure of social distance between Uganda districts and the relative importance of cultural association in influencing the choices made. In elucidating the basic structure only major flows were considered. For this reason a nodal flow analysis was adopted to identify first-order patterns of preferred movement between districts and the characteristics of any nodal systems (Nystuen and Dacey, 1961, pp. 30–42).

Districts were initially ranked on the basis of their volume of incoming flow. First-order nodal flows were defined by the direction of the largest outgoing flow from each district (that is, the maximum value in each row of the matrices, apart from the principal diagonal) where the destination was a higher ranking district. An 'independent' district was one whose largest flow was to a lower ranking district. Within the network of major connections an independent nodal system was defined as the area comprising an 'independent' district and the various subordinate districts oriented to it. By this procedure the basic structure of association between districts as defined by preferred migration was identified and measured.

The pattern of first-order flows extracted from each matrix revealed a high degree of consistency, respondents from the South and East indicating a strong intra-regional preference while, by contrast, students from the West and North showed a stronger preference for districts beyond the home region (Fig. 6.4). Within the combined group of school-children preferred movement was of two kinds – short-distance between contiguous districts, and fairly long-distance, focusing on the shore of Lake Victoria (Fig. 6.4A). Only four nodal districts emerged, emphasizing the high level of consensus. These were West and East Mengo in the South, Bugisu in the East and Bunyoro in the West. The latter three were nodal only for contiguous districts, suggesting a fairly localized importance. By contrast West Mengo, the district of the capital city on the fertile lakeshore, was of national significance being the focus of both short-distance flows from contiguous Southern districts and of long-distance flows from the West and North. The direction of nodal flows suggested the existence of two systems of preferred movement – a major system focusing on West Mengo and, nesting within it, a subsidiary localized system confined to Eastern students and focusing on Bugisu, the densely populated district of major coffee production on the foothills of Mount Elgon. Among students of the West and North the cultural pull of contiguous districts was outweighed by the economic and, more particularly for this age-group, the educational attractions within the district of the capital city with which they were familiar through the journey to school. It is conceivable that many students had friends or relatives in this area due to the long migration tradition from the North and West to the South, a social factor which may have influenced their preferences (Dak, 1968).

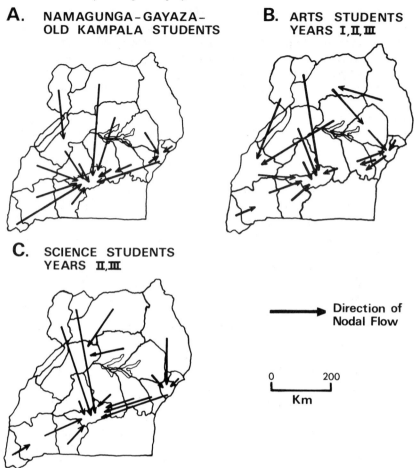

A. NAMAGUNGA-GAYAZA-
OLD KAMPALA STUDENTS

B. ARTS STUDENTS
YEARS I, II, III

C. SCIENCE STUDENTS
YEARS II, III

⟶ Direction of
Nodal Flow

0   200
Km

Fig. 6.4 Patterns of preferred movement between districts: first-order nodal flows.

Among Arts students a similar pattern emerged with short-distance movement between contiguous districts in this instance being characteristic of students from all regions supplemented by long-distance flows to West Mengo and Toro (Fig. 6.4B). Seven nodal districts emerged across the national area, a reflection of the greater short-distance preference. Of these only Teso, Toro and West Mengo extended their influence beyond the regional level. The direction of nodal flows indicated two independent systems dividing the country along a north–south axis. As with school-children the major system concentrated on West Mengo. By a series of direct and indirect links through the subsidiary node, Toro, it was the focus for much of the North and West. However, an independent, more localized, system could also be identified in the East, focusing on Bugisu.

Among Arts students a localized preference was particularly characteristic, the attraction of Buganda and West Mengo being weaker than among school students. Although it remained nodal for Westerners, West Mengo was the dominant focus for only one Northern district and no Eastern districts. The results are surprising in view of the fact that all respondents had spent upwards of one year in the national capital. This variation perhaps reflects the influence exerted by age on the motives for the decision, the attraction of West Mengo among the younger group of secondary students reflecting their desire to attend Makerere, while university students looked beyond education to employment which many perceived in their home area.

With regard to the levels of consensus among students from any one region the greatest divergences occurred among Northerners who had a diffuse pattern of preference. Until recently the poor quality of communications has hindered personal contact between Northern peoples. Such contact among Eastern, Western and Southern groups with a shared Bantu cultural and linguistic tradition and a long history of economic interdependence may have served to structure a more integrated view within these groups. The links shown by Northerners to East and West perhaps reflect the natural routes in these directions: the physical barrier of Lake Kyoga has hindered cultural assimilation with the South.

Among Science students only a restricted analysis could be undertaken due to the lack of respondents from certain districts. However, from the results obtained a pattern closely reflecting that of school students was evident with an emphasis on inter-regional movement (Fig. 6.4C). Localized systems focusing on Ankole and Bunyoro in the West, and on Bugisu in the East, were subsidiary to, and linked with, the major system centred on West Mengo. The cultural bias of the home area was less evident among Science than Arts students, perhaps a reflection of their more localized employment opportunities as previously suggested.

In summary, two significant results emerged from this analysis. Firstly, the analysis demonstrated the overwhelming importance which students attached to their home area, thereby confirming the findings of similar studies elsewhere (Gould and White, 1968; Johnston, 1971). Physical separation from home at regular periods during the academic year in culturally varied institutions had not weakened the significance of ethnic identity. Secondly, students from each region with the exception of Northerners exhibited a coherent preference pattern, either intra-regional in nature or inter-regional orientated to the district of the capital city of which university students, at least, had direct experience. A positive image of West Mengo shared by students from many districts reduced the frictional effect of physical and social distance. By adopting nodal flow analysis the basic structure of preferred movement was uncovered. The direction of nodal flows identified three major receiving areas – Toro, Bugisu and West Mengo. The attraction of Toro in the West to respondents from the West and North reinforces a long-established rural–rural migration movement which has taken place into this district (Masser and Gould, 1975). By contrast the position of Bugisu in the East is somewhat anomalous. While being a leading area for the production of high value *arabica* coffee, it is a densely populated district of net out-migration offering little employment to immigrants (Southall, 1967). Nevertheless its economic and social advantages had contributed to its importance as a node of preferred migration. The overwhelming attraction of West Mengo confirms a tradition of population movement observed throughout the national area (Masser and Gould, 1975).

During the course of the questionnaire respondents indicated a precise location of preference over their first five district choices which provided valuable information on the relative importance of alternative rural and urban areas. Clearly, students perceived their employment opportunities within urban areas. Over 80 per cent of the respondents in each sample attached overwhelming importance to the district headquarters or, in the case of West Mengo, to the capital city. As regards future migration patterns to be expected on the basis of preference only a two-fold pattern emerged either within or between districts. Rural–urban movement accounted for 35 per cent of respondents while inter-urban flow was characteristic of some 50 per cent. Thus, while the familiarity and security of the home area was an important factor in the early choices, a significant distinction was made by students between the traditional local rural or small town community, and the larger urban centres where appropriate employment was more likely to be found.

The role of nationality

In concluding this analysis of migration preferences it was decided that the importance attached to cultural background and personal experience should be tested further by a comparison between the choices made by native and non-native respondents. The initial classification of respondents by nationality provided a means of assessing the importance of this factor. As a basis for objective comparison the responses made by individuals within each sample were initially summarized by calculating the mean rating assigned to each district, together with the standard deviation of the mean (Fig. 6.5 provides an example of

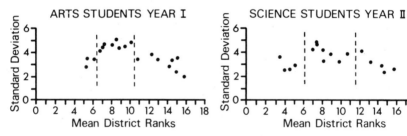

Fig. 6.5 Summarized preference patterns.

the results). The wide range of district mean values recorded for all samples, broadly from 2.0 to 15.0, indicated strong spatial biases in the choice pattern, while reference to the inverted 'U' of each graph emphasized a high degree of consensus towards most and least preferred districts with a greater variability among choices in the indifference zone.

The wide range of mean values obtained permitted precise grouping of districts on the three-fold basis outlined above: that is, districts with a low mean, positively preferred; districts with a high mean, strongly disliked; middle-rank districts, regarded with indifference. Districts were grouped by the following procedure. An overall mean value and standard deviation were calculated as a yardstick against which to compare the means of individual groups. Adopting the 0.01 significance level as the threshold, district groupings were obtained by testing the significance of the difference between individual means and the national norm in a positive and negative direction. In all cases sufficient discrimination had been made between districts to produce a threefold classification illustrated by the vertical dashed lines on Fig. 6.5.

In view of this common structure in the choice pattern, a characteristic confirmed by similar studies conducted elsewhere (Gould, P., 1967; Gould and White, 1968), a comparison of responses between samples was justified. By means of a cluster analysis procedure (Davis, J. C., 1973, pp. 466–73) the 11 samples were grouped on the basis of their similarity in mean rank. A standardized Euclidean distance coefficient was adopted to measure the degree of similarity between samples for two reasons. Firstly, unlike the correlation coefficient, it is not constrained within the range of + 1 to − 1. Secondly, studies hitherto suggest that distance measures yield lower distortion in the results than do correlation matrices (Davis, J. C., 1973, p. 466). A weighted pair-group method of clustering was adopted to arrange the samples into a hierarchy, and, to facilitate lengthy calculations, the appropriate computer program was used in the analysis. As shown in Fig. 6.6 the following distance values were selected as bases for grouping samples into mutually similar clusters:

First-order group: Samples which combined within the distance range of 0.50 and 0.99
Second-order group: 1.00–1.49
Third-order group: 1.50–1.99

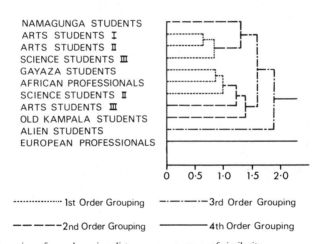

Fig. 6.6   Clustering of samples using distance as a measure of similarity.

In view of the increasing distortion at successive levels in the clustering procedure a low cut-off point was selected to define the groups, so that the distance was not identified at which the inevitable fourth-order group is produced.[3] At the first-order level two small clusters appeared forming the basis of separate groups at the second level. Linkage at the third level incorporated 10 of the 11 samples within the classification, the exception being expatriate professionals who remained separate throughout the analysis.

From the hierarchical classification significant results emerged. As predicted, the greatest variation in patterns of preference occurred between Ugandans and non-Ugandans, findings substantiated by cross-national studies conducted elsewhere (Sonnenfeld, 1967; Murton, 1972). While differences emerged within culture groups, of greater significance was this native/non-native division. The Ugandan samples clustered early in the analysis. By contrast alien students did not join the classification until the third-order level while European expatriates remained separate throughout. Among the last-named group a combination of maturity and European cultural background put decision-making on a different basis from the dominant African groups – hence the independent position of the Europeans. This was exemplified in the higher value attached to scenically attractive, though relatively underdeveloped peripheral districts such as Kigezi and Karamoja which students associated with unemployment and economic backwardness.

From this study of migration preferences valuable information was obtained concerning the attributes of population and place which influence the decision. A methodology was adopted which would test specific hypotheses concerning the underlying structure and spatial characteristics of preferred movement and, while the unrepresentative nature of the respondents questioned precludes conclusive results, nevertheless significant observations may be made. In general terms knowledge gained by the educational élite through direct experience of Uganda was fundamentally important in determining the choice pattern. On a more specific level, however, cultural differentiation influenced the respondents' relative evaluation of those districts of which they had personal knowledge and hence the precise areas selected for desired employment and residence. Within this context nationality played a primary role in discriminating between sample preferences, while among the Ugandan respondents an additional sub-structure existed which was influenced by their diverse spatial origins. The dominant pattern of preferred migration generated by the latter confirmed earlier findings that movement to the major zone of economic activity, including the capital city, is not an inevitable consequence of educational development. The ethnic tie with the home environment remains sufficiently strong to encourage return movement following education, given that the required employment opportunities are available. However, the pull of the urban location shared by all respondents has important implications concerning future movements of population and levels of urban growth.

Conclusions

Some reference should be made to the implications of this study within the framework of African development. The spatial characteristics of occupational preferences among this small 'élite' sector of the population are of considerable significance in national planning. In Uganda, as in other developing countries, policy-makers are confronted with the possibility of assigning skilled personnel, administrators and technologists to fixed locations throughout the country.[4] Since independence attempts have been made to create a unified state out of considerable cultural diversity. However, many difficulties emerge in the use of spatial assignment to achieve this end. Should personal preferences be respected or should they be compromised in the interests of development? The problem has been widely discussed elsewhere. For example, in 1972 in Nigeria in relation to assignment between alternative urban–rural locations, the Federal Minister for Housing and Works, analysing 'self-created' unemployment, suggested that:

> Unless we are able to decide whether education is aimed at making us find pleasure out of nothing, or at enabling us to contribute our own quotas to the economic development of our community, there will continue to be cold attitudes

towards working in rural areas, and the labour sectors in such areas will continue to be understaffed (*Daily Sketch*, Ibadan, 1972).

From this study of migration preference insight has been gained into the influence of the attributes of population and place. The role of past mobility in influencing attitudes to possible future migration destinations has been clearly displayed. That these patterns conform closely to the traditional movements of population within Uganda raises important issues for policy-makers and planners concerning the future spread of economic development.

By adopting a micro-level approach a clearer understanding of the forces and constraints behind movement has been possible. However, two limitations of the present study did emerge and could be rectified in future work. The first concerned the sampling procedure, where a greater range of secondary and university students selected from throughout the national area would provide a more accurate assessment of the influence of home location on the choices made. Secondly, as regards questionnaire design, more needs to be known about the precise occupational aspirations and socio-economic background of young people and the extent to which these factors influence spatial decision-making. Only then will the true impact of migration on demographic, social and economic conditions be made explicit. This survey has provided a direction for future, more detailed study.

Notes

1. Until the political unrest in 1972 certain Ugandan students received government travel bursaries to attend both secondary school and Makerere university, thus alleviating the financial burden involved in advanced education. While no figures are available on the number of bursaries awarded, it can nevertheless be assumed that the majority of students received no financial assistance. On these grounds it may be inferred that economic status was a significant force in educational selection.
2. On the basis of a Manpower Survey carried out by the Central Planning Bureau in 1962 all forms of employment requiring a minimum educational qualification of the school certificate (achieved at the end of four years in a senior secondary school) were placed within the category of high-level manpower.
3. By the weighted pair-group technique the similarity matrix is recomputed at each level in the clustering procedure, mutually similar pairs being treated as one sample through the process of arithmetic averaging. As a result, when single samples are combined within clusters they exert a greater influence on the similarity matrix than do samples which linked earlier. Thus distortion due to averaging becomes increasingly apparent at successive levels in the hierarchical classification.
4. Since the survey was carried out in 1972 political changes within Uganda have affected both the education system and the employment structure. No information on these changes is available.

Acknowledgements

The author is grateful to the Social Science Research Council for financial support during this research, and to Professor B. W. Langlands for making available the facilities of the Geography Department at Makerere University. She is indebted to Dr K. J. Tinkler for his assistance during the survey and analysis. The interest expressed by Dr M. A. Hirst was also most valuable.

Chapter 7

Migration and land as aspects of underdevelopment: an approach to agricultural migration in Bolivia

P . E . Buksmann

In this chapter migration, land tenure and economic development are discussed as three closely related variables in the context of Bolivia. The objective is to examine the influences of in-migration and land tenure on the responses of peasant cultivators to opportunities to improve their agricultural production. The fieldwork on which this chapter is based was conducted in several communities within a 15-kilometre radius of the town of Monteagudo in the province of Hernando Siles, the department of Chuquisaca in south-east Bolivia (see Fig. 7.1) in an area which has been affected by the Bolivian land reform.

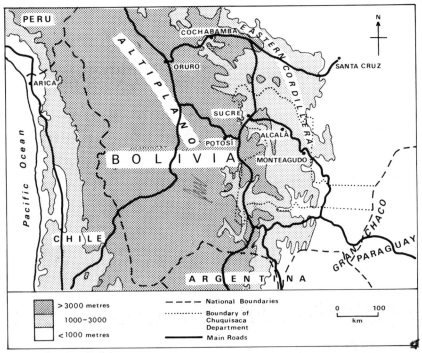

Fig. 7.1 Southern Bolivia.

In this area migration is important, not just as a phenomenon which has produced changes in both origin and destination areas, but also as one aspect of the changing relationship between rural dwellers and the land which they work. Because economic opportunities for rural dwellers, particularly small cultivators, are fundamentally determined by their access to land, any economic development – or underdevelopment – is also a direct function of that access. Any factors which influence access to land also influence the opportunities available for rural cultivators: two such factors which are significant in this study are in-migration and land (tenure) reform. In-migration has increased the pressure of population on the land: land reform has modified the economic and social relationships between rural producers and the land base. As a result of the operation of these two factors access to land for small cultivators has become increasingly limited.

Migration, land tenure and underdevelopment

Land (tenure) reform may be defined as a reorganization of the 'rights, duties, liberties and exposures of individuals and groups [to] land and water', (Dorner, 1972, p. 17). In Latin America the distribution of ownership rights to large areas of rural land has been traditionally concentrated among land-holding 'élites' (United Nations, 1954, p. 37). Land (tenure) reforms have attempted to create more equal distributions of land-ownership rights, and also to create holdings adequate for some surplus production of agricultural commodities by small cultivators over and above that required for use by the cultivators' own families. The term 'agrarian' reform, in contrast, has included reforms of all rural institutional frameworks which affect the lives and livelihoods of rural dwellers.

In many Third World countries certain methodological approaches to economic development attempt to define the significant relationships between land tenure patterns and economic development. Such approaches begin by explaining how 'feudal' land tenure types act as obstacles to the efficient development of agriculture: if this explanation is accepted it then becomes both logically and ideologically necessary to reorganize these land tenure systems in order to stimulate domestic agricultural production of both staple foodstuffs and of cash crops for export. Revenue from agricultural exports can then be used to purchase manufactured goods and machinery for the development of a domestic industrial sector (Johnston and Southworth, 1967, p. 4). However, such a neat conceptualization makes no explicit distinction between the 'traditional' and 'modern' sectors characteristic of Third World agricultural systems, and leads to the identification of relationships between agriculture and economic development which are spurious or deliberately misleading.

While it is undeniable that agriculture can make a substantial contribution to economic development it is the modern agricultural sector which produces the agricultural commodities for export and which is likely to benefit most from land reform aimed at economic growth. Traditional agriculture, producing mainly for domestic consumption, tends to receive little benefit, such that while the export sector of agriculture consolidates its dominance through modernization, traditional agriculture is still confronted with fundamental problems of access to land.

In Latin America land tenure reforms have been a significant feature of attempts to modify or abolish 'feudal' agrarian structures as a first step towards promoting economic development. However, to argue that the task of those 'genuinely concerned with economic development [is to] effect the transition from an overwhelmingly subsistence to a predominantly commercial type of agriculture' (Sen, 1974, p. 26) is misleading because traditional agriculture is thereby unequivocally equated with subsistence production. The application of such an argument would be likely to initiate processes of 'modernization' which would have disruptive or destructive effects on patterns of social organization which, in traditional sectors of agriculture, are firmly based on existing patterns of land tenure. Furthermore, such 'modernization' processes tend to make the small producers more marginal to the national economy rather than to integrate them into it.

This marginality of small rural producers, deriving from the inegalitarian patterns of land-holding and made worse by inappropriate and unsuitable approaches to economic development in agriculture, is further exacerbated by population pressures. Yet rather than approaching this real problem of marginality as resulting from conditions in the countryside, research attention has been directed primarily to examining the results of this phenomenon in the creation of migration flows from rural to urban areas, in the selectivity of migration, in the nature of the migration process, and in the formation, economic, social and political dimensions of shanty towns in and around the major cities of Latin America. High rates of urban population increase have diverted research away from the investigation of the myriad effects of migration in rural communities (Preston, 1969, p. 282) and towards studies of the impact of migration in urban areas.

Furthermore, although the predominance of economic motives for rural–urban migration is often discussed (Stoltman and Ball, 1970), only a few observers have proposed improving economic conditions in the countryside. The responsiveness of migration to spatial differences in wages has been examined in different national contexts (for example in Jamaica by Adams, N. A., 1969; in Colombia by Schultz, 1971, p. 163): in Schultz's study it was found that even if rural wages were increased by one-half (with city wages constant) rural out-migration would only be reduced by one-quarter (Schultz, 1971, p. 161). Nevertheless, unless some attempt is made to redress wage imbalances between rural and urban sectors, to exhort peasants to stay on the land is futile (Adams, N. A., 1969, p. 151). As long as these imbalances are sufficiently large then peasants will migrate, and the imbalances are likely to remain large if population pressure in the countryside is high or increasing since this will keep wages down.

Planned agrarian reform or colonization programmes 'cannot be expected to absorb the whole of the excess rural labour force, particularly the more marginal part of it' (Economic Commission for Latin America, 1971, p. 89), so excessive numbers of rural labourers will mean that wage increases are unlikely to occur and, if they do occur, will offer no permanent solution to disparities in standards of living in the countryside: wage increases would only alleviate the hardship of the privileged few who would receive them, and then only in the short term. It is difficult, therefore, to argue with the view that:

> Population increase combines with a number of other forces . . . to make the pre-existing patterns of land tenure, cultivation, marketing, neighbourhood ties and urban–rural relationships less and less viable. In their present combinations, these forces point to widening disparities between rural population groups able to cope with change and the 'marginalized' remainder (Economic Commission for Latin America, 1971, p. 89).

There are, however, two schools of thought on the relationship of population and economic development in Latin America (Peláes and Martine, 1974, p. 117). The first argues that any economic progress achieved is undermined and absorbed to a significant degree by population growth. The second argues that population growth rates in Latin America are irrelevant in view of the low density of population and the potential for economic growth which is higher than population growth rates. In reform programmes redistributions of land are often combined with attempts to promote the movement of people, especially the 'marginalized' groups, from overcrowded rural areas to regions where population pressures on land are less severe (Odell and Preston, 1973, pp. 93–4). In areas of highland Andean Latin America, where rural populations exhibit considerable concentration in valleys and basins (James, 1969, p. 5) and where agrarian reform is a major force (Smith, 1971, p. 263), there is simply not enough land to distribute to all those eligible for it. Consequently, between 1950 and 1960, while 14 million people moved from rural to urban areas in Latin America, other internal migrations to rural areas demonstrated 'the dynamic importance of frontier settlement influenced by government programmes as well as privately generated schemes' (Thomas, R. N., 1971, p. 105).

These large movements of rural dwellers from the overcrowded highland areas to virtually uninhabited lowland zones suggest that the measures which have so far been applied to improve conditions in traditionally long-settled rural areas cannot have been effective without export of labour. Nevertheless, even planned colonization projects can reproduce old dependency patterns in which small producers are forced to work on larger farms to supplement their income; and this perpetuates systems of land tenure and social relations which are contrary to the aims of settlement programmes (Jacoby, 1971, pp. 283–4).

Land tenure reform, economic underdevelopment and migration in Bolivia

Bolivia provides a particularly good example of the 'intimate' though 'undetermined' relationships (Peláes and Martine, 1974, p. 95) between economic development strategies, population and both the traditional and modern sectors of agriculture. Here we are primarily concerned with the traditional sector.

The role of migration in post-revolutionary Bolivia was specifically defined in the reform decree of 1952 when the revolutionary government came to power. Migration was considered necessary on three counts: firstly, in order to produce a more 'rational' distribution of population; secondly, to strengthen national unity; and thirdly, to integrate the potentially rich agricultural area of the eastern lowlands more closely with the rest of the country. As one of the objectives of the agrarian reform of 1953, domestic currents of migration of rural dwellers, which had been concentrated in the highland areas, were encouraged towards these eastern lowlands (Heath, 1959, pp. 20ff).

After the agrarian reform two significant migration streams of rural dwellers did, in fact, take place. The first was a movement of young people to urban centres, and the second was the officially encouraged movement (although occurring spontaneously) from the overcrowded highland valleys towards the lowlands. In the north the plains of the Beni received many migrants (Osborne, 1964, p. 77), while further south the area around Santa Cruz was a popular destination. Movement to this latter area was to some extent facilitated by the completion of the Santa Cruz–Cochabamba highway in 1953 which was part of the attempt to unify the country both economically and politically. Despite high rates of return migration among settlers in the lowlands in the early years of colonization (Heath, 1959, p. 21), the early 1960s witnessed a greater desire among migrants to stay (Zondag, 1966, p. 160). However, further south, the Gran Chaco, strategically placed on the border with Paraguay, did not emerge as a popular zone for settlement despite the presence of the extensive sub-Andean oil belt which passes through it (Osborne, 1964, p. 156). Instead migration from the southern highlands of this area of Bolivia tended to be temporary and over short distances. Periodic migrations to work in the sugar-cane harvest were, and remain, the dominant patterns, since:

> as long as economic opportunities are not sufficient to be an incentive to migrate permanently those who move into newly opened lowland areas will be predominantly families from regions close by (Erasmus, 1969, p. 150).

Problems confronted those migrants from highland areas who moved to the lowlands. Not the least of these was the 'fear of sickness and dislike of the hot climate' (Erasmus, 1969, p. 150), although for those who returned to their original highland communities social and family ties and the need to develop different food habits may have been more important problems than climatic differences (Zondag, 1966, p. 160). Most migration and settlement has resulted from spontaneous rather than government-directed movements of population, since in a poor country such as Bolivia infrastructural services are minimal and government control over migration and colonization is thus likely to be weak.

In spite of the heavy out-migration from the highland areas in response to population pressure the success of the 1953 agrarian reform has been thwarted in the highlands by the continuing presence of a landlord class and their continuing dominance of the peasants who have remained (Graeff, 1974, p. 33). The land tenure system in pre-revolutionary Bolivia was dominated by large estates. The 1950 Bolivian agricultural census reported that estates larger than 500 hectares comprised at most 8 per cent of all farm units yet covered 95 per cent of the total area in farms (Ferragut, 1963, p. 82) and were probably controlled by an oligarchy of only 4 per cent of all landowners. Farms of less than 10 hectares made up 60 per cent of the total number of farms, yet covered only 0.41 per cent of the total farm area. The agrarian reform attempted to destroy the large estates as the controlling social, economic and political structure in the countryside. However, the uneven spatial impact of the agrarian reform and the inevitable delays in its application because of the complicated nature and formality of its procedures weakened its radical 'bite'. Consequently many landlords have been able to retain possession of their estates intact, even in major centres of agrarian reform such as Cochabamba, often under the guise of natural pastures or as a so-called 'agricultural enterprise'. In more isolated and inaccessible regions of the country the 1953 reform brought little change or improvement for the peasants who remained largely subsistence producers.

In terms of a broad economic and social restructuring of the country Bolivia's agrarian reform was intended to integrate the different regions of the country more closely. To some extent this has been achieved by the development of new nucleated rural settlements with weekly markets (Odell and Preston, 1973, p. 85) which have stimulated the geographical mobility of the peasants (Clark, R. J., 1968, pp. 166–7). In addition, the emphasis and encouragement given by the agrarian reform decree to the colonization of vast areas of tropical and sub-tropical plains showed the strategic and military significance of settling these lowland areas by migration.

The Bolivian land reform has had some successes, particularly in terms of population redistribution and land colonization, but there have been regional variations in the application of the reform measures, especially with regard to the question of land tenure. Nevertheless, the reform partly fulfilled the obligations of the revolutionary government to its supporters among the peasant masses. It can only be speculated how much more explosive the rural situation might have become if no reform had been carried out.

The Monteagudo case study area

The Monteagudo area, chosen as a case study of the effects of recent migration on agrarian structures, is located in the south-eastern lowlands of Bolivia in an area which borders the Gran Chaco (Fig. 7.1). Topographically, Monteagudo is situated within the eastern cordillera (James, 1969, p. 506), or what is often called the sub-Andean belt (Acción Cultural Loyola, 1974, p. 13) – the final series of north–south-trending mountain ranges (average height 1,500 metres) before the eastern tropical lowlands are reached. The situation of Monteagudo at the junction between highland and lowland areas and on a major north–south routeway has contributed towards its emergence as an economic and political focal point and has also stimulated population growth through in-migration in recent decades. In colonial times the eastern cordillera formed a major trade route linking Lima with the rich mining areas of Bolivia, particularly the silver mines of Potosí (James, 1969, p. 519). Some vestiges of the historical significance of this route still remain in the annual droves of mules and horses which originate in Argentina and pass through Monteagudo on their way to the annual livestock fair in Alcalá.

Until the 1920s the whole province of Hernando Siles, in which Monteagudo lies, was very much a 'frontier' region inhabited predominantly by *Chiriguano* Indians[1] (Acción Cultural Loyola, 1974, p. 56), who provided *peón*[2] labour on the pre-reform estates. Estates in the vicinity of Monteagudo concentrated on cattle-rearing until widespread outbreaks of cattle diseases and of smallpox among the *Chiriguano* labourers in the late 1940s and early 1950s reduced the numbers of both cattle and labour so much that large areas within estates stood empty and vacant. At the time of the land reform, therefore, the area was not virgin territory, for the land had been divided up and exploited in the past, although the population density was low.

Migration into the study area has been a prominent feature of local demography, especially since the agrarian reform, although there were already some migrants before 1953. Migrants have come almost exclusively from more mountainous areas to the west, leaving their infertile, stony plots in the highlands in search of better land to cultivate elsewhere. Once in the Monteagudo area these migrants form the mass of small producers whose agricultural system is one of subsistence crop cultivation in which only a very small and variable proportion of production is sold. Maize is the dominant crop, both by virtue of the area under its cultivation and by the volume and value of total production (Acción Cultural Loyola, 1974, p. 269).

Agricultural systems within the study area have evolved within a varied and mixed range of land tenure categories. However, the operators of the land can be classified according to three basic types of tenure. Firstly there are those who own large estates and are known as *patrones* or *dueños* (landlords); secondly there are those who own and work small plots and are known as *propietarios pequeños* (smallholder owners); and thirdly there are those who work land which they do not own. Among this latter group are *arrenderos* (tenants) as well as *arrimantes*, *arrendatarios*, and those holding land *en cuidado*, and *alquilado* or *anticrético* tenures.[3] Most of these provide some labour services to the landlord or landowner in return for usufruct rights to a plot of land.

The nature and evolution of land tenure patterns in the south-east of Bolivia in general, and in the vicinity of Monteagudo in particular, were affected quite considerably by the 1953 agrarian reform, although certain changes predate that reform. While estate-dominated patterns of land tenure have continued in existence, albeit in weakened form, since the reform the old social and economic relationships based on land tenure have been substantially altered. The main changes produced in land tenure systems occurred in the organization of labour regimes on estates. In general labour obligations and the services performed on estates in the south-east were small in number and comparatively light. Estates close to Monteagudo had the second lowest number of days worked per year by tenants in the whole of southern Bolivia (6 days against a maximum elsewhere of 350 days). Furthermore, some of these estates were apparently unique in the complete absence of labour obligations other than field labour (Erasmus, 1967, p. 354; 1969, p. 87). However these obligations were modified, extended or even added to, as the numbers of tenants on estates changed due to in-migration.

The continuing and increasing pressure of the local rural population on land for cultivation has increased land values. Recent migrants have had to accept land under insecure and precarious conditions of tenure unless they already had friends or relatives resident in the area who were able to lease them some land. As land for the most part is still held by large estates only marginal land is available for cultivation by these recent arrivals. This means that such people are more concerned with, and devote their energies towards, subsistence cultivation on marginal land rather than towards commercial or cash crop production. Continued in-migration has favoured only a minority of rural producers in terms of agricultural economic development, the beneficiaries being primarily those with long periods of residence in the area and who therefore had superior access to land, access which they have since maintained. Recent migrants to Monteagudo are under-represented among those who are able to benefit from development opportunities there, and this is all the more significant since Monteagudo is the planned regional focus in the south-east for future economic development: in particular it is intended to create an agro-industrial growth pole there by the commercial development of the maize-and-hog sector of local agriculture. However, the potential benefits of such a development project can apply to only a minority of local producers; the majority are likely to be unaffected because of the nature of the inter-relationships between in-migration, land tenure and economic development, and particularly through the timing of migration.

The imbalance between the increasing rural population seeking land to cultivate and the availability of such land tends to produce agricultural systems that are characterized by under-employment of labour. Many small producers therefore seek extra income by hiring themselves out to other farmers as labourers or for work on town-based projects, where the rates of pay are superior although only short-term employment is available. Such extra work is in addition to the changes in tenants' obligations to their landlords which have come about with increased rural population pressure. These changes have taken the form of increases in the number of field days of labour demanded from tenants, such increases coinciding with recognizable influxes of migrants into the study area, particularly during the 1950s, and despite the intentions of the agrarian reform. For example, on one estate in the pre-reform years the *yanapacu* system[4] had existed and tenants had had to devote two days of labour each week to this, the obligation later being reduced to ten days of estate labour per year from each tenant; as a result of in-migration at the time of the reform the obligation was increased again to one day per week, although payment was also introduced at the rate of 10 *pesos* (about 17 US cents) per day plus meals and a ration of coca leaves.

It can be argued that a combination of the widespread livestock diseases, the reduction of Indian *peóns* on the estates and the threat of imminent land reform in the later 1940s and early 1950s forced the estate-owners to some extent to anticipate the reform of 1953 by introducing *arriendo* tenures on their estates as the most rapid method of 're-populating' them. Such tenures are all those under which the tenant is obliged to perform labour or other services for the landlord in exchange for access to land for cultivation. The estate-owners also hoped that, by bringing land back into cultivation, when the agrarian reform did eventually occur sentences of expropriation would be less severe than might have been the case if the land was unused. The re-population of the estates took place by means of migrant flows to Monteagudo from the Andean foothill areas to the west and north-west. The old cattle-ranching system had required relatively little labour except that provided by the Indian *peóns*: the tenantry was small and worked under the *yanapacu* share-cropping arrangements. With the reduction in the Indian *peóns* and the arrival of migrants agricultural systems began to change. Labour obligations were modified in form and duration in accordance with whether there were now more or fewer tenants than there had once been *peóns* to carry out the labour obligations required by the estate-owners.

It is therefore possible to see a complex pattern of inter-relationships between migration and agricultural land tenure systems. On the one hand it was the offer of tenancies that brought in the migrants, and on the other hand it was the scale of immigration that led to a shortage of tenancies and the re-imposition of more restrictive controls on access to land. The agrarian reform was not flexible enough to deal with such complex patterns of land tenure relationships which, under continuing pressure from new migrants, produced increasing socio-economic differentiation among small rural producers in the study area and in south-east Bolivia in general. Such differentiation did not allow all small producers to benefit equally from programmes of agricultural economic development, since differential access to land is the most important aspect of the local rural socio-economic structure, both as a result of the persistence of unequal access from the pre-reform period and of continued in-migration.

The field study in Monteagudo

Two four-month periods were spent in the field. The first, in 1975, was exploratory with the major objective being to assess the nature of local agrarian change and its impact on different categories of rural cultivators. The criteria used to differentiate these cultivators were their land tenure status and their areas of land worked. It became clear, during this period of field investigation, that in-migration, largely since the agrarian reform, had been influential in determining the degree to which different groups of peasant cultivators had been affected by agrarian change.

In the second fieldwork period in 1976 it was therefore hypothesized that length of residence in the study area was also of importance in explaining the nature and extent of agricultural change among small producers, in addition to the two criteria of land tenure and land area. It was expected that rural cultivators who had been longest resident in the study area would have better access to land than more recent arrivals; that those cultivators with superior access to land would exhibit more change towards commercialized production than those with inferior land access; and that those with the better land access would therefore have experienced the most improvement in their levels of socio-economic welfare. Only the first two of these specific hypotheses are examined here.

All information collected during the field periods was obtained through interviews with peasants using informal questionnaire techniques. Rural people in developing countries are often suspicious and distrustful of outsiders since their contact with authority figures, officials and institutions is usually less frequent and direct than is the case for urban dwellers. In the study area this suspicion among respondents meant that initially interviews had to be carried out as conversations without the simultaneous recording of information: the obvious disadvantage of this process was the practical limitation of interview time to an average of 20 minutes so that information could be satisfactorily recorded at the termination of the discussion. During the later stages of fieldwork simultaneous recording of information was possible once the interviewer was known to the respondents. In 1975 105 peasants were interviewed using a single questionnaire: in 1976 three questionnaires were administered, the main one to 127 respondents, the second (dealing with detailed place of residence and livestock information) to 47 peasants and the third to 18 residents of the new peasant town of Candúa (Fig. 7.2).

It is often difficult to obtain a random sample of informants in rural areas where settlement patterns are dominated by isolated farmsteads and recent maps at suitable scales are non-existent. There are also practical problems over transportation in the field especially, as here, where the absence of bridges over the numerous rivers makes any travel difficult. In such circumstances a representative rather than a random sample is a realistic aim.

In the present study informants were selected from communities displaying the influence of a wide range of micro-climatic and topographic controls on agriculture. The informants were chosen to cover the range of land tenure types found in the area and also to provide a sufficient cross-section of lengths of local residence from one or two months up to 40 years or more, including also some who had been born locally.

One distinct problem of analysis of the data from such informal question-naires of a peasant population is that of gaps in many of the questionnaire responses. Informants may be unable or unwilling to supply specific information: for example, they may not know exactly how old they are and so may round off their age to the nearest five years. They are also frequently reluctant to provide exact figures for livestock and land, this reticence being based on the belief that the information will be used to take the land away from them. Nevertheless, most

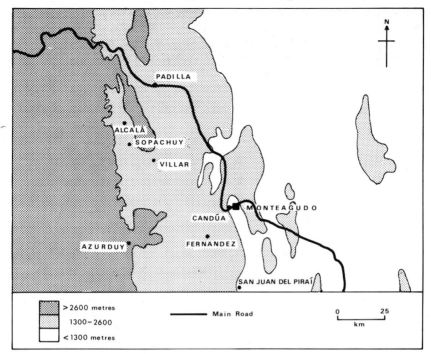

Fig. 7.2 The Monteagudo study area.

of the data collected were amenable to the use of non-parametric statistical tests.

The role of migration in the study area highlighted two problems during the data collection. These problems were, firstly, the need for a working, as opposed to a theoretical, definition of migration; and secondly, the validity of the reasons given by the informants for their migrations.

Migration is usually presented as a movement from any origin point to any destination point, but in much rural-to-rural migration, as in the present study, the migrations are really between areas rather than between points. If rural migrants make several short local moves from farm to village to town in the origin before final departure from it, and similar movements from town to village to farm in the destination area, then how relevant is a concept of migration based on movement between origin and destination points when this fails to exploit the importance of the major inter-regional move? In Monteagudo, even where migrants had friends and relatives to receive them, such migrants later moved within the study area according to where land was available for cultivation or to seek less onerous and more secure conditions of tenure. The major movement into the area was regarded as the important one in this study.

The second problem concerned the reasons given for migration: the majority of respondents' reasons reflected an intention on their part to farm fertile land, to raise better livestock more easily and to improve their living standards in general. But the conclusion was inescapable that the migrants had not been able to fulfil these expectations. The migrants were reluctant to admit that economic possibilities in Monteagudo were disappointing and that in some respects they were little better off than before their moves. The more fertile land and the easier rearing of livestock may have been true, but these reasons for migration did not occur to the migrants until after their moves: the chief motive for moving was probably to improve living standards and, despite some agricultural benefits, this had not generally happened. Migration had thus not necessarily resulted in the improvement of the economic and financial situation of the migrants: in order to gauge why not it is necessary to consider in detail the relationships hypothesized earlier between access to land, commercialization of production and length of residence in the study area.

Migration into the Monteagudo area – results of data analysis

The migrants

Over 80 per cent of the informants interviewed in the study area in 1976 had migrated to Monteagudo, the majority having arrived in the 23 years since the agrarian reform. In-migrants to the study area came almost exclusively from rural communities smaller in size and more distant from large towns than the communities that they now live in. As mentioned earlier, migration was often in stages. The first stage was a move from a rural community to the nearest large town where the migrants spent some time working as labourers or learning the rudiments of a trade, and thereby more easily financing the next stage of their journey which was most frequently direct to Monteagudo. If the migrant had no friends or relatives in the area he usually lived close to or in the town while he looked around for land to cultivate: other migrants on arrival in the study area lived in Candúa before moving out to plots in the countryside.

Migrants originated predominantly from mountainous areas to the north-west, west and south-west of Monteagudo. Padilla and its surroundings contributed over 30 per cent of the migrants while Villar, Azurduy, Sopachuy (see Fig. 7.2) and San Juan del Piraí to the south-west each contributed between 6 and 10 per cent: in total these five locations were the sources of 62 per cent of the migrants. The average distance travelled by migrants from the highlands to Monteagudo was 79 kilometres.

The reasons given by migrants for coming to Monteagudo were extremely varied (Table 7.1). However, almost 50 per cent of their reasons reflected the difficulties of cultivation and the marginality of the land base in the highland communities. A further 14.5 per cent of the reasons given concerned the problems of raising livestock, so that agricultural problems were most significant as reasons for migrating and the migrants said that they came to Monteagudo in the hope of better conditions for agriculture.

Migration into the area really began in the years immediately after the Chaco War (1933–36). Migration streams later gathered momentum (Table 7.2) as the growing town of Monteagudo, with its agricultural marketing function, became a centre of information diffusion to the areas of San Juan del Piraí, Azurduy, Fernandez, Padilla and even Potosí, the news of land availability being carried by farmers who came from those places to Monteagudo to sell produce and to purchase manufactured goods. The arrival of the largest numbers of migrants took place from 1956, the time-lag after the reform decree of 1953 being due to delay in its implementation and consequent uncertainty. The questionnaire responses showed that often migrants had relatives or knew former neighbours

Table 7.1 Reasons for migration to Monteagudo

	Frequency*	Percentage of total
Land/physical factors at origin		
Poor land therefore poor harvests	42	
Poor land	13	47.1
Overcrowding	4	
Others	6	
Livestock/pasture problems at origin		
Livestock pests and diseases	11	14.5
Lack of pasture/difficulties of stock-raising	9	
Family and related factors		
Family already in Monteagudo	5	
Large family at origin	4	13.8
Death or divorce in family	4	
Others	6	
'Forced' migration		
Forced to move, or bad treatment, by landlord	10	9.4
Others	3	
Came to give children education	9	6.5
Marketing, distance, access problems at origin	4	2.9
Other reasons	8	5.8

*Frequencies refer to the number of respondents giving each reason. As some gave more than one reason for migration the frequency total (138) is greater than the total of informants (101).
Data source: 1976 questionnaire survey.

Table 7.2 Arrival dates and length of residence in Monteagudo

Arrival period	Length of residence (years)	Absolute percentage of respondents	Cumulative percentage
1931–35	41–45	2.2	2.2
1936–40	36–40	5.5	7.7
1941–45	31–35	2.2	9.9
1946–50	26–30	6.6	16.5
1951–55	21–25	2.2	18.7
1956–60	16–20	19.8	38.5
1961–65	11–15	13.2	51.7
1966–70	6–10	22.0	73.7
1971–76	0–5	26.4	100.1

Data source: 1976 questionnaire survey.

who were now living in Monteagudo and who were able to help them when they arrived.

Migration and access to land

In-migration substantially influenced the ease of access to land. One way in which this was apparent was in the comparison between the tenure pattern in the area before 1953 of those respondents who were already in Monteagudo then and the tenure pattern of the total set of respondents in 1975 (Table 7.3). Although the proportion of owners has risen there has also been a spreading out of the lower end of the land tenure social status hierarchy, with insecure tenures being created which did not exist before the agrarian reform and before the big influx of migrants began. As the pressure on cultivable land has increased the ease of access to land has tended, despite the increase in owners, to decrease.

At the time of the agarian reform there was abundant land available for

Table 7.3 Land tenure status, pre-reform and 1975

Tenure categories	Pre-reform, percentage of respondents	1975, percentage of respondents
Owner	21.5	47.8
Foster child of landlord	1.1	–
Tenant	62.4	21.7
Estate labourer (*peón*)	1.1	–
Working land of family	1.1	3.3
Working land of father	12.9	3.3
Sharecropper	–	8.7
Hired land	–	7.6
*Anticrético**	–	1.1
*Arrendatario**	–	1.1
*Arrimante**	–	1.1
*Alquilado** or *en cuidad**	–	2.2
Agricultural labourers	–	2.2

Note: The horizontal division into categories is based on similarities in tenure and degree of security. The tenure categories are placed in descending order of security through the table.
*For explanation see note 3, p. 128.
Data source: 1975 questionnaire survey.

cultivation. Even in 1963 squatters on vacant land in the vicinity of Monteagudo were not being evicted (Erasmus, 1969, p. 118). However, by the time of the field surveys in 1975 and 1976 informants were complaining that land for cultivation was in increasingly short supply and, where available at all, was of poor quality and obtainable only on short-term leases.

However, the land tenure status of in-migrants has tended to change with longer periods of residence and, for the individual long-stay migrant, has tended to improve over time even despite current land shortages. Migrants move within the study area as new opportunities become available to them, but for the latest in-migrants their low status means that only short leases of one or two years' duration are possible so they move more frequently from plot to plot and from landlord to landlord. The effect of continued in-migration on land tenure systems in Monteagudo can be demonstrated by comparing the present tenure status of past migrants with the length of their periods of residence. Table 7.4 shows that the proportion of non-owners has steadily increased among migrants who arrived in any five-year period after 1956. The relatively low proportion of owners among recent migrants compared to that among the migrants arriving in the 1956–60 period also stands out. A comparison of the frequencies of present-day owners and non-owners among arrivals in the 1956–60 and 1971–76 periods using the chi-square test produced a significant difference at the 0.025 level,

Table 7.4 Length of residence and tenure status

Arrival period	Length of residence (years)	Owners		Non-owners		Mixed tenure	
		Number	Per cent of period's migrants	Number	Per cent of period's migrants	Number	Per cent of period's migrants
1931–55	21–45	10	63	5	31	1	6
1956–60	16–20	9	56	3	19	4	25
1961–65	11–15	5	45	5	45	1	9
1966–70	6–10	9	47	9	47	1	5
1971–76	0–5	7	29	15	63	2	8

Data source: 1976 questionnaire survey.

indicating that the present tenure status of past migrants is not random but is likely instead to be a function of the length of time spent in Monteagudo. The longer a migrant has been in Monteagudo the better his tenure is.

It was expected that length of residence would also influence the area of land held by migrants for cultivation. Yet only those migrants who had arrived in the last five years held appreciably less land than earlier arrivals, although all migrants were disadvantaged compared to those born in the area (Table 7.5). However, a comparison of the land areas held by those coming before and after the reform shows appreciable differences with those arriving in the period 1956–60 being particularly favoured at a time when the migratory pressure on land had not yet built up. Although, in the questionnaire survey even these favoured migrants talked of the problems of present-day access to land, with the acquisition of additional land for cultivation made more difficult because of overcrowding. More recent migrants perceived the problem of access to land more in terms of the precarious short-term tenures which they were offered, as well as the marginal quality and small sizes of plots available.

Table 7.5 Length of residence and area of land held

Arrival period	Length of residence (years)	Mean area of land held (hectares)		
		Five-year groups	Decades	Life/pre-/post-reform
–	Life	–	–	12.9
1931–35	41–45	5.0	5.0	
1936–40	36–40	4.0	4.8	
1941–45	31–35	6.5		4.8
1946–50	26–30	4.3	4.7	
1951–55	21–25	6.0		
1956–60	16–20	7.8	7.1	
1961–65	11–15	5.9		5.5
1966–70	6–10	6.2	4.3	
1971–76	0–5	2.7		

Data source: 1976 questionnaire survey.

Some of the poor correspondence between length of residence and areas of land held can be attributed to the attitudes of landlords to their former tenants. Cases existed on all estates in the study area where it was clear that landlords were reluctant to recognize some tenants as 'long-standing' and thereby, in the terms of normal moral obligations, eligible for more land: often such tenants had been those who had acted as leaders within the community or who had been in some past dispute with the landlord. Land tenure, land area and residence relationships were also influenced by the practice of landlords offering for sale plots of land which had been cleared and cultivated by long-standing tenants, thereby forcing those tenants to move to other parts of the estates or, at least, reducing substantially the area of land cultivated by the tenants. Such processes brought about imbalances in the expected relationships linking length of residence to both tenure status and land areas held by cultivators.

Migration and opportunities for commercial agricultural production

A further influence of migration on access to land can be explored by examining the degree to which the small rural cultivators were actively involved in experimenting with and adopting measures to improve their agriculture.

Certainly on balance there were better and more opportunities in agriculture in Monteagudo than ever existed in the migrants' home communities, but the increasingly restrictive land tenures that came into existence in Monteagudo as migration progressed severely limited the scope for improving agricultural production. Migrants who worked small marginal plots under precarious and insecure conditions of tenure have, of necessity, had to concentrate their productive energies on subsistence cultivation. Consequently in-migration to the study area has not provided the conditions favourable to the production of the more commercially orientated crops that are needed if the Monteagudo area is to become an agro-industrial complex as the government planners hope.

The relationship between in-migration and agricultural economic development in the study area cannot be considered except in the context of the locally prevailing patterns of land tenure. In order to examine the relevance of these inter-relationships the local introduction of improved hog-rearing[5] practices will be considered here, as an example of the kind of commercial opportunities which were available to the peasants and the nature of the responses made to those opportunities.

Five factors are particularly significant in the production of hogs by small farmers. Most fundamental is the area of land 'surplus' to family requirements which can be utilized for the production of maize as hog-feed. Secondly, family size itself determines family requirements for land for maize and, thirdly, also governs the availability of family members to feed and watch over the hogs. Fourthly, the cultivator has to consider the potential effects of inclement weather conditions on maize harvests. Fifthly, the sale of hogs, to whom, at what stage of fattening, and at what price, determines both the rate of return and the economic feasibility of hog production.

In 1976 53 per cent of all informants had sold, or expected to sell, hogs. All respondents kept hogs, and those not selling in 1976 fell into two groups – those who usually sold but would not in that year (28 per cent), and those who raised hogs exclusively for their own consumption (19 per cent). When sellers and non-sellers of hogs were controlled for tenure type affiliation owners of land were proportionately dominant among the sellers (see Table 7.6). A 2×2 contingency table comparing the frequencies of owners and non-owners of land among sellers and non-sellers of hogs gave a chi-square value significant at the 0.001 level, strongly suggesting that owners of land were much more likely to sell hogs than were non-owners. However, by using chi-square to compare the frequencies of owners and non-owners in the two groups of non-sellers it was found that there were significantly (0.05 level) more non-owners than owners who, in 1976, did not sell hogs but usually did. This suggests that not all non-owners of land were unable to produce hogs for commercial sale: it was their marginality as agricultural producers which affected their hog production so that, when the

Table 7.6 Sales of hogs, 1976, according to tenure types

	Sold hogs in 1976	Did not sell hogs in 1976	
		Normally sold	Never sold
Absolute totals	42	22	15
Of which: Per cent owners	59.5	18.2	46.7
Per cent non-owners	23.8	72.7	33.3
Per cent others or not known	16.7	9.1	20.0

Data source: 1976 questionnaire survey.

cumulative effect of the five factors outlined above was adverse, they could not produce for sale.

Most cultivators did not produce substantial numbers of hogs for sale despite concerted official efforts to facilitate all aspects of hog-raising, production and marketing. Almost 60 per cent of hog-sellers in 1976 raised less than 5 animals and only 5 per cent sold, or expected to sell, over 20. Tenure status alone was a weak determinant of how many hogs were sold, but the actual area of land held by sellers was more significant: among sellers of less than 5 hogs owners of land held, on average, 84 per cent more land than non-owners: among sellers of from 6 to 10 hogs owners held, on average, 89 per cent more land than non-owners.

Migration influenced hog production and sale through its influence on migrants' access to land. Owners of land tended to be the longer-resident migrants (Table 7.4) and, given the nature of the marginal land increasingly occupied by recent migrants, the opportunity to develop agricultural activities other than subsistence ones principally favoured the longer-resident migrant land-owners. This group had secure land access and was able to innovate and to produce beyond subsistence needs. The agro-industrial development of hog production could therefore only benefit a minority of rural producers, and the whole scheme itself could only operate at a low level because of the inability of many producers to go beyond subsistence cultivation.

However, the general lack of success with improved hog-rearing practices among small rural producers was also the result of several other related factors. Improved hog-rearing practices were intended for adoption as a 'package' and the adoption of one item without the others was unlikely to produce any substantial improvements in hog production. Furthermore, the costs of the recommended pure and cross-bred stock were prohibitive compared to local stock. But more importantly, cultivators were accustomed not to buy in hogs for fattening, but to raise and maintain their own stocks, culling and selling animals in accordance with the cash needs and maize stores of the household. Neither were they used to penning or corralling hogs, but instead allowed them to roam freely to find additional food by foraging. Indeed, ex-tenants on estates in the study area who received land grants through the reform were also given rights to grazing land in accordance with traditional livestock-rearing practices. Ex-tenants had rights of access, in common with ex-landlords, to the large areas of uncultivated and rough grazing land which were characteristic of the estates before the reform. For such cultivators to pen hogs and to provide them with artificial feed appeared illogical, given the particularly favourable access of the producers to land for grazing and foraging by their animals.

Recent migrants found considerable difficulty in raising hogs because they did not have access to land for grazing and foraging and were therefore unable to take full advantage of the opportunities available to improve hog-rearing, for their prime concern was the need to meet family subsistence requirements for maize from whatever land was available. Under these circumstances it was very difficult for recent migrants to compete effectively with longer-term residents and therefore the new opportunities for commercial agriculture favoured the longer-resident migrants with their better access to land.

The areas of migrant origin

The attraction of streams of migrants to Monteagudo and the development of the town itself as an agro-industrial centre did not automatically imply the demise or abandonment of the smaller population centres of the more isolated highland areas from which many of the migrants originated. The relatively short migration distances travelled by most migrants suggest that few of their home communities were completely isolated, and even before the agrarian reform some highland dwellers used to travel to sell produce in Monteagudo or other market centres. Road construction has been particularly important in the influence it has had on the development of trade in agricultural produce and manufactured goods within the region as a whole. The influx of the trucker-merchants who usually follow such improvements in road links has facilitated the increased geographical mobility of rural dwellers by providing them with vehicular services and at the same time the means to pay for the use of them through the sale of agricultural produce.

The departure of migrants from their home communities can therefore have positive as well as negative effects there. It has been argued that those migrants who leave are often the more dynamic individuals and the ones who remain comprise the more conservative elements within the community (Preston, 1969, p. 284). Additionally it has been suggested that it is individuals from larger farms who migrate because they are more able to finance moves than are those who farm smaller plots (Adams, D. W., 1968, pp. 533–4). However, if it is the poorer families on small plots who remain then the ratio of population to cultivable land is little affected. Although out-migration may provide the opportunity for smaller cultivators to work for, or rent from, those who remain on the larger farms this also produces ideal conditions for the development or perpetuation of dependency relations among producers. Among respondents in Monteagudo most migrants had left some of their family in the home community: land parcels there were rarely sold or disposed of, the more common practices being to arrange some rental agreement with an interested party, or simply to leave the land to be farmed by other family members.

Visits back and forth between home community and Monteagudo, although not frequent, were not uncommon. In periodic visits to their highland communities of origin migrants passed on information and experiences of different crops and methods of cultivation and thereby brought new knowledge to cultivators who might otherwise have remained unaware of recent developments. However, it is possible that if only conservative elements remained in the highland communities they may be unresponsive to new ideas and innovation (Economic Commission for Latin America, 1961, p. 39).

The effects of out-migration on sending communities can also produce negative repercussions. To some extent these depend on the numbers of able-bodied men and women who leave any one particular agricultural district. If out-migration reduces the number of potential workers below the level required to perform fundamental agricultural tasks then agricultural production will suffer (Miracle and Berry, 1970, pp. 88–92). Usually, however, the 'reserve army' of underemployed agricultural workers is large enough to replace 'lost' workers, in which case decreases in agricultural production are unlikely to be severe. Additionally, there may exist communal or reciprocal labour arrangements in the communities, such arrangements being implemented when needs arise.

Migration can be beneficial to the sending community when it reduces the sizes of those families which must be supported from small plots. Furthermore, migration does not always select the youngest and most able individuals: among informants in Monteagudo a few cases were encountered where parents had migrated in middle age while their adult children remained in the home community. Out-migration, however, does become detrimental when complete families leave and as a result land is left vacant and disused as population declines.

Ironically, as relatives and friends of the original migrants continue to arrive in Monteagudo the local conditions that formed the push factors in the motivation of the original migration from the highlands are replicated in Monteagudo as population pressures on land there dictate that household plots are sub-divided to accommodate new arrivals.

In-migration and exploitation in Monteagudo

The continuing migration of peasants into Monteagudo has increased the pressure of population on the finite area of cultivable land available – a situation which has provided opportunities for the exploitation of migrant agriculturalists by landlords and other landowners. The distance of the study from more active areas of agrarian reform, and the lengthy legal procedures and confusions over rights and titles to land where reform has been operated, also produce ideal conditions for the exploitation of small cultivators. For example, until the legal processes of the agrarian reform are all completed on any particular estate the landlord can demand that a tenant vacate his plot or move to another part of the estate if a buyer for the plot appears: this was a common ploy used by landlords to prevent any household becoming too entrenched on a particular plot. Should a plot where such an eviction has occurred be sold but the reform arbitrators eventually award the ownership rights to the original tenant instead, then the whole procedure becomes legally complex. Few tenants have sufficient cash resources to finance the legal process through to its conclusion so that the question of ownership is often not finally settled in favour of the small cultivator.

A little more than half the cultivators in the study area did not own the land they worked, and these peasants were often exploited by their landlords who could always find new tenants on unequal terms from among the new migrants. It has been the presence of such migrants that has enabled the landlords to perpetuate, or even to strengthen, their power of exploitation over their tenants.

On one estate, for example, in order to clear the land of dense scrub and thicket the landlord leased the flatter areas to peasants for two-year periods in return for 35 days of paid labour per year for the benefit of the estate. The plots leased rarely exceeded 2 hectares and a tenant at best could clear and plant only about 1 hectare of land in his first year. Such newly cleared land often had to be cultivated by hoe rather than by plough as the stumps and roots of trees had to be left to rot in the ground. In 1976 the landlord extended the labour obligation to 45 days, explaining to his tenants that the extra 10 days were in lieu of *porcentaje* – the payment of a percentage of the harvest from a tenant's plot (Erasmus, 1969, p. 94) – a system which was prohibited by the agrarian reform along with other 'taxes' on the agricultural production of tenants.

On other estates intimidation of varying degrees of subtlety by landlords kept some older tenants and recent migrant arrivals in states of subordination. For example, some of the ex-tenants of one estate were still accustomed to give their old landlord 'presents' of chickens and eggs in order to remain in his good favour. On another estate some cultivators still paid *catastros* amounting to 20 per cent of their harvest. It was also common for tenants working land which had once formed part of an estate to continue to provide several days of 'token' labour service each year to the present owner of that land. A 22-year-old migrant who had been in the study area just one month and had managed to lease a plot from a local landowner indicated that he would be expected to give her a few bags of maize as well as his contractual payment.

These examples illustrate some of the ways in which rural cultivators in the study area were still being exploited by a land-owning élite. Recent migrants were in some cases forced to pay various 'taxes' on their agricultural produce, to provide labour service, or to show some deference to landlords by the provision of 'gifts'. Longer residents without titles of ownership could 'lose' some of their cultivated land or be moved to other parts of estates at the whim of the landlord. All such practices tended to maintain the small rural cultivators in a state of physical and psychological insecurity (Shanin, 1971, p. 15).

Conclusions

From the results of the questionnaires carried out in Monteagudo it has been seen that the continued presence of landlords in the countryside and the ways in which their economic dominance was maintained kept rural cultivators who did not own land in a very subordinate position. Recent migrant arrivals were particularly vulnerable. Attempts to 'modernize' peasant agriculture were of dubious success because the continued exploitation of rural cultivators by landlords was a serious obstacle to such cultivators engaging in anything other than subsistence agriculture: secondarily, their energies were concentrated on holding on to what land they had rather than improving technologies of production. Inequalities in access to land still determined to a considerable extent those peasants who benefited most, least or not at all from development efforts.

The role of migration in this agricultural pattern was of great importance. Traditional agricultural systems tend to change more slowly and unevenly than agricultural systems characteristic of more 'modern' sectors, and in the study area uneven rural development partly resulted from, and was reinforced by, in-migration. Without the increased population pressure on land resources it is unlikely that the continued exploitation of non-land-owning cultivators by landlords and landowners would have occurred to such an extent. Certainly the new categories of land tenure (for this area) would not have come about without such pressure from migrants. The existence of identifiable categories of cultivators based on access to land and related through systems of dependency are one result of the 'unevenness' of rural development. Only those cultivators with superior access to land found it easier to take advantage of the available opportunities to improve their systems of production, and the date of migration to Monteagudo was of great importance in influencing ease of access to land. The longer a migrant had resided in the study area the better was his access to land and the more freedom he had to pursue other than purely subsistence activities.

Inequality in access to land was promoted by the scale of in-migration, and the reflection of this inequality can be seen in the development of a more complex hierarchical division of rural cultivators, thus widening rather than narrowing socio-economic differences. In-migration has achieved this by increasing the pressure of the population on the land resources available. Probably both the date of migration and the length of residence are of importance in determining the migrant's access to land in Monteagudo. For those arriving in the 1950s there was, at that time, more land available, and on less restrictive tenures, than has been the case more recently. On arrival in the study area the in-migrant at that time was, therefore, probably more favourably placed than the in-migrant today. For all migrants the time spent in the area was important in permitting a search for better land, a chance to demonstrate obedience to the landlord, and even a chance to save money towards land purchase. However, because of the build-up of population pressure through further in-migration the recent migrant not only starts from a lower level in the land tenure hierarchy than did the migrant of the 1950s, but the future opportunities for upward movement through that hierarchy are likely to be fewer. It is not until after a reasonably secure place in that hierarchy has been found that the migrant cultivator can consider the adoption of improved agricultural practices and start to produce for the commercial market as well as for his own subsistence.

It could be argued that the uniqueness of events in the study area effectively precludes its comparison with other areas influenced by agrarian reform. Furthermore, it could be pointed out that pre- and post-reform land tenure patterns in south and south-eastern parts of lowland Bolivia differ significantly from those of the highland Andean zones. However, the conclusions from the Monteagudo study, especially those concerning the power of landlords, echo those from other areas of Bolivia (Graeff, 1974), while the methods used by landlords to maintain their control over access to land, and the phenomenon of increasing socio-economic differentiation among peasants resulting from increased population pressure are also similar in rural Egypt (Abdel-Fadil, 1975). The general problems with which this chapter has been concerned are by no means unfamiliar to the social scientist.

This particular case study has attempted to illustrate how a migration stream into an area where the availability of land was fixed, or at least strictly controlled, produced modifications in agriculture and land tenure systems and, at the same time, created conditions favourable to the reappearance of mechanisms for the exploitation of rural cultivators by landlords and landowners. The relationships examined between migration, land tenure systems and the economic (under) development of traditional agriculture have indicated how some pre-reform land tenure patterns and social relations between landlords, landowners and peasants have been modified yet maintained, largely through the creation of population pressure. Rural institutional structures of this type present serious obstacles to authentic economic development in agriculture for the benefit of the majority rather than of the few, and also present obstacles to the development of a commercial agriculture of sufficient scale to act as a stimulus to general economic development.

In-migration has benefited landlords and landowners by increasing the demands made on the cultivable land of which they controlled the supply. As in-migration has continued they have been permitted to exchange access to land for ever more precarious and onerous conditions of tenure and more demanding labour services. These conditions do not allow recent migrants to engage in anything other than agricultural production for their own subsistence. Future influxes of migrants will reduce even further any opportunities for socio-economic progress as only more marginal land will be available for cultivation. Only those longer-resident migrants with more secure tenures of cultivated plots large enough and of such quality as to produce above subsistence levels of production can be expected to improve their agriculture in such conditions.

Migration, land tenure and agricultural development in this study area were intimately related. The relationships showed that when migration increased the population pressure on cultivable land access to land became unequal for the small cultivators, with systems of dependency developing between owners of land and non-owners and between longer residents and recent migrants. In such circumstances the development of the 'modern' agricultural sector, which had been one of the official aims in encouraging migration to Monteagudo, became extremely difficult. The problems have been brought about by both in-migration and the landlord system, although further in-migration has exacerbated and worsened the situation. A reduction of in-migration would help by stopping the creation of further agricultural marginality and peasant exploitation, but such a measure could only be a palliative. Only a more equal pattern of access to land and the removal of the landlord interest can now rectify the problems created by past in-migration and offer any real likelihood of progress in agriculture and of benefit for the small producers.

Notes

1. 'These are presumably remnants of the Chiriguano, a tribe who have occupied parts of south-eastern Bolivia since late in the fifteenth century, and who are culturally, linguistically, and historically related to the Guaraní' (Heath, 1959, p. 77).
2. A *peón* was an agricultural labourer on the pre-reform estates. They often had no access to land for cultivation themselves and although 'paid' for their labour on a daily basis they rarely saw any actual cash: instead the landlord provided them with rations and clothing.
3. An *arrimante* is literally the tenant of a tenant. In the study area such a person might be a recent in-migrant who works, for himself, land belonging to a tenant or a former tenant of an estate in return for a few days of labour on the landlord–tenant's plot. An *arrendatario* is an individual who has established himself on cultivated land belonging to a landlord or other landowner in exchange for some small services (see Acción Cultural Loyola, 1974, p. 99). Land held *en cuidado* is being looked after while the owner himself is absent, while land which is *alquilado* is literally 'hired' by the incumbent for cultivation for one or two years from a landowner, after which time the land must be vacated or a new contract agreed. Under an *anticrético* tenure agreement the peasant gives an agreed sum of money to the landlord at the start of the tenure period in exchange for land: the money is returned to the peasant at the end of the lease period.
4. The *yanapacu* system was one by which each estate tenant was given a certain quantity of seed to plant, tend and harvest for the benefit of the landlord. 'The amount of time required for *yanapacu* service was consistently estimated at between 80 and 85 days [per year] nearly everywhere it had been employed' (Erasmus, 1969, p. 96).
5. Hogs are male swine of a breed resembling the wild boar. They are bred for slaughter as meat.

Chapter 8

Labour migration and suburban expansion in the north of England: Sheffield in the 1860s and 1870s

P . Cromar

In the conditions of the nineteenth century in Britain the rate of growth of urban areas can be broadly correlated with the development of industrial capitalism. However, it would be wrong to see this development solely in terms of a large employer and a factory type of organization, for as late as 1870 the immediate employer was often not a large capitalist but rather an intermediate sub-contractor who was both an employee and a small employer (Dobb, 1946; Samuel, 1977). Indeed for most of the working class in this period, and certainly until 1890, the money bond between the worker and the capitalist was obscured (Lane, 1974; Saville, 1957). The special significance of the Industrial Revolution lies in the transformation not just of the structure of industry, but also of the social relations of production, both occurring as a result of technical change at a certain crucial level. It was not enough for the commodity of labour power merely to exist, it had also to be available in adequate quantities in the places where it was most needed. Since capitalist development is uneven in both time and space this meant that the mobility of the labouring population was essential to the continuing development of industrial capitalism. Further, the development of capitalism necessarily entails a concentration and centralization of capital in the geographical as well as the economic sphere and this means a concentration and centralization of economic life in large industrial units and in large urban agglomerations, resulting in an increased demand for labour in urban areas. It is part of the aim of this chapter to investigate the relationships between the patterns and processes of labour migration, the satisfaction of the demand for labour in urban areas, and the continued development of industrial capitalism.

Traditional work on labour migration

The seminal work on nineteenth-century migration was done by Ravenstein (1876; 1885; 1889), and Grigg (1977) provides an exhaustive review not only of this original work but also of the studies done since on internal migration in nineteenth-century England and Wales. Most of this body of work deals with the actual patterns and processes of labour migration without relating these patterns and processes to the wider questions of economic development, although there are exceptions and it is to these that attention will initially be given before outlining a possible alternative theoretical framework for the analysis of labour migration in the nineteenth century.

Cairncross (1953) notes a steady drift from the countryside to the town from the 1840s to the 1870s with no new courses of migration being followed until the 1880s. He also notes that the centres of outflow were in close juxtaposition to the centres of attraction and that the towns, which were swelling with the growth of the railway system and of urban industry, drew on the natural increase of their rural hinterland. At the same time, he says, centres of attraction in America and the colonies competed for migrants, such that local urban expansion and colonization tended to alternate with one another in successive decades because this competition was intermittent. Furthermore, he suggests that fluctuations in rural outflow had little to do with agricultural prosperity or depression, but that the main cause of rural depopulation was the building of railways and the consequent revolution in transport (p. 75). This is in marked contrast with Saville (1957) who says that the increase in the mobility of labour brought about by the railway was an accelerating rather than an initiating factor. Cairncross (1953, p. 75) goes on to develop his explanation of the importance of railway building by its provision of employment and the stimulation of employment, putting towns in need of more metal workers and engineers, although there seems no reason why this employment should have been filled by rural migrants. He does suggest that railway building 'increased mobility, both by taking men longer distances to assist in the work of construction, and by making journeys to the town easier and cheaper . . . displaced rural labour found a cure for unemployment by moving to the towns and to America' (p. 75). Finally, he notes that there was a preponderance of short-distance migration, although there may also have been a 'large centripetal movement from the rural periphery to the urban core in earlier years' (p. 79), but this is masked by the use of the printed returns of the census which only publish data on the place of birth by counties and so fail to distinguish intra-county migration.

Cairncross, however, fails to consider some crucial questions. Why were the patterns of migration fixed from 1840 to 1870 (if indeed they were)? What happened to cause the change to 'unfamiliar courses'? Why is industry urban in capitalism? Why were the areas of depression in close juxtaposition to the areas of growth? Why was the competition from America and the colonies intermittent? Why should rural outflow have had anything to do with agricultural prosperity or depression since the peasantry had ceased to exist to a large extent anyway, and impoverished agricultural labour was being displaced in a secular manner as capital penetrated more and more into agriculture? Might it be that improved transport is an immediate, superficial cause of rural depopulation for which there are deeper structural reasons?

Brinley Thomas (1972) develops Cairncross's arguments about the competition for migrants from America and the colonies by the explicit consideration of international capital flows and internal migration. Thomas suggests that when capital is exported to America this brings about a fall in construction at home which then encourages the rural proletariat to emigrate to the United States of America instead of migrating internally to urban areas. His whole explanation is a rather mechanistic one, being related to long swings in the economy which he defines as fluctuations in the rate at which the whole network of urban infrastructure is developed. This argument is valuable in that it focuses attention on capital flows and the international nature of industrial capitalism, but it is lacking in explanation of why these changes in capital flows occur. What causes changes in the development of the capital and consumer goods sectors and how does this development affect the rate and direction of migration?

Saville (1957) adopts a much more integrated approach whereby, with various qualifications, the growth of towns in nineteenth-century England and Wales is seen as an index to the development of the 'industrial state' and the social relationships which accompanied the new industrial order. He notes three major factors in the growth of towns: (1) a high rate of natural increase of the urban population; (2) continuous inflow from rural areas; (3) immigration from outside, notably Scotland, Ireland and occasionally the outside world. The main physical characteristics of internal migration are seen as a constant movement of population from the countryside to urban areas, and a movement of population that is mostly short-distance in character. However, Saville's work, though valuable, is mainly on a county level, and this makes much more difficult the analysis of spatial and temporal differences in urban growth rates, and certainly does not allow any analysis of urban-to-urban migration which may have been of increasing importance in the late nineteenth century. In fact a large amount of work has been done showing the predominance of short-distance migration, nearly all relying on published tables of the census (Grigg, 1977, p. 44, note 2) although some have used census enumerators' books (Anderson, M., 1971; Pooley, 1977; Dennis, 1977) or rate books (Holmes, 1973), but there has been little attempt to relate the specific patterns of urban growth to a more general framework of economic development in the nineteenth century. Furthermore, very little is known as yet about the nature of early suburban migration, whether in terms of the patterns and processes of that migration which Grigg (1977, pp. 51, 53) suggests is a major field of research, or in the broader terms of its role in the development of industrial capitalism. However, before going on to consider a particular case study of suburban growth it is necessary to outline a theoretical understanding of the relationships between labour migration and the development of industrial capitalism.

A theoretical framework

In the nineteenth century the mainspring of capitalist development seems to have been not only the uneven development of industry and agriculture, but also the uneven and combined development of different regions within the important capitalist countries. The resultant release of money capital via the progressive penetration of agriculture by capitalist commodity circulation, and of producers separated from the land and the soil, led to the continuous drain of money capital to the major industrial districts, where evicted ex-peasants now formed an industrial reserve army. In the first century after the Industrial Revolution the productivity of labour in the consumer goods sector was generally higher than in the capital goods sector. The genesis of industrial capitalism must be described as the machine-industrial production of consumer goods by means of hand-made machines. The result of this was that the whole inner dynamic of industrial capitalism in this epoch was concentrated on accelerating capital accumulation in the consumer goods sector at the expense of accumulation in the capital goods sector. In other words, it was those areas favourable for consumer goods production, especially textiles, which exhibited the highest growth rates in this epoch – for example the cotton towns of Lancashire and the woollen towns of the West Riding of Yorkshire.

The turning point in this pattern of urban growth occurred about 1847 as a result of two concurrent and combined changes in the operation of industrial capitalism. Firstly, the capital goods sector went over from man-made production of stream-driven motors to the machine production of steam-driven motors. The consequent transformation of the entire production process in this sector caused a massive increase in the productivity of labour in the particular part of the capital goods sector which produced fixed capital (machines). At the same time a transformation occurred in the technology of the part producing circulating capital, especially raw materials, primarily through improvements in transport technology. Together these processes determined a massive increase in the productivity of labour in the capital goods sector while the change in production technology in the consumer goods sector was limited to the replacement of man-made steam-driven motors by machine-made steam-driven motors, and this could hardly lead to a fundamental change in the productivity of labour in that sector. Secondly, the progressive introduction of machine-made steam-driven machines from 1847 to 1873, combined with the growing generalization of railway construction in this period (the period of 'railway mania'), absorbed colossal amounts of capital (Hobsbawm, 1969). This large transfer of capital began to consolidate the predominance of the capital goods sector over the consumer goods sector, and the productivity of labour in the former gradually approached that of the latter and then rapidly overtook it. The result was a dramatic change in the direction of flow of capital investment away from the consumer goods sector and into the capital goods sector. The new boom industries were now those producing capital goods: iron and steel, heavy engineering and railways. Moreover the specific nature of the fixed capital produced in the capital goods sector meant that it was produced mainly on order and not for sale on an anonymous market. Production sites were accordingly adjusted to cater for maximum orders, with the obvious problems of over-capacity in the future.

At the same time as this massive change in the direction of flow of capital investment was making itself felt at the inter-urban scale, with attendant changes in the patterns of labour migration, there were also massive changes at the intra-urban scale. The economic developments of the second half of the nineteenth century, especially those of commerce and the railways, brought about dramatic changes in land use within cities, and most especially city centres. Residential areas were cleared for the extension of railway lines, the building of stations and goods yards (Kellett, 1969), the erection of huge warehouses, and for the provision of commercial offices. The consequence of these developments was a vast increase in land values in the centre. Compared to the commercial rent derived from business premises the profits to be obtained from house property, except in extreme cases of rack-renting, were insignificant, and so a marked transformation in the land-use patterns of cities took place. This transformation of the commercial centre did not result from the harmonious adjustment of the forces of supply and demand, but was much more conditioned by the uneven development of space in industrial capitalism whereby employment opportunities become more and more spatially concentrated while those seeking to live near these opportunities also increase in numbers. The result was that the old centres of cities began to lose population by migration, while the suburbs started to grow massively. What we need to know about is the nature of this early suburban migration. Did the populations of the early suburbs migrate from the old city centres or did they migrate directly into the suburbs from outside the city? Was this vast migration from the central districts a result of workers moving out in pursuit of better economic opportunities or was it the result of demolition and the forcible eviction of a labour force whose workplace remained located in the centre? Even to begin to answer these and other questions it is necessary to look more closely at actual suburban growth, within the framework of the development of industrial capitalism. Migration should perhaps be studied not only in relation to the structure of the dominant industry, or 'leading sector', but also with regard to the social relations of that particular industry.

In this respect Sheffield provides a valuable area for case study since the iron and steel industry, on which its growth was based, was composed of two completely different sectors – the light trades comprising mainly the cutlery and hand-tool-making industries, and the heavy trades manufacturing industrial steel, heavy engineering and armaments (Pollard, 1959). The former was very much petty commodity production, although on a decreasing scale and with increasing dependence on large-scale enterprise; the social relations surrounding this production were very different from those around the large capitalist

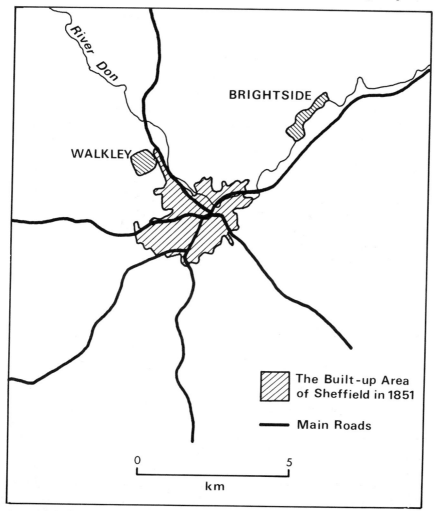

Fig. 8.1   The location of Brightside and Walkley, Yorkshire.

enterprises in the latter sector. The light trades of Sheffield were strongly artisan-unionized and these unions were very sectional with small local memberships. There was little conflict with the bourgeoisie since there was little barrier to upward (or downward) social movement, and little distinction between employee and employer as the artisans had not yet lost their ownership of the means of production. The light trades remained a complex of specialized workshop and outwork production where the indispensable craftsman or specialized operative not only was more important, but saw himself to be more important (Hobsbawm, 1964; Thompson, 1968). The labour supply was frequently restricted by the unions, sometimes by industrial sabotage (Pollard, 1959), often as a defensive mechanism against the introduction of the machine and the factory system with the depression of a special form of sub-contracting outworker as a result of the inevitable dilution of skill. In the light trades low wages and long hours seemed to be related to economic or organizational weakness on the part of the workers and the unions held that their existence might make a difference of up to 50 per cent to wage rates. It is around these particular forms of industrial structure and social relations of production that Walkley grew up as a working-class suburb after 1860.

By contrast Brightside, another working-class suburb of the same period, was very dependent on the heavy sector which had expanded massively after 1860 with the greatest boom of the century in the heavy sector occurring between 1870 and 1873. Here technological change, the migration of capital and the irregularity of armaments contracts encouraged the iron and steel firms to employ a contractor system. The sole task of the contractor was to supply labour while the firms supplied the money for materials and machinery. Pollard (1959) suggests that most of this labour force was immigrant, attracted by high wages or quick advancement despite the conditions of short-time working and the temporary lack of housing.

With this outline in mind it is now possible to investigate more closely the patterns and processes of labour migration to the two Sheffield suburbs of Brightside and Walkley in the 1860s and 1870s, the decades of most rapid population growth in Sheffield. Figure 8.1 shows the location of the two suburbs in relation to the city centre of Sheffield.

Data sources

The major sources for gross figures of migration are 'The birthplaces of the people' in the *General Reports of the Censuses*, 1851–1901, which give the county of birth; the *Annual Reports of the Registrar General*, 1837–1901; and the *Decennial Supplements* to these. Much of the work on migration has used these publications, the use of which is explained by Baines (1972). However, there are well-known limitations to the usefulness of such material; they give no indication of the actual timing of migration; they do not show whether the movement from birthplace to place of enumeration was direct or indirect (the 'step by step' hypothesis of Ravenstein); the available statistics only allow analysis at the county level and this is clearly inadequate for an investigation into the patterns and processes of suburban growth. What alternative sources are available to enable more detailed research to be undertaken?

The census enumerators' books are the most important source of detailed information, although other sources have been suggested and used, not only as checks on the accuracy of the information in the enumerators' books but also as sources in themselves. Poll books are of limited value as a check on the validity of census returns because they may well exclude large numbers of the working class who were not qualified to vote. It is possible to use parish registers (Küchemann *et al.*, 1967; Constant, 1948; Perry, 1969), but it is extremely laborious and hardly worth while to undertake for its own sake. Trade directories, which are available for most large towns after the middle of the nineteenth century, may be used to check the accuracy of the occupation listed in the census schedules, but there is a tendency for directories only to upgrade the census and this may well reflect the advertising nature of the directory. Also the entries in the directory are mainly concerned with the commercial structure of the town and so will give details of the more prosperous artisans, the traders and the professional and middle classes rather than the bulk of the working class. Rate books have been suggested (Holmes, 1973) as a source for the study not only of the structure of house-property ownership, but also of inter-censal migration since the use of census material alone may grossly underestimate the total amount of migration. This point is well taken, but within the context of this study it was decided to rely mainly on the census enumerators' books, although a random sample was taken from the 1871 rate book for each suburb in an attempt to gain some insight into the nature of house-property ownership in the two suburbs.

For the purposes of the census the country was divided into registration districts based on the Poor Law unions (set up under the 1834 Amendment to the Poor Law) and the sub-districts derived from them. The registrars and their staffs selected enumeration districts of a suitable size within these registration districts and also chose enumerators to visit them. The lists of these were submitted to the Census Office for approval. In the week preceding the census night each enumerator delivered blank forms, known as schedules, to every householder in their district. They collected these forms the morning after census night and after checking them and filling in those with no information by making inquiries on the spot, they took them home where they transcribed them into books of forms which were very similar in design to the householders' schedules. It is these books which have been preserved and are made available for public inspection, subject to the 100 years rule of confidentiality.[1]

The census enumerators' books contain information under the headings of schedule number, street, personal name, relation to head of household, marital condition, age (male or female), occupation and birthplace. Tillott (1972) gives a very detailed account of the various sources of inaccuracy in these enumerators' books and M. Anderson (1972a) proposes a set of rules for using them. It is pointed out that the fundamental unit for analysis should be the household rather than the house and that addresses cannot be used consistently to identify houses, this only being possible where addresses are precisely given and contemporary maps, street plans and directories are available – such reconstruction seems hardly worth recommending. Birthplace data, Tillott suggests, are subject to clerical error rather than anything more serious, but there are major problems occurring with the use of data relating to occupation. First of all there is the problem of unemployment, rarely mentioned in the returns, so that occupation does not necessarily reflect economic status. Secondly, the distinction between master and man is often unclear and is made more difficult by the question referring to occupation being posed in terms of the guild system.

Thirdly, the indication of place of work or name of industry or employer occurs only by chance and so is difficult to use in a systematic manner. Fourthly, although many employers of labour record the numbers they employed, in accordance with the instructions, many did not. Finally, many occupations are unspecified.

Despite the multiplicity of these problems there has been a lot of work done on processing the information available in the enumerators' books to produce social groups. The most common method is to refer occupations to the 1951 General Register Office's classification of occupations and to note to which of the five social classes each has been allocated. The chief proponent of this scheme has been Armstrong (1966; 1968), but his original proposals met with a certain amount of criticism, notably from Floud and Schofield (1968) and Harris (1968), the latter on the grounds that the original 1951 scheme was 'a lousy classification for any sociological purpose' and that class III was so large and cumbersome as to be meaningless. Armstrong (1972) demonstrated the superiority of the 1951 classification over other Register Office classifications, especially those of 1911 and 1931, and gave a clear guide as to how the 1951 scheme should be used in empirical enquiries and listed a number of modifications to allow of greater use when dealing with nineteenth-century problems. He also made a strong plea for everyone else to use this classification, if not exclusively then alongside any alternative that they might propose or devise for their own particular purposes. Royle (1977) suggests further modifications to Armstrong's scheme thereby making the 1951 classification more suitable for nineteenth-century studies. In the following analysis Armstrong's scheme has been modified not only to take account of the particular circumstances of the Sheffield trades, but also to follow Foster's (1974, p. 292) classification in terms of craft/skilled *vis-à-vis* semi-skilled/labourer with union strength on the prevention of entry to any particular trade being viewed as of great importance in terms of the social relations involved in each industry.

Data collection

In nearly every migration study using material derived from the census enumerators' books it has been found necessary to use some sort of sampling framework. This has been done not only to save time, but also to allow a more detailed enquiry to be undertaken, although this latter is feasible only if it is possible to discover what is needed by looking only at a part of the evidence. Where interest is focused on the typical rather than the bizarre, use of a sampling framework will provide an acceptable summary of the evidence with only a fraction of the time and effort, if the exercise is carried out properly (Schofield, 1972). Laserwitz (1971) suggests that a sample: (1) must give a precise picture of the population from which it is drawn; (2) must be obtained by a probability process so that statistical techniques can be used to describe and analyse the sample data and relate them to the population from which they came; (3) should be as small as conditions of precision permit, as economical as possible and gathered as quickly as its various measurement techniques permit. It should also be borne in mind that the sampling framework should not only yield estimates of population means, percentages and totals, but must also obtain measurements for sub-classes of a population, for instance those engaged in the heavy trades in Brightside, or the light trades in Walkley.

Having decided to use a sampling framework the next problems are of which is the most appropriate framework to use, closely followed by the size of the sample required to give precise results. The most basic sampling procedure is that of simple random sampling, which requires a clear definition of a population to be sampled, a complete listing of all its elements, and the assumption that all such elements are statistically independent of each other. These basic requirements seriously restrict the opportunities for the practical use of simple random sampling, but nevertheless a knowledge of simple random sampling is necessary for an understanding of other types of sampling framework (Schofield, 1972). In practice the most widely used sampling framework, at least for initial investigations, seems to be systematic sampling. A systematic sample is drawn by taking every kth item in sequence in the population. For example, a sample of households can be drawn from the census enumerators' books by taking every seventh household (k = 7). The sampling interval, k, can be any size, depending on the number of items required in the sample size. When working with microfilm, which cannot be numbered, it is often more convenient to draw a systematic sample than a random one, simply by counting through the population as the sample is drawn. Nevertheless there is a price to be paid for this easier framework and this appears in the form of a major danger which must be guarded against: periodicity, where if there is any rhythm in the way the population has been listed, then there is a danger that the sample interval may be to some extent in phase with it, thereby systematically (or periodically) distorting the representativeness of the sample. In most practical situations it is by no means clear whether periodicities are present or not, or, if present, how marked and regular they are. Periodicity in systematic samples remains a source of possible bias which is difficult to evaluate, but in practice it is ignored and the precision of the systematic sample is estimated as if the sample had been drawn randomly.

It is important to consider the precision that will be required of the sample estimates before any sampling is undertaken. This is a necessary step, for on the one hand there is no point in drawing a larger sample than is necessary to attain an estimate of the required precision, while on the other hand it is advisable to ensure before drawing a sample that the largest practicable sample will in fact yield estimates that are precise enough to be useful. Schofield (1972) suggests that in most cases it is not difficult to decide upon the degree of precision appropriate to the context and says that if the field of enquiry is a new one a fairly rough estimate may suffice. He then outlines (pp. 161–5) a series of formulae designed to give estimates of required sample sizes, but it is important to remember that these only refer to simple random sampling frameworks and are not particularly appropriate in connection with a systematic sample. In this latter case published studies have commonly used a fixed percentage systematic sample of the census enumerators' books (Shaw, 1977; Pooley, 1977; Royle, 1977) and this is the procedure followed here. In order to allow some sort of statistical analysis of the derived data it was thought desirable to use a larger sample framework for Brightside in 1861 than for the other areas since it had a markedly smaller population. A systematic sample of households, with a random start, was drawn from the appropriate enumerators' books, with a 33⅓ per cent sample for Brightside 1861, and 20 per cent samples for Walkley 1861, Brightside 1871 and Walkley 1871. This yielded information on 112 households, 148 households, 165 households and 314 households respectively, raw data being collected on 739 large file cards. Fairly obviously this mass of data needs to be structured and organized in some way so as to facilitate analysis.

Data structuring

In recent years there has been a more concerted attack on the material available in the census enumerators' books aided by improved techniques of data manipulation, whether by computerization, mechanical data-processing machinery or by the use of much labour, the latter being especially appropriate to those researchers in extra-mural departments who can use their students as a source of labour-power. For most researchers, though, it is computerization which will allow the enumerators' books to be used more fully. Unfortunately, much of the published work on computerizing the census (Dyos and Baker, 1968; Anderson, M., 1972a) has used the data from the census in an uncoded form so that names, occupations and birthplaces appear in alphabetical form and this is not only very wasteful of computer storage space and compilation time, but also makes any succeeding analysis very difficult. To overcome these problems a rather different form of data and file structure was devised using a system of direct-access files.

There were four main objectives in the creation of this new system: (1) to preserve the accuracy of the data; (2) to preserve the inter-relationships within the data; (3) to minimize storage requirements; (4) to minimize computer search time. A series of direct-access files was used to achieve these objectives, each file containing pointers to other files storing related data. The general structure is shown in Fig. 8.2.

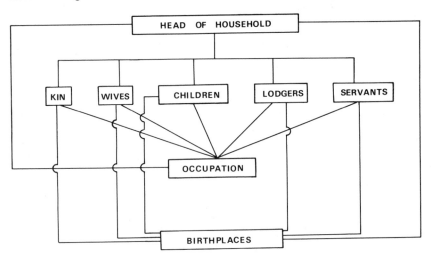

Fig. 8.2   General file structure.

The master file is that of the 'head of household' and it contains not only information on the head and the household, but also various pointers which provide linkages to the other files. The data stored in this file are arranged as follows:

columns 1–16   NAME, a two-element array in alphabetic
columns 17–32   ADDRESS, a two-element array in alphabetic

column 34	Area, a number 1, 2, 3, 4 referring to Brightside 1861, Walkley 1861, Brightside 1871, Walkley 1871 respectively. This allows the use of a 'do loop' in any program, so enabling all four areas to be analysed at the same running of the program.
columns 36–7	AGE, a two-figure number
columns 39–41	OCCUPATIONS, a three-figure number referring to the OCCUPATION file.
columns 43–4	BIRTHPLACES, a two-figure number referring to the BIRTHPLACE file.
column 46	MARITAL STATUS, a number 0, 1, 2 or 3. 0 where the column is empty in the enumerator's book, 1 = married, 2 = widower, 3 = unmarried. If the value is 1 this allows access to the WIVES file.
column 48	RURAL/URBAN ORIGIN, a number 1 or 2 referring to rural or urban origin respectively. Urban origins were derived from Cairncross (1953, p. 67) with slight additions.
columns 51–2	FAMILY SIZE, a two-figure number.
columns 54–5	HOUSEHOLD SIZE, a two-figure number.
column 57	STAGE IN LIFE-CYCLE, a number 0, 1, 2, 3, 4, 5 or 6. 0 applies where the question is inappropriate; 1 to 6 according to the classification in M. Anderson (1972b, p. 60), but modified to allow for one-parent families.
column 59	LODGERS, a single-figure number which acts as a pointer to the LODGERS file.
column 61	KIN, a single-figure number which acts as a pointer to the KIN file.
column 63	SERVANTS, a single-figure number which acts as a pointer to the SERVANTS file.
columns 65–8	FOOD WEIGHTING, a measure to relate a family's size, age and sex composition to its food requirements. By marrying household data from the census to information on wages, prices and employment it should be possible to obtain some insight into the incidence of poverty, (Bowley and Burnett-Hurst, 1915; Foster, 1974). The weights are derived direct from Bowley and Burnett-Hurst.
column 70	DID FAMILY MOVE FROM OUTSIDE SHEFFIELD? a number 1 or 2 representing the answer 'yes' and 'no' respectively. Family mobility is obviously a thorny problem and this column represents an attempt to recognize the problem within the limitations imposed by the data. An answer of 'yes' is coded if the household still has children at home, some or all of whom were not born in either the respective area or Sheffield itself. By looking at the ages and birthplaces of the children of these mobile families it is possible to gain some insight into spatial and temporal migration patterns. The proportion of mobile families in the sample is almost certain to be an underestimate since the census does not provide information on family members who were not resident in the household on census night. The number 0 is used when there are no children in that household.
columns 73–4	CHILDREN, a two-figure number which acts as a pointer to the CHILDREN file.

In all cases on this master file the pointers to other files are set to zero (apart from the WIVES file) for any of the attributes which are not present for a particular head of household. Where the pointer is not zero then that refers to the number of lodgers, kin, servants or children in that particular household.

The WIVES, LODGERS, KIN, SERVANTS and CHILDREN files are all structured in a similar manner to that part of the master file referring to the head of household himself, and their internal ordering corresponds exactly to their appearance in the master file. All files record the information available in the enumerators' schedules in the sequence name, age, occupation (coded), birthplace (coded), rural/urban origin, while the KIN file also records the relationship to the head of the household, again coded, but not referring to another file. It is necessary to take care when dealing with the encoding of kin, for in the enumerators' books the terms daughter-in-law and son-in-law often refer to step-daughter and step-son.

The OCCUPATIONS and BIRTHPLACES files were set up because traditional list-processing methods require the excessive duplication of large amounts of text while alphabetical sorting is extremely wasteful of computer time. By using a direct-access data structure each occupation and birthplace is stored only once, so allowing the efficient retention of a large number of definitions while sorting is much easier since it is done numerically.

In this particular study the initial OCCUPATIONS file was set up using a possible 1,000 records (although this number was extendable) with each record referring to a specific occupation, defined by a maximum of 32 letters and spaces. For example record number 001 had the occupation of file cutter, record number 300 had the occupation of coal miner. A further structural element of the file arrangement was that distinct blocks of numbers referred to particular sub-groups of occupations defined partly on an industrial basis and partly with reference to the other criteria mentioned previously. So numbers 001 to 099 referred to occupations in the light trades; 100 to 199 referred to skilled occupations in the heavy trades; 200 to 299 were occupations requiring a definite degree of skill and for which there was some degree of control over the entry to that trade or craft, especially those in the building, engineering and metal trades; 300 to 399 were occupations which required a modicum of skill but which had no control over entry to the trade – miners, potmakers, brickmakers for example; 400 to 499 general labourers, carters, building and metal labourers; 500 to 599 tradesmen and shopkeepers; 600 farmers; 601 to 699 small manufacturers, employing less than 25 people; 700 to 799 clerical workers; 800 to 899 large manufacturers employing more than 25 people, professional people, officers in the armed services; 900 to 999 predominantly female occupations. Further sub-divisions were distinguished within each particular group, especially in the light trades where, for instance, the file trades occupied records 001 to 008, the saw trades 013 to 017, the table knife trades 051 to 057.

The initial BIRTHPLACES file was set up using 51 records (again extendable), each record referring to a particular birthplace defined by a maximum of 32 letters and spaces. The definitions were organized in such a way as to facilitate analysis of the problems of suburban migration discussed earlier. So 01 referred to Walkley, 02 Brightside, 03 Sheffield itself, 04 within 8 kilometres of Sheffield. The other records referred to the county or country of origin of the enumerated individual. Data about rural or urban origin had already been included in the various individual files (HEAD OF HOUSEHOLD, WIVES, CHILDREN, SERVANTS, KIN and LODGERS) while data referring to familial mobility had been included in the HEAD OF HOUSEHOLD file. By using data from this last category, in association with data from the CHILDREN file, it is possible to discover a little more about the temporal patterns of migration into Brightside and Walkley.

Data analysis

The initial task in this study of suburban migration is to discover the spatial distribution of the birthplaces of the enumerated population and to see if there are any significant differences in the migration fields of the two suburbs in question. For this purpose the HEAD OF HOUSEHOLD, WIVES, LODGERS, SERVANTS and KIN files were numerically sorted into the various categories defined in the BIRTHPLACES file. The CHILDREN file was not used since it was felt that children would have little choice with regard to whether they migrated or not, although their presence or absence, and age, may well have affected the decision of the family to migrate. Figure 8.3 and Table 8.1 show the spatial distribution of the birthplaces of the sample of the inhabitants of Brightside and Walkley for both 1861 and 1871.

Table 8.1 Birthplaces, Brightside and Walkley inhabitants, 1861 and 1871

	Brightside		Walkley	
	1861	1871	1861	1871
Sample total	283	430	352	782
Percentage from:				
Sheffield	17.0	16.0	52.8	57.2
Within 8 km. of Sheffield	25.4	9.1	15.3	12.1
Rest of England and Wales	55.8	67.9	30.4	27.6
Ireland	1.4	5.8	1.1	1.5
Other	0.4	1.2	0.3	1.5

Data source: Census enumerators' books.

Immediately apparent is the overwhelming dominance of Sheffield-born inhabitants in Walkley for both 1861 and 1871, while in Brightside the majority of inhabitants had been born more than 8 kilometres from Sheffield for both 1861 and 1871. In all four cases there seems to be some sort of distance decay effect with neighbouring counties providing more migrants than those further away. It is necessary, however, to discover whether the differences between Walkley and Brightside are significant or whether they could be attributable to sampling errors. Further, it would be useful to know if there are any significant changes in these distributions between 1861 and 1871, and whether there are any significant differences, either spatial or temporal, between the migration fields of men and women. One way of answering these questions is to use a combination of contingency tables and a statistic – chi-square.

Table 8.2 shows the migration data set out in a two-way array where the 713 individuals from the samples of the census enumerators' books for Brightside in 1861 and 1871 are classified for both birthplace and year of enumeration. Direct

Table 8.2 Birthplaces, Brightside inhabitants, 1861 and 1871

Year of enumeration	Birthplaces of inhabitants			Totals
	Sheffield	Within 8 km of Sheffield	Other	
Brightside 1861	48	72	163	283
	(46.44)	(44.06)	(192.50)	
Brightside 1871	69	39	322	430
	(70.56)	(66.94)	(292.50)	
Totals	117	111	485	713

Note: Main entries are observations: chi-square expectations in parentheses.
Data source: Samples of census enumerators' books.

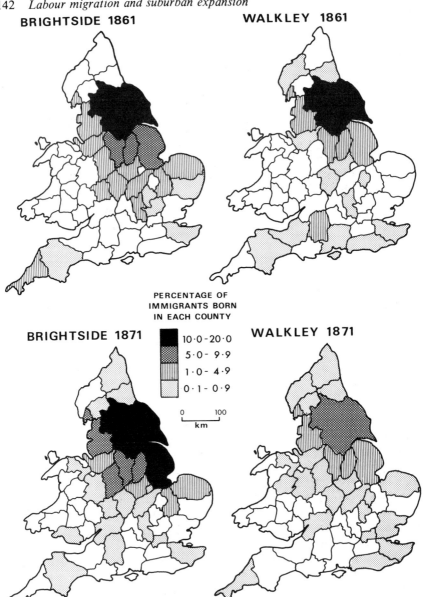

BRIGHTSIDE 1861

WALKLEY 1861

PERCENTAGE OF
IMMIGRANTS BORN
IN EACH COUNTY

BRIGHTSIDE 1871

10·0 - 20·0
5·0 - 9·9
1·0 - 4·9
0·1 - 0·9

0   100
k m

WALKLEY 1871

Fig. 8.3 Birthplaces of enumerated persons (excluding children) in Brightside and Walkley, 1861 and 1871.
Data source: Samples of census enumerators' books, 1861 and 1871.

comparison of the observed and expected numbers gives an immediate clue to possible sources of difference in the two distributions. So in Table 8.2 there is a large discrepancy between the numbers of inhabitants born within 8 kilometres of Sheffield and those born elsewhere in 1861 and 1871. Use of a chi-square statistic gives a value of 36.96 with 2 degrees of freedom, indicating that there is only one chance in a thousand that the difference in the distribution of the birthplaces of the sampled inhabitants of Brightside in 1861 and 1871 is not a real difference. In other words, there is a significant difference in the migration fields of Brightside, 1861 and Brightside, 1871. Similar tests show that Brightside and Walkley had significantly different migration fields for both 1861 and 1871 (both significant at the 0.001 level) while there is no significant difference between the migration fields of Walkley, 1861 and Walkley, 1871. In view of the suggestions in the literature that there may be a difference in the migration characteristics of men and women the data were further sub-divided into sets containing heads of households only and sets containing wives only. It was found that again there were significant differences between the migration fields of Brightside heads for 1861 and 1871 (at the 0.05 level) and between the migration fields of Brightside wives for the same years (at the 0.001 level). There were no significant differences between Walkley, 1861, and Walkley, 1871, in respect of the migration fields of either the heads of households or their wives. In none of the four sample sets (Brightside, 1861; Brightside, 1871; Walkley, 1861; and Walkley, 1871) was there any significant difference between the migration fields of heads of households and their wives. At this level of investigation then, where the birthplaces of inhabitants are classified as Sheffield, within 8 kilometres of Sheffield, or other, there are no significant differences between the migration fields of men and their wives.

Similar differences between Brightside and Walkley were found for both 1861 and 1871 when the question of rural or urban origin of heads of households and their wives was considered. In all four cases Brightside migrants were found to be predominantly rural in origin, all differences being significant at the 0.001 level. Within the particular suburbs the only significant difference was between the origins of Walkley wives in 1861 and 1871. Table 8.3 shows that Walkley wives

Table 8.3 Rural/urban origins, Walkley wives, 1861 and 1871

Year of enumeration	Origin of wives		Totals
	Rural	Urban	
Walkley 1861	62	79	141
	(49.80)	(91.20)	
Walkley 1871	92	203	295
	(104.20)	(190.80)	
Totals	154	282	436

Note: Main entries are observations: chi-square expectations in parentheses.
Data source: Samples of census enumerators' books.

were even more dominantly urban in origin in 1871 than they were in 1861 (the value of chi-square is 6.83, significant at the 0.001 level). In terms of the degree of family mobility, as defined above, it was found that Brightside families tended to be more mobile than Walkley families for both 1861 (significant at the 0.05 level) and 1871 (significant at the 0.001 level). Within each particular suburb there was no statistically significant difference between the degree of family mobility in 1861 and 1871. It was also found for Brightside, 1861 (at the 0.01 level), Walkley, 1861 (at the 0.01 level) and Walkley, 1871 (at the 0.001 level) that if a family was mobile it was more likely to have a head of rural origin. There was no statistically significant difference between the origins of the heads of mobile families in Brightside, 1871. In order to investigate the reasons for these different migration patterns it is necessary to look more closely at the occupational structure of each area and also to look at the social relations surrounding production in the main industries in the two areas.

Figure 8.4 shows the basic occupational structure for each of the four areas while Table 8.4 gives a more complete breakdown of this data, with distinct groups shown in the case of skilled workers. Fairly obviously both suburbs were

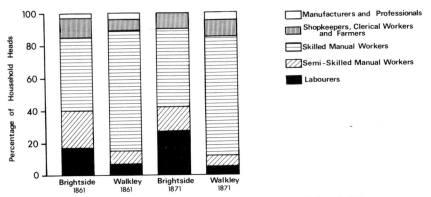

Fig. 8.4 Occupations of household heads, Brightside and Walkley, 1861 and 1871.
Data source: Samples of census enumerators' books, 1861 and 1871.

massively working class in composition, with Walkley's population being predominantly occupied in the light trades and Brightside's, although to a less dominant extent, in the heavy trades. An initial analysis, again by means of contingency tables and chi-square, with the sample classified according to craft, semi-skilled or labourer in the manner described above, and ignoring those in other categories, shows that there were significant differences between Brightside

Table 8.4 Occupational structures, Brightside and Walkley, 1861 and 1871

Occupational group	Number of household heads in each group			
	1861		1871	
	Brightside	Walkley	Brightside	Walkley
Light trades	7	83	6	184
Heavy iron	27	5	40	9
Building and engineering	16	18	32	35
Semi-skilled	25	11	24	23
Labourers	19	10	44	14
Shopkeepers	4	6	9	14
Farmers	5	–	3	–
Manufacturers	3	6	–	9
Clerical	5	5	6	19
Magnates	–	–	–	5
Totals	111	144	164	312

Data source: Samples of census enumerators' books.

and Walkley for both 1861 and 1871 (both significant at the 0.001 level) in terms of the possession of skill. Within each area there were no significant differences between the two census-year samples. Why might this be so? Perhaps it could be suggested that the more skilled a person was the more regular his employment was likely to be, especially in industries where employment fluctuated markedly, either seasonally as in the cutlery trade, or cyclically as in the heavy trades (notably those making armaments or railway lines and equipment). The skilled man would be more likely to be kept on when trade was slack, whereas semi-skilled or unskilled men would be much more vulnerable to the fluctuations of activity in any particular sector of industry. An initial hypothesis could then be formulated that the skilled working class were less mobile than the rest of the working class since the skilled had more regular and secure employment and would tend to stay where they were once they had a job, while the semi-skilled and labourers were more prone to irregularity of employment and so would tend to move frequently in search of work. This might explain why Walkley, whose inhabitants were more skilled than those of Brightside, had significantly fewer mobile families than Brightside. However, when the sub-group of mobile families was considered it was found that only in the sub-set for Walkley, 1871 were the semi-skilled and labourers more mobile than one would expect on probability grounds (chi-square significant at the 0.05 level). In all the other cases there was no significant difference between the heads of mobile families and others in terms of their possession of skill. Obviously the relationship between mobility and skill is a complex one.

When the question of the inter-relationships between rural or urban origins and the possession of skill is considered some revealing insights emerge. For Brightside, 1861, there were no significant differences, but Table 8.5 shows that

Table 8.5 Rural/urban origins and possession of skill, Brightside, 1871

Rural or urban origin	Possession of skill			Totals
	Heavy iron skilled	Other skilled	Semi-skilled and labourer	
Rural	28 (27.17)	20 (26.47)	53 (47.37)	101
Urban	11 (11.83)	18 (11.53)	15 (20.63)	44
Totals	39	38	68	145

Note: Main entries are observations: chi-square expectations in parentheses.
Data source: Samples of census enumerators' books.

in Brightside, 1871 there were more semi-skilled and labourers of rural origin than expected and fewer in the 'other skilled' category, while the distribution of those skilled in the heavy trades was very much as expected. For Walkley, 1861, Table 8.6 shows that the origins of those engaged in skilled work in the light

Table 8.6 Rural/urban origins and possession of skill, Walkley, 1861

Rural or urban origin	Possession of skill			Totals
	Light trades skilled	Other skilled	Semi-skilled and labourer	
Rural	22 (32.68)	15 (9.06)	13 (8.27)	50
Urban	61 (50.32)	8 (13.94)	8 (12.73)	77
Totals	83	23	21	127

Note: Main entries are observations: chi-square expectations in parentheses.
Data source: Samples of census enumerators' books.

trades were significantly more urban than expected while those engaged in other skilled trades and the semi-skilled and labourers were more rural in origin than expected (significant at the 0.001 level). The same pattern emerges for Walkley, 1871, again significant at the 0.001 level. The Brightside, 1871, difference is significant at the 0.05 level. So skill in the light trades in Walkley was predominantly associated with inhabitants of an urban origin while in Brightside the semi-skilled and labourers were predominantly of a rural origin. Perhaps this was a result of a process whereby the initial requirements of the particular industry meant that labour was attracted from particular areas where the necessary skills were to be found. For instance, the expanding cutlery industry would originally have drawn its labour force from those areas where the population possessed the required skills, in this case either Sheffield and its environs or other large towns. However, once this initial labour force had been attracted the social structure of the suburb might now have been such as to reinforce these migration patterns and so further influence that social structure. It might well be that the original spatial distribution of particular skills meant that a growing industry would attract its labour from specific areas and the impact of this migration would result in a social structure which reinforced those same channels of migration. Is there any evidence for these inter-relationships between the social relations of an industry, the particular migration fields resulting from these and then the combination of both of these factors, operating through the social structure, in accentuating the influence of migration on a particular area?

In the cutlery industry of Sheffield the social relations surrounding production were not those of capitalist employer and wage labourer, but were in fact much more complicated and diffuse. Where men could be employers one day and employees the next, where access to the elements of fixed capital was controlled by a *rentier* group who hired out places in their grinding 'hulls' or forges by the week, the day or even the hour, to men working on their own account, it was a complicated division of labour which was the essence of industrial production. This division of labour, based upon possession of a particular skill, where, for example, four trades were required to make a file (forger, hardener, grinder and cutter), was at once both a source of strength and an element of weakness. Until about 1867, when they came into closer contact with the national trade union movement, the local organized societies continued to view their labour market in the narrowest of terms. They viewed their prime function as one of controlling the labour market. In order to maintain this control it was necessary to regulate entry into the trade, to maintain comprehensive friendly benefits, to oppose machinery and trade frauds, and to attempt to impose a closed shop upon employers. So long as the unions remained successful the operation of these policies would restrict recruitment to the industry to those from Sheffield and its environs, who, it can be assumed, would be associated with the unions anyway, or to those from urban origins where similar guild-type organizations would be in existence. Also the success of the unions rested largely on the social cohesion of their members, and again this cohesion was likely to be increased if migration could be restricted to workers who were already unionized. In fact, of the 22 persons in the sample of rural origin engaged in the light trades in Walkley in 1861 15 were born within 8 kilometres of Sheffield, and in 1871 of the 52 of rural origin 32 were born within 8 kilometres of Sheffield. Such a spatial concentration of origins may well have reflected and reinforced the power of the local trade unions to restrict entry to the trade.

By the 1860s and 1870s, however, the traditional handicraft basis of the light trades was beginning to be undermined, not only by the development of the industry itself towards a more capitalist structure, but also by the introduction of machinery which progressively de-skilled the workers and exposed the inherent weakness of their sectional unions in terms of organized collective bargaining. However, the effects of these changes were not the same throughout the light trades, but were initially concentrated in the file trades and after the defeat of the 'Great File Strike' in 1866 (Pollard, 1959) the pace of these changes was accelerated. In the saw trades the importance of social cohesion was exemplified by the difficulty of the authorities in obtaining evidence against those involved in the 'Sheffield Outrages' (Pollard, 1959). So the social structure of the area had a massive impact on the migration field of that area and then that migration reinforced the social structure. The particular structure of the light trades, and the social relations surrounding that production, seem to have been of great importance in ensuring that the migration field of Walkley was predominantly urban, and especially from Sheffield and its surrounding district. In fact, in the particular circumstances of the organization of labour in the light trades, female labour from within the family may have made a very necessary contribution to the household economy. This might explain the increasingly dominant urban origin of the Walkley wives in 1871 since they might well have come from families engaged in the light trades and so would be familiar with the nature of the work involved.

In distinct contrast to the conditions in Walkley the specific characteristics of the heavy trades in Brightside, while not actually deterring union growth, certainly discouraged union expansion. The use of the contractor system whereby the firms supplied money for materials and machinery while the contractor supplied labour only, allied with the highly cyclical nature of the heavy trades, meant that the turnover of labour power was very rapid. Howard (1976) suggests that the smelters and rollers were in charge of relatively large-scale projects, sometimes involving hundreds of men. Once orders were completed, the large gangs of men engaged on these would be dismissed and sent into unemployment. The contractor sometimes combined the task of employment agent with that of production manager, with the additional responsibility of training the personnel. As such any employee had to remain on good terms with the contractor if he wished to keep his employment. Moreover, the particular hierarchical organization of the labour process – smelter, first hand labourer, second hand labourer and third hand labourer – meant that if promotion was to be achieved, and with it not only increased wages but also the increased chance of regularity of employment, there had to be a similarly good relationship with the production manager. There could be no common interest between first hand labourers and the rest. In such a situation of essentially casual employment, except for those at the top of the hierarchy, there would be a marked tendency for a massive turnover of labour as well as the importation of non-union labour at crucial times, either to break strikes or to expand the labour force at the time of a cyclical upswing. The period 1860–70 in fact saw the biggest boom of the nineteenth century in the heavy trades and large amounts of labour moved to Brightside in search of employment. In the main this labour was of rural origin, as has been shown above, for rural labour was well known as being fairly docile and poorly unionized (Stedman Jones, 1971). In such a situation of the weakness of trade unions in the heavy trades and a social structure dominated by semi-skilled and unskilled workers of rural origin there was little that the existing workers could do to protect their employment from the importation of workers with similar characteristics. The needs of heavy industry for a particular sort of labour encouraged migration from particular geographical areas; this migration created a specific social and economic structure in Brightside which interacted with the social relations surrounding production there and reinforced the channels of migration flow.

In terms of the actual temporal patterns of migration the analysis is obviously made more difficult by the dearth of information. While it is impossible to glean any information from the census enumerators' books about non-mobile families whose head is from Sheffield, or for those households with no children, there are two possible sources of information about the other households: that relating to mobile families, as defined above, where by noting the age of the youngest child in the family born elsewhere it is possible to say that that family was definitely not in Sheffield that number of years ago; for non-mobile families whose head is not from Sheffield, by noting the age of the eldest child born in Sheffield it is possible to say that that family definitely was in Sheffield that number of years ago. Table 8.7 shows this information. For mobile families, which form the most

Table 8.7 Temporal patterns of migration, Walkley and Brightside, 1861 and 1871

Area	Mobile families: definitely not in Sheffield ten years ago	Non-mobile families with head of household not from Sheffield: definitely in Sheffield more than ten years ago	Total number of households
Brightside 1861	27	17	112
Brightside 1871	54	14	165
Walkley 1861	24	15	148
Walkley 1871	29	42	314

Data source: Samples of census enumerators' books.

satisfactory group to deal with, analysis by contingency tables and chi-square shows that there is no significant difference between Brightside, 1861, and Brightside, 1871, nor between Brightside, 1861, and Walkley, 1861. However, there is a difference between Walkley, 1861, and Walkley, 1871, significant at the 0.05 level showing that Walkley's population in 1871 contained fewer mobile families. The difference between Brightside, 1871, and Walkley, 1871 (significant at the 0.001 level), shows that Brightside was now much more dependent on migration from outside Sheffield than was Walkley. These results would tentatively suggest that the inhabitants of Walkley migrated there from Sheffield, whether they had been born in Sheffield or not, while the inhabitants of Brightside were more likely to have settled there directly. These results may again reflect the way in which the social relations surrounding the dominant industry in an area, and the labour requirements of that industry, encouraged migration from particular geographical areas and how that migration in turn had a marked impact on the social and economic structure of the area leading to a reinforcement of the original migration channels. Of course these relations are not frozen in time and may well change. One possibility might be a change in the strength (or weakness) of the local trade unions, especially in their ability to control the influx of labour. If the union was heavily defeated then the social cohesion, which had been a great part of its strength, might disappear and the effects of this on the social structure of the area might result in the in-migration of labour from non-traditional areas.

In an attempt to gain some possible insights into the reasons for migration extra information was collected from sources other than the census enumerators' books. A random sample of 100 was taken from the 1871 rate books for both Brightside Bierlow (for Brightside) and Nether Hallam (for Walkley). Table 8.8 gives the results. The much higher level of home ownership in Walkley would

Table 8.8 House ownership and rental values, Brightside and Walkley, 1871

Area	Sample size	Number of owner-occupiers	Average gross estimated rental value	
			All houses	Excluding owner-occupiers
Walkley	100	23	£7.96 (±0.45)	£6.96 (±0.34)
Brightside	100	4	£7.96 (±0.32)	£7.89 (±0.33)

Note: Standard errors of estimates are shown in parentheses.
Data source: Random sample of rate books, Brightside Bierlow and Nether Hallam.

suggest that those who moved there were considerably better off than those in Brightside, as well as suggesting a further reason for the lower mobility of Walkley families than those in Brightside. However, when the owner-occupiers are excluded from the sample it is seen that the average gross estimated rental value in Walkley is significantly lower than that in Brightside, although the high level in Brightside may well reflect the housing shortage there (Pollard, 1959). Certainly when the figures for shared accommodation are analysed (Table 8.9) it is found

Table 8.9 Shared working-class households, Brightside and Walkley, 1861 and 1871

Area	Working-class households			
	Number with lodgers	Number with kin	Number with lodgers and/or kin	Total number
Brightside 1861	16	10	25	94
Brightside 1871	36	21	54	146
Walkley 1861	17	9	25	127
Walkley 1871	33	40	71	265

Data source: Samples of census enumerators' books.

that Brightside, 1871, had more shared accommodation than Walkley, 1871 (significant at the 0.05 level), but this difference was dominated by those households with lodgers rather than kin. Walkley, 1871, had significantly more households sharing with kin than Walkley, 1861 (significant at the 0.05 level), and this may well reflect some sort of social security mechanism aming the population of Walkley, especially in the light trades, as a response to the onset of depression. This depression was not uniform in its impact on the light trades, but was especially important in the file trades where the introduction of machinery was having a noticeable effect, mainly by de-skilling the workers and so reducing the level of wages that their labour power could command. This, combined with the defeat in the 'Great File Strike' of 1866, may well have increased the impoverishment of those in the file trades (in 1861 of the 24 households whose head was in the file trades only 3 shared accommodation; in 1871 27 out of 56 did so).

At the same time the trade directories show that the majority of employment in the light trades remained located in the city centre although there were some workshops and factories set up in Walkley itself. It seems apparent that the motives for migration to Walkley were very complex. Undoubtedly some of the migration was undertaken by artisans moving out of the city centre in pursuit of better economic opportunities, while another part, the larger part, involved the out-movement of workers whose place of employment remained in the centre, but for whom housing was no longer available at a price they could afford. At the same time the development of the light trades themselves towards a more capitalist structure was reflected in the differentiation of the artisans with, on the one hand, small capitalist employers investing in house property in the suburbs, and on the other hand, a decline in status for the majority of workers, fighting a defensive battle against the introduction of machinery and their subsequent impoverishment. So part of the migration from the city centre to Walkley was undertaken by those better-off artisans who were undergoing a process of *embourgeoisement* while most moves were undertaken by artisans who were undergoing a process of proletarianization.

Summary and conclusions

Labour migration in nineteenth-century England and Wales has been studied within a theoretical framework which encompasses the development of industrial capitalism. It has been suggested, moreover, that when looking at actual detailed case studies migration should perhaps be studied not only in relation to the type and structure of the dominant industry, or 'leading sector', in that area, but also with regard to the social relations surrounding production in that particular industry. Once this background has been established use of the census enumerators' books, as well as other sources, enables much detailed information to be added to any proposed explanation of the patterns and processes of labour migration. In particular it is possible to analyse the ways in which the demands of an industry for specific types of labour create particular patterns of migration, and then the way in which that migration has a specific impact on the social and economic structure of the recipient area (and also on the sending area) which may well result in the reinforcement of the original migration channels.

In this particular case study the use of the census enumerators' books, allied with the more efficient method of data storage and structuring outlined, has enabled some light to be cast upon the different patterns and processes of migration associated with the two working-class suburbs of Brightside and Walkley. The first distinction was that the migration fields of Walkley and Brightside were significantly different for both 1861 and 1871, Walkley being dominated by Sheffield-born migrants while the majority of Brightside inhabitants had been born more than 8 kilometres from Sheffield. There was no significant difference in the migration fields of heads or their wives within any particular area, although the same significant differences occur between Walkley and Brightside. Walkley inhabitants were predominantly urban in origin while those of Brightside were predominantly rural. Brightside families tended to be more mobile than Walkley families. The initial hypothesis that these differences in mobility might be attributable to the possession of skill, with the skilled working class being less mobile than the semi-skilled and unskilled, because the employment of these latter groups was less regular in nature, was found to be rather too simplistic to explain these complex relationships. By considering the social relations surrounding production in the light trades on the one hand, and the heavy iron and steel industries on the other, and examining the relationships between these social relations, the original migration flows, the impact of that migration on the social and economic structure, and then the influence of that social and economic structure on later migration, some tentative explanations of the differences have been proposed. In terms of the actual temporal patterns of migration it seems likely that the inhabitants of Walkley moved there from Sheffield, whether or not they had been born in Sheffield, while the inhabitants of Brightside were more likely to have settled there directly. The reasons for these differences may well be bound up in the development of the dominant industries themselves and the changing social relations surrounding these developments.

Notes

1. The Public Record Office houses the originals of these books, but many municipal libraries in large towns have microfilms of the books relating to their local area, often for the 1841, 1851, 1861 and 1871 censuses. If they do not have microfilms they are undoubtedly able to help in the specification of the details of place, enumeration district and folio number required in order to obtain copies of the books from the Public Record Office.

Acknowledgements

The author wishes to thank Michael Blakemore, Lecturer in Geography at the University of Bristol, for help in devising the computer file system used in this study.

Chapter 9

Migration, marriage and the collapse of traditional peasant society in France

P. E. Ogden

Rural France since the mid-nineteenth century has experienced social and cultural change of revolutionary proportions. The gradual breakdown of formerly isolated peasant communities has followed the spread of urbanization and of rural depopulation. Economic modernization and integration at the national level have introduced new links between town and countryside and, in a process that Eugen Weber (1977) has recently likened to colonization, the land of Balzac's 'savages' has gradually been subjugated to urban, and expecially Parisian, influences. The regional peasant economies of bewildering diversity of the 1860s where French was hardly spoken, where roads were few and markets distant, where the village or *commune* marked the limits of social intercourse for the majority, gave way to a new rural France. An essential element in this transformation was migration, and it is to the geographical impact of migration and the changing nature of mobility and social contact patterns in rural France that this chapter gives attention.

This study is set firmly within a context of rural depopulation and seeks to show how the undermining of traditional patterns of social contact in one of France's most impoverished regions – the eastern Massif Central – has taken place. An important theme developed in this essay is the way in which the pattern of marriage distances may be used to measure the extent of rural isolation in the mid-nineteenth century and to plot the expansion of social contacts, both local and long distance, up to the 1970s. The argument is prefaced, first, by a discussion of the general nature of change over the period and, secondly, by an analysis of the extent of rural out-migration and of the variable contribution of in-migration to village populations. In this last context, particular attention is given to the role which marriage itself plays in shaping migration. While general remarks are made for France as a whole the majority of original research material is drawn from work on the department of the Ardèche which has experienced traumatic social, economic and cultural transformation over this period.

Migration and the collapse of the peasant economy in France

Between 1851 and 1968 the proportion of the French population living in the countryside declined from 74 per cent to 34 per cent so that, despite a rising national population, there were about 12 million fewer rural dwellers. Many departments lost over 50 per cent of their rural populations (Merlin, 1971) in a century characterized by rural decay and rapid urban growth. As rural depopulation took hold there was no region, and scarcely a village, that by the First World War had not sent some of its inhabitants to the cities. The Paris region grew more than three-fold (6 million people) from the mid-nineteenth to the mid-twentieth century (Pourcher, 1964) and provided a major focus for migrants. The capital gradually strengthened its administrative, economic and cultural grip on the provinces and, although its influence varied by region, there were few departments that by 1911 had not established direct migratory links with it (Ogden and Winchester, 1975). Equally, urban centres in the provinces – Lyon, Marseille, Bordeaux and so forth – came increasingly to exercise influence over their rural hinterlands and to aid the process of integration of peasant society into urban life. Nevertheless, rural decay came later to France than to other parts of Western Europe and many rural areas remained in 1914 very much more isolated and backward than in, say, England or Germany. Fundamental change came to many regions, indeed, only after the Second World War since which time the crisis in the peasant economy has been felt everywhere with force.

This process of change has naturally attracted a great deal of scholarly attention and, while it is not an aim of this chapter to provide a detailed bibliographical review, a number of important works should be noted. The recent completion of Zeldin's monumental *France, 1848–1945* (Zeldin, 1973; 1977) provides a general framework against which all contributions to the history of the period must henceforth be set; while Dupeux (1976) provides a more modest introduction. For more specifically rural themes, E. Weber (1977) and two volumes of the *Histoire de la France Rurale* by Agulhon *et al.* (1976) and Gervais *et al.* (1976) are invaluable. Merlin (1971) and Clément and Vieille (1960) have provided informative overviews of the process of rural depopulation while Wright's (1964) or Mendras's (1958; 1967) treatment of the peasantry in the twentieth century may be used as useful background to the many regional studies of rural change in France. Studies of individual communities abound, for example by Higonnet (1971) and Wylie (1957; 1966).

The nature of peasant society in the mid-nineteenth century, against which change may be measured, has been well established. 'Vast parts of . . . France', particularly the mountainous areas with which this paper is concerned, 'were inhabited by savages'. No words from the lips of contemporary observers were too harsh to describe the peasantry of a century ago: 'the peasant is . . . sin, original sin, still persistent and visible in all its naïve brutality'; 'lazy, greedy, avaricious and suspicious' (quoted in Weber, E., 1977, p. 4). The bonds of a common patois, of strongly localized culture and of geographical isolation were sufficient to ensure that rural France was made up of a number of largely independent and very distinctive regions. Thus in Lozère in 1864 when school-children were asked by a visiting inspector in what country their department was situated they could not say (Zeldin, 1977, p. 1).

Although geographical isolation was widespread, especially in the poorest, often mountainous, regions, it would be wrong to convey the impression of an entirely immobile traditional society. There was, as we shall see, much permanent migration from village to village, fostered for example by the nature of land-holding, by the existence of local crafts and rural industry or by marriage. In addition, of course, rural communities were to some extent dependent on short-range but intensive movements to markets or fairs, which for at least some of the population created contacts beyond the immediate horizons of the village. Long before real transformation began to take effect many areas had sent seasonal migrants over quite long distances both to other agricultural areas and to the cities (Chatelain, 1976). But in all these cases of mobility it may be cogently argued that they strengthened cultural distinctiveness and helped a region to remain 'isolated' from the world outside. Thus, even where movement was to the city, as in the case of the masons from the Creuse (Corbin, 1971), the migrants often maintained close ties among themselves and integrated only very slowly in urban life. It may well be that the links forged merely laid the basis for subsequent patterns of permanent rural out-migration rather than contributing directly to cultural change. As Eugen Weber (1977, p. 281) has argued, 'such passages from stability to movement then back to a new mobility suggest that the crux of traditional society is not immobility but mobility of an impenetrable sort'. For in providing temporary relief from abject poverty seasonal migration helped the traditional system to keep going. Thus while we may agree with Augé-Laribé's (1955, p. 166) judgement that 'village populations are often regarded as much more immobile, more firmly fixed to the soil, than they have ever been in reality' and endorse Wylie's (1968, p. 79) insistence on the volume of migratory flux in village communities, the effects of this mobility need to be carefully qualified.

For it was permanent out-migration from the countryside that began to effect real change, aided by the great increase in ease of communications in the later nineteenth century. It was this accelerating flood of migration in many regions that began to do more than simply skim off a surplus population and to dig deeply into the roots of local society and break down the distinctions between urban and rural France. Migration itself was, indeed, merely a reflection of deep-rooted economic change: the shift from a peasant subsistent to a centralizing, urban, capitalist economy. The expansion of cities both caused, and was aided by, the flight from the land. The attractions of urban life were matched by a growing discontent with rural conditions and by periodic local agricultural crises. All was made easier, too, by the growth of roads and railways opening up the countryside and by schools which both taught all children French and introduced them to the opportunities that instruction made available. Temporary migrants had helped in the spread of literacy and political ideas while military service uprooted from the countryside a large section of peasant youth at an early and impressionable age. Although change often took a long time to permeate into some regions, all had reached their maximum rural[1] populations by the eve of the First World War, since which time decline had been headlong. As Fig. 9.1A shows, many departments have been losing population since the 1850s and most (Fig. 9.1B) have lost more than 40 per cent of their rural populations at the time of the maximum. Many departments had indeed maintained growth only by natural increase and Agulhon *et al.* (1976, pp. 80–1) show that rural out-migration began to take hold from the 1830s, with at least 790,000 people leaving the countryside between 1831 and 1851. The most depopulated areas are in southern and eastern France, especially in the Massif Central, the Alps and the Pyrenees. The department of Ardèche, for which detailed research findings are presented here, was seventh out of 90 departments ranked according to rural population loss from the maximum to 1962 (Merlin, 1971, pp. 12–13). By the 1930s, indeed, only 16 of the French departments had larger total populations than ever before. As Gravier (1947) so effectively showed in his study of France and the 'French desert', France was unique among European states in that between 1851 and 1931 overall population increase meant, in fact, population decline for 95 per cent of the national territory (see

A.   DATE OF RURAL POPULATION MAXIMUM

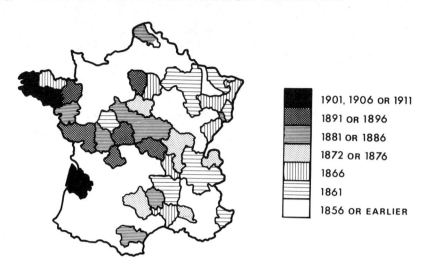

1901, 1906 OR 1911
1891 OR 1896
1881 OR 1886
1872 OR 1876
1866
1861
1856 OR EARLIER

B.   PERCENTAGE DECLINE OF RURAL POPULATION
FROM MAXIMUM TO 1962

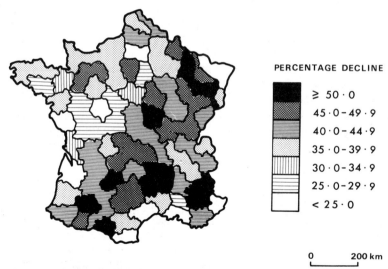

PERCENTAGE DECLINE

≥ 50·0
45·0 – 49·9
40·0 – 44·9
35·0 – 39·9
30·0 – 34·9
25·0 – 29·9
< 25·0

0   200 km

Fig. 9.1   Decline of rural population in France.
Source: Merlin, 1971.

also Ogden, 1975a) and this trend of widespread population loss has continued up to the present.

The extent to which increased mobility has affected the population as a whole is shown in Fig. 9.2 which gives the proportion of men and women at age 45 who were living outside their department of birth for generations born between 1816 and 1926. This figure has grown in both cases from around 20 per cent to about 40 per cent. The effects of these changes have been profound: French rural

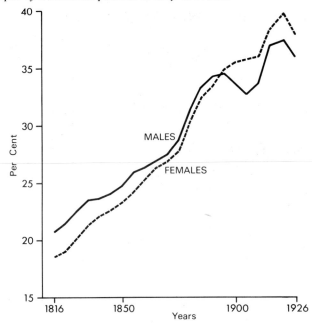

Fig. 9.2 Percentage of those aged 45 living outside their department of birth, for generations born 1816–1926, France.
Source: Tugault, 1973, p. 36.

society of the 1970s in many respects bears very little resemblance to that of the mid-nineteenth century. While the French population as a whole is better fed, better paid, more literate and mobile and able to look forward to a longer life than at any time in its history, depopulation has weakened or destroyed almost every aspect of traditional village society. In the worst-affected areas declining agriculture, an ageing population and reductions in the provision of schools and social services have been accompanied by the seasonal influx of second-home owners. The complex and profound influences of urbanization in its broadest sense have at once removed the bases of the peasant economy and irreversibly altered the life-style of France's rural population today.

Rural depopulation and the changing structure of village communities

Within the broad context of profound change we may begin to look more closely at the transformation of one area over this period. The Ardèche exemplifies the theme of this essay: a very poor, densely populated, predominantly peasant area of the mid-nineteenth century has been gradually sapped by out-migration. The enclosed, isolated populations of the valleys and plateaux that make up the area were in the early nineteenth century in many respects similar to Weber's descriptions of the peasantry as a whole: badly nourished and illiterate, speaking a local dialect, out of touch with any area beyond immediately local horizons, but with a rich and diverse cultural tradition (see for example Bozon, 1961; 1966; Siegfried, 1949). However, it was not an entirely immobile society, for seasonal migration and local mobility associated with industry, trips to markets and fairs, as well as the general population 'turnover' of permanent movements into and out of the *communes*, had long formed part of the social framework. It was not until mass out-migration took hold that traditional society began to crumble.

The department is distinctive in that it straddles a great variety of environmental and agricultural systems from the high plateaux of the Massif Central proper in the west to the Rhône valley which forms the eastern boundary of the department. Figure 9.3 shows the general location of the Ardèche and also of the 70 *communes*[2] which have been studied in detail as a basis for this analysis. Two aspects are treated in the present section: first, the pace and volume of out-migration; and, secondly, the extent of in-migration to the village communities,

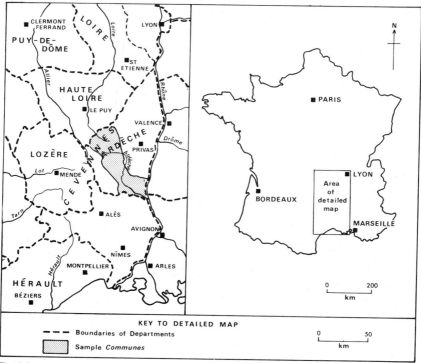

Fig. 9.3 Location of the Ardèche study area.

even in the context of rural depopulation, is examined in order to give an impression of the migratory structure of the 'residual' population at different periods. This is preceded by some comments on sources available for the study as a whole.

Sources

Sources for the study of post-Revolutionary French demographic history are as varied as they are incomplete. In matters of mobility, there is no one source or group of sources that give an accurate or detailed picture. The use of marriage distance – the distance between places of residence of the bride and groom at the time of marriage – as an index of social contact patterns (pp. 164–76) follows in part from the nature of the source. Here civil marriage records for the period 1863–1970 have been used, for they are complete for all communities and record almost exactly the same information throughout: age of each partner, places of birth and residence, occupation, and place of residence and occupation of the parents of the bride and groom. A sample of almost 9,000 marriages has been used here.

For the study of the pattern of in-migration and 'turnover' in the *communes* data on birth-place have been extracted from the *listes nominatives*. These lists, established in principle for each *commune* at the time of the census, usually give name, age, occupation and birth-place. For the department of the Ardèche all nineteenth-century lists have been destroyed and so use is made here of those for 1911, in fact a useful date for summarizing conditions prevailing before the First World War, and for 1968.

The volume and destinations of out-migrants pose the most difficult problems: no source gives accurate and consistent information over long periods. For volume and general destinations (by department) birth-place tabulations of successive censuses are useful, as too are tabulations by last place of residence. In addition, electoral lists, against which successive changes of residence are marked, have been used in some studies and are referred to below. Fuller discussion of these sources may be found in, for example, Merlin (1971) and Pitié (1971).

The pace and extent of rural depopulation

As Table 9.1 and Fig. 9.4 show, the decline of population, especially in the sample *communes*, has been dramatic. The department as a whole reached its maximum in 1861, since when it has lost over one-third of its population. Within the study areas decline has been more marked still: a net population loss of over 46,000 out of a population of under 80,000 in 1861. In individual *communes*, the percentage decline over the century has meant that communities have almost totally disintegrated: thus, in the Cévennes, Valgorge declined from a maximum of 1,459 to 353 in 1975 (− 76 per cent) while neighbouring Beaumont dropped from 1,367 in 1841 to 162 by 1975 (a loss of 88 per cent). While dates of population maximum varied considerably – between the 1840s in the Cévennes and the 1890s in the high plateaux – the rate of decline accelerated in all areas during the twentieth century. Thus, while the sample *communes* lost only 15 per cent between 1861 and 1901, there was a further decline of 51 per cent between 1901 and 1975.

This should not, though, lead us to underestimate the extent of migration during the nineteenth century. Two factors helped to camouflage its influence: first, a high rate of natural increase in many areas helped to stave off net population decline for several decades; secondly, peasant populations were generally so densely distributed that even continuous and heavy out-migration during several decades could fail to have a general impact. The balance between natural increase and migration is notoriously difficult to estimate at this period,

Table 9.1 Population change, Ardèche and sample *communes* 1861–1975

	1861	1901	Percentage change 1861–1901	1975	Percentage change 1861–1975
Ardèche	388,529	353,564	−9.00	257,065	−33.84
Sample *communes*	79,805	67,707	−15.16	33,086	−58.54

Data source: Population censuses, 1861–1975.

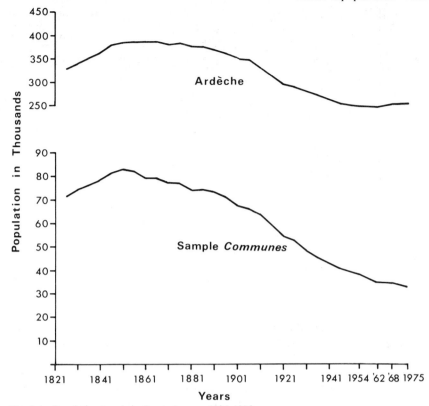

Fig. 9.4 Population trends in the study area, 1826–1975.

but the calculations of Bozon (1961, pp. 290–3) for the period 1830–1930 are of interest. His data have been re-aggregated to fit our present sample *communes* and the general balance of the components of population change is shown in Fig. 9.5. It is clear that out-migration from the area was important from the 1830s onwards and that natural increase contributed to population stability until the end of the century. From 1900 onwards rapid net loss was fostered by both out-migration and an excess of deaths over births.

It is more difficult still to penetrate beyond net balances of change in order to arrive at some indication of the total number of people moving into and out of the *communes* over the century. Birth-place tables from the census give us generalized figures at the departmental level: we know, for example, that of the 412,631 people born in the Ardèche and still alive in 1911, 117,762 were living outside the department. But it is more difficult to monitor the continuous process of migration and to count individuals, although this is clearly most important: painstaking reconstruction of migration in the sample *communes* between 1962 and 1968 showed that while net population loss was 1,025, of which 340 was natural decrease and 685 net out-migration, these figures mask at least 5,789 in- and out-migrants and a total of 3,304 births and deaths.

It follows that the measurement of exact destinations is also difficult. Here the electoral registers are used for this purpose as an illustration of the spatial form of the migration field. Place of re-registration is marked against place of birth for individuals and in this case data have been gathered for all people born in one

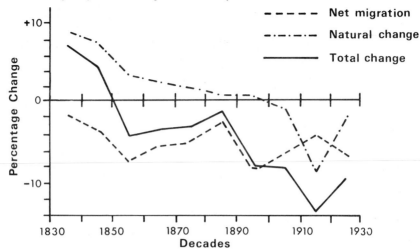

Fig. 9.5 Components of change in sample *communes*, 1830–1930.
Source: after Bozon, 1961.

commune – Burzet – between 1870 and 1950,[3] for whom the number of usable
entries amounts to a little over 1,000. Figures 9.6A, B and C show the pattern of
destinations at three different scales: within the Ardèche (A), within the nine
most attractive, neighbouring departments (B) and in the rest of France (C). The
most remarkable factor is the great spilling out of population downhill: areas to
the west and north within the Ardèche are largely unattractive and the main poles
of concentration are the minor urban centres like Aubenas within the department
and a variety of towns within the Rhône valley: Valence, Montélimar, Avignon
and Nîmes. The role of Lyon is particularly important, and it is the single most
attractive destination. Beyond the immediate departments migrants from Burzet
are represented in 36 departments in which, with the exception of Paris, there is
marked attachment to the south and south-east.

   The shortcomings in the source – especially the inconsistency with which date
of migration and migration stages are given – do limit its usefulness and draw
attention to how difficult it is to plot accurately and in detail the developing
process of out-migration. But Fig. 9.6 does serve the general purpose of showing
the way in which out-migration over the century from the approximate date of
population maximum has opened up formerly tightly knit rural communities,
dispersing their inhabitants widely throughout the country.

In-migration and the village community

Against this background of extreme rural depopulation a question rarely asked is
the extent to which the 'residual' population at any one moment is itself a product
of migration. Did the villages provide simply an immobile backcloth of people
who had never moved since birth, or can we find evidence of permanent
migration fostered by the traditional economic and social pattern? The study of
birth-places of the resident population may elucidate this problem. At the
departmental level less than 10 per cent of the population in 1911 had been born
outside the Ardèche, making it one of only 16 departments where more than 90
per cent of the population was born in the department of residence. By 1962,

A. WITHIN ARDÈCHE

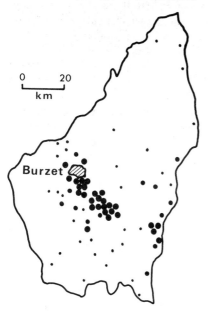

Burzet

0   20
km

B. WITHIN REGION

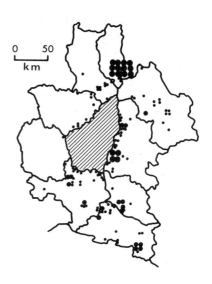

0   50
km

C. REST OF FRANCE

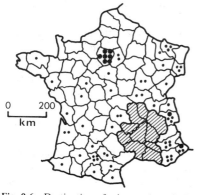

0   200
km

- ● 10 migrants
- • 5 migrants
- · 1 migrant

Fig. 9.6 Destination of migrants born in Burzet, 1870–1951.
Data source: Fichier electoral.

though, almost one-quarter – 60,000 out of a population of 248,000 – were in-migrants in this sense. For the sample *communes*, aggregate birth-places have been calculated from the *Listes Nominatives* of the 1911 and 1968 censuses. This is not a simple task of interpretation for, as Jollivet (1965) has shown, birth-place is a complicated measure which gives no impression of migration stages or date of migration and whose very definition is tied to administrative units of widely varying population and territorial bases. But, in the absence of better sources, birth-place data do have the advantage of providing a useful indication of the extent to which the population of a particular community has moved. Certain refinements make data interpretation easier: children are excluded, since any moves they may have made will generally be confined to those within the family. Also, because of the changing demographic structure which tends to exaggerate the significance of women in the oldest age-groups in the population by the late 1960s, particular attention is given to married couples.

Of all adults (over 21) living in the sample *communes* in 1911 66 per cent were born in the *commune* (see Table 9.2). By 1968 the comparable figure had fallen to 46 per cent. This indicates a relative increase in mobility and a generally high level of movement for so rural and depopulated an area. There was considerable variation within the *communes*: in 1911 figures varied from a maximum of 96 per cent to a minimum of 24 per cent and in 1968 from a maximum of 82 per cent to a minimum of 21 per cent. The *communes* were neither uniform nor generally stable. But the influence of permanent in-migration on the community bites even deeper than these figures suggest because, of course, the 55 per cent of in-migrants in 1968 were not all in the same households or married to each other. In order to illustrate the role of migration throughout the population the birthplaces of the adult, married population are analysed in two ways. First, simple totals may be calculated of the proportion of the total married men and women born in their *commune* of residence (Table 9.2(b)) at each date and for both agricultural and non-agricultural households. Secondly, the couples may be classified into three main groups: those where both husband and wife were born in the *commune* of residence, those where neither was and those where one partner was born in and one outside the *commune* (see Table 9.2 (a)).

Table 9.2(a) thus shows that the core, stable element in the population – the proportion of married couples where both partners were born in the *commune* of residence – is remarkably low. By 1968 only 17 per cent of all couples came into this category. In other words, over 80 per cent of all couples were 'affected' by migration in the sense that one or other of the partners was born outside the *commune* of residence. Even in 1911 this figure stood at a little under 60 per cent. As well as showing the extent to which mobility existed and increased over time this method also hints at the major mechanisms which produced this high degree of local 'flux'. The isolation of couples where both partners were in-migrants produces relatively low figures too, indicating that migration for marriage itself was an important factor: only 17 per cent in 1911 and 36 per cent of all couples in 1968 came into that category. Individual *communes* provide interesting examples of the interplay of various factors: Beaumont, for instance, in an isolated valley in the Cévennes, had 80 per cent of its 1911 population living in their *commune* of birth. Although only 67 per cent of all couples had both partners born in the *commune*, in only 3 per cent were both partners born outside. We may conclude, therefore, that the role of marriage was, and is, crucial.[4] In most *communes*, indeed, a large number of couples was neither totally migratory nor totally non-migratory, in the sense defined here, but were characterized by just one of the partners having moved.

These points are further emphasized if we look at the contrast between the agricultural and non-agricultural populations and at the contribution of women to in-migration. In the case of Beaumont in 1911, 91 per cent of all married men had not moved since birth compared to 72 per cent of women (70 per cent and 50 per cent in the non-agricultural occupations). Table 9.2 shows these contrasts to be even more valid for the total sample of *communes*: almost half of all 'non-agricultural' couples in 1968 were cases where both partners were born outside

Table 9.2 Summary indicators of migration in sample *communes* in 1911 and 1968

(a) All adults and married couples

	All adults, Percentage born in *commune*	Couples								
		Per cent where both partners born in *commune*			Per cent where one partner born outside *commune*			Per cent where both partners born outside *commune*		
	Total	Total	Agric.	Non-Agric.	Total	Agric.	Non-Agric.	Total	Agric.	Non-Agric.
1911	65.57	42.07	47.70	27.54	41.01	42.75	33.77	16.92	9.55	38.69
1968	45.66	17.13	26.87	12.10	46.96	57.11	41.10	35.91	16.02	46.80

(b) Total married population – percentage born in commune of residence

	Total population			Agricultural			Non-agricultural		
	Total	M	F	Total	M	F	Total	M	F
1911	62.64	71.26	54.03	69.07	79.18	58.96	46.02	50.77	41.23
1968	40.39	47.88	32.80	55.42	69.21	42.18	32.93	38.54	28.32

Note: Agricultural and non-agricultural households defined according to occupation of husband.

the *commune*, compared to 16 per cent among couples in agriculture (see Table 9.2(a)). Women were markedly more migratory than men, especially in the agricultural population: thus in the total married population in 1911, 71 per cent of men but only 54 per cent of women were born in their *commune* of residence (see Table 9.2(b)). The male peasant population was by far the most stable, even in 1968, and the female non-agricultural population the most migratory: by 1968 only three wives in ten in this group had not changed residence since birth.

Much of this mobility was over very short distances: Fig. 9.6A, for example, shows that out-migration from Burzet was in fact in-migration for neighbouring communities. The reasons behind movement were diverse: the type of land-holding in some areas induced short-range peasant movements, while local textile industries encouraged migration of both men and women, especially before the Second World War. Within this diversity, it is certain that the movement of women for marriage was one essential element in the exchange of population between communities. It was generally women who moved into their husband's *commune* of birth. Assuming that the proportion of the married population born outside the *commune* who are women is an indicator of the role of migration for marriage, this may be correlated with other factors for each of the 70 *communes*. Results for 1968 show a negative correlation ($r = -0.51$) with the total size of the *commune*, but a positive correlation ($r = +0.61$) with the proportion of the population engaged in agriculture, with the total proportion of the adult population born in the *commune* of residence ($r = +0.52$) and with the importance of local movements in the migration field ($r = +0.65$) – all significant at the 0.01 level. In short, movement for marriage is most important in the small agricultural community which has attracted a low proportion of in-migrants.

This analysis provides a useful method for looking in detail at the cumulative effect in a community of several generations of movement for marriage and for other purposes. It reflects a diverse set of individual migration histories and is a useful reminder of the complexity of local population exchange which persisted even when the dominant trend was of out-migration. It is in this light that we may now turn to the wider investigation of social contact patterns and, in particular, to the way in which contacts were established between these communities and other areas, in view of the large-scale migration systems that have come to exist since the mid-nineteenth century.

Marriage distance and the decline of rural isolation in the Ardèche, 1860–1970

Marriage distance is used both as a surrogate measure of patterns of social contact and as an indicator of the direct influence of migration on marriage itself. It is argued here neither that marriage distance is the only indicator of isolation nor that it adequately summarizes all forms of mobility and contact. It is seen, rather, as one of the few indicators which may be measured very accurately over long periods of time for the whole of the present sample of villages, and it seems a reasonable assumption that marriage distance reflects neighbourhood knowledge or information fields as expressed geographically. The *Actes de Mariage* are complete and comparable for the whole period of modernization covered by this essay and allow us to plot in great detail the way in which the marriage field has changed over the last century. In addition, marriage itself was a vital part of the social system in traditional society, and the relationships between marriage distance and wider aspects of the demographic system of France and Western Europe have been developed elsewhere (Ogden, 1973; 1974; 1975b).

Marriage distance has been used in a number of different contexts: within geography it has been developed as a basis for the simulation of diffusion processes (for example Morrill and Pitts, 1967; Marble and Nystuen, 1963). A second group of studies has been concerned more directly with economic and social relationships both in urban and rural contexts and with the structure of the marriage field *per se*. Examples of urban studies include Ramsøy (1966), and D. A. Coleman (1973), while rural studies with a social bias include work on Dorset (Perry, 1969), the USA (Anderson, W. A., 1934) and in France (Morel, 1972; Girard, 1964). A third group of studies has sought links within the narrower context of demography and genetics, including Harrison and Boyce (1972), Alström and Lindelius (1966) and, in France, Sutter (1958), or Sutter and Goux (1962). The last of these is particularly interesting for it gives a general view of the way in which isolation and inter-marriage have declined in France as a whole.

The present analysis draws upon marriages which took place in the 70 *communes* at four five-year periods: 1863–67, 1903–07, 1933–37 and 1966–70. The spatial expression of the marriage field is discussed at two scales: first, endogamous and 'local' marriages up to 50 kilometres where the continuous spatial field ends; and secondly, long-distance contacts. A last section looks at the role of occupation and social groups.

Local contact patterns and their evolution

The evolution of the proportion of marriages where both partners were resident in the same *commune* prior to marriage (see Fig. 9.7) gives an overall view of trends in isolation:[5] the figure has declined from a peak of 66 per cent in the 1840s to 26 per cent by the 1960s. This decline in endogamy has been fairly continuous since the mid-nineteenth century with a sharp fall since the Second World War. The endogamy rate did, though, decline less sharply during the later

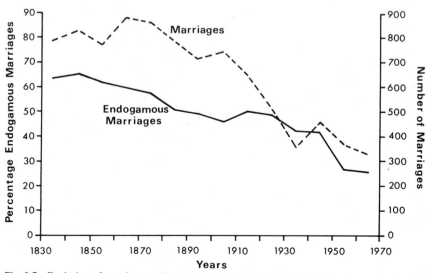

Fig. 9.7 Evolution of marriages and endogamy in an eight-*commune* sample.

nineteenth century than did the total number of marriages, which might have reinforced the trend to increased consanguinity suggested by Rambaud (1962) and others.

Beyond fairly basic temporal comparisons this figure alone is not very useful for comparing *communes* (see Perry, 1969, p. 126) given the wide differences in their population or areal sizes. Such comparisons are best achieved by looking at the features of the marriage distance field as a whole. For a few *communes*, though, it is possible to measure contact within the *commune*, where addresses in the marriage registers are given down to the level of individual farmsteads and hamlets. In the case of the *commune* of Burzet, for example, which in 1861 had a population – mainly peasant – of 2,774, no fewer than 57 separate residence places within the *commune* were recorded in the marriages of the 1860s. These have been mapped in Fig. 9.8 to give an impression of the high intensity of movement at this very local scale in traditional society: between 1863 and 1872 64 per cent of all marriages took place in the *commune* and of these three-quarters involved movement of less than 2 kilometres, indicating the extremely restricted nature of mobility for a considerable proportion of the population. This intensity of social interaction was much reduced over the following century as a result of the opening up of the area to a wider field of communication with more distant areas and because the very decline and ageing of the population meant that there was an ever diminishing possibility of young people of a particular *commune*, and still less of a small hamlet, finding a husband or wife within the confines of that settlement.

The degree of isolation in the mid-nineteenth century and the way it broke down may be better illustrated by reference to marriages contracted beyond the

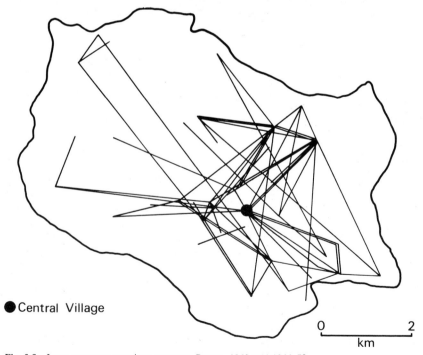

● Central Village

0   2
km

Fig. 9.8 Intra-*commune* marriage contacts, Burzet, 1863 and 1866–72.

limits of the *commune*. Table 9.3 shows the general evolution of the marriage field and indicates that as the proportion of marriages within the *commune* fell from 52 per cent to 16 per cent it was the proportion of long-distance contacts that increased, rather than those taking place within 50 kilometres. Distances for all marriages occurring within this last 'local' band have been measured for each of the 70 *communes*. The nature of rural isolation in the mid-nineteenth century and its erosion is illustrated in several different ways in Figs. 9.9 and 9.10. In Fig. 9.9 the cumulative frequency of marriage distances over successive kilometre bands is shown, first, for all marriages both within and beyond the *commune* and, secondly, for 'local' exogamous marriages up to 50 kilometres only. In Fig. 9.10 semi-log regression equations have been fitted to the pattern of 'local' exogamous marriages in two ways: first, to the general relationship between marriage and distance; and secondly, population densities at each period have been built into the distance axis in order to give an impression of the number of people, or 'neighbourhood population size' within which interaction takes place.[6] The b values resulting from the regression analysis give a convenient comparison between the different curves (see Table 9.4).

Table 9.3 Evolution of marriage distances 1863–1970, all sample *communes*

	Number of marriages	Per cent marriages within commune	Per cent marriages up to 50 km.	Per cent marriages over 50 km.
1863–67	2,919	51.90	43.99	4.11
1903–07	2,554	39.24	47.22	13.54
1933–37	1,670	34.74	45.99	19.27
1966–70	1,287	16.13	56.67	27.20

Table 9.4 Regression equations for marriage fields 1863–1970, all sample *communes*

	Geographical distance			Neighbourhood population size		
	r	log a	b	Population density/km²*	log a	b
1863–67	−0.97	3.135	−0.123	56	3.073	−0.350
1903–07	−0.98	2.961	−0.105	48	2.909	−0.347
1933–37	−0.96	2.953	−0.108	34	2.899	−0.507
1966–70	−0.73	2.392	−0.057	25	2.363	−0.363

*Density figures for 1861, 1901, 1931, 1968.

The overwhelming friction effect of distance on patterns of contact is shown very clearly in the 1860s: more than 90 per cent of all marriages fell within 20 kilometres and indeed over 80 per cent within 10 kilometres (see Fig. 9.9A). The extremely high degree of correlation between marriage frequency and distance is further shown in the correlation values in Table 9.4. In some *communes*, especially those in the most withdrawn valleys of the Cévennes and on the high plateaux of the Massif proper, mobility for marriage was even more restricted and the great majority of marriages took place within 5 kilometres. The study of marriage in such areas provides eloquent support for Siegfried's (1949, p. 96) view that the high plateaux 'constitute a special region cut off from society by geographical and social isolation'. Such areas, even in the 1860s, were in sharp contrast to the *communes* bordering on the Rhône and Languedoc which were more receptive to 'outside ideas'.

The evolution of the local field of contact is also shown in Figs 9.9 and 9.10. Looking first at the 'total' marriage distance distribution (Fig. 9.9A) it is clear that there has been a general opening up of the area begun in the 1860s and continued progessively over the century. Thus the proportion of total marriages falling within 20 kilometres fell from over 90 per cent to under 60 per cent by the 1960s, linked to a general decline in endogamy and a great increase in long-distance contact. The most profound changes have undoubtedly taken place since the Second World War. Changes in the mobility pattern have not, though, led to a general, continuous expansion of the spatial field. As village populations declined there has been little proportional increase in contact with the local area, but instead a direct expansion of links with urban areas. Improvements in communications locally do not seem to have had as marked an effect as has been observed elsewhere (for example in Dorset by Perry, 1969).

This is shown most clearly in Fig. 9.9B where the cumulative frequency of exogamous marriage distances falling within 50 kilometres shows how little change there was in this respect between the mid-nineteenth century and the 1930s: the proportion of marriages within 10 kilometres remained at between 60 and 70 per cent and the proportion at longer distances increased only slightly. The general form of the distance decay curves reinforces this point: Fig. 9.10A and Table 9.4 show that the slope of the regression line decreased somewhat between the 1860s and 1903–07 but remained stable up to the 1930s. In some areas, indeed, if the overall sample is sub-divided, there is a decline in the spatial extent of the 'local' field so that the average distance travelled in the 1930s was actually less than in the 1860s (see Ogden, 1973, p. 37). Again, the most significant changes came after 1945 when the spatial extent of the marriage field expanded substantially: the proportion of local exogamous marriages within 10 kilometres declined to 45 per cent and the general slope of the regression line (see Fig. 9.10A) shows a considerable flattening out. In all parts of the study area any contraction of the marriage field had stopped, indicating perhaps that at this stage, as depopulation had advanced so greatly, a threshold level was reached where the available choice of partners was so restricted as to involve of necessity a search over a wider field.

This point is further illustrated if the regression model is modified slightly, to take account of changing population densities over time, in order to give an idea of 'neighbourhood population size' within which interaction took place. For, although from period to period the simple geographical distribution of marriage contacts may be similar, population density and the actual range of choice may vary. To give such a complementary view, therefore, the method adopted in Fig. 9.10B and Table 9.4 is simply to replace distance with population occurring in successive kilometre bands at the different periods and to refit the lines on this basis.[7] The results show that 'neighbourhood' sizes in fact declined at each successive period from the 1860s to the 1930s as the expansion of geographical distances failed to keep pace with declining population. Only after the Second World War did neighbourhood size begin to increase, and even in the 1960s it was considerably below the levels of the 1860s. Thus while the extent to which the population was in contact with neighbouring areas undoubtedly increased over the century, the actual size of the population within which interaction took place declined.[8]

The stability or contraction of the extent of this 'local' contact field is eloquent evidence of the run-down of the local economy. Just as depopulation was engendered by the collapse of agriculture and rural industry, so the general decline in the need for and frequency of markets and fairs, for example, contributed to an actual decline in the social dealings which communities had

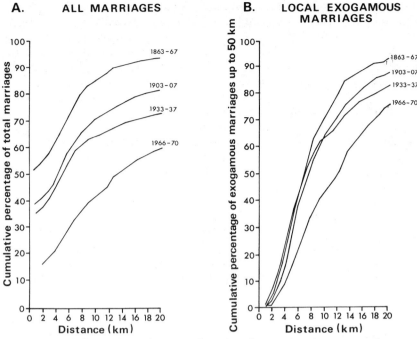

Fig. 9.9 Cumulative percentage frequency of marriage distances, sample *communes* of Ardèche.

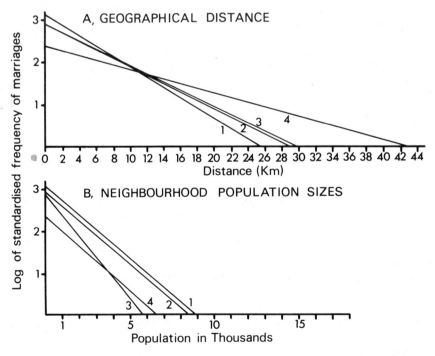

1, 1863-67   2, 1903-07   3, 1933-37   4, 1966-70

Fig. 9.10 Evolution of marriage fields, sample *communes* of Ardèche.

with surrounding villages and townships. While the general improvement in communications made movement less arduous (see especially Weber, E., 1977, Ch. 12) and no doubt helped in the erosion of isolation to some extent, after that date the extent of decline in the local economy (see for the Ardèche Bozon, 1961 and Reynier, 1934) seems to have cancelled out this effect. To be added to this are, of course, factors such as the decline of the traditional village social functions such as the *bals* which had long played a vital role in local demography (Morel, 1972, p. 74 shows that the majority of marriages were the direct result of local dances). The same is true of other village *fêtes* scattered liberally throughout the year: the importance of these is evident from contemporary regional literature (Francus, 1885, pp. 314–15) and Bozon (1961, p. 184) notes that it was in particular the '*fêtes votives*' which 'brought in, often from great distances, young people who did the rounds of all the celebrations in the area'. Equally, the decline of such activities as the silk industry in the Cévennes, whose factories had long employed a large, predominantly young, female population travelling over considerable distances, undoubtedly affected also the pattern of marriage distance. The decline in seasonal migration for harvest and so on also contributed, while permanent migration within the 'local' area often did not go outside the established field of contact (see the spatial bias in Fig. 9.6A).

The growth of long-distance contacts

The real contributor to the decline of rural isolation has been, then, not a gradual spreading out of local contacts but a rapid expansion of long-distance links brought about principally by migration. As Table 9.3 showed, the proportion of contacts beyond 50 kilometres rose from 4 per cent to 27 per cent over the century and the number of departments with which links were recorded rose from 19 to 50 (Fig. 9.11). Distance itself at this scale becomes less relevant for, as Morel (1972, p. 67) has shown for Picardy, beyond the local region knowledge is generally restricted to towns and cities whose real distance from home is frequently distorted by incomplete information and differently perceived attractiveness. In the present case one is reminded of Zeldin's (1977, p. 75) remark for another region that 'the paradox of Savoy was that it contained a mass of isolated and inaccessible valleys but that it also had a tradition of migration, so that Savoyards often had more contact with distant cities than with their own immediate neighbours'. This was increasingly the case in the Ardèche.

For the mid-nineteenth century, though the proportion was very low, contacts were nevertheless recorded with 19 different departments. The most frequent contacts were with the contiguous departments to the south and east, to the Languedoc and Mediterranean coasts in general and above all to the Gard, Drôme, Vaucluse and Bouches-du-Rhône. A strong axis of contact is already apparent around the Rhône valley, centred particularly on Lyon, while the departments to the west scarcely count (there were no contacts at all with Haute Loire, Cantal, Aveyron or Puy-de-Dôme). Finally, contacts were beginning, although in small numbers, with the departments of the Paris basin. External contacts varied considerably within the study areas: the high plateaux had almost no contact beyond the department in the 1860s (1 per cent of all marriages compared to 6 per cent – covering 14 departments – in the Cévennes).

The reasons underlying this pattern include, first, seasonal migration: movements had long been established in the Ardèche (Bozon, 1961, pp. 138ff)

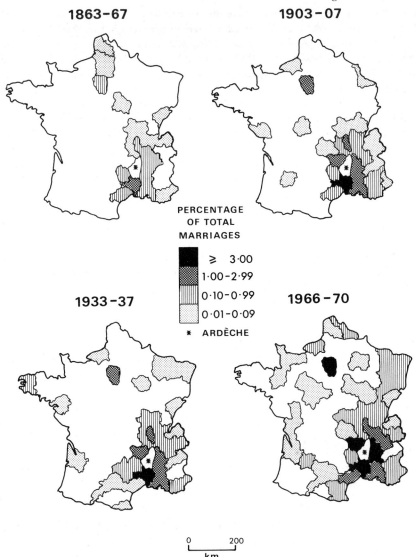

1863-67

1903-07

PERCENTAGE
OF TOTAL
MARRIAGES

≥ 3·00
1·00-2·99
0·10-0·99
0·01-0·09
* ARDÈCHE

1933-37

1966-70

0   200
km

Fig. 9.11 External marriage contacts, sample *communes* of Ardèche.

and increased during the early nineteenth century as the growth of population at home and of demand for labour in other areas grew. Some agricultural migrants went well beyond the departmental borders while other seasonal migrants went to the mines of Alès or Bessèges in the Gard. General reservations about the effects of these movements expressed above (p. 154) apply, but it is not unlikely that a few of the thousands of young migrants (Boyer, 1932) may have found marriage partners. A further factor was the growth of the local silk industry during the eighteenth and nineteenth centuries which for a few *communes* and for certain sectors of the population was, through strong commercial links, responsible for the generation of many and varied contacts with Lyon. The most important reason of all, though, was the growing influence of permanent migration from the area both to neighbouring, more prosperous departments (as the analysis of Burzet, pp. 159–60, has shown) and increasingly to the larger urban centres of Lyon, Marseille and Paris. The general outline of the spatial extent of contact was already set by the 1860s and Fig. 9.11 shows that subsequent periods saw an intensification of this pattern. Marriage contacts provide, indeed, a very interesting indication, long sought for in studies of rural–urban migration, of contacts retained with the local area.

Marriage distance itself is based on the place of residence of partners at the time of marriage, but in the period 1863–67 over 60 per cent of long-distance contacts in fact concerned people born in the area. Thus a miner living in Robiac (Gard) returns to Laboule, his *commune* of birth, for marriage; a girl living in Nîmes (Gard) returns to her native Valgorge; a guard with the SNCF at Chasse (Isère) returns to Chauzon; a '*garçon de café*' native of Lentillères returns from Bessèges (Gard) to the neighbouring village of Chanzeaux. By this process the sample *communes* in Ardèche had, by the 1960s, contacts with more than half the departments of metropolitan France. In addition – and this is an important point for the discussion in the earlier part of this chapter – marriage itself fostered out-migration, for the great majority of couples whose marriage came into this category subsequently left the area permanently.

The effects of out-migration on the marriage distance pattern become more complex over time. The proportion of those marriage partners living at long distances who were in fact born in the department declined to 52 per cent at the beginning of the present century, to 28 per cent in the 1930s and to 8 per cent in the 1960s. This may in part be due to an expansion of genuine contacts with distant cities, but it is due also to a 'chain effect' where although the young person concerned may not have been born in the Ardèche his parents may have been, and close contact is maintained with the original village. A close scrutiny of individual family histories shows this frequently to be the case. In addition, the general flux of migration in the sample *communes* has increased considerably over the century so that even between birth and time of marriage several places of residence may be interposed. For example, an Italian immigrant coming to work as an agricultural labourer may subsequently have moved to Paris but may still marry a girl from the Ardèche. Permutations springing from the cumulative effects of in- and out-migration are numerous, and the nature of links with foreign areas is a further aspect of this. Particularly notable are links with Algeria, evident briefly in the 1860s and, to a much greater extent, in the 1900s and 1930s (when Tunisia and Morocco also entered the scene), subsequently receding considerably by the 1960s. This is a clear reflection of the great waves of emigration to North Africa. A corollary of this is the way in which return migration from North Africa may contribute to the complex pattern of the 1960s. It may be difficult to guess why a girl from the village of Joyeuse marries a miner from the Nord, until one sees that they have a common birth-place in Algeria, and are therefore *pieds noirs*.

Changes in occupational structures within the area – especially since 1945 – have greatly contributed, too, to the pattern of long-distance contact: the drastic reduction of the peasant population has meant that the much greater variety of occupations is often associated with a very complex mobility structure, in the sense both of the day-to-day movements and contacts associated with the job, and of permanent migratory moves that the job may entail. The general weakening of the peasantry has been associated with an increase of population in the larger urban and semi-urban *communes*, where the likelihood of contact with distant centres is greater. Where the occupational structure remains fairly simple and the urban population small, then the 1960s pattern approximates more closely to that of the nineteenth century, especially in the highest, most mountainous, areas. The general economic decline locally, which contributed, as we have seen, to the stagnation and even contraction of the local marriage field no doubt contributed also in significant measure to the need to establish contacts at greater distances. Other contributory factors are as diverse as the importance of military service and the growth of higher education. Many students now go to university in, for example, Grenoble or Lyon, meet their spouses there and return home for marriage. The possibilities for geographically varied contacts are extensive and have kept pace with the growing economic and social diversity of the area.

A distinctly post-Second World War phenomenon is the influence of tourism and second-home expansion. The coincidence of greatly increased urban affluence and the desertion of rural houses by out-migration has produced a great increase in the number of second homes: by 1975 over 50 per cent of the houses in many of the sample *communes* came into this category. This new form of seasonal migration is a key link between urban and rural communities and its importance has become so great that its effects on marriage distances, although minor, are nevertheless evident. In this particular area, for example, there has been a considerable influx of foreigners and the period 1966–70 saw the appearance of two Belgian and two German temporary residents who married local girls. Equally, there seems to be an increasing number of instances where a marriage takes place between a couple who have no apparent links with the *commune* either by birth or residence, except perhaps a summer visit. The general effect of this factor is to reinforce spatial patterns of external contact, for it is very often from the cities to which the majority of out-migrants went that most tourists and second-home owners come.

This section has shown, then, that long-distance contacts, particularly with urban areas, have come to form an essential and increasingly important aspect of the marriage field. This is symptomatic of the breakdown of the rural isolation of the nineteenth century, is in large part a direct reflection of the complex impact of migration on the peasant community and family structure, and is eloquent illustration of Eugen Weber's general thesis of the gradual absorption of rural regions into the wider socio-economic whole. A clear rift thus develops in the spatial structure of a community's information field: besides a fairly close association with the neighbouring areas, contact has been increasingly with distant urban centres. Marriage distance is one of the few convenient measures of the extent to which rural–urban contacts existed and are developed. The overall effect of a century of change is that no villages, and few families, in the Ardèche now remain isolated from contact with areas outside the department, and the traditional form of the marriage pattern of close liaison within only a tightly knit group of villages has been largely submerged.

Occupational group and the marriage pattern

Marriage distance may also be used as an indicator of interaction between different social groups, and the changing balance of occupations is itself a reflection of the impact of migration on community structure. One example may be developed here by re-classifying the marriages according to the occupational status of the bridegroom, paying particular attention to the broad differences between agricultural and non-agricultural groups. Table 9.5 shows how dramatic the general trend away from the land has been, especially in these predominantly young age-groups: 'non-agricultural' marriages increased from less than one-quarter in the 1860s to nearly 90 per cent a century later. The number of 'agricultural' marriages declined from 2,268 in the first quinquennium to 124 by 1966–70.

It is clear from both Table 9.5 and Fig. 9.12 – which again graphs both the total marriage field and the 'local' exogamous marriages only – that at all periods marriages among the agricultural population have been geographically much more tightly circumscribed than the rest. Thus the proportion of endogamous marriages has been consistently higher, and the proportion of contacts beyond 50 kilometres consistently lower, in the peasant population. Among 'local' marriages the fall-off with distance was consistently less marked among the non-agricultural groups at all periods (see Fig. 9.12B). Several factors need to be noted. First, those in industrial, commercial or service occupations had greater opportunities and need to travel both locally and further afield and, except on relatively rare social occasions, or trips to the local market, the peasant tended to be 'rooted to the soil'. Secondly, given the possibility of a strong tendency to marry within a particular occupational or social group, the opportunity to do so is naturally restricted by the small size of, for example, the artisan groups in the nineteenth-century village, and this may again lead to the search for a partner over longer distances. In addition, the influence of out-migration was strong, for many of the 'non-agricultural' marriages in fact involved a man who had left for a distant location and who returned to marry: he had almost inevitably taken up an occupation outside agriculture and so the influence of out-migration would apply more to the non-agricultural than to the agricultural sector, as defined here. Time, moreover, as Fig. 9.12 shows, accentuated differences between the two groups and, while there was a fairly constant widening of the marriage distance distribution for the non-agricultural population, the changes in the agricultural sector were more confused. There was, for example, very little change between the 1860s and 1930s for the agricultural population, while since the Second World War there has been some widening of the marriage horizon, although only to the level of the non-agricultural marriages of the mid-nineteenth century (contrast curves 4a and 1b in Fig. 9.12B).

The question also arises of the extent to which inter-marriage took place within occupational and social groups, irrespective of the effect of geographical

Table 9.5 Occupational group and marriage distances 1863–1970, all sample *communes*

		1863–67	1903–07	1933–37	1966–70
Percentage of marriages where groom in non-agricultural occupation		22.30	36.47	46.18	89.53
Percentage marriages within *commune*	(a)	52.82	43.97	40.69	26.61
	(b)	48.69	31.12	27.82	14.91
Percentage 'local' marriages 0–50 km	(a)	45.37	51.16	50.83	66.94
	(b)	39.17	40.26	40.53	55.47
Percentage marriages over 50 km	(a)	1.81	4.87	8.47	6.45
	(b)	12.14	28.62	31.85	29.62

(a)=agricultural population; (b)=non-agricultural population.

A.   ALL MARRIAGES

B.   LOCAL EXOGAMOUS MARRIAGES

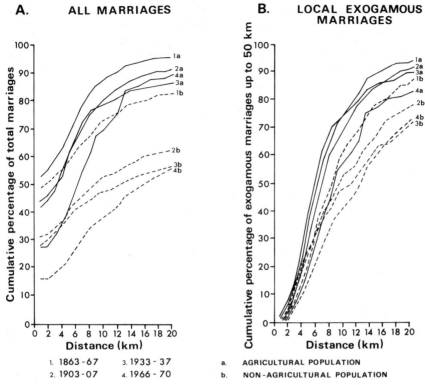

Fig. 9.12 Cumulative percentage frequency of marriage distances by occupation, sample *communes* of Ardèche.

distance. Clearly, valuable indications may be obtained by matching the occupation of the groom with that of the bride's father. It is possible, for example, to reconstruct the degree of inter-marriage among artisans, shop-keepers or minor industrialists in the mid-nineteenth-century villages and to see how these patterns were affected by subsequent change. One aspect is selected here for comment, that of the changing role of the peasant groups themselves.

From the point of view of the other crafts and occupations there has been a decline in their distinctiveness, and clear examples of occupational inter-marriage become rather less obvious. The case of agriculture, however, has become more, rather than less, distinctive over the century. The pursuit of an agricultural occupation very often brings with it both at national and at local scales the risk of remaining unmarried. As early as the 1860s there is clear evidence to suggest an increasing tendency for girls to marry out of agriculture. An analysis of marriages for the sample *communes* for 1863–67 shows that while there were frequent examples of men exercising a wide range of occupations marrying the daughters of farmers, there were rather fewer instances of farmers taking as brides daughters from other groups.

This growing isolation of the farming community has been accentuated as the impact of migration has made itself felt with particular severity on the agricultural sector. Celibacy rates for the study areas amply reflect the disaffection with farming as a way of life (Ogden, 1973; Jegouzo, 1972; Jegouzo and Brangeon, 1974). A brief look at the marriage of peasant farmers between

1966 and 1970 shows that over 70 per cent of those who did marry married the daughters of farmers, a particularly high figure in view of the generally diminishing size of the agricultural community. Moreover, of the remainder there is a clear predominance of occupations of brides' fathers which lie towards the lower end of the social spectrum. For example, as well as those who married into families in activities directly related to agriculture (such as cattle dealers or foresters), the occupations most represented are *ouvriers* of various kinds – transport workers, joiners, factory workers and building workers. Many of the latter are of course but one generation removed from the land. By contrast, a similar analysis of the marital fortunes of the daughters of peasant farmers for the same period shows that a very small proportion married farmers. Of 412 brides whose fathers worked the land, only 63 (15.3 per cent) married a farmer. This is partly because out-migration has brought about a certain decline in the 'supply' of farmers, but more especially, and this seems the more evident when one bears in mind the very high levels of male celibacy in the agricultural population, a lack of demand from girls to marry into agriculture. This represents a clear avoidance by women of marrying into the peasant life, rather than the avoidance of any particular class or social group. This is indeed what Jegouzo (1972) has referred to as 'professional exogamy' within a general system of 'social homogamy': that is to say that women do not refuse to marry men of agricultural origin but simply those among them who still work the land. It is, therefore, not so much a symptom of upward social mobility as of a clear repudiation of the peasant way of life. This has consequences for the general marriage pattern, for it not only implies that women may feel obliged to search further afield for a marriage partner, but also that the high levels of male celibacy in the agricultural population are at least in part attributable to this cause. One may add, therefore, a certain element of isolation by occupation to the general picture of an agricultural population severely isolated by geographical distance.

Conclusions

Evidence presented in this chapter has underlined the complexity of patterns of migration and social contact associated with rural change in France over the last century. Migration itself has had a marked geographical effect on social and economic structures as the peasant economy collapsed, regional cultures disintegrated and the grip of the cities tightened. At the broadest level the discussion here has helped to elucidate for one particular case the way in which modern France was moulded from a mass of distinctive regional peasant societies. The emphasis of this study on mobility and marriage and on the use of particular sources is, of course, only one of many approaches to the same problem. In general, migration and changes in levels of personal mobility are but a reflection of more profound changes in economic structures and need to be seen in the broad context of French social change over the century. The aim here has been to provide a detailed view of the changing extent of mobility, of the nature of rural isolation in the nineteenth century and of the pace and extent of its erosion. In using marriage distance as a specific indicator of change it has in addition sought to contribute to the understanding of the role of marriage *per se* in bringing links between communities and to point to some of the implications of such an approach for interpreting, for example, demographic change or the interplay of social and spatial mobility.

A number of specific conclusions follow from the research material presented in this chapter. First, it is clear that although the extent and impact of rural depopulation in the department of Ardèche, selected for special study here, have been very pronounced, Ardèche is not unrepresentative of trends in the French countryside as a whole since the mid-nineteenth century. The pace of change has, of course, varied considerably from region to region. Although the most profound changes have come only since the end of the First World War and, indeed, in some cases only since 1945, there is no doubt that migration from the countryside was important long before net population loss made itself felt. Thus, as Fig. 9.5 has shown for the Ardèche, the effects of out-migration were masked for several decades in the nineteenth century by a continuing surplus of births over deaths. Certainly the volume of migration and the range of destinations of migrants were among the most important influences leading to the breakdown of rural isolation.

Secondly, the detailed study of the extent of permanent movement into the sample *communes* pointed to the high degree of local population flux even in a context of severe rural depopulation, and largely refuted the notion that population loss took place against a backcloth of immobility in the traditional economy. Although the great majority of this movement was over short distances, birth-place information does show how deeply local movement affected the 'residual' populations and proved a useful method of looking at the cumulative effect of several generations of movement for marriage and for other purposes.

Thirdly, the analysis of marriage distance provided a useful measure both of the nature of the marriage pattern itself and of the general impact of profound change on the spatial pattern of social contacts and information flow. It was clear that in the 1860s, although mobility over long distances was certainly fostered for some members of the community by factors as diverse as seasonal migration or the existence of local industry, for the majority movement for marriage was limited to very narrow horizons. The erosion of this relative isolation over the century was not, though, a simple matter of the gradual spread of contacts over surrounding areas in response to the decline of the village or to improved communications. In dividing the marriage field into local marriages (less than 50 kilometres) and long-distance contacts it became clear that the former scarcely changed, and indeed in some cases actually contracted, up to the Second World War. This stagnation or contraction of the spatial extent of local contacts defined simply in terms of geographical distance was reinforced by the measures of 'neighbourhood population size' within which interaction took place. The results were eloquent illustration of the way in which depopulation gradually eroded the formerly close mesh of social contacts between villages as the peasant economy decayed. Real expansion of this 'local' field of marriage movement came only after 1945. By far the most significant change throughout the period was the rapid increase in contact with urban centres throughout France. Marriage was seen to be both an accurate indicator of the extent to which migrants retained contact with their areas of origin and was, in its own right, a contributor to out-migration. For the majority of girls, marrying a man from outside the department meant that they subsequently migrated themselves.

Lastly, it was shown that the spatial extent of social contact was much influenced by occupational group. At all periods the peasant population was less mobile than those employed outside agriculture and marriage partners were sought over a much narrower range. The peasant groups became, in a sense, more and more distinctive over time, for as their numbers declined the trend among the young has been resolutely against marrying into the peasant life, creating high levels of celibacy among the remaining male agricultural population.

In general terms, therefore, the analysis has shown how a century of change and a continuous flow of migrants from the area have so affected economic and social structures as to create a very different pattern of marriage, information flow and social contact in the 1960s and 1970s compared to that of a century before.

Notes

1. The usual French census definition of 'rural' is of any *commune* in which less than 2,000 people live in the chief settlement: this definition has varied from time to time.
2. The sample *communes* numbered 70 in 1863 but 75 by 1968 because of sub-division.
3. Only the first recorded place of residence after birth is used here. The major disadvantages in the use of these data are listed in, for example, Pitié, 1971, and Merlin, 1971. They include the fact that only the migration of voters is covered; that much depends on re-registration which is not compulsory; that they thus cover only a small percentage of total migrants; and that no date of migration is given.
4. The manipulation of figures in this way needs to be done with care. This conclusion may be an oversimplification for the fact that both partners were born outside the *commune* does not necessarily mean that they moved in together: they could, for example, have come independently as children. But, despite disadvantages, it is a convenient measure for disaggregated overall levels of mobility.
5. Based on only eight *communes* because of the enormous task of collating data for each of the 130 years illustrated.
6. A negative exponential function has been fitted to the data in the form $\log y = \log a - bD$, where y is a measure of marriage frequency and D is distance (see Taylor, 1975, for a discussion of this function). A double-log function was also fitted but proved less satisfactory. The y-axes in Figs 9.10A and 9.10B are identical; but in Fig. 9.10B the x-axis has been transformed to take account of different population densities at each of the four periods. The y-axes show the absolute number of marriages per square kilometre for successive bands away from the place of origin, thus standardizing the data to take account of the increasing area within each successive band: these standardized values were then transformed by conversion to logarithms. In Fig. 9.10A the x-axis shows the mid-point of the distance band of successive rings from the place of origin. In Fig. 9.10B the average population density figures shown in Table 9.4 have been used, for each period in turn, to convert the x-axis from a measure of distance to a measure of population at distance, distance and population size being assumed to be perfectly correlated. Hence the correlation coefficients shown in Table 9.4 remain the same for both sets of regression analyses, the different ordering of the regression lines between Figs 9.10A and 9.10B being brought about solely by changes in average population density over time.
7. Other more complex methods of approaching the same problem are discussed in Harrison and Boyce (1972) and Ogden (1973).
8. It is difficult to be sure to what extent population density is itself important in determining the location of marriage contacts once a certain minimum threshold level is attained. The purpose here is to provide a complementary interpretation of the extent of contact fields, not to suggest any relationship between the marriage pattern and population size.

Acknowledgements

I am grateful to the Zaharoff Bequest (University of Oxford) and the French Government for financial assistance, and to Jean Gottmann, Theodore Zeldin and Jacques Bethemont for valuable guidance. I am indebted also to the departmental archivist in the Ardèche, the directors of INSEE in Lyon and Paris and the staff of the *Tribunal de Grande Instance* in the Ardèche for allowing me access to information.

Chapter 10

Migration and social segregation in Birmingham and the West Midlands Region

R. I. Woods

Two of the aims of role-playing *Homo sociologicus* are to avoid contact with his social inferiors and to promote contact with his peers. This he achieves in a number of ways: for instance by choosing his friends in a certain way; by restricting the activities of his children, and thereby influencing their potential marriage partners; and by selecting a dwelling in an area where a large number of his peer-group already live. This last-mentioned aspect leads to the spatial concentration of certain social groups in some towns rather than others, in particular parts of urban areas, and in certain rural areas. The process of residential social segregation is closely linked with selective migration which can both create new concentrations of social groups and maintain pre-existing patterns.

Clearly, this initial outline is too simple because not all social groups are able to choose where they wish to live; many groups are constrained by economic and social pressures to reside in a restricted number of areas. Property developers, planners, local housing authorities, and financial institutions, such as building societies, also have an important influence in promoting and perpetuating residential social segregation over and above the aims and objectives of the individual. For some social groups, however, particularly the élite, there is a considerable range of choice. The spatial concentration of this group in certain neighbourhoods and its migration to new or similar districts will determine the location of the high-status residential areas. Other less economically or politically influential groups will then be left to limit their activities to those areas which remain once the élite has made its choice (Speare, *et al.*, 1974).

In this chapter it is intended to examine the relationship between migration and social segregation, to explore the impact of selective migration on the spatial separation of social classes, and to suggest how new high status residential areas are established and old ones abandoned. The period of study is largely that since the Second World War and the location is Birmingham and the West Midlands Region.[1]

The study is divided into three parts. The first deals with the definition of social segregation and the nature of the relationship it has with migration. The second part will be used to show the existence of social segregation in general in Birmingham and the West Midlands Region at a variety of scales, dealing particularly with the spatial concentration of the élite group. The third part will attempt to link the pattern of segregation with intra-urban and urban–rural migration and by so doing illustrate the impact of intra-regional migration as an initiator and perpetuator of segregation.

Segregation and migration

The term 'segregation', like the terms 'class', 'status' and 'discrimination', poses very difficult definitional problems. The word implies separation, being apart, isolated. Not only does it reflect a state of affairs, but it also indicates movement; segregation is a process. As a technical term segregation is used with different emphasis by sociologists and geographers. The former stress the connotation of social isolation; the exclusion from membership of organizations, families, clubs and so forth; even the lack of political representation. Geographers, on the other hand, emphasize the aspect of spatial separation, the clustering of individuals and groups in certain areas. Both of these approaches beg the question of whether segregation occurs because the members of a group wish to isolate or separate themselves or are forced to do so by the pressure of non-members.

Blalock (1967, p. 15) has argued that segregation can be used to assess the extent of discrimination: that while the former is measurable the latter cannot be directly quantified. However, this view raises at least one difficulty, as R. Brown (1973, p. 11), has pointed out. It is important to know whether segregation, in the spatial sense, has been produced and maintained by discriminatory practices or whether it is merely geographical clustering. Most geographers take a pragmatic view on this problem: 'as a working hypothesis, it can be assumed that the degree of dispersal or segregation of the minority group along the spectrum from complete similarity with the host community at one end to complete segregation at the other, is an index of social integration' (Peach, 1968, p. 83, referring to West Indians in Britain).

The position taken in this chapter is that discrimination leads to social isolation; that one aspect of that isolation is usually spatial separation; and that spatial separation does not necessarily mean social isolation. Nor does spatial mixing imply social integration, but rather the degree of social isolation and spatial separation are significantly and positively correlated, but not perfectly so. Spatial separation will be used to assess social isolation, but not the level of discrimination.

Taking this view means that segregation, through spatial separation, can be measured. The index of dissimilarity (ID) and the index of segregation (IS) both compare the conformity of the distribution of two population groups among a set of areas (Duncan and Duncan, 1955a): ID deals with non-overlapping groups and IS with overlapping ones. They may be defined thus:

$$ID_{xy} = 0.5 \sum_{i=1}^{n} \left| \frac{x_i \cdot 100}{\sum_{i=1}^{n} x_i} - \frac{y_i \cdot 100}{\sum_{i=1}^{n} y_i} \right|, \tag{10.1}$$

and

$$IS_{ty} = \frac{ID_{ty}}{1 - \frac{\sum_{i=1}^{n} y_i}{\sum_{i=1}^{n} t_i}}, \tag{10.2}$$

where x_i = a population group x occurring in area i,
   y_i = a population group y occurring in area i,
   t_i = the total population of area i,
   x and y are mutually exclusive groups,
   n = the total number of areas in the spatial system (i = 1, 2, 3, ... , n).

Both ID and IS range from 0 to 100 – from complete distributional conformity to complete separation. By using these indices one can measure the degree to which the distributions of pairs of population groups are matched over a set of areas. If an ID equals 80, for instance, it means that there is a high level of spatial separation and thus, perhaps, a similarly high level of social isolation between the two population groups. However, it is important to recognize the disturbing effect that the spatial arrangement and the number of areas in the spatial system can have on both indices (Woods, 1976).

The relationship between segregation and migration, particularly intra-urban migration, has been examined by a large number of sociologists and geographers. Three aspects have proved of major significance. Firstly, the notion of 'place utility' is important in the understanding of how potential migrants perceive their current environment, of how they react to that environment (possibly by leaving it), and how they perceive the relative advantages of potential destinations (Rossi, 1955; Brown and Longbrake, 1970; Horton and Reynolds, 1971). Secondly, migration streams appear to be sectorally biased and take place from one residential area to a set of other areas further out from the centre of the urban area but within a narrow wedge (Adams, J. S., 1969; Johnston, 1972). Thirdly, migration is age and class selective and therefore can lead to changes in both the demography and the social structure at origin and destination (Schnore, 1964; Taeuber and Taeuber, 1964; Goldstein and Mayer, 1965; Johnston, 1966; Simmons, 1968): in particular, age selectivity works through the variable of 'stage in the life-cycle' to make young married couples and the newly retired, for instance, more mobile than other groups (Robson, 1973, p. 229). These three aspects have proved important in the case of American, Canadian, Australian and New Zealand cities, but their significance has been little discussed at the regional scale and with particular reference to the British case (Herbert, 1973). The study reported here seeks to extend the scale of analysis and to focus attention on an example in Britain.

Social segregation in Birmingham and the West Midlands Region

Since the Second World War the population of Birmingham has declined (1951 – 1,114,000; 1961 – 1,111,000; 1971 – 1,015,000) while that of the region as a whole has increased (1951 – 4,423,000; 1961 – 4,758,000; 1971 – 5,110,000); the population decline in Birmingham is partly the result of intra-regional movement. The city has experienced massive redevelopment schemes which have transformed the inner areas and some of the outer suburbs, while the region has seen rapid expansion of many of the small towns within commuting distance of the conurbation (Sutcliffe and Smith, 1974; Joyce, 1977; Lambert *et al.*, 1978). Within this context of central decline and peripheral growth, a pattern typical of other British regions and particularly the South East and North West, social segregation has been perpetuated and even strengthened at both the urban and regional scales.

This observation may be demonstrated by using evidence from the 1961 and 1971 population censuses of England and Wales. Since the 1911 census Registrars-General have attempted to combine occupation groups to create five social classes and, more recently, 17 socio-economic groups (S.E.G.s). Further, since the 1961 census small area enumeration district (E.D.) data has been made available for British cities. Birmingham was divided into some 1,200 E.D.s in

1961, 2,000 in 1971. Although the E.D.s were thus not common to both censuses it is possible to group them and thereby form a set of 484 amalgamated areas which permit the comparison of results for 1961 and 1971. The specially tabulated enumeration district data for the 1961 census provided information on S.E.G.s, but the 17 groups were combined into six categories (referred to here as categories A to F). These combinations are shown in Table 10.1. Although the 1971 census gave enumeration district data on all 17 S.E.G.s they have also been combined into the six categories for comparison with 1961.

Table 10.1 Combinations of socio-economic groups (S.E.G.s)

Categories	S.E.G.s	Description
A	3, 4	Professional workers – self-employed and employees
B	1, 2, 13	Managers, employers, farmers
C	5, 6	Intermediate non-manual, junior non-manual workers
D	8, 9, 12, 14	Foremen, skilled manual workers
E	7, 10, 15	Personal service, semi-skilled and agricultural workers
F	11, 16, 17	Unskilled manual, armed forces, unclassified workers

The same six categories have been used to classify occupational data for the local authorities in the West Midlands Region. In 1961 the region was divided into 121 areas and in 1971, after some local government reorganization, 93 areas were in use (the most important local authorities are shown in Fig. 10.1 for 1971). These two sets of areas are not strictly comparable in the same way that the amalgamated areas are, but they can be used as frameworks for the analysis of the distribution of social groups at particular points in time. Table 10.2 shows the number of economically active and retired males in the six categories defined in

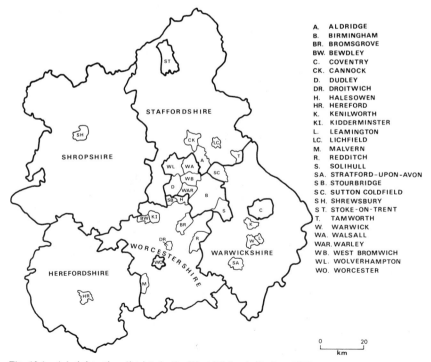

A.   ALDRIDGE
B.   BIRMINGHAM
BR. BROMSGROVE
BW. BEWDLEY
C.   COVENTRY
CK. CANNOCK
D.   DUDLEY
DR. DROITWICH
H.   HALESOWEN
HR. HEREFORD
K.   KENILWORTH
KI. KIDDERMINSTER
L.   LEAMINGTON
LC. LICHFIELD
M.   MALVERN
R.   REDDITCH
S.   SOLIHULL
SA. STRATFORD-UPON-AVON
SB. STOURBRIDGE
SC. SUTTON COLDFIELD
SH. SHREWSBURY
ST. STOKE-ON-TRENT
T.   TAMWORTH
W.   WARWICK
WA. WALSALL
WAR. WARLEY
WB. WEST BROMWICH
WL. WOLVERHAMPTON
WO. WORCESTER

Fig. 10.1 Administrative districts in the West Midlands Region, 1971.

Table 10.2 Economically active and retired males in six social categories, Birmingham and the West Midlands Region, 1961 and 1971 (10 per cent samples).

Social categories	Birmingham				West Midlands Region			
	1961		1971		1961		1971	
	No.	Per cent	No.	Per cent	No.	Per cent	No.	Per cent
A	1,061	2.91	1,031	3.29	5,530	3.51	6,891	4.37
B	2,492	6.84	2,436	7.76	14,522	9.22	17,567	11.15
C	5,153	14.15	4,567	14.56	21,452	13.62	23,338	14.82
D	16,641	45.69	13,429	42.80	70,361	44.68	68,148	43.26
E	6,981	19.17	6,304	20.09	29,413	18.68	26,859	17.05
F	4,096	11.25	3,606	11.49	16,213	10.29	14,719	9.34
Total	36,424		31,373		157,491		157,522	

Data source: Population Censuses of England and Wales, 1961 and 1971.

Table 10.1 for Birmingham and the West Midlands Region in 1961 and 1971. Although the overall distribution was similar between time periods and between the two spatial scales, with over 40 per cent of the economically active and retired males in the skilled manual category of occupations (category D), Birmingham's overall share of the total declined from 23.1 to 19.9 per cent between 1961 and 1971.

Indices of dissimilarity and segregation may be calculated for the 484 amalgamated areas for Birmingham, and for the 121 and 93 local authority areas (including Birmingham) into which the West Midlands Region was divided in 1961 and 1971 respectively, in order to measure the degree of segregation, in the sense of spatial separation, that existed between the six categories of S.E.G.s. These indices are shown in Table 10.3. In both Birmingham and the West

Table 10.3 Indices of dissimilarity and segregation for social categories, Birmingham and the West Midlands Region, 1961 and 1971

Indices of dissimilarity, Birmingham*

Social categories		1971 A	B	C	D	E	F
1961	A	–	33.63	38.74	53.51	52.76	63.22
	B	36.95	–	20.69	33.29	35.07	46.33
	C	41.97	26.72	–	21.41	25.36	37.64
	D	52.64	38.51	25.81	–	21.30	24.02
	E	56.16	43.95	31.35	15.34	–	32.23
	F	59.44	47.82	38.72	24.41	23.60	–

Indices of segregation, Birmingham*

	A	B	C	D	E	F
1961	48.99	35.88	24.94	15.13	18.26	25.91
1971	48.76	36.45	24.75	14.21	18.04	27.28

Indices of segregation, West Midlands Region†

	A	B	C	D	E	F
1961	43.20	46.97	26.95	26.75	22.96	30.94
1971	37.32	41.29	18.29	21.98	25.77	27.79

*Based on 484 amalgamated areas.
†Based on 121 local authority areas for 1961, 93 local authority areas for 1971.
Data source: Population Censuses of England and Wales, 1961 and 1971, special tabulations.

Midlands Region in both 1961 and 1971 the same patterns of social segregation occurred. Professionals, managers and employers (categories A and B) were the most spatially separated occupational groups, although in the region category A members were less segregated than were those of category B. Further, the reversed J-shaped curve which reflects the higher segregation of persons in the extremes of the social class hierarchy, and which was identified by Duncan and Duncan (1955b) in the 1950s, is clearly in evidence. Figure 10.2 shows four of these reversed J-shaped curves.

The indices of segregation show that in Birmingham there has been only a slight change in social segregation between 1961 and 1971, although the matrix of indices of dissimilarity between categories does reveal some more substantial changes, for example between categories A and F. The number of persons in each category clearly influences the potential for separation, but Birmingham and the West Midlands Region do seem to represent, nonetheless, the typical pattern of social class segregation to be found in America and Australasia (Peach, 1975).

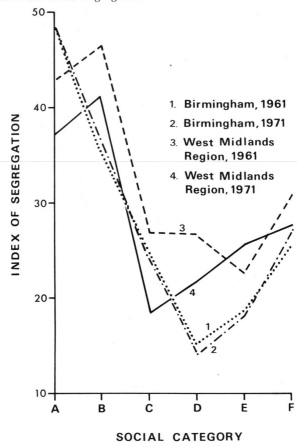

Fig. 10.2 Indices of segregation for social categories, Birmingham and the West Midlands Region, 1961 and 1971.
Data source: Population Censuses of England and Wales, 1961 and 1971, special tabulations.

The measures presented in Table 10.3 and illustrated in Fig. 10.2 give an impression of the magnitude of segregation, but they need to be supplemented by analysis of the changing distribution of social groups in residential space. In this context only categories A and B will be considered in any depth for it is largely from those census-defined groups that the élite of Birmingham society is drawn. Figure 10.3 shows the spatial concentration of members of social category A in Birmingham in 1961 and 1971 by amalgamated areas. The distribution has a very clear bias towards the south and particularly the south-west of the city centre – that is in Edgbaston, Harborne, Selly Oak, Quinton, Moseley, King's Heath and Hall Green wards. To the north of the city centre there are concentrations in Handsworth Wood (Sandwell ward), Erdington and Washwood Heath.

The first-mentioned area, Edgbaston, was developed and has been preserved as a high-status residential area by the Calthorpe Estate Trust (Giles, 1976). The trust's policy has been to maintain the area in low-density housing and to ensure the quality of building standards. Because of this the area has been preserved as a very desirable residential neighbourhood despite its proximity to the city centre whilst other areas, parts of Harborne and Moseley for instance, have recently

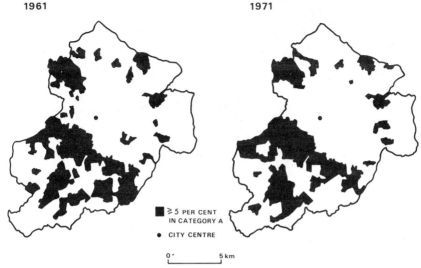

Fig. 10.3 Percentage economically active and retired males in social category A, Birmingham, 1961 and 1971 (amalgamated areas).
Data source: Population Censuses of England and Wales, 1961 and 1971, special tabulations.

become the scene of the multi-occupation of dwellings where many of the larger Victorian houses have been converted into flats. The residential desirability of these areas for the social élite has therefore diminished, although the influence on the concentration of such social groups is not fully reflected by Fig. 10.3 which merely deals with the crude distribution by amalgamated areas.

Changes have also taken place at the regional scale. Figure 10.4 shows the percentage concentration of those in category A and category B (see Table 10.1) in 1961 and 1971 by the 121 and 93 local authority areas, respectively, in the West Midlands Region. Figure 10.4 suggests that a number of observations are valid. Firstly, only in a very small number of local authorities did category A groups (professionals) represent a substantial proportion (over 9 per cent) in either year. Those areas were Sutton Coldfield and Solihull, to the immediate north-east and south-east of Birmingham respectively; Kenilworth, to the south of Coventry; Malvern, in Worcestershire; and Church Stretton, in Shropshire. The last two of these are retirement areas while the first three are suburban dormitory towns for Birmingham and Coventry. Secondly, there is clearly a desirable residential area for members of both category A and B to the west, south-west and south of the West Midlands Conurbation, that is in south-west Staffordshire, north-east Worcestershire and north-west Warwickshire. These areas are the major ones for the concentration of those in category B (managers and employers). Thirdly, despite boundary changes, the Worcestershire–Warwickshire belt appears to have become even better established in the 1960s while the differences between the south-western edge and the north-eastern edge of the conurbation have been perpetuated, and perhaps even widened during the decade.

The analysis of data derived from population censuses shows that in Birmingham and the West Midlands Region as a whole segregation by social class is quite distinctive. Further, those in professional and managerial categories of occupations have tended to live in certain areas in Birmingham and the region

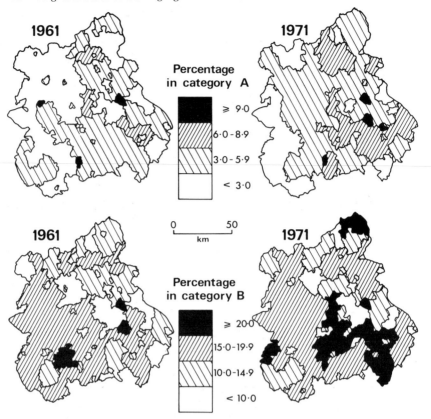

Fig. 10.4 Percentage economically active and retired males in social category A and social category B, West Midlands Region, 1961 and 1971 (administrative districts).
Data source: Population Censuses of England and Wales, 1961 and 1971, special tabulations.

– areas which are mainly to the south of the city centre and to the south of the conurbation respectively. Certainly there are exceptions to this generalization, but both the pattern and the trend are clear.

Further analysis is restricted by the limitations of census data. For example, it is impossible to use British census data to show the intra-local authority pattern of migration; similarly, data on migrations between local authorities does not provide detailed comparative information on occupations and thus on social class. For these reasons any empirical analysis of the association between migration and social segregation must employ special and alternative sources of data, such as local 'Who's Who' listings. Birmingham is fortunate in this particular respect because a local firm of booksellers, Cornish Brothers, began to publish a 'Who's Who' list for the city shortly after the First World War. This function was taken over by the *Birmingham Post and Mail* newspaper organization after the Second World War. Thus, for the years 1920, 1930, 1940, 1950, 1960 and 1970 lists of the local élite are available in the form of 'Who's Who' directories.

'Who's Who' listings offer opportunities, but they also have drawbacks. For instance, it can never be established which criteria the compilers used to select the notables to be included. Leaders of the local community are generally those involved; whether they are businessmen, professionals, politicians or those who have established their fame by other means, such as sportsmen. On the other hand the opportunities afforded by these sources are obvious: they give addresses, occupations, ages, educational backgrounds of individuals and, by comparing lists, allow one to establish who has, or has not, moved residence during a period of time.

In this instance the Birmingham 'Who's Who' lists were used to establish precisely which areas were the high status ones in 1920, 1930, 1940, 1950, 1960 and 1970; and to show how residential migration occurred in the decades 1950–60 and 1960–70 by comparing the 1950, 1960 and 1970 lists. Figure 10.5 shows the distribution of those areas which had more than or equal to 0.5 per cent of the total 'Who's Who' list living in Birmingham, Sutton Coldfield and Solihull (i.e. 153 in 1920; 224 in 1930; 316 in 1940; 848 in 1950; 1,164 in 1960; and 1,155 in 1970).[2] The shaded areas are made up of 500 metre squares each of which has more than or equal to 0.5 per cent of a particular year's total list.

These six cross-sections reveal that the relative distribution of Birmingham's social élite has both contracted and expanded within the continuous built-up area of the West Midlands Conurbation. In the north of Birmingham the élite has withdrawn from parts of Handsworth and Erdington, while the same could be said of Moseley to the south of the city centre. However, Sutton Coldfield to the north-east, and Solihull, to the south-east, have both experienced relative and absolute growth in importance. Edgbaston still remains one of the most important high status residential areas.

Figure 10.5 complements Fig. 10.3, but allows longer temporal comparison and provides a means of locating precisely the residences of those in the local social élite. With Fig. 10.4 and Table 10.3 they show how social groups are spatially separated (Table 10.3) and how at the urban and regional scales the pattern of segregation takes on a spatial connotation with the concentration of élite groups in only a small number of residential areas where they represent if not a majority then at least a significant minority. How has intra-urban and intra-regional migration created or sustained this pattern?

Officers to the south; men to the north

The 'Who's Who' listings from the *Birmingham Post and Mail Year Books* for 1950, 1960 and 1970 can be employed to show the pattern of movements in 1950–60 and 1960–70 by establishing lists of those included in both 1950 and 1960 and those included in both 1960 and 1970, and then by creating two additional lists of movers 1950–60 and 1960–70. These two movement patterns will be considered here at three different scales – within the conurbation; between the conurbation and the remainder of the region; and between the region and other regions in England and Wales. Table 10.4 gives the number of moves involved at these scales. Of the 731 and 840 matching entries in 1950–60 and 1960–70, 33.5 and 34.4 per cent respectively changed residences; 57.6 and 61.6 per cent of the moves were within the West Midlands Conurbation, effectively Birmingham, Sutton Coldfield and Solihull; 24.5 and 27.0 per cent respectively were moves between the conurbation and the rest of the West Midlands Region. Although turnover rates remained similar in the 1950s and 1960s, the percentage moving

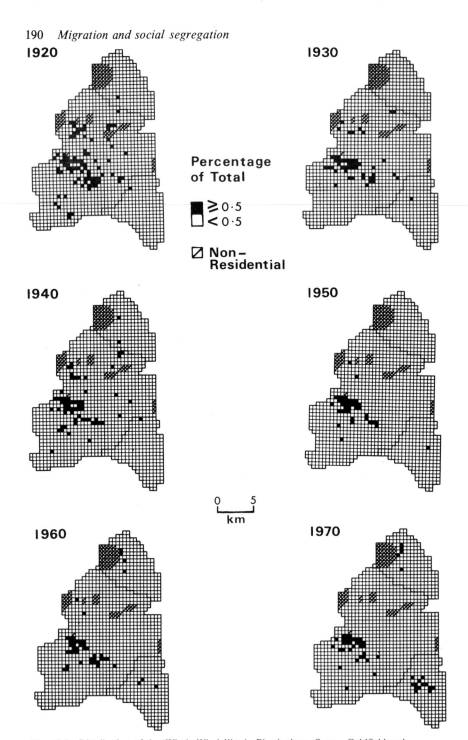

Fig. 10.5 Distribution of the 'Who's Who' élite in Birmingham, Sutton Coldfield and Solihull.
Data source: Cornish Brothers' Year Books and *Birmingham Post and Mail Year Books.*

Table 10.4   Analysis of the 'Who's Who' lists for Birmingham, 1950, 1960 and 1970

		1950–60	1960–70
	Matching entries*	731	840
Of whom:	Movers	245	289
Of whom:	Movers within the conurbation	141	178
	Conurbation-region movers†	60	78
	Movers between the region and the rest of England and Wales‡	44	33

*All those occurring on the lists of both years considered.
†Movement between the conurbation and the rest of the West Midlands Region outside the conurbation. Also includes moves within the region.
‡Also includes moves between regions other than the West Midlands.
Data source; Birmingham Post and Mail Year Books for 1950, 1960 and 1970.

within the conurbation and between the conurbation and the region was higher in the latter decade.

The pattern of intra-urban migration within the conurbation is shown in Fig. 10.6. Most of the moves were of very short distance, often within the same high-status residential area whether Edgbaston, Sutton Coldfield or Solihull. Double-log regression equations can be fitted to the relationship between interaction (I)

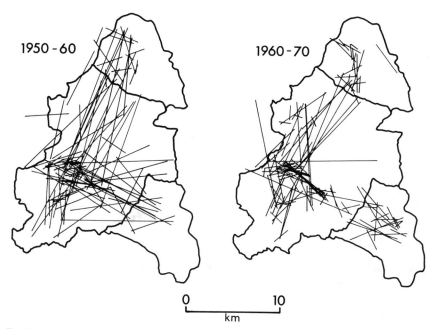

Fig. 10.6   Intra-urban migration of the 'Who's Who' élite in Birmingham, Sutton Coldfield and Solihull, 1950–60 and 1960–70.
Data source: Birmingham Post and Mail Year Books.

and distance (D) to summarize the changing influence of distance on migration during the 1950s and 1960s.[3] These equations are:

1950–60 $\log I = 0.2939 - 1.5756 \log D$,
1960–70 $\log I = 0.4895 - 1.8957 \log D$.

They show that the slope of the regression line steepened from one decade to the next and thus that more moves were taking place over shorter distances (the regression equations only apply to moves of less than 20 kilometres).

The impression created by Fig. 10.6 and the regression equations is one of contraction – moves increasingly occurring within rather than between high status neighbourhoods – and of the abandonment of some former high status areas. There is little sign of strong sectoral bias occurring at this scale, at least among the élite. At the regional scale, however, sectoral bias is perhaps the most important aspect of the movement pattern. Figure 10.7 shows the origins and

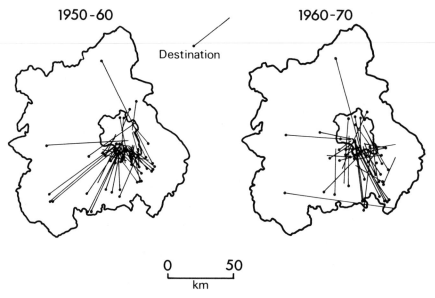

Fig. 10.7   Intra-regional migration of the 'Who's Who' élite in the West Midlands Region, 1950–60 and 1960–70.
Data source: Birmingham Post and Mail Year Books.

destinations of movers between the conurbation and the region in 1950–60 and 1960–70. Most of the destinations lie in western Warwickshire and eastern Worcestershire to the south of the conurbation. Many are small commuter villages (Belbroughton, Alcester, Barnt Green, Henley-in-Arden, Hampton-in-Arden for instance), but others are small towns (Bewdley, Kidderminster, Bromsgrove, Droitwich, Stratford-upon-Avon, Warwick, Kenilworth). Certainly there are few moves from the Birmingham–Sutton Coldfield–Solihull part of the conurbation to Staffordshire and the northern part of the region in general. The regional pattern of élite migration both reflects and helps to reinforce the structure of social segregation at that scale and the spatial concentration of those in professional and managerial occupations in a small number of specific residential areas. This point may be illustrated by comparing Figs 10.4 and 10.7.

Migration between the West Midlands Region and the remainder of England and Wales is shown in Fig. 10.8. Once again the southward stream of movement is quite pronounced. The South Coast towns, London and the Home Counties, and those counties adjacent to the southern edge of the West Midlands Region are the most important destinations for élite migrants.

Why does migration occur to create the form of pattern illustrated in Figs 10.6, 10.7 and 10.8? Naturally this question cannot be answered in full, but

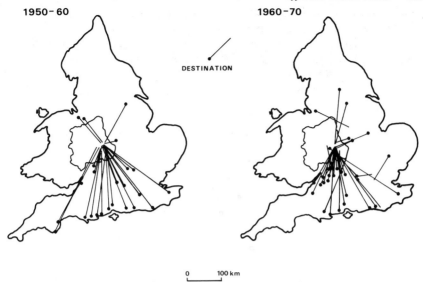

Fig. 10.8 Migration between the West Midlands Region and the remainder of England and Wales of the 'Who's Who' élite, 1950–60 and 1960–70.
Data source: Birmingham Post and Mail Year Books.

certain relationships can be suggested. It is possible that much of the long-distance migration is associated with either change of employment or retirement. The former has been discussed by Hart (1970) and by Johnson *et al.* (1974) among others and will not be dealt with here. However, retirement, and stage in the life-cycle in general, can be considered in some detail with the aid of the 'Who's Who' listings.

Of those 840 matching entries (see Table 10.4) in the 1960 and 1970 lists, 781 give information on age, and of the entries for the 289 movers 282 do so. Age-specific probabilities of migration in the ten-year period 1960–70 can be calculated using this data. These probabilities are shown in Fig. 10.9 graphed

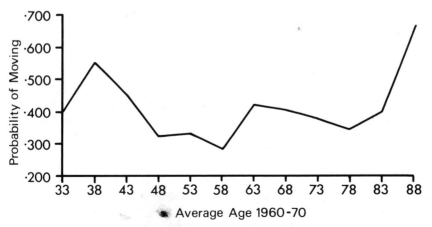

Fig. 10.9 Age-specific probabilities of members of the 'Who's Who' élite migrating in the period 1960–70.
Data source: Birmingham Post and Mail Year Books.

against the average ages of members of the élite group in the 1960s. If stage in the life-cycle were to have a significant bearing on the probability of becoming a migrant then one would expect to find that certain age-groups were more mobile than others. The 30s, early 60s and 80s would correspond quite well with expected mobile ages, although the last-mentioned is likely to be of negligible significance in terms of absolute numbers moving. Early career and retirement migration are phenomena which have often been observed. However, the data used to construct Fig. 10.9 may be analysed more rigorously. A null hypothesis was set up: that there was no significant difference between the age structure of movers and those in the total matched entries list for 1960–70. The null hypothesis was accepted at the 0.01 level of significance after testing with the Kolmogorov-Smirnov one-sample two-tailed significance test (Siegel, 1956, p. 47). There is no significant difference between the ages of movers and those in the total list of movers and stayers; movers are a random sample of those in the total list in terms of age structure. On the statistical evidence, therefore, there would seem little reason to interpret élite migration in Birmingham and the West Midlands Region in the light of stage of life-cycle models, although this conclusion does belie the visual impression created by Fig. 10.9, which is perhaps the result of small sample sizes in both younger and older age-groups.

Why do the captains of industry appear only to migrate southwards when they leave the conurbation? A number of factors are important in answering this question, some of which create arguments of the classic 'chicken and egg' variety. One of the aims of this study has been to illustrate the reinforcing impact that socially selective migration can have in perpetuating, or even sharpening, social segregation. In the context of the West Midlands Region social segregation already existed in the 1950s, but it has been strengthened by the movement of the élite and other members of similar social groups. The north Worcestershire and north-west Warwickshire area has become a high status residential area by a cumulative process of self-selection and migration.

How did the initial emphasis occur? One important aspect seems to have been the very concentration of high-status residential areas to the south of the city centre in Birmingham, in Edgbaston particularly, and more recently in Solihull. The sectoral bias of residential search behaviour could therefore have operated at the regional scale, although not at the intra-urban, to generate migration to the north Worcestershire and north–west Warwickshire area. However, this particular point cannot be fully substantiated without the aid of survey research in each particular destination area (see Pahl, 1965; 1970a, pp. 69–111).

A second important aspect is that of the attitudes of local authorities in the region. The administrative counties of Shropshire, Warwickshire, Herefordshire and Worcestershire (now Hereford and Worcester) have tended to defend their rural–agricultural image both in and beyond the conurbation's 'green belt'. By contrast, Birmingham, Coventry, Stoke-on-Trent, Wolverhampton and the other authorities that were formerly independent county boroughs have been cast in the role of land-hungry imperialists perpetually striving to encroach on pieces of the 'green belt'. The administrative county of Staffordshire, which until the 1960s included many of the small Black Country boroughs, has had a peculiarly urban-industrial tradition in terms of its economic structure and electoral voting pattern. Sutton Coldfield, although physically and economically part of Birmingham, was in the administrative county of Warwickshire until

1974, as was Solihull (motto *Urbs in Rure*) until it became a county borough in the 1960s.

This divergence of outlook among local authorities was evident in the *Developing Strategy for the West Midlands* (West Midlands Regional Study, 1971) which reflected ideas current in the 1960s. Redditch and Droitwich were to be the only planned residential growth areas to the south of the conurbation, excluding developments on its immediate edge. Telford New Town (to the north-west in Shropshire), Cannock, Lichfield and Tamworth (to the north in Staffordshire), together with Chelmsley Wood (to the east in Warwickshire) were to be the main planned population growth areas in the region. The local authorities' attitudes were crucial in determining this strategy for only Staffordshire saw itself as an area of major growth potential while the other county authorities tended to be more defensive. Although Worcestershire and Warwickshire attempted to restrict expansion in the sector south-west from the conurbation their activities have only made the area more attractive to potential migrants in the élite and other high status groups. Staffordshire's policies have tended to have the opposite effect and in consequence those in categories C, D and E (see Table 10.1) have been attracted, but particularly young couples in those S.E.G.s who were seeking to enter the owner-occupied sector of the housing market and those willing to take part in overspill schemes to expanded towns, such as Tamworth.

The economic and environmental character of the county authorities in the West Midlands Region has led to the creation of a recognizable degree of social differentiation between the residential areas to the immediate south-west and north-east of the conurbation. These differences have been maintained by, firstly, a process of socially selective migration which has operated during the 1950s and 1960s (see Fig. 10.7) and, secondly, local authority housing and planning policies which are themselves some reflection of divergent economic and social changes which have occurred since the Industrial Revolution.

Conclusions

This study has attempted to substantiate, by empirical means, the relationship between the pattern of social segregation and the behavioural process of migration. It has been shown that in Birmingham and the West Midlands Region in 1961 and 1971 social groups, classified in terms of occupation, were segregating themselves in residential space. Certain areas in the conurbation and the region had emerged as high status residential areas, while other districts had either failed to maintain their status or had never been regarded as desirable places in which to live by those with professional or managerial occupations, and by the social élite in particular.

The availability of 'Who's Who' listings provided a means of identifying precisely the areas within the West Midlands Conurbation, but particularly Birmingham, Sutton Coldfield and Solihull, where the élite lived in 1920, 1930, 1940, 1950, 1960 and 1970. Comparison of the 1950, 1960 and 1970 lists permitted the description of migration patterns for 1950–60 and 1960–70 at the intra-urban, conurbation-region and inter-regional scales. The patterns of these moves (Fig. 10.6, 10.7 and 10.8) revealed that at the intra-urban scale, where all moves were less than 20 kilometres in length, there were relatively fewer longer-distance moves between high status neighbourhoods in the 1960s than in the 1950s. Furthermore a number of areas to the north of Birmingham's city centre and at least one to the south lost their appeal as residential areas for the social élite and these areas experienced the familiar process of 'filtering down'. Finally, the pattern of intra-urban movement of the élite did not exhibit sectoral bias, but merely interaction between a handful of precisely defined neighbourhoods which did not happen to be strung out along sectors from the conurbation centre.

At the conurbation-region scale the pattern of sectoral bias is very evident. Élite migration does help to support the level of social segregation at the regional scale by maintaining the distinction between, on the one hand, north Worcestershire with north-west Warwickshire and, on the other hand, south Staffordshire. Analysis at the inter-regional scale also revealed a distinctive pattern of southerly, rather than northerly, migration on the part of the élite groups in both the 1950s and the 1960s.

A number of factors, it was suggested, could have led to these patterns of social segregation maintaining migration, and of migration maintaining the patterns of social segregation. Stage in the life-cycle did not prove to be a statistically significant factor in leading to élite migration. In terms of the factors which could have led to the observed spatial patterns two were given particular attention. The first was the pre-existing tendency for the high-status residential areas to be located in the southern part of Birmingham – that is in districts with easy access to the north Worcestershire and north-west Warwickshire area, access which would probably have led to the inclusion of this semi-rural area within the 'action space' of potential migrants.

The second factor which, it was suggested, could have had an important influence in establishing discrepancies between the north-east and the south-west edges of the conurbation was the attitude of local authorities in the region, particularly between pro-expansionist Staffordshire and the more restrictive county authorities, notably Worcestershire and Warwickshire.

Finally, the evidence presented in this particular case study has a number of implications for the general theory of migration behaviour, as well as its pattern and impact. Sectoral bias in residential migration streams has been identified, but only at a particular intra-regional scale. The pattern of intra-urban migration did not exhibit this particular phenomenon. Migration streams in the West Midlands Region are certainly class selective, but for the group examined age did not seem to be as important an aspect of the mover-stayer question as might have been expected. In short, the sectoral bias phenomenon can appear and disappear by changing the scale of analysis; the link between social segregation and migration is a regional as well as a purely urban association; and age is not always a good indicator of whether a person will become a migrant or not in the near future.

Notes

1. After local government reorganization in 1974 the West Midlands Region was divided into Staffordshire, Shropshire, Warwickshire, Hereford and Worcester, and the West Midlands Metropolitan County (including Birmingham, Coventry and the Black Country Metropolitan Districts). The local authority names used in this chapter, and shown in Fig. 10.1, refer to the pre-1974 areas and to county boroughs, municipal boroughs and administrative counties from that period.

2. Figure 10.5 shows the relative concentration of members of the 'Who's Who' élite even though this may mean that for the pre-Second World War distributions a larger number of squares will be shaded as having more than 0.5 per cent of a year's total list living in them. This procedure does mean that every square with a listed person living in it will be shaded in the 1920 map.
3. Interaction (I) is the relative density of moves per unit area, and distance (D) is measured in terms· of the mid-points of kilometre distance bands. The Pareto, double-log, relationship was found to provide the most suitable best-fit regression line (see Woods, 1979, Ch. 7).

Acknowledgements

The author wishes to thank the Social Science Research Council for financial assistance in the purchase of census data under project HR 1774/1.

Chapter 11

Migration loss and the residual community: a study in rural France 1962-75

P. E. White

The study of the impact of migration loss

Within the general inter-disciplinary field of migration study the dominant pattern has traditionally been a concern with the migrant himself or with migrants as a distinct group within the population. It can be argued that this concern has manifested itself in three particular branches of study: investigation of the motivations for movement; analysis of the spatial patterns of movement once it occurs; and description of the effects of the migration in the places of destination.

Nowhere have these three strands of migration study been so clearly apparent as in the study of migration from rural areas, and especially in rural–urban migration. The analysis of motivations has become a major behavioural study dealing with the psychology, aspirations and attitudes of the migrants, exemplified in such studies as those by Hannan (1970) on Irish rural youth and Galtung (1971) in Sicily. The spatial patterning of population movement has emerged in recent years as a major concern of geographers, and rural–urban movement has been subsumed within this general field (Olsson, 1965; Courgeau, 1970). The description of the reception of rural migrants in the city has led to many research papers although no suitable summary exists since Beijer's work (1963).

There is, however, one further aspect of migration study that has been relatively neglected – the study of the effects of emigration on the areas left behind. As Lowenthal and Comitas (1962, p. 196) have pointed out:

> People who move are much more frequently considered as immigrants than as emigrants.

One result of a more general acceptance of a systems approach to the study of migration (Mabogunje, 1970) might, perhaps, be a greater awareness of the inter-relationships between what have in the past sometimes been seen as discrete elements of migration study. In the scope of a single chapter such as this it is impossible to consider in its totality a whole migration system, but an attempt will be made to redress the customary balance of interest by providing a case study of the areas and communities left behind by rural migrants.

Net migration loss of population from rural areas has a very long history in the nations of the developed world (Saville, 1957; Merlin, 1971; Beale, 1964) although in the measurement of such loss there have often been problems of the definition of 'rural' areas, or 'non-metropolitan' areas as they are known in some countries. Many causal factors have been examined to explain this general population loss – agricultural mechanization, improved rural education standards leading to greater aspirations, the attraction of relatively high urban wage levels, dissatisfaction with rural community life and so on: almost all local or national studies of rural migration produce their own lists of important 'causes'. It is important, however, to see the general large-scale reduction in rural population levels against the background of major social, demographic and economic changes occurring in other sectors of local or national life. In Britain, for example, the rural population reached its peak in 1851 (Saville, 1957), and although the absolute numbers living in rural areas have not varied markedly since then (Clout, 1972, p. 12), there has been population growth in 'peri-urban' areas matched by a heavy loss of population in more remote districts. This net loss of population has occurred contemporaneously with the fertility decline of the later stages of the demographic transition, with the general attainment of adult literacy after the Education Acts of the late nineteenth century, with the great increase in personal mobility afforded by the bicycle and later by the private car, and with the general rise in personal living standards from national economic growth and modernization.

Similarly, in other countries of the developed world population loss from rural areas has been but one of the whole series of major transformations of the national way of life over the last century or so. Any analysis of the effects of that large-scale rural emigration on the communities left behind is therefore made more complex by the need to relate the changes in the rural world to those in the wider national realm in an attempt to disentangle the effects of emigration from the effects of other developments.

A further complexity in the study of the effect of migration loss arises from the fact that such loss is always 'net' loss. The existence of migration counter-streams has been attested ever since Ravenstein's (1885) 'laws' were put forward and it is generally acknowledged that rural communities, far from being the stable entities often imagined, have always had a great volume of in- as well as out-migration, whether for agricultural employment, to take up craft apprenticeships or for marriage purposes (Blayo, 1970; Schofield, 1970; Jollivet, 1965). Even in areas of profound migration loss account must be taken of flows of incoming population (Pitié, 1971, p. 38) which may either, for example in the case of farm servants, help to reduce the general effects of net loss or, as in the case of retirement migration, serve to exacerbate and amplify certain of those effects.

As with the impact of all migration, the selectivity and characteristics of the migrants are of the greatest importance in conditioning the effects of migration in the residual communities left behind. Net migration loss from rural communities has generally been found to have certain common features (Merlin, 1971, pp. 67–92). The two most common are that most migrants are young, usually in the 18–30 age-group (Beale, 1964, p. 269; Beteille, 1972, p. 531); and that there are generally imbalances between the sexes in migration, with females exceeding males in some areas (Bariou, 1974; Jones, 1965, p. 36) and males exceeding females in others (Barata, 1975, p. 64; Pérez-Díaz, 1973, p. 12). Other aspects of selectivity sometimes investigated include educational achievement (Hannan, 1969, pp. 206–7), position in the local rural social hierarchy (Iszaevich, 1975, p. 304), and whether or not the migrant is a social innovator (Galtung, 1971, pp. 190–1). Whatever the particular type of selectivity operating in any rural area it is most unlikely that the in-migrants to the area will be of the same type as the out-migrants, if only because the in-migrants must be valuing something in the local rural environment which the out-migrants view as disadvantageous. It is from an appreciation of this that one can understand the counter-flow of urban–rural retirement migration against the rural–urban flow of the young (Cribier, 1975).

It is, of course, possible that the net loss of migrants from a rural area may have effects which may be either beneficial or detrimental to the residual community. In the case of Spain it has been argued by several authors that emigration from agricultural communities helped to maintain a *status quo*. Douglass (1975, p. 120), for example, found that:

> The Basque system of domestic group organization depends upon migration and emigration of excess membership.

In Castile rural migration was a useful safety valve in times of agricultural difficulty (Pérez-Díaz, 1974, p. 51): rural social structures were stabilized and demographic growth was nullified at a time of high natural increase (Iszaevich, 1975, p. 303).

In general it can be argued that it has been with the onset of the fertility decline that rural migration loss has become a problem rather than a cure – from the nineteenth century in Britain and France, from the inter-war years in most of Southern Europe. While high rates of population increase were occurring – the result of high fertility and low mortality – the rural exodus helped to maintain a stable rural population and social community. But once fertility started to fall in rural communities (and that fall in fertility was partly the result of age and sex selective out-migration in the past) the continuation of rural migration loss has reduced total populations and undermined the existence of corporate institutions. The future consequences of zero population growth, or even national population decline, could be extremely serious for rural areas if migration loss continues (Riemann, 1975). Despite the continued growth of rural populations in some peri-urban regions (Commins, 1978, p. 80), national or regional figures mask severe population decline in many more remote rural areas.

France, given the earliness of its fertility decline, has suffered more than most from the rural exodus, with the rural populations of all departments having reached their maxima by the census year 1911 (Merlin, 1971, p. 14), and with many rural regions having lost population consistently in every decade since the mid-nineteenth century (Larivière, 1971, p. 601). It is in France, therefore, that the long-term effects of the rural exodus on the residual communities can best be seen.

Studies of residual communities have painted similar, if fragmentary, pictures of the areas left behind by the migrants. The demographic effects are basically two-fold: ageing of the population (Drudy, 1978, p. 58), and the creation of imbalances between the sexes (Bourdieu, 1962). It is important to remember, however, that the first of these phenomena – ageing – occurs against a background of general national population ageing in the countries of the developed world (Paillat, 1976).

Socially, rural migration loss often results in a loss of potential innovators (Jones, 1965, pp. 42–3) and of social leadership (Capo and Fonti, 1965, p. 270). The residual communities may thus become internally homogeneous in psycho-social outlook (Wylie *et al.*, 1968, p. 101) with that outlook being dominantly a negative one towards the future of the community (Leonard and Hannon, 1977, p. 389).

Economically the reduction in population brought about by migration loss reduces the scope for, and viability of, commercial activity, which may cause further migration loss (Reiter, 1972, p. 42). The reduced tax base may give difficulties in maintaining even the most elementary public services (Ruiz, 1972, p. 31), especially if the remaining population is disproportionately old and impoverished (Gade, 1970, p. 75). In total, the effects of migration loss may be such that demographically, socially, and in terms of economic potential there is little possibility of future stabilization, let alone growth or development.

It is the aim of the present chapter to make a detailed study of recent migration changes in a rural region in Southern Normandy, France, with a view to identifying the actual patterns of selectivity that have operated among migrants both into and out of the studied villages, and to examine the way in which the observed patterns of selectivity have led to changes in the structures of the residual communities during the period under investigation.

The Normandy study area

The French planning region of Lower Normandy consists of three departments – Calvados, Manche and Orne. All of these, together with the department of Mayenne to the south in the Pays de la Loire region, achieved their rural population maxima at the time of the census of 1856 (Merlin, 1971) and they have each experienced a reduction of between 35 and 45 per cent in their rural populations since that date. That population decline is still continuing and between the censuses of 1962 and 1975 the total rural populations in both Orne and Mayenne (the two departments in which the present study area lies) fell by 9.5 per cent and 6.9 per cent respectively.[1] In both departments the rural population was growing by natural increase, but these increases were cancelled out by high rates of net migration loss (0.86 per cent per annum in Orne, and 0.70 per cent per annum in Mayenne). Both departments therefore have what Fel (1974) has described as the 'agricultural fundamental type' of population structure, characteristic of much of Western France, where fertility is still relatively high despite a long history of out-migration and consequent population decline. Rural migration loss has thus been both a historical and a continuing recent phenomenon in the two departments and this is especially true for the individual *communes* selected for detailed study.

Of the seven *communes* studied five are in Orne and two in Mayenne (see Fig. 11.1) The choice of *communes* was made randomly from among those having the necessary census documents for each of the three most recent censuses. A stratified random sample was taken to ensure that each size-group of local rural *communes* was satisfactorily represented. Agriculture is the most important single employment sector in each *commune* although there are alternative employment opportunities: Juvigny-sous-Andaine, Neuilly-le-Vendin and St Aignan-de-Couptrain, the three largest *communes* in the sample, each have retailing and commercial employment; all the *communes* are satisfactorily placed for commuting to the nearby small industrial centres of La Ferté-Macé, Domfront and Flers. Until the early 1970s several men from La Coulonche worked in a nearby iron mine, since closed, while in Haleine itself there is a small electro-chemical works. The nearby spa village of Bagnoles-de-l'Orne provides seasonal employment for several *communes*.

Long-term decline has reduced the populations of individual villages

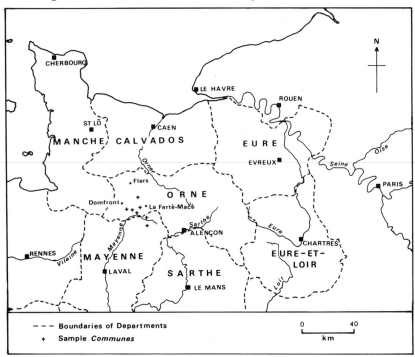

Fig. 11.1   Location of Normandy study area.

Table 11.1   Population change, sample *communes*, 1962–1975

	1962 total population	1968 total population	1975 total population	Percentage change 1962–75
La Coulonche	475	429	347	−26.9
Haleine	266	245	245	− 7.9
Juvigny-s-A.*	889	843	915	+ 2.9
Lucé	184	149	137	−25.5
Neuilly-le-V.	540	456	415	−23.1
St Aignan-de-C.	522	462	445	−14.8
St Michel-des-A.	324	298	273	−15.7
Total	3,200	2,882	2,777	−13.2

*The population figures given throughout this chapter for Juvigny exclude the residents of an orthopaedic institute.
Data source: Listes nominatives de recensement.

markedly: Haleine, for example, has lost 56 per cent of its 1836 maximum population of 540. Table 11.1 shows the population totals and rates of change over the period 1962 to 1975 studied. Globally, and in several of the *communes* individually, the rate of decline was greater between 1962 and 1968 than in the following period, the major exception being La Coulonche which was then affected by the mine closure. Only in the largest *commune* – Juvigny-sous-Andaine – did the population actually rise during the period under examination.

Data sources and study methods

The student of migration and its effects is well provided for in rural France and several sources have been used in the present study. The most useful sources are the *listes nominatives de recensement*, still filled in by most village mayors, or their secretaries, at the time of each population census. The documents form a complete list of inhabitants of each *commune* arranged by households, and showing also the individual's date of birth, his place of birth, his occupation and his relationship to the head of the household.[2] The *listes* form a vital source for detailed local study of migration (see for example Blayo, 1970; Pinchemel, 1957) for by the comparison of one list with another a picture of each inter-censal immigrant and emigrant can be built up. The *listes* also give a useful description of the population, household and occupational structure of each *commune* at successive censuses. Unfortunately the construction of a *liste nominative* is no longer compulsory for local administrations, and fewer *communes* are now keeping up the tradition: in the seven sampled *communes*, however, *listes* were still being produced at the 1975 census.[3]

The technique for identifying migrants between censuses is the same as that used for identifying emigrants and immigrants from electoral registers in England (Johnston, 1967): new names at the second date can be regarded as immigrants, and names that disappear between the two dates as those of emigrants. In England problems occur from marriages, deaths and those coming to electoral age (Dunn and Swindell, 1972): in France the problems of such spurious 'migrations' resulting from birth, marriage or death can be dealt with by consulting the civil registration documents (the *État Civil*) for the inter-censal period for each village. These show not only the vital events within the *commune* but also births elsewhere (for example in maternity hospitals) occurring to women normally resident in the *commune*, as well as deaths elsewhere of those normally resident. These civil registers therefore provide a complete check on the presumed inter-censal migrations and allow the final detailed migrant list to be free of errors.

In dealing with inter-censal migrations there are four categories of movement for which data are usually obtained only with difficulty: out-migrations of those born since the previous census, in-migrations of those who then die before the next census, the movements of those who arrive and depart during the inter-censal interval, and those who depart only to return before the next census. The use of the civil registers allows the first two of these to be dealt with accurately. For the third group limited information is only available if a family event occurred during the stay in the *commune* – a birth, marriage or death – for with the registration of these events details are also given of certain proximate relatives – parents for births and marriages, spouse or offspring for deaths.[4] Hence, although a complete picture of migration remains a Utopia, the use of the civil registration documents enables the inclusion of certain categories of movement which are normally omitted from studies comparing lists of the populations present in two different years. Further detail on 'in-and-out' movements could have been obtained (but for the adult population only) from a detailed year-by-year comparison of electoral registers – a time-consuming task. This might also have provided evidence of some of the 'out-and-return' migrants who, in the present study, were only identified if children were born to them but not registered in the *commune* under investigation.

In the latter part of this chapter reference is made to the documents of the *commune* administrations, notably the budgetary documents, as a useful source of information. The use and meaning of these documents will be outlined in a later section.

The balance-sheet of population change

Table 11.1 has already demonstrated that the populations of six of the study communes declined between 1962 and 1975. Using the methods outlined in the previous section it is now possible to demonstrate how these population movements were made up in terms of the migratory and natural balances. In Table 11.2 the individual figures of births, deaths, out- and in-migration for each *commune* for the two study periods have been rendered into rates per thousand resident population per annum to enable comparisons to be made, both between *communes* and between the two inter-censal periods of six and seven years' duration.

The first thing to be noticed in Table 11.2 is that for every case considered, except that of Juvigny in 1968–75, there has been net migration loss, often at relatively high levels. The net rate of migration loss, however, bears little relationship to the gross total rate of all migration for both emigration and immigration are substantial: indeed, if the emigration and immigration rates are added together it can be found that for the two *communes* of Haleine and St Michel over 10 per cent of the population was in movement each year. In assessing the impact of net migration loss, therefore, attention must be paid to both the emigrant and the immigrant component of the net change.

The second major conclusion from Table 11.2 is that the migration component is generally of much greater importance in the total population change of the parishes concerned than is the rate of natural change. In 7 cases out of the 14 presented, significant net migration loss has reversed a picture of stability or population growth engendered by natural increase, while in a further 5 cases (Haleine, Neuilly and St Michel in 1962–68; La Coulonche and Neuilly in 1968–75) migration loss exceeds and reinforces natural loss to give a population structure tending towards true depopulation, demonstrating the assertion by Lowenthal and Comitas (1962, p. 197) that depopulation results more from emigration than from natural loss.

The table demonstrates that two *communes*, St Aignan and Lucé, belonged, in both time periods, to Fel's (1974) 'agricultural fundamental' population structure of migration loss nullifying natural gain: Haleine and Neuilly belong to Fel's structure of 'abandonment' – both migration and natural loss. St Michel is on the brink between the two structures while La Coulonche takes the natural progression (Duboscq, 1972) towards abandonment. Only in Juvigny, the largest *commune*, has there been a real recent revival.

This recent revival in Juvigny is to some extent reflected in the general picture of the seven *communes*. Apart from the case of La Coulonche with its mine closure the other *communes* all had lower emigration rates during the second inter-censal period than during the first, and four of them, including La Coulonche, had higher rates of immigration. The migration balance, although negative, has been reduced, as has happened throughout France (Rochas, 1977, p. 16). Various reasons for this may be suggested: it may be the success of official initiatives in developing new local industrial employment, particularly at the town of Domfront (Fig. 11.1); or it may be, as Fel (1974, p. 61) has suggested, that the rural demographic reservoir for migration is now emptying so that populations are starting to stabilize at a level where there is equilibrium between the agricultural resources and their human exploiters. Some evidence on these alternative explanations may be gleaned from the examination of the patterns of migrant selectivity in the two inter-censal periods.

Table 11.2 Population balance sheet, 1962–75 (All figures are rates per thousand per annum)

	1962–68						1968–75					
	Births	Deaths	Natural balance	Emigration	Immigration	Migration balance	Births	Deaths	Natural balance	Emigration	Immigration	Migration balance
La Coulonche	17.3	11.8	+5.5	45.7	23.2	−22.5	10.3	11.8	−1.5	52.3	23.9	−28.4
Haleine	13.7	17.6	−3.9	65.1	54.0	−11.1	12.8	15.2	−2.4	57.7	57.1	− 0.6
Juvigny-s-A.	17.8	11.7	+6.1	47.2	32.7	−14.5	13.5	8.6	+4.9	37.2	43.1	+ 5.9
Lucé	12.0	9.0	+3.0	50.9	16.0	−34.9	13.0	9.0	+4.0	36.0	16.0	−20.0
Neuilly-le-V.	13.6	16.7	−3.1	57.6	31.1	−26.5	10.2	15.4	−5.2	49.5	41.6	− 7.9
St Aignan-de-C.	18.0	12.2	+5.8	57.6	30.5	−27.1	18.9	11.0	+7.9	41.9	29.3	−12.6
St Michel-des-A.	9.1	13.4	−4.3	64.8	52.5	−12.3	13.0	13.0	−	57.4	44.5	−12.9
Total	15.8	13.2	+2.6	53.9	33.6	−20.3	13.3	11.5	+1.8	45.7	38.0	− 7.7

The selectivity of migration

Using the data sources outlined above, three specific aspects of selectivity were examined in these seven villages – the aspects of sex and age selectivity, and of selectivity by occupational classes. The first two of these aspects are of obvious significance in examining the demographic effects of migration, while occupational selectivity may be important in a wide range of both economic and social effects, the latter in areas such as this where agricultural factors may be important in the social structure of a community. The data would enable a wide range of other selective factors to be examined – such as whether families or individuals move, whether migration differs between outlying hamlets and village centres – but these aspects are not examined here.

Age and sex selectivity

The sex selectivity of the migrants could be easily dealt with, in simple terms, by relating the emigrants to the original population structure and by relating immigrants to the structure at the end of the relevant period. However, sex and age selectivity really need to be dealt with together because of their mutual interdependence. Given the irregular French inter-censal interval certain standard demographic accounting models (Rees and Wilson, 1973; 1975) cannot be applied unless the census year age-groups are made compatible with the inter-censal interval, which, in this case, would lead to non-comparability of results between the two periods under consideration.

The procedure adopted here was to construct, for each village, for the census years 1962 and 1968, a complete age and sex breakdown of the population using five-year age-groups. This structure was then up-dated, year by year, up to the next census date – 1968 or 1975. In the up-dating account was made of the ageing of the population according to their known birth-dates, of deaths occurring to individuals of known ages, of births in each year, and of both out- and in-migration by the precise year of movement where this was known (for example at the time of marriage). Where no precise information was available on the date of migration of an individual or family the move was assumed to have occurred exactly half-way through the inter-censal period. In this way a reference population was obtained for each year and a summation could be made of the aggregate number of individual person-years spent in any five-year age-group during an inter-censal period. Age- and sex-specific emigration rates were calculated on the basis of the total number of migrants from a five-year age-group during an inter-censal period against the total of the reference populations in that age-group summed for the start of each year of that inter-censal period: for immigration rates the comparison was with the reference populations at the end of each year. For certain purposes described later age-specific death and fertility rates were calculated using the aggregates of person-years.

The patterns of age selective emigration are shown in Fig. 11.2 where the emigration rates have been produced in a form showing, for individuals in any five-year age-group, the annual probability of migration for the two individual inter-censal periods and for the total period 1962–75. The data in Fig. 11.2 are for the seven study *communes* combined.

All the male and female curves show the expected pattern of very high migration probability in the young adult age-groups 15–29, and for both sexes there is also an increase in migration probability after the age of 70, following a period of low mobility in middle age. Although this was not explicitly investigated in this study there is local evidence that much of this migration of the old is extremely local, either to the small towns or to live with offspring or other relations. The extent of this migration of the old is probably under-represented in larger-scale studies. The importance of age selectivity is shown by the fact that if the 1962–75 aggregate curves are examined the male peak migration probability (at age-group 20–24) is nearly eight times that of the trough (age-group 50–54); while for females the peak is nine times that of the trough, which occurs in the 55–59 age-group.

A comparison of the 1962–75 curves for males and females reveals several interesting points. Most importantly, there is a profound difference in the 15–19 age-group where the female migration probability of 0.114 is nearly 80 per cent higher than the male rate of 0.064. This may indicate that males, after leaving school, are more likely to work locally for a few years before departing. Between the ages of 25 and 44 the male probability slightly exceeds that of females; there is then similarity in the age-groups 45–69 after which males become more migratory once more, perhaps a reflection of their lower ability to look after themselves in old age, or an indication of the success of French agricultural policy in persuading older farmers to retire from the land instead of working it

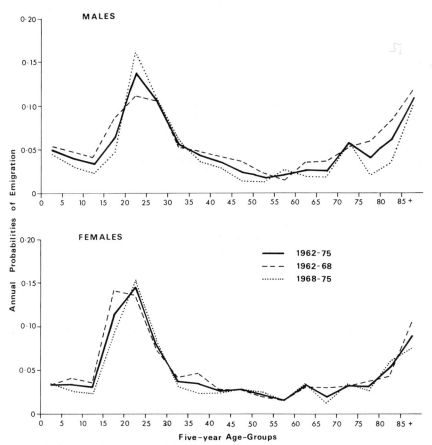

Fig. 11.2   Patterns of age selective emigration.

until their death (International Labour Office, 1971, p. 383). The dominant sex difference in emigration, however, must be identified as the tendency of females to start their major migration movement earlier than the males: this was particularly true for the 1962–68 inter-censal period where the female peak occurred in the 15–19 age-group, five years before the male.

The comparison of the two inter-censal periods shows that male emigration has recently become much more concentrated in the 20–24 age-group, the reduction in migration among the 15–19s perhaps being the result of longer educational training. For almost all age-groups after 35 the probability of male emigration fell between the two inter-censal periods so that in 1968–75 the peak was over 12 times as great as the trough.

The recent male tendency towards more concentration on emigration in the 20–24 age-group is also shown for females, and in this way the migrational habits of the two sexes are becoming more similar. From the age of 40 onwards the female emigration probabilities differ very little between the two periods.

Hence, although the basic patterns of both male and female migration selectivity remain similar through the two periods examined, the gross reduction in emigration referred to earlier in connection with Table 11.2 has occurred largely through a reduction in the migration of males over 35, and has occurred against a picture of the heightened intensity of emigration in the young adult age-group, a pattern very similar to that of rural France as a whole (Rochas, 1977, p. 16).

Looking at individual *communes* is problematic because of the small migrant totals in some cases, but it is notable that it is in Juvigny, the largest *commune*, that the young adult migration peak is least marked (a 1962–75 peak probability per annum of moving of 0.123 for males 20–24: females 0.111 for the same age-group). In Neuilly the probabilities for this same age-group reach 0.208 for males and 0.220 for females. Clearly there are marked differences between *communes*.

Without any form of immigration such high levels of population loss as occur in the young adult sector of the population pyramid would rapidly lead to total depopulation. Immigration, then, as well as being a normal process, is also a necessary one to help to maintain some demographic balance.

The immigration rates shown in Fig. 11.3 have been calculated to show, for the population in each age-group at the end of each year, the probability of individuals present then having arrived during the course of the preceding year. As in Fig. 11.2, the data are for the seven study *communes* combined.

As with the emigration rates there is a peak of mobility in the young adult age-groups, although with both males and females reaching the maximum immigration probabilities in the five-year age-group after the peak emigration rate. There is also a distinct pattern of high mobility for the 0–4 age-group, and, for females only, the post–75 increase in mobility that was noted for emigrants. There is no evidence here to suggest that this might be one of the rural areas of France affected by retirement migration. The fact that females are more migratory than males after the age of 70, as measured through immigration, is probably a reflection of the combined effects of the customary male/female disparity in age-at-marriage, and the earlier ages of death of men followed by the movement of widows to live with relations.

Other features notable from the comparison of the male and female 1962–75 rates include the high female immigration rate for the 20–24 age-group, almost certainly caused in part by movement at the time of marriage; and the fact that

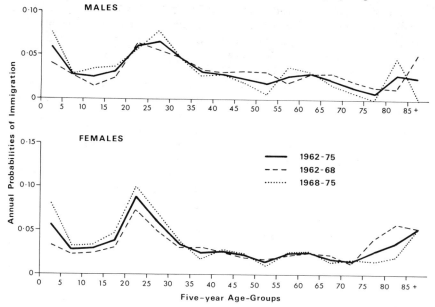

Fig. 11.3 Patterns of age selective immigration.

throughout the age-groups 35–74 the male and female immigration rates are almost identical. In an area such as this while emigration may involve single people, even in the middle age-groups, there is little immigration of adults that is not of married couples.

Comparison of the two inter-censal periods shows that, in general, for all age-groups up to 34 there was an increase in rates of immigration over the period studied. Beyond the age of 35 temporal change in age-specific immigration has

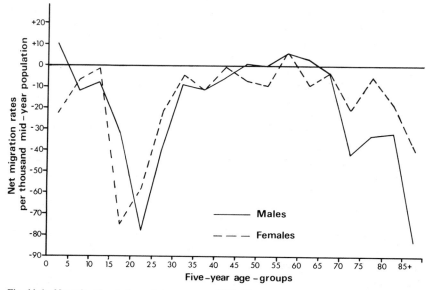

Fig. 11.4 Net migration balance by age-group, 1962–75.

been less straightforward and is less open to interpretation. It seems to be the case, therefore, that the increase in the immigration rate referred to in connection with Table 11.2 has come about as a result of greater movement by young adults and families with young children: again there is nothing to suggest retirement migration to the area. For the young there has therefore been an increase in the intensity of migration both out of and into the *communes* in the study area.

Age-specific net migration rates per thousand resident mid-year population are shown in Fig. 11.4. Despite the presence of immigration there are heavy rates of net loss in the age-groups between 15 and 29 for both males and females. The high rates of net migration loss of males over 70 also stand out, although it must be remembered that the absolute numbers involved in such moves are very small.

The analysis of the age and sex selectivity of migration therefore shows that, over the seven sampled *communes* as a whole, there is a distinct process of selectivity operating, more especially in emigration, which results in a distinctive pattern of migratory net loss to the communities. The importance of migration in the young adult classes has been demonstrated, and some light has been shed on the changes in the nature of age and sex selectivity between the two time-periods covered.

Occupational selectivity

It is possible to use the available data sources to obtain an idea of the occupational structure of the movers, although the information relates only to the occupation at the time of the last census before leaving, in the case of emigrants, or the first census after arrival, in the case of immigrants, rather than to the actual occupation at the time of movement. Obviously there may be occupational changes between the census date and migration, and one important category of movers is neglected – those who were at school at one census date and had left before the next: nothing is known about whether they took up local employment for a year or two before making a residential move.

Nevertheless some useful information is obtainable, and in the analysis here the occupational structure has been broken into seven sectors: agriculture and forestry; agricultural processing (including sawmilling, dairy-workers and so on); industry and mechanical trades; personal service (housekeepers, servants, cooks and other related occupations); the liberal professions; commerce and retailing (including such food-processing activities as baking and pork-butchery which, in the French rural context, are intimately linked to retailing); and finally office workers such as clerks, secretaries and cashiers. The agricultural sector is, unfortunately, the one where the greatest inaccuracies may creep into the figures with confusion over the status of 'family workers' on farms.

It is most useful to produce rates of migration from occupational groups which take into account both the original numerical importance of each group and the ages of the migrants. In Table 11.3 data for the two inter-censal periods has been combined such that the figures show, for each occupation, the percentage of males in that sector at the start of each year who have migrated by the end of the year, with the figures also being broken down into four age-groups. No entry is made in the table where the total number of emigrants during the period was less than five, although such emigrants are incorporated in the calculations of totals.

Emigration was generally low from agriculture – a somewhat surprising

Table 11.3 Male emigration by occupation and age, 1962–1975

	Percentage moving per annum*				
	Age up to 30	30–44	45–59	60+	Total
Agriculture	6.6	2.5	1.8	2.8	3.2
Agricultural processing	11.6				8.9
Industry	9.8	4.4	1.9		6.3
Professions	14.1	6.5			7.3
Commerce	10.1	4.0	2.5		5.1
Office work	9.2				5.6
Total	8.6	3.3	2.0	2.6	4.3

*Figures omitted from table for all categories with less than five migrants.

finding which deserves further investigation. Only for the over 60s was male agricultural emigration higher than total emigration for the age-group, and this was expected since retirement from farming would commonly involve moving in order to relinquish a farm in such an area of generally small family holdings. Two explanations can be suggested for the apparent overall low rate of emigration from agriculture: either the picture is a genuine one reflecting low rates of farm mobility, in which case local conditions of farm tenure and farm size may be important considerations; or those involved in agriculture commonly move into another occupation before finally leaving their village. More detailed investigation would be needed to clarify which interpretation is correct. The other occupational sector with relatively low mobility – commerce – may indicate that in those walks of life where there is a high capital investment, for example in a shop or a farm, there is a greater degree of inertia. Otherwise the figures provide few surprises – professionals have the generally higher mobility of the middle classes, and throughout the table there is the expected general decline in emigration according to age.

To complete the picture of male migration according to occupations it is necessary to consider Table 11.4 which shows, again for the two inter-censal periods combined, the percentage of those in each occupational group at the end of the year who have moved in during the course of the year. Once again there is the expected fall-off in this measure of mobility with greater age, and this is consistent throughout the table. As with the emigrants of Table 11.3, the mobility rate among the male agricultural population is much lower than in all other sectors and, once again, the professional group have by far the highest mobility, as measured through immigration.

The conclusion from the consideration of Tables 11.3 and 11.4 must be that the differential mobility levels of the different employment sectors are likely to

Table 11.4 Male immigration by occupation and age, 1962–1975

	Percentage arriving per annum*				
	Age up to 30	30–44	45–59	60+	Total
Agriculture	4.0	2.4	1.4	1.1	2.1
Agricultural processing	5.0	5.0	2.1		3.6
Industry	7.0	3.5	3.1		5.0
Professions	11.9	9.6			8.9
Commerce	7.2	6.6	2.1		5.4
Office work					3.2
Total	6.3	3.8	2.1	1.9	3.8

*Figures omitted from table for all categories with less than five migrants.

result in changes in the occupational structures of individual *communes* as a result of migration.

Although the number of occupied females migrating was much lower than the totals of occupied males the selectivity of occupational migration was similar. Agriculture had low mobility in general, although with a relatively high immigration rate for the under 29s – almost certainly a reflection of marriage into a farming life. Both personal service and the professions were associated with high mobility, particularly for immigrants.

The general picture of occupational selectivity in migration is thus one of differential mobility according to type of occupation, with agriculture being particularly notable as the sector from which direct emigration is low and to which immigration is of low importance. It must be added, however, that although agriculture has a low rate of migration the absolute numbers moving are relatively large. As with the characteristics of the age of those moving the fact here is that migration does not deal with a random cross-section of the population but is instead highly selective. It is to the effects of that selectivity that attention must now be given.

Demographic effects of migration loss

In the analysis of the demographic effects of migration distinct problems arise. The first of these concerns the other external variables which have been affecting the residual communities – in the case of the demographic effects of migration it is necessary to take some account also of secular trends in the evolution of both mortality and fertility which may be, but to an unknown extent, independent of migration.

Following from this comes the second problem which is that of attempting, in a dynamic field such as the evolution of population structure, to produce an understanding of the impact of migration during a time period of n years from a consideration solely of the population at time t, the original date, compared to the population at time t + n. During that period of n years the population will have altered as a result of births and deaths, even without the complications introduced by selective emigration and immigration.

A third problem is that the effects of migration are likely to be, in part, long-term. The emigration of 20-year-olds now will deplete a particular age-cohort for a further 60 years or so, as well as having an immediate effect on fertility. Similarly, certain features of population structure at the present time will have been induced by migrations occurring in the past. In a study of only two inter-censal periods only short-term impacts can be identified.

The procedure that has been adopted here has been to produce a simulation of the evolution of the populations of each *commune* for each inter-censal period, the simulation being based on an assumption of no emigration or immigration at all. Hence if a simulation of the population evolution of a *commune* from 1962 to 1968 is made, based on the known 1962 census population structure, the difference between the simulated 1968 population structure and the actual census structure of that year can be interpreted as being the measure of the effect of net migration.

In order to provide a simulation for the evolution of village populations under conditions of no migration detailed rates of age-specific mortality and female age-specific fertility were required.[5] In the case of mortality, separate annual age-specific mortality rates were calculated for the two sexes for the two inter-censal periods using the pattern of ages at death built up from the local analysis of civil registration records compared with the annual reference populations described earlier (p. 206). In order to eliminate minor aberrations in certain age-classes caused by small sample sizes the mortality rates that were finally used were standardized half-way between the local rates and the French national rates for the years 1965 and 1971 for the two inter-censal periods respectively.

Similarly, local female age-specific fertility rates were calculated for each inter-censal period, although for these the sample sizes were large enough to eliminate the need for standardization against French national data. The sex ratio at birth was also obtained.

In simulating the evolution of the small populations of the *communes* of the study area a probabilistic technique had to be used since annual mortality or fertility rates applied to the small populations in most age-groups would invariably yield no deaths or births. The mortality and fertility rates were therefore read as the probabilities of dying or giving birth within a year. For each age-group at the start of each year three-figure random numbers were examined up to the total number of individuals in that age-group: each set of random numbers that was less than the relevant mortality or fertility three-figure probability represented one demographic event.[6] The process was repeated for each year of the inter-censal periods, with the population being aged from year to year according to their known birth-dates as recorded in the base census. From this probabilistic method of simulating populations for 1968 and 1975 the final population structures are one sample from a variety of structures that could occur using different sets of random numbers. Therefore, in the comparison of the simulated populations, in which there was no migration, with the actual migration-affected populations, the use of certain statistical significance tests is justifiable.[7]

If there had been no migration at all the simulations show that the 1962 total population of 3,200 could have grown to 3,247 in 1968 (the actual 1968 population was 2,882 so that the true net loss attributable to migration is 365): that actual 1968 population of 2,882 could have risen to 2,890 in 1975 (true net migration loss of 113 actually brought the 1975 total down to 2,777 – see Table 11.1).

Figure 11.5 provides an illustration of the effects of migration on the population structure of the seven *communes* combined for the first inter-censal interval in displaying the differences between the population structure that might have resulted in 1968 under conditions of no migration with the structure that did actually occur. Certain features of these structures are common to the whole of France – the effect of the First World War losses in the male age-groups over 75: the deficit in the 50–54 age-group resulting from low fertility during that war; and the dearth of births during the Second World War reflected in the 25–29 age-groups. In the last of these groups, however, net migration loss is also of great importance in reducing numbers, especially for females: net migration loss further reduces an already small cohort.

In general the net balance of migration results in an increase in the proportions in age-groups over 35. The age-group 30–34 appears to be the pivot, and below the age of 30 the proportions in most age-groups are generally reduced by net migration loss. The one major exception is the age-group 0–4 where, in the short

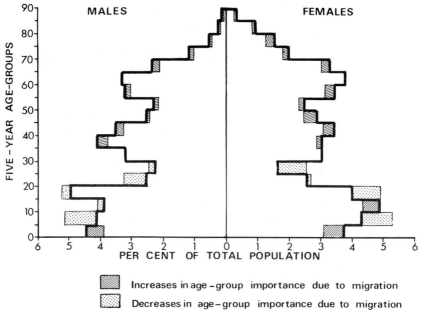

Increases in age-group importance due to migration

Decreases in age-group importance due to migration

Fig. 11.5   Actual population structure, 1968 and migration effects, 1962–68.

term, the proportions are increased by migration, this probably being the result, in the period shown, of changes in the distribution of the female population in the child-bearing age-groups. The effect of migration on age structure can be summed up as being an enhancement of the relative importance of the middle-aged and elderly and a reduction in the importance of children and young adults.

The age structure can be represented by the mean age of the population and it is possible to test whether there is a significant difference between the mean ages of the simulated populations and the mean ages of the actual populations for the same census years: the statistic used is the calculation of Student's t for one sample against a given mean – in this case the sample is the simulated population and the given mean is the mean age of the actual population for the same year.[8] Between 1962 and 1968 the mean age of the population in the seven *communes* rose by 0.03 years from 34.42 to 34.45 years by natural change alone; migration caused a further increase of 1.37 years to 35.82 years. For the second inter-censal interval natural processes alone would have led to a reduction in mean age by 0.48 years, but this was outweighed by the migration effect which took the mean age to 37.04 years. In all cases for all *communes* migration led to an increase in average age, and the significance levels for these increases are given in Table 11.5. Despite the generally lower levels of migration in the second inter-censal period the effects of migration on the age of the population are more distinct then – the result of the more intensive age selectivity operating in the 1968–75 period. Particularly interesting are the figures for La Coulonche which was affected by the mine closure already mentioned: in the seven-year period between 1968 and 1975 migration led to an increase of the mean age of the population by 5.11 years to reach, in 1975, a mean of 40.04 years: the only other *commune* with an average age of over 40 was Lucé, the smallest *commune*, at 40.02. The importance of the effect of migration on age is illustrated by a

Table 11.5 Significance levels for increases in average age of populations due to migration

	1962–68			1968–75		
	Males	Females	Total	Males	Females	Total
La Coulonche	0.05	n.s.	0.05	0.005	0.001	0.001
Haleine	n.s.	n.s.	n.s.	0.05	n.s.	0.10
Juvigny-s-A.	n.s.	n.s.	n.s.	n.s.	n.s.	n.s.
Lucé	n.s.	0.05	0.05	0.01	n.s.	0.05
Neuilly-le-V.	n.s.	0.005	0.005	0.05	n.s.	0.05
St Aignan-de-C.	n.s.	n.s.	n.s.	n.s.	n.s.	n.s.
St Michel-des-A.	n.s.	n.s.	0.10	0.05	0.10	0.01
Total	0.01	0.01	0.005	0.005	0.05	0.001

n.s. Not significant.

correlation coefficient, r_s, of $+0.72$ (significant at the 0.05 level) between the rate of net migration between 1968 and 1975 and the average age of the population in 1975: the higher the rate of migration loss the older the residual population.

An important aspect of population ageing is the increase in both the numbers and the proportion of those who are retired (International Labour Office, 1971). Increases in numbers can lead to a strain on welfare facilities (Bracey, 1970, p. 35), and increases in the proportion of aged may affect the stability of social structures. In the study area the absolute number of those over 60 rose from 517 in 1962 to 634 in 1975, and this despite the overall reduction in population. In terms of the proportion of the total population that was over 60 there was an increase from 16.16 per cent in 1962 to 22.91 per cent in 1975. Obviously this increase in both absolute numbers and percentages could have come about both by natural processes, for example increased longevity, or by the effects of migration. Since the numbers involved in migration among the aged are relatively small it is likely that the increase in the absolute numbers of the old is largely the result of natural factors, but the increase in their importance in the population is the result of migration. This runs against established demographic theory which argues that the single most important factor causing demographic ageing is the decline in fertility (Coale, 1957). As with other branches of population study the scale of the population under consideration appears to be highly significant.

Again it was possible to test the difference between the simulated closed populations and the actual migration-affected populations to determine whether migration had a significant effect on the balance between over-60s and under-60s. A chi-square test was used with the observed values as the simulated absolute numbers of under 60s and over 60s and the expected values calculated from the actual under/over 60 balance for the same year to match the simulated population total. The significance levels were generally low. For the first inter-censal period it could be accepted at the 0.05 significance level that migration had increased the total proportion of elderly within the seven *communes*, but there were few results of significance for the individual *communes*. For the second time-period the significance level increased to 0.001 for the total population and stood at 0.005 for the proportions of both elderly males and females taken individually. As with the mean age the *commune* of La Coulonche provided an extreme case where, during the 1968–75 inter-censal period, the proportion of over 60s rose by 7.10 per cent due to migration reaching, in 1975, 25.94 per cent of the total population.

During the relatively short time-periods under investigation migration was not shown to have any significant effect on the proportion of under 15s within the population. It is likely, however, that in a study covering a longer period the reduction of the numbers of child-bearing women as a result of migration would produce a commensurate reduction in the importance of children within the population.

One further demographic feature that was examined was the extent of a shift in the sex ratio in the population that might result from migration: it is generally believed that a common outcome of migration from rural communities is a changed sex balance (Clout, 1976, p. 41). However, in this study area, despite differences in certain age-groups, as discussed earlier (pp. 207–8), there is little overall difference between the two sexes in either immigration or emigration (Figs 11.2 and 11.3). Consequently a chi-square test showed no significant differences between the sex balances of the simulated closed populations and those of the actual, migration-affected, ones.

In the analysis of migrant selectivity (pp. 210–2) it was shown that there were marked differentials for occupational groups and ages within them. The impact of those differentials occurs in changing both the numbers employed and the age distribution within certain employment sectors.

The dominant employment trend for males during the period studied has been the reduction in the importance of agriculture: in 1962 57.5 per cent of the male labour-force was on the land, but this proportion had fallen to 40.6 per cent by 1975. As in much of the rest of France the importance of hired agricultural labour has fallen particularly quickly during this period (Mathieu, 1974). In terms of absolute numbers the local male agricultural population fell from 553 to 294 for the seven *communes* together. The sector to gain most in importance (from 23.1 per cent to 33.1 per cent of the male labour-force) was industry, although in absolute terms the increase was meagre – only 18 persons: in other words the industrial sector held its own against a general background of decline. In the reduction of agricultural employment migration loss has played a major role. Table 11.6 gives details of the net migration balances in each occupational sector and age-group and it can be seen that despite the generally low mobility of the agriculturally employed population (pp. 210–1) that occupational sector suffered a heavy net loss through migration. In fact 45.2 per cent of the reduction in agricultural employment between 1962 and 1975 can be directly ascribed to the effect of migration, the remaining reduction being caused by what might be

Table 11.6   Male occupational net migration, absolute figures, 1962–1975

	Age up to 30	30–44	45–59	60+	Total
Agriculture	−62	−16	−19	−20	−117
Agricultural processing	− 3	+ 6	+ 1	0	+ 4
Industry	−17	− 7	+13	+ 1	− 10
Personal service	+ 2	0	− 1	− 1	0
Professions	− 2	+ 8	+ 1	+ 2	+ 9
Commerce	− 2	+ 2	− 3	+ 2	− 1
Office work	− 2	0	+ 1	0	− 1
Total	−86	− 7	− 7	−16	−116

called 'internal' factors – retirement, changed occupations or employment selectivity among school-leavers. In no sector other than agriculture was net migration of any real importance in effecting changes in the total employment in the sector: for all other sectors the 'internal' factors affecting employment were far more significant than was the net migration balance. The agricultural population stands apart in being relatively immobile, but is one in which emigrants, when they do leave, are not replaced by newcomers.

Apart from information on the net migration balance for occupational groups, Table 11.6 also deals with four specific age-groups. The combined effect of occupational and age selectivity is to produce certain changes in the age structures of the employed population. Over the full 13-year period the average age of the male working population scarcely changed (40.54 years in 1962, 40.58 years in 1975); but the average age in both the agricultural sector and all other sectors combined rose (the increased importance of the non-agricultural sectors enabling the overall mean to remain unchanged). The mean age of males in agriculture rose from 43.33 to 45.82 years; while the mean for all other occupations rose from 36.75 to 37.01 years. Hence the difference between the average age in agriculture and in other occupations rose during the period from 6.58 to 8.81 years. It has already been pointed out that migration has been the cause of the ageing of the population, and that migration has played a major role in reducing the importance of agriculture: the further role of migration in increasing the demographic individuality of agriculture must now be added to that list. That effect of migration is brought about by the overwhelming net loss from the youngest occupied age-group, although undoubtedly this is coupled to the increased reluctance of school-leavers to go into agriculture anyway (Chevalier, 1975).

The demographic and related effects of migration have thus been several and varied in nature. Net loss of population through migration has resulted in general population loss in the area studied, since the small natural increases that have occurred have been insufficient to outweigh the balance of migration. That general population loss has been accompanied by an ageing of the residual populations, in large part the result of the age-specific nature of migration both out of and into the *communes* studied. Not only has the average age of the populations been significantly increased but the importance of the older age-groups, both numerically and as a proportion of the total population, has been enhanced. Within the employed age-groups differential migration helped to bring about a distinctive change in the occupational structure of the area, with emigration providing a means for achieving the governmentally desired reduction in the agricultural labour-force. It can be argued that, to date, insufficient alternative employment opportunities have been created locally, since the numbers employed in sectors outside agriculture scarcely grew during the period studied. Emigration does not need to play such a large role in the reduction of agricultural employment – it is a sufficient cause but not a necessary one.

Migration loss and local administration

It is a distinctive feature of the rural scene in France that each *commune* is largely self-governing, raising its own local revenue from property taxes and administering a range of services and amenities with this income. Among the regular costs of the *communes* certain are especially onerous – the cost of maintenance of the municipally owned buildings such as the school and *mairie* (the parish office); the cost of social welfare payments to local residents (in which the *commune* shares responsibility with the state); the cost of maintenance of the local road network; and the cost of administration itself, including the cost of remuneration of the personnel employed.

The services provided by the local administration vary quite widely between the seven *communes* studied: La Coulonche does not yet have a piped water supply, in Lucé the school closed down in the early 1970s, and only in St Aignan and Juvigny are the *mairies* open daily. In certain cases, such as Haleine, the secretary of the *commune* is shared with other villages, elsewhere the secretary is also the village school-teacher, as at La Coulonche. Since 1959 *communes* have been encouraged to band together in syndicates in order to allow the provision of local amenities to take place on a more efficient scale (Detton and Hourticq, 1975, p. 109). Each of the seven *communes* studied belongs to at least one syndicate, the services provided by these including road repairs, fire service, youth facilities and the secretarial personnel of the individual *communes* themselves; but although each *commune* contributes financially to the syndicates each retains complete individuality in most budgetary respects and raises its own rate income.[9]

It is possible to examine the effects of migration on the cost of local administration through an examination of the annual administrative accounts of each *commune*, drawn up at the end of each financial year: these were examined, when available, for the three census years 1962, 1968 and 1975. Despite the allegiance of individual *communes* to specific syndicates for certain purposes the total annual expenditure figures are comparable for five of the *communes*: the exceptions are Lucé, where a very much reduced scale of services is provided, and Juvigny where, by virtue of being both a larger village and the chief place of a *canton*, the next highest administrative unit after the *commune*, the range of services is wider.

The most important fact to emerge from the examination of the accounts for 1975 is that *per capita* current account expenditure increases with decreases in population size: the correlation coefficient, -0.73, is significant at the 0.05 level. For example, in St Aignan (population 445) the *per capita* cost of current account expenditure by the *commune* was 403 francs: in St Michel (population 273) it was 474 francs. A similar overall relationship between population size and *per capita* administrative costs also exists for 1962 and 1968, although based on smaller numbers of available accounts. If, as has already been shown to be the case, migration significantly reduces the population sizes of the individual *communes* it also, therefore, increases the burden of local administrative costs for those left behind – the demands on the *commune* funds, such as road repairs, do not necessarily decrease at the same time or at the same rate as the decrease in population size.

A second aspect of migration which is of importance to local administrations is the role of migration in the ageing of the population, and particularly in increasing the proportions of over 60s. Social welfare payments are made to groups other than the aged, such as the unemployed, and the position is complicated by the separate existence of certain social security funds for agriculture, but the evidence is that overwhelmingly the over 60s are the biggest drain on the social welfare sector of the budgets of the *communes*.[10] As *commune* populations have aged, so welfare payments have become more important: in 1962 such payments were about 10 per cent of total current account outlays; by 1975 the median percentage was 12.7 in La Coulonche, rising to a maximum of 23.5 per cent in Haleine which was also the *commune* with the highest proportion of elderly – 29.8 per cent. The correlation coefficient for the relationship between the proportion of elderly and the *per capita* expenditure on social welfare was +0.74, significant at the 0.05 level. Migration effect is obviously not the only cause of increases in social welfare – the level of provision of such services has increased nationally during the period considered (International Labour Office, 1971) – but the ageing of the population has played an important role. Between 1962 and 1968 the total *per capita* expenditure on social welfare rose by 76 per cent (the equivalent rise in retail prices for France was 25 per cent): between 1968 and 1975 the rise was 202 per cent, compared to a retail price index rise of 71 per cent: in 1975, on average, the local social welfare sum spent per inhabitant of each *commune* was just over 48 francs.

Obviously the money to meet these increases in expenditure must come from somewhere. In France the two chief sources of *commune* income are, at present, the salaries tax (which replaced the old local commercial turnover tax in 1968), and the *centimes additionels*, which are based on a form of property rating. It is with the *centimes additionels* that the revenue burden falls on the local inhabitants, differential rates being payable on four categories of property – built-up land, non-built-up land, dwellings, and land used for commercial and industrial activity. The migration loss of population from the villages has meant that the reduced residual population has had to pay higher rates to support a pattern of service provision which has not been reduced in step with the population fall but which has, in some sectors, had to increase to provide for new demand as in the social welfare sector. In the 1962–68 period the average rates locally paid per head rose by only 11 per cent compared to the general national retail price index rise of 25 per cent, the effect of the change from the local turnover tax to the tax on salaries, redistributed nationally, being to reduce the pressure to increase the contribution of the *centimes additionels*. During the 1968–75 period, however, this contribution rose by an average of 106 per cent compared to the general national retail price index rise of 71 per cent. The cost to the residual populations of local government service provision therefore rose faster than the general national rate of price rises. Migration must be put forward as an important cause of this increasing financial inefficiency, both through the lowering of overall population totals and through its effects in changing the structure of the population towards more service-consuming sectors.

Conclusion: migration loss and the residual community

The seven *communes* that have been studied here have been experiencing, with the exception of the largest (Juvigny), a steady rate of depopulation over the last few years, a rate which is not untypical of many rural areas not just in France but in other European countries as well (for example see Kühne, 1974). That depopulation has been occurring through the effect of a negative migration balance rather than through natural loss of population, but despite the overall dominance of emigration the incidence of immigration plays an important, and even vital, role in conditioning the general trend of population evolution and maintaining demographic communities.

Migration both to and from the seven *communes* has been shown to be highly selective both by age and by occupation, but there are certain important differences in the extent and nature of selectivity between emigration and immigration: of great importance here is the fact that emigration is increasingly concentrated in the young adult age-group, but that with immigration the age distribution is less peaked with a more even distribution of movement by age. Of the occupational sectors agriculturalists were shown to be relatively immobile although with the dominant migrations affecting the sector being, as expected, in the young adult age-group.

Apart from the general reduction in population totals the other most important demographic effect of migration was the ageing of the population, measured both through average age and through changes in the proportion of over 60s. These changes in the population structures were shown to differ significantly from the changes that might have occurred had no migration taken place. It must be stressed, however, that the time-period examined was a short one and that migration loss is likely to have further long-term effects, particularly in changing the balance of natural change in the population. In the occupation categories examined migration was seen to contribute to the reduction of agricultural employment and also to the increased individuality of the agricultural population in terms of its age structure, which confirms findings elsewhere (Locoh, 1970). Both the general reduction in the total numbers and the ageing of the residual populations resulting from migration were found to be important in reducing the financial efficiency of local government and in increasing its cost to the remaining residents of the *communes*.

It is often argued (for example by Franklin, 1971, p. 12) that rural migration is not always disadvantageous to the rural community. Certainly this must be said to be the case in the studies of Spain mentioned earlier where emigration is needed to maintain stability. In areas in the final stage of the demographic transition with generally low fertility and mortality rates, as in the area of Normandy studied here, any imbalance between emigration and immigration must inevitably bring about changes in the population structure, and especially so where both emigration and immigration are markedly selective of participants. Pronounced changes in the population structure bring with them difficulties of the provision of various forms of local government services or amenities, whether it be of welfare services for the aged or of educational facilities for the young. Where such changes in the population structure are allied to falling populations, brought about by migration, certain facilities may become redundant with a consequent writing-off of capital investment as, for example, in the closing of the school in Lucé or in the closure of small private shops in several of the villages. Some of these closures are almost inevitable in a situation where a reduction in the labour force in agriculture, and a concomitant increase in labour efficiency, are seen as desirable and practicable, and where that reduction in the agricultural labour-force is being brought about by migration loss. Were the reduction of the agricultural labour force to be achieved by occupational transfers *in situ* migration loss and amenity closures would not be inevitable. It is perhaps a verdict on the recent local industrial implantation in Normandy, particularly in the town of Domfront, that it has not yet been on a sufficient scale to enable that local occupational transfer to occur which might stop the migration loss from the surrounding villages.[11]

Commins (1978) has shown that in the developed world many national governments are now adopting planning criteria which argue in a positive way for the maintenance and well-being of the population of rural areas, although the precise objectives vary from country to country. The present study has demonstrated that while net migration loss continues, population stability and levels of social amenity provision are threatened, and the long-term outlook is depopulation. In particular the strength of migration selectivity of the young is a notably important factor. In order that rural populations may be stabilized and standards of social provision rise it seems essential to halt this massive pattern of migration loss.

One way in which the French have attempted to improve the possibilities of rural stability has been through the introduction of larger-scale administrative systems, encouraging a programme of *commune* fusions under the 1971 law. This should enable the modernization of rural service provision to take place with greater cost-effectiveness (for example in water supply, refuse disposal or rural road maintenance), but progress in this programme is, at present, slow (Gervais *et al.*, 1976) because of the strength of tradition and of local objections to the replacement of a distinctly personal system of rural local government with a more anonymous, less local, structure.

Yet such measures can only be palliatives to make minor adjustments in response to population losses of the past and to increased expectations of service provision at the present. Inasmuch as continued migration loss is reducing the viability and stability of rural communities for the future, more large-scale curative measures are needed including national reorientations of economic planning. In the present north-west European situation of low rates of natural increase in population, Rochas (1977) has clearly demonstrated that only by halting urban growth can the rural exodus, particularly of the young, be reduced. With further declines in the agricultural labour force almost inevitable in the future in response to structural change and modernization of the farming sector in much of Europe, the provision of new forms of rural employment must be a major priority, in order to halt rural migration loss, and thereby to counteract the deleterious effects of past migration loss on the rural communities left behind.

Notes

1. 'Rural population' is defined as being the total number living in *communes* where the chief settlement has less than 2,000 inhabitants.
2. There are minor changes to the types of information given from one census to the next, and there are variations between villages in the completeness of the information recorded at any one census.
3. For Juvigny no *liste* was produced in 1968 and for the purposes of this study a list of inhabitants was constructed for that year from information given at the 1975 census, from the *liste électorale* and from the civil registration records.
4. In most cases only the names of the migrants in this category are recorded in the registers with no further personal details.
5. It is, of course, likely that such age-specific rates are themselves affected by migration: this would be particularly true for fertility rates where migration may deprive women of marriage partners.
6. Hence if the probability of dying was 0.034 and the number in the age-group was 15, then 15 three-figure random numbers were examined and any that were less than 034 were counted as deaths. The number 000 was read as 1000.
7. It may appear that there is no way of knowing whether a large number of simulations carried out under these rules would yield any specific sample distribution. In practice, however, the results of the exercise are, in part, predictable. Where the probability of a demographic event is small the annual distribution of such events approximates to a Poisson distribution, but when the results for the individual years are summed to give the figure for the six- or seven-year period the resulting distributions are approximately normal. Where the probability of a demographic

event is high, for example for births to women aged 25–29, both the annual and period totals of events are normally distributed. If in a single set of simulations, as carried out in this chapter, the final predicted population totals within each age-group for each individual *commune* are part of a normal distribution the sums of the predicted population totals by age-group for the seven *communes* are likely to approximate to the mean of all possible totals, although for individual *communes* there may be some variation from the possible mean.

8. A Kolmogorov–Smirnov test could have been used to test the difference between the total population structures. The test on the means was preferred here because it gave an indication of the actual population ageing.

9. Since 1971 French rural *communes* have been encouraged to fuse together completely (de Kervasdoué *et al.*, 1976): there has been opposition to this policy in Orne, although in Mayenne there have been several successful fusions within a few kilometres of the study area.

10. It is also likely that the increasing proportion of the elderly in the population affects the volume of purchasing power and sets off negative multipliers in the local commercial sector.

11. No information is available in this study on where the migrants go to and it is possible that some of the moves are local to the small nearby industrial towns of Domfront, Flers and La Ferté-Macé. If that is the case it is of regional significance but does not alter the effects of migration loss in the nearby villages.

Acknowledgements

Data collection in France was carried out in 1977 under the funding of a British Academy West European Grant. The author wishes to thank the mayors and secretaries of each of the *communes* visited, especially Mlle Rallu and Mme Letourneur of Juvigny, Mme Grimaux of Haleine, M. Chedeville of La Coulonche, and M. Gasté of St Aignan, as well as the staff of the *Archives Départementales* at Alençon and Laval. Much help in data collection and analysis was given by Elizabeth White. Professor R. J. Johnston made useful comments on an earlier version of the chapter.

Further reading

These remarks are intended as a guide to the use of the references which follow. They indicate the most important works on certain migration topics and on migration within certain geographical areas.

Useful collections of papers on various aspects of migration can be found in Jackson, J. A. (1969); Kosiński and Prothero (1975); and Brown and Neuberger (1977). On behavioural concepts in migration analysis the student is recommended to read Wolpert (1965); Brown and Longbrake (1970); and Lieber (1978). Rossi's book (1955) remains an important study of motivations for movement, while Michelson's study (1977) of residential search procedures can also be recommended. Lee (1966) provides a brief general overview of several themes in migration analysis, and Willis (1974) gives a more detailed consideration to important points. Zelinsky (1971) discusses the way in which the character of migration flows changes over time. Ravenstein's major contribution to migration study is discussed and evaluated in Grigg (1977). On the question of the relationship between migration and distance Hägerstrand (1957) is essential reading, while more recent discussion of the topic may be found in Cavalli-Sforza (1962); Morrill (1963); Olsson (1965); and Taylor (1975). Stouffer's paper (1960) on intervening opportunities is also relevant here, while Courgeau (1970) provides a detailed examination of distance questions in the case of migration within France. The most important example of a general systems approach to migration analysis is given by Mabogunje (1970). Methods of migration analysis are referred to in Woods (1979).

Among the studies of migration in Britain, Patten (1973) gives a useful general overview of pre-industrial mobility and Clark, P., (1972) provides more detailed examples. Redford's book (1926) remains an important examination of population movement in the early nineteenth century, and both Pooley (1977) and Dennis (1977) show the extent and impact of migration in Victorian cities. Saville's volume (1957) is a major discussion of rural–urban movement in Britain. Among the literature on recent migrations Hart (1970) and Peach (1968) may be recommended.

Papers on European migration as a whole are contained in Salt and Clout (1976). Böhning (1972) summarizes the importance of labour migration in the continent. Morrill's work (1965) on the growth of the urban system in Sweden is an important methodological contribution to migration analysis. Beijer (1963) provides a compendium of material on the movement of rural populations to cities, while Ogden and Winchester (1975) consider in detail patterns of migrant segregation in Paris in 1911. Migrants to Paris are also the subject of a study by Pourcher (1964) which makes use of a massive questionnaire survey. Merlin's book (1971) is unequalled as a study of rural migration in one country – in this case France. Douglass (1975) considers in detail the relationship between migration, agriculture and community in two villages of the Basque country of Spain. On a much larger scale B. Thomas' major study (1954) of the relationship between transatlantic migration and economic development on both sides of that ocean can still be recommended.

Africa has been particularly well studied by population geographers interested in migration and the student interested in migration in the Third World might be advised to concentrate his attention on the African continent. Hance (1970) provides a useful general overview of migration and urbanization; while detailed national examples are given by Caldwell (1969) and by de Graft-Johnson (1974) for Ghana, and by Riddell (1970b) for Sierra Leone. East Africa has been the context for important studies by Masser and Gould (1975); Claeson (1974); and Hirst (1976).

On migration in Latin America, Thomas, R. N., (1971) provides a useful summary of major research lines.

The student interested in migration should also consult *GeoAbstracts, Series D*, published six times a year, which has a section dealing with population migration, and the bibliographical journal *Population Index*.

References

Abdel-Fadil, M. (1975) *Development, Income Distribution and Social Change in Rural Egypt, 1952-1970* (Cambridge: Cambridge U.P.).

Abel, W. (1973) *Crises Agraires en Europe (XIIIe-XXe Siècle)* (Paris: Flammarion).

Acción Cultural Loyola (1974) *Estudio Socio-Económico de la Provincia Hernando Siles* (Sucre: Comité de Desarrollo de Chuquisaca).

Adams, D. W. (1968) 'Rural migration and agricultural development in Colombia', *Economic Development and Cultural Change*, **17**, pp. 527-39.

Adams, J. S. (1969) 'Directional bias in intra-urban migration', *Economic Geography*, **45**, pp. 302-23.

Adams, N. A. (1969) 'Internal migration in Jamaica: an economic analysis', *Social and Economic Studies*, **18**, pp. 137-51.

Agulhon, M., Désert, G. and **Specklin, R.** (1976) *Histoire de la France Rurale,* Tome 3, *Apogée et Crise de la Civilisation Paysanne, 1789-1914* (Paris: Seuil).

Alström, C. H. and **Lindelius, R.** (1966) 'A study of the population movement in nine Swedish subpopulations in 1800-49 from the genetico-statistical viewpoint', *Acta Genetica et Statistica Medica*, **16** (Supplement), pp. 1-44.

Álvarez, J. E. and **Antolín, R. P.** (1973) 'Los movimentos migratorios españoles durante el decenio, 1961-1970', *Geographica*, **15**, pp. 105-42.

Anderson, M. (1971) *Family Structure in Nineteenth Century Lancashire* (Cambridge: Cambridge U.P.).

Anderson, M. (1972a) 'Standard tabulation procedures for the census enumerators' books, 1851-1891', in Wrigley, E. A. (ed.), *Nineteenth Century Society*, pp. 134-45 (Cambridge: Cambridge U.P.).

Anderson, M. (1972b) 'The study of family structure', in Wrigley, E. A. (ed.), *Nineteenth Century Society*, pp. 47-81 (Cambridge: Cambridge U.P.).

Anderson, W. A. (1934) *Mobility of Rural Families*, Bulletin No. 607, Cornell Agricultural Station.

Armstrong, W. A. (1966) 'Social structure from the early census returns', in Wrigley, E. A. (ed.), *An Introduction to English Historical Demography*, pp. 209-37 (London: Weidenfeld and Nicolson).

Armstrong, W. A. (1968) 'The interpretation of census enumerators' books for Victorian towns', in Dyos, H. J. (ed.), *The Study of Urban History*, pp. 67-85 (London: Arnold).

Armstrong, W. A. (1972) 'The use of information about occupation', in Wrigley, E. A. (ed.), *Nineteenth Century Society*, pp. 191-310 (Cambridge: Cambridge U.P.).

Arriaga, E. E. (1968) 'Components of city growth in selected Latin American countries', *Milbank Memorial Fund Quarterly*, **46**, pp. 237-52.

Augé-Laribé, M. (1955) *La Révolution Agricole* (Paris: A. Michel).

Bagley, C. (1971) 'Immigrant minorities in the Netherlands: integration and assimilation', *International Migration Review*, **5**, pp. 18-35.

Baines, D. E. (1972) 'The use of published census data in migration studies', in Wrigley, E. A. (ed.), *Nineteenth Century Society*, pp. 311-35, (Cambridge: Cambridge U.P.).

Barata, O. S. (1975) 'A emigração e o êxodo rural en Portugal', *Boletim, Sociedade de Geografia de Lisboa*, **93**, pp. 37-69.

Bariou, R. (1974) 'Dépeuplement, exode, dépopulation en Bretagne centrale: l'exemple de la Haute-Cornouaille', *Norois*, **21**, pp. 527-39.

Beale, C. L. (1964) 'Rural depopulation in the United States: some demographic consequences of agricultural adjustments', *Demography*, **1**, pp. 264-72.

Beals, R. E., Levy, M. B. and **Moses, L. N.** (1967) 'Rationality and migration in Ghana', *Review of Economics and Statistics*, **49**, pp. 480-6.

Beaujeu-Garnier, J. (1970) 'Large over-populated cities in the underdeveloped world', in Zelinsky, W., Kosiński, L. and Prothero, R. M. (eds), *Geography and a Crowding World*, pp. 269-78 (New York: Oxford U.P.).

Beech, G. T. (1964) *A Rural Society in Medieval France: The Gatine of Poitu in the Eleventh and Twelfth Centuries* (Baltimore: Johns Hopkins U.P.).

Beijer, G. (1963) *Rural Migrants in Urban Setting* (The Hague: Martinus Nijhoff).

Bennassar, B. and **Jacquart, J.** (1972) *Le XVIe Siècle* (Paris: A. Colin).

Bernard, L. (1970) *The Emerging City: Paris in the Age of Louis XIV* (Durham, North Carolina: Duke U.P.).

Beteille, R. (1972) 'Les mouvements migratoires récent dans un département à dominante rurale: la Charente', *Norois*, **19**, pp. 519–39.

Bićanić, R. (1964) 'Three concepts of agricultural overpopulation', in Dixey, R. N. (ed.), *International Explorations of Agricultural Economics*, pp. 9–22 (Ames: Iowa State U.P.).

Bird, H. (1976) 'Residential mobility and preference patterns in the public sector of the housing market', *Transactions, Institute of British Geographers,* New Series, **1**, pp. 20–33.

Blalock, H. M. (1967) *Toward a Theory of Minority Group Relations* (New York: Wiley).

Blayo, Y. (1970) 'La mobilité dans un village de la Brie vers le milieu du XIXe siècle', *Population*, **25**, pp. 573–605.

Bogue, D. J. (1977) 'A migrant's-eye view of the costs and benefits of migration to a metropolis', in Brown, A. A. and Neuberger, E. (eds), *Internal Migration: A Comparative Perspective*, pp. 167–82 (New York: Academic Press).

Böhning, W. R. (1970) 'Foreign workers in post-war Germany', *New Atlantis*, **2**, pp. 12–38.

Böhning, W. R. (1972) *The Migration of Workers in the United Kingdom and the European Community* (Oxford: Oxford U.P.).

Böhning, W. R. (1974) 'Migration of workers as an element in employment policy', *New Community*, **3**, pp. 6–25.

Bourdieu, P. (1962) 'Célibat et condition paysanne', *Etudes Rurales*, **5**, pp. 32–135.

Bourgeois-Pichat, J. (1965) 'The general development of the population of France since the eighteenth century', in Glass, D. V. and Eversley, D. E. C. (eds), *Population in History*, pp. 474–506 (London: Arnold).

Bourgeois-Pichat, J. (1974) 'France', in Berelson, B. (ed.), *Population Policy in Developed Countries*, pp. 545–91 (New York: McGraw-Hill).

Bowley, A. L. and **Burnett-Hurst, A. R.** (1915) *Livelihood and Poverty* (London: Bell).

Boyce, A. J., Küchemann, C. F. and **Harrison, G. A.** (1971) 'Population structure and movement patterns', in Brass, W. (ed.) *Biological Aspects of Demography*, pp. 1–9 (London: Taylor and Francis).

Boyer, A. (1932) 'Migrations saisonnières dans le canton de Burzet (Ardèche)', *Revue de Géographie Alpine*, **20**, pp. 341–60.

Bozon, P. (1961) *La Vie Rurale en Vivarais* (Valence: Impr. Réunies).

Bozon, P. (1966) *Histoire du Peuple Vivariois* (Valence: Impr. Réunies).

Bracey, H. E. (1970) *People and the Countryside* (London: Routledge and Kegan Paul).

Braudel, F. (1972) *The Mediterranean and the Mediterranean World in the Age of Philip II*, Vol. 1 (London: Collins).

Bridenbaugh, C. (1968) *Vexed and Troubled Englishmen, 1590–1642* (Oxford: Clarendon Press).

Briggs, J. W. (1978) *An Italian Passage: Immigrants to Three American Cities, 1890–1930* (New Haven: Yale U.P.).

Brown, A. A. and **Neuberger, E.** (eds) (1977) *Internal Migration: A Comparative Perspective* (New York: Academic Press).

Brown, L. A., Horton, F. E. and **Wittick, R. I.** (1970) 'On place utility and the normative allocation of intra-urban migrants', *Demography*, **7**, pp. 175–83.

Brown, L. A. and **Longbrake, D. B.** (1970) 'Migration flows in intra-urban space: place utility considerations', *Annals, Association of American Geographers*, **60**, pp. 368–84.

Brown, L. A. and **Moore, E. G.** (1970) 'The intra-urban migration process: a perspective', *Geografiska Annaler*, **52B**, pp. 1–13.

Brown, L. M. (1969) 'Modern Hull', in Allison, K. J. (ed.), *A History of the County of York, East Riding*, Vol. 1: *The City of Kingston upon Hull*, pp. 215–87 (Oxford: Oxford U.P.).

Brown, R. (1973) *Rules and Laws in Sociology* (London: Routledge and Kegan Paul).

Butland, G. J. (1966) 'Frontiers of settlement in South America', *Revista Geographica*, **65**, pp. 93–108.

Byerlee, D. (1974) 'Rural–urban migration in Africa: theory, policy and research implications', *International Migration Review*, **8**, pp. 543–66.

Cairncross, A. K. (1953) *Home and Foreign Investment, 1870–1913; Studies in Capital Accumulation* (Cambridge: Cambridge U.P.).

Caldwell, J. C. (1968) 'Determinants of rural–urban migration in Ghana', *Population Studies*, **22**, pp. 361–77.

Caldwell, J. C. (1969) *African Rural–Urban Migration: The Movement to Ghana's Towns* (Canberra: Australian National U.P.).

Callaway, A. (1963) 'Unemployment among African school leavers', *Journal of Modern African Studies*, **1**, pp. 351–71.

Capo, E. and **Fonti, G. M.** (1965) 'L'exode rural vers les grandes villes', *Sociologia Ruralis*, **5**, pp. 267–87.

Carron, M. A. (1965) 'Prélude à l'exode rural en France: les migrations anciennes des travailleurs creusois', *Revue d'Histoire Economique et Sociale*, **43**, pp. 289–320.

Carus-Wilson, E. M. (1965) 'The first half century of the borough of Stratford-upon-Avon', *Economic History Review*, 2nd Series, **18**, pp. 46–63.

Castle, E. B. (1966) *Growing up in East Africa* (Oxford: Oxford U.P.).

Castle, E. B. *et al.* (1963) *Education in Uganda* (Entebbe: Government Printer).

Castles, G. and **Castles, S.** (1971) 'Immigrant workers and class structure in France', *Race*, **12**, pp. 303–15.

Castles, S. and **Kosack, G.** (1973) *Immigrant Workers and Class Structures in Western Europe* (Oxford: Oxford U.P.).

Cavalli-Sforza, L. L. (1962) 'The distribution of migration distances', in Sutter, J. (ed.), *Human Displacements*, pp. 139–58 (Monte Carlo: Hachette).

Chalklin, C. W. (1974) *The Provincial Towns of Georgian England, 1740–1820*, (London: Arnold).

Chambers, J. D. (1960) 'Population change in a provincial town: Nottingham, 1700–1800', in Pressnell, L. S. (ed.), *Studies in the Industrial Revolution*, pp. 97–124 (London: Athlone Press).

Chandler, T. and **Fox, G.** (1974) *3000 Years of Urban Growth* (London: Academic Press).

Chatelain, A. (1976) *Les Migrants Temporaires en France de 1800 à 1914* (Lille: P.U.L.).

Chesswass, J. D. (1966) *Educational Planning and Development in Uganda* (Paris: UNESCO International Institute for Educational Planning).

Chevalier, J. (1975) 'Le village et les migrants. Mutation professionnelle des jeunes agriculteurs et perception de l'espace rural', *Etudes Rurales*, **58**, pp. 63–82.

Claeson, C.-F. (1974) 'Inter-regional population movement and cumulative demographic disparity: an analysis of census data in Tanzania', *Geografiska Annaler*, **56B**, pp. 105–20.

Claeson, C.-F. and **Egero, B.** (1972a) *Migration in Tanzania. A Review Based on the 1967 Population Census*, Research Notes No. 11, University of Dar es Salaam, Bureau of Resource Assessment and Land Use Planning.

Claeson, C.-F. and **Egero, B.** (1972b) 'Migration and the urban population – analysis of population census data for Tanzania', *Geografiska Annaler*, **54B**, pp. 1–18.

Clark, P. (1972) 'The migrant in Kentish towns, 1580–1640', in Clark, P. and Slack, P. (eds), *Crisis and Order in English Towns*, pp. 117–63 (London: Routledge and Kegan Paul).

Clark, R. J. (1968) 'Land reform and peasant market participation on the North Highlands of Bolivia', *Land Economics*, **44**, pp. 153–72.

Clarke, J. I. (1965) 'Sex ratios in Sierra Leone', *Bulletin-Journal of the Sierra Leone Geographical Association*, **9**, pp. 72–7.

Clément, P. and **Vieille, P.** (1960) 'L'exode rural. Historique, causes et conditions, sélectivité, perspectives', *Etudes de Comptabilité Nationale*, pp. 57–130 (Paris: Impr. Nationale).

Cliff, A. D., Martin, R. L. and **Ord, J. K.** (1974) 'Evaluating the friction of distance parameter in gravity models', *Regional Studies*, **8**, pp. 281–6.

Clout, H. D. (1972) *Rural Geography: An Introductory Survey* (Oxford: Pergamon).

Clout, H. D. (1976) 'Rural–urban migration in Western Europe', in Salt, J. and Clout, H. D. (eds), *Migration in Post-War Europe. Geographical Essays*, pp. 30–51 (Oxford: Oxford U.P.).

Coale, A. J. (1957) 'How the age distribution of a human population is determined', *Cold Spring Harbor Symposia on Quantitative Biology*, **22**, pp. 83–9.

Coleman, D. A. (1973) 'Marriage movement in British cities', in Roberts, D. F. and Sunderland, E. (eds), *Genetic Variation in Britain*, pp. 33–57 (London: Taylor and Francis).

Coleman, D. C. (1977) *The Economy of England, 1450–1750* (Oxford: Oxford U.P.).

Commins, P. (1978) 'Socio-economic adjustments to rural depopulation', *Regional Studies*, **12**, pp. 79–94.

Connell, K. H. (1950) *The Population of Ireland, 1750–1845* (Oxford: Clarendon Press).

Constant, A. (1948) 'The geographical background of inter-village population movements in Northamptonshire and Huntingdonshire, 1754–1943', *Geography*, **33**, pp. 78–88.

Corbin, A. (1971) 'Migrations temporaires et société rurale au XIXᵉ siècle: le cas du Limousin', *Revue Historique*, **246**, pp. 293–334.

Cornwall, J. (1970) 'English population in the early sixteenth century', *Economic History Review*, 2nd Series, **23**, pp. 32–44.

Courgeau, D. (1970) *Les Champs Migratoires en France*, Cahier de l'I.N.E.D. No. 58 (Paris: P.U.F.).

Courgeau, D. (1976) 'Quantitative, demographic, and geographic approaches to internal migration', *Environment and Planning*, **8A**, pp. 261–9.

Cousens, S. H. (1960) 'The regional pattern of emigration during the Great Irish Famine, 1846–1851', *Transactions, Institute of British Geographers*, **28**, pp. 119–34.

Cribier, F. (1975) 'Retirement migration in France', in Kosiński, L. A. and Prothero, R. M. (eds), *People on the Move*, pp. 361–73 (London: Methuen).

Croix, A. (1974) *Nantes et le Pays Nantais au XVIᵉ Siècle: Étude Démographique* (Paris: S.E.V.P.E.N.).

Cullen, L. M. (1972) *An Economic History of Ireland since 1660* (London: Batsford).

Cummings, F. H. (1975) 'Internal migration and regional development planning; Thailand, the Philippines and Indonesia', *Journal of Tropical Geography*, **41**, pp. 16–27.

Currie, J. and **Maas, J. van L.** (1974) 'Uganda secondary school graduates: postponement of labour market entry', *Greylands Educational Journal*, **9**, pp. 14–31.

Curry, L. (1972) 'A spatial analysis of gravity flows', *Regional Studies*, **6**, pp. 131–47.

Dak, O. (1968) *A Geographical Analysis of the Distribution of Migrants in Uganda*, Occasional Paper No. 11, Makerere University, Department of Geography.

Davis, J. C. (1973) *Statistics and Data Analysis in Geology* (New York: Wiley).

Davis, K. (1963) 'The theory of change and response in modern demographic history', *Population Index*, **29**, pp. 345–66.

Davis, K. (1965) 'The urbanization of the human population', *Scientific American*, **213**, pp. 41–53.

Davis, K. and **Golden, H. H.** (1954) 'Urbanization and the development of pre-industrial areas', *Economic Development and Cultural Change*, **3**, pp. 1–26.

Davis, R. (1973) *The Rise of the Atlantic Economies* (London: Weidenfeld and Nicolson).

Deane, P. and **Cole, W. A.** (1962) *British Economic Growth, 1688–1959* (Cambridge: Cambridge U.P.).

Demko, G. J. (1969) *The Russian Colonization of Kazakhstan, 1896–1916*, Indiana University Publications, Uralic and Altaic Series, Vol. 99.

Dennis, R. J. (1977) 'Inter-censal mobility in a Victorian city', *Transactions, Institute of British Geographers*, New Series, **2**, pp. 349–63.

Derry, D. K. (1973) *A History of Modern Norway, 1814–1972* (Oxford: Clarendon Press).

Desai, R. (1963) *Indian Immigrants in Britain* (Oxford: Oxford U.P.).

Detton, H. and **Hourticq, J.** (1975) *L'Administration Régionale et Locale de la France*, 7th edition (Paris: P.U.F.).

Dobb, M. (1946) *Studies in the Development of Capitalism* (London: Routledge and Kegan Paul).

Doolittle, I. G. (1975) 'The effects of the plague on a provincial town in the sixteenth and seventeenth centuries', *Medical History*, **19**, pp. 333–41.

Dorner, P. (1972) *Land Reform and Economic Development* (Harmondsworth: Penguin).

Douglass, W. A. (1970) 'Peasant emigrants: reactors or actors?', in Spencer, R. F. (ed.), *Migration and Anthropology*, pp. 21–35 (Seattle: Washington U.P.).

Douglass, W. A. (1975) *Echalar and Murelaga: Opportunity and Exodus in Two Spanish Basque Villages* (London: Hurst).

Downs, R. M. (1969) 'Geographic space perception: past approaches and future prospects', *Progress in Geography*, **2**, pp. 65–108.

Dozier, C. L. (1969) *Land Development and Colonization in Latin America: Case Studies of Peru, Bolivia and Mexico* (London: Praeger).

Drake, M. (1969) *Population and Society in Norway, 1735–1865* (Cambridge: Cambridge U.P.).

Drudy, P. J. (1978) 'Depopulation in a prosperous agricultural sub-region', *Regional Studies*, **12**, pp. 49–60.

Duboscq, P. (1972) 'La mobilité rurale en Aquitaine: essai d'analyse logique', *L'Espace Géographique*, **1**, pp. 23–42.

Duby, G. (1962) *Rural Economy and Country Life in the Medieval West* (London: Arnold).

Duncan, O. D. and **Duncan, B.** (1955a) 'A methodological analysis of segregation indices', *American Sociological Review*, **20**, pp. 210–17.

Duncan, O. D. and **Duncan, B.** (1955b) 'Residential distribution and occupational stratification', *American Journal of Sociology*, **60**, pp. 493–506.

Dunn, M. C. and **Swindell, K.** (1972) 'Electoral registers and rural migration: a case study from Herefordshire', *Area*, **4**, pp. 39–42.

Duocastella, R. (1970) 'Problems of adjustment in the case of internal migration: an example in Spain', in Jansen, C. J. (ed.), *Readings in the Sociology of Migration*, pp. 319–37 (Oxford: Pergamon).

Dupeux, G. (1974) 'La croissance urbaine en France au XIXe siècle', *Revue d'Histoire Économique et Sociale*, **52**, pp. 173–89.

Dupeux, G. (1976) *French Society, 1789–1970* (London: Methuen).

Dyer, A. R. (1973) *The City of Worcester in the Sixteenth Century* (Leicester: Leicester U.P.).

Dyos, H. J. and **Baker, A. B. M.** (1968) 'The possibilities of computerising census data', in Dyos, H. J. (ed.), *The Study of Urban History*, pp. 87–112 (London: Arnold).

Economic Commission for Latin America (1961) 'The demographic situation in Latin America', *Economic Bulletin for Latin America*, **6**, pp. 13–53.

Economic Commission for Latin America (1971) 'Population trends and policy alternatives in Latin America', *Economic Bulletin for Latin America*, **16**, pp. 71–104.

Edmond-Smith, J. (1972) 'West Indian workers in France', *New Community*, **1**, pp. 444–50.

Eldridge, H. T. (1965) 'Primary, secondary and return migration in the United States, 1955–60', *Demography*, **2**, pp. 444–55.

Emery, F. V. (1973) 'England circa 1600', in Darby, H. C. (ed.), *A New Historical Geography of England*, pp. 248–301 (Cambridge: Cambridge U.P.).

Erasmus, C. J. (1967) 'Upper limits of peasantry and agrarian reform: Bolivia, Venezuela and Mexico compared', *Ethnology*, **6**, pp. 349–80.

Erasmus, C. J. (1969) 'Land reform and social revolution in Southern Bolivia: the valleys of Chuquisaca and Tarija', in Heath, D. B., Erasmus, C. J. and Buechler, H. C. (eds), *Land Reform and Social Revolution in Bolivia*, pp. 63–165 (New York: Praeger).

Everitt, A. (1967) 'The marketing of agricultural produce', in Thirsk, J. (ed.), *The Agricultural History of England and Wales*, Vol. IV: *1540–1640*, pp. 466–592 (Cambridge: Cambridge U.P.).

228 *References*

Ewusi, K. (1974) 'The growth rate of urban centres in Ghana and its implications for rural–urban migration', *Nigerian Journal of Economic and Social Studies*, **16**, pp. 479–91.

Farmer, B. H. (1957) *Pioneer Peasant Colonization in Ceylon* (Oxford: Oxford U.P.).

Farmer, B. H. (1974) *Agricultural Colonization in India since Independence* (Oxford: Oxford U.P.).

Fel, A. (1974) 'Types d'évolution démographique de la France rurale', *Geographia Polonica*, **29**, pp. 55–62.

Ferragut, C. (1963) 'La reforma agraria Boliviana: sus antecedentes, fundamentos, aplicaciones y resultados', *Revista Interamericana de Ciencias Sociales*, **2**, pp. 78–151.

Floud, R. C. and Schofield, R. S. (1968) 'Social structure from the early census returns: a comment', *Economic History Review*, 2nd Series, **21**, pp. 607–9.

Foster, J. (1974) *Class Struggle and the Industrial Revolution: Early Industrial Capitalism in Three English Towns* (London: Weidenfeld and Nicolson).

Francus, Dr (Mazon, A.) (1885) *Voyage le Long de la Rivière d'Ardèche* (Privas: Impr. du Patriote), reprinted 1970 (Aubenas: Lienhart).

Franklin, S. H. (1971) *Rural Societies* (London: Macmillan).

Frederiksen, A. V. K. (1976) *Familierekonstitution: en Modelstudie over Befolkningsforholdene: Sejerø Sogn, 1663–1813* (Copenhagen: Akademisk Forlag).

Friedl, E. (1976) 'Kinship, class and selective migration', in Peristiany, J. G. (ed.), *Mediterranean Family Structures*, pp. 363–88 (Cambridge: Cambridge U.P.).

Friedlander, D. (1969) 'Demographic responses and population change', *Demography*, **6**, pp. 355–81.

Friedman, J. and Sullivan, F. (1974) 'The absorption of labour in the urban economy: the case of developing countries', *Economic Development and Cultural Change*, **22**, pp. 385–413.

Gade, O. (1970) 'Geographic research and human spatial interaction theory: a review of pertinent studies in migration', in Spencer, R. F. (ed.), *Migration and Anthropology*, pp. 75–9 (Seattle: Washington U.P.).

Gale, S. (1973)'Explanations, theory and models of migration', *Economic Geography*, **49**, pp. 257–74.

Galtung, J. (1971) *Members of Two Worlds: A Development Study of Three Villages in Western Sicily* (Oslo: Universitetsforlaget).

Gautier, E. and Henry, L. (1958) *La Population de Crulai, Paroisse Normande: Étude Historique*, Cahier de l'I.N.E.D. No. 33 (Paris: P.U.F.).

Geiger, F. (1975) 'Zur Konzentration von Gastarbeiten in alten Dorfkernen: Fallstudie aus dem Verdichtungsraum Stuttgart', *Geographische Rundschau*, **2**, pp. 61–71.

Gervais, M., Jollivet, M. and Tavernier, Y. (1976) *Histoire de la France Rurale*. Tome 4, *La Fin de la France Paysanne de 1914 à nos Jours* (Paris: Seuil).

Getis, A. and Boots, B. (1978) *Models of Spatial Processes* (Cambridge: Cambridge U.P.).

Giles, B. O. (1976) 'High status neighbourhoods in Birmingham', *West Midlands Studies*, **9**, pp. 10–33.

Girard, A. (1964) *Le Choix du Conjoint: Une Enquête Psycho-Sociologique en France*, Cahier de l'I.N.E.D. No. 44, (Paris: P.U.F.).

Gist, N. P. and Clark, C. D. (1938) 'Intelligence as a selective factor in rural–urban migration', *American Journal of Sociology*, **44**, pp. 36–58.

Goddard, A. D., Gould, W. T. S. and Masser, F. I. (1975) 'Census data and migration analysis in Tropical Africa', *Geografiska Annaler*, **57B**, pp. 26–41.

Goldstein, S. (1964) 'The extent of repeat migration: an analysis based on the Danish Population Register', *Journal, American Statistical Association*, **59**, pp. 1121–32.

Goldstein, S. (1973) 'Interrelations between migration and fertility in Thailand', *Demography*, **10**, pp. 225–41.

Goldstein, S. and Mayer, K. B. (1965) 'The impact of migration on the socio-economic structure of cities and suburbs', *Sociology and Social Research*, **50**, pp. 5–23.

Goldthorpe, J. E. (1965) *An African Élite: Makerere College Students, 1922–1960*, East African Studies No. 17 (Nairobi: Oxford U. P. for East African Institute of Social Research).

Goldthorpe, J. E. and Wilson, F. B. (1960) *Tribal Maps of East Africa and Zanzibar*, East African Studies No. 13 (Kampala: East African Institute of Social Research).

Goodey, B. R. (1968) *A Pilot Study of the Geographical Perception of North Dakota Students* (Grand Forks: University of North Dakota).

Goodey, B. R. (1971) *Perception of the Environment: An Introduction to the Literature*, Occasional Paper No. 17, Centre for Urban and Regional Studies, University of Birmingham.

Gosal, G. S. and Krishnan, G. (1975) 'Patterns of internal migration in India', in Kosiński, L. and Prothero, R. M. (eds), *People on the Move*, pp. 193–206 (London: Methuen).

Gottmann, J. (1952) *La Politique des États et Leur Géographie* (Paris: A. Colin).

Gould, P. (1967) 'Structuring information on spatio-temporal preferences', *Journal of Regional Science*, **7**, pp. 259–74.

Gould, P. (1969) 'The structuring of space preferences in Tanzania', *Area*, **4**, pp. 29–35.

Gould, P. and White, R. (1968) 'The mental maps of British school leavers', *Regional Studies*, **2**, pp. 161–82.

Gould, P. and White, R. (1974) *Mental Maps* (Harmondsworth: Penguin).

Gould, W. T. S. (1971) 'Geography and educational opportunity in tropical Africa', *Tijdschrift voor Economische en Sociale Geografie*, **62**, pp. 82–9.

Gould, W. T. S. (1973a) *Movement of School Children and Provision of Secondary Schools in Uganda*, Working Paper No. 3, African Population Mobility Project, Department of Geography, University of Liverpool.

Gould, W. T. S. (1973b) *Secondary School Admissions Policies in Eastern Africa: Some Regional Issues*, Working Paper No. 9, African Population Mobility Project, Department of Geography, University of Liverpool.

Gould, W. T. S. and **Prothero, R. M.** (1975) 'Space and time in African population mobility', in Kosiński, L. A. and Prothero, R. M. (eds), *People on the Move*, pp. 39–50 (London: Methuen).

Graeff, P. (1974) *The Effects of Continued Landlord Presence in the Bolivian Countryside During the Post-Reform Era: Lessons to be Learned*, Land Tenure Centre No. 103, Madison, University of Wisconsin.

Graft-Johnson, K. T. de (1974) 'Population growth and rural–urban migration with special reference to Ghana', *International Labour Review*, 109, pp. 471–85.

Grandstaff, P. J. (1975) 'Recent Soviet experience and Western "laws" of population migration', *International Migration Review*, 9, pp. 479–97.

Gravier, J.-F. (1947) *Paris et le Désert Français* (Paris: Editions Le Portulan).

Greenwood, M. J. (1970) 'Lagged response in the decision to migrate', *Journal of Regional Science*, 10, pp. 375–84.

Grigg, D. B. (1974a) 'Agricultural populations and economic development', *Tijdschrift voor Economische en Sociale Geografie*, 65, pp. 414–20.

Grigg, D. B. (1974b) 'The growth and distribution of the world's arable land, 1870–1970', *Geography*, 59, pp. 104–10.

Grigg, D. B. (1975) 'The world's agricultural labour force, 1800–1970', *Geography*, 60, pp. 194–202.

Grigg, D. B. (1976) 'Population pressure and agricultural change', *Progress in Geography*, 8, pp. 135–76.

Grigg, D. B. (1977) 'E. G. Ravenstein and the "laws of migration"', *Journal of Historical Geography*, 3, pp. 41–54.

Grigg, D. B. (in press) *Population Growth and Agrarian Change* (Cambridge: Cambridge U.P.).

Gugler, J. (1968) 'The impact of labour migration on society and economy in sub-Saharan Africa', *African Social Research*, 6, pp. 463–86.

Gugler, J. (1969) 'On the theory of rural–urban migration: the case of sub-Saharan Africa', in Jackson, J. A. (ed.), *Migration*, pp. 134–55 (Cambridge: Cambridge U.P.).

Hägerstrand, T. (1957) 'Migration and area', in Hannerberg, D. *et al.* (eds), *Migration in Sweden*, pp. 27–158, Lund Studies in Geography, 13B (Lund: Gleerup).

Hägerstrand, T. (1967) *Innovation Diffusion as a Spatial Process* (Chicago: Chicago U.P.).

Halsey, A. H. (1978) *Change in British Society* (Oxford: Oxford U.P.).

Hance, W. A. (1967) *African Economic Development* (London: Pall Mall).

Hance, W. A. (1970) *Population, Migration and Urbanization in Africa* (New York: Columbia U.P.).

Hannan, D. F. (1969) 'Migration motives and migration differentials among Irish rural youth', *Sociologia Ruralis*, 9, pp. 195–220.

Hannan, D. F. (1970) *Rural Exodus: A Study of the Forces Influencing the Large-Scale Migration of Irish Rural Youth* (London: Chapman).

Harris, C. (1968) 'Contributions to the discussion of Armstrong's paper', in Dyos, H. J. (ed.), *The Study of Urban History*, pp. 147–48 (London: Arnold)

Harrison, G. A. and **Boyce, A. J.** (1972) 'Migration, exchange and the genetic structure of populations', in Harrison, G. A. and Boyce, A. J. (eds), *The Structure of Human Populations*, pp. 128–45 (Oxford: Clarendon Press).

Hart, R. A. (1970) 'A model of inter-regional migration in England and Wales', *Regional Studies*, 4, pp. 279–96.

Hart, R. A. (1973) 'Economic expectations and the decision to migrate: an analysis by socio-economic group', *Regional Studies*, 7, pp. 271–85.

Haynes, R. M. (1974) 'Application of exponential distance decay to human and animal activities', *Geografiska Annaler*, 56B, pp. 90–104.

Heath, D. B. (1959) 'Land reform in Bolivia', *Inter-American Economic Affairs*, 12, pp. 3–27.

Helleiner, K. F. (1967) 'The population of Europe from the Black Death to the eve of the vital revolution', in Rich, E. E. and Wilson, C. H. (eds), *The Cambridge Economic History of Europe*, Vol. 4: *The Economy of Expanding Europe in the Sixteenth and Seventeenth Centuries*, pp. 1–95 (Cambridge: Cambridge U.P.).

Herbert, D. T. (1973) 'Residential mobility and preference: a study of Swansea', in Clark, B. D. and Gleave, M. B. (eds), *Social Patterns in Cities*, pp. 103–21, Special Publication No. 5, Institute of British Geographers.

Herlihy, D. (1970) 'The Tuscan town in the Quattrocento: demographic profile', *Medievalia et Humanistica*, New Series, 1, pp. 81–109.

Hicks, J. R. (1971) *The Social Framework: An Introduction to Economics* (Oxford: Clarendon Press).

Higonnet, P. L. R. (1971) *Pont de Montvert: Social Structure and Politics in a French Village, 1700–1914* (Cambridge, Mass.: Harvard U.P.).

Hirst, M. A. (1970) 'Tribal migration in East Africa: a review and analysis', *Geografiska Annaler*, 52B, pp. 153–64.

Hirst, M. A. (1972a) 'Evolution of a method for establishing net migration patterns in East Africa', *Nigerian Geographical Journal*, **15**, pp. 107–14.

Hirst, M. A. (1972b) 'Tribal mixture and migration in Tanzania: an evaluation and analysis of census tribal data', *Canadian Geographer*, **16**, pp. 230–47.

Hirst, M. A. (1975) 'The distribution of migrants in Kampala', *East African Geographical Review*, **13**, pp. 37–57.

Hirst, M. A. (1976) 'A Markovian analysis of inter-regional migration in Uganda', *Geografiska Annaler*, **58B**, pp. 79–94.

Ho, J. (1972) 'Les travailleurs étrangers en Allemagne', *Population*, **27**, pp. 308–12.

Hobsbawm, E. J. (1964) *Labouring Men – Studies in the History of Labour* (London: Weidenfeld and Nicolson).

Hobsbawm, E. J. (1969) *Industry and Empire* (Harmondsworth: Penguin).

Hodne, F. (1976) *An Economic History of Norway, 1815–70* (Oslo: Tapir).

Hofsten, E. and Lundström, H. (1976) *Swedish Population History: Main Trends from 1750 to 1970*, Urval No. 8, National Central Bureau of Statistics (Stockholm: Liber Förlag).

Holderness, B. A. (1970) 'Personal mobility in some rural parishes of Yorkshire, 1777–1822', *Yorkshire Archaeological Journal*, **42**, pp. 444–54.

Hollander, A. den (1960) 'The Great Hungarian Plain: a European frontier area', *Comparative Studies in Society and History*, **3**, pp. 74–88.

Hollingsworth, T. H. (1970) 'Historical studies of migration', *Annales de Démographie Historique*, **6**, pp. 87–96.

Holmes, J. H. and Haggett, P. (1977) 'Graph theory interpretation of flow matrices: a note on maximization procedures for identifying significant links', *Geographical Analysis*, **9**, pp. 388–99.

Holmes, R. S. (1973) 'Ownership and migration from a study of rate books', *Area*, **5**, pp. 242–51.

Horton, F. E. and Reynolds, D. R. (1971), 'Effects of urban spatial structure on individual behaviour', *Economic Geography*, **47**, pp. 36–48.

Hoselitz, B. F. (1957) 'Population pressure, industrialization and social mobility', *Population Studies*, **11**, pp. 123–35.

Hoskins, W. G. (1976) *The Age of Plunder: King Henry's England, 1500–1547* (London: Longman).

Howard, N. P. (1976) 'Cooling the heat. A history of the rise of trade unionism in the South Yorkshire iron and steel industry, from the origins to the First World War', in Pollard, S. and Holmes, C. (eds), *Essays in the Economic and Social History of South Yorkshire*, pp. 59–73 (Sheffield: South Yorkshire County Council).

Hunter, J. M. (1965) 'Regional patterns of population growth in Ghana, 1948–1960', in Whittow, J. B. and Wood, P. D. (eds), *Essays in Geography for Austin Miller*, pp. 272–90 (Reading: University of Reading).

Hutton, C. (1973) *Reluctant Farmers? A Study of Unemployment and Planned Rural Development in Uganda* (Nairobi: East African Publishing House).

Hvidt, K. (1975) *Flight to America: The Social Background of 300,000 Danish Emigrants* (London: Academic Press).

Immigrant Statistics Unit (1978) 'Marriage and birth patterns among the New Commonwealth and Pakistani population', *Population Trends*, **11**, pp. 5–9.

International Labour Office (1971) 'The social situation of old people in rural areas', *Sociologia Ruralis*, **11**, pp. 374–400.

Iszaevich, A. (1975) 'Emigrants, spinsters and priests: the dynamics of demography of Spanish peasant societies', *Journal of Peasant Studies*, **2**, pp. 292–312.

Jackson, J. A. (ed.) (1969) *Migration* (Cambridge: Cambridge U.P.).

Jackson, L. E. and Johnston, R. J. (1974) 'Underlying regularities to mental maps: an investigation of relationships among age, experience and spatial preferences', *Geographical Analysis*, **6**, pp. 69–84.

Jackson, V. J. (1968) *Population in the Countryside: Growth and Stagnation in the Cotswolds* (London: Cass).

Jacoby, E. H. (1971) *Man and Land: The Fundamental Issue in Development* (London: Deutsch).

James, P. E. (1969) *Latin America*, 4th edition (New York: Odyssey Press).

Jegouzo, G. (1972) 'L'ampleur du célibat chez les agriculteurs', *Économie et Statistique*, **34**, pp. 13–22.

Jegouzo, G. and Brangeon, J.-L. (1974) 'Célibat paysan et pauvreté', *Économie et Statistique*, **58**, pp. 3–13.

Johnson, J. H. (1967) 'Harvest migration from nineteenth century Ireland', *Transactions, Institute of British Geographers*, **41**, pp. 97–112.

Johnson, J. H., Salt, J. and Wood, P. A. (1974) *Housing and Migration of Labour in England and Wales* (Farnborough: Saxon House).

Johnston, B. F. and Southworth, H. M. (1967) 'Agricultural development: problems and issues', in Southworth, H. M. and Johnston, B. F. (eds), *Agricultural Development and Economic Growth* (Ithaca, N.Y.: Cornell U.P.).

Johnston, R. J. (1966) 'The location of high status residential areas', *Geografiska Annaler*, **48B**, pp. 23–35.

Johnston, R. J. (1967) 'A reconaissance survey of population change in Nidderdale, 1951–1961',

Transactions, Institute of British Geographers, **41**, pp. 113–23.

Johnston, R. J. (1971) 'Residential preferences of New Zealand school children', *New Zealand Journal of Geography*, **50**, pp. 13–23.

Johnston, R. J. (1972) 'Activity spaces and residential preferences: some tests of the hypothesis of sectoral mental maps', *Economic Geography*, **48**, pp. 199–211.

Johnston, R. J. (1973) 'On friction of distance and regression coefficients', *Area*, **5**, pp. 187–191.

Johnston, R. J. (1976) 'On regression coefficients in comparative studies of the "frictions of distance"', *Tijdschrift voor Economische en Sociale Geografie*, **67**, pp. 15–28.

Johnston, R. J. (1978) *Multivariate Statistical Analysis in Geography* (London: Longman).

Johnston, R. J. and **Perry, P.J.** (1972) 'Déviation directionelle dans les aires de contact: deux exemples de relations matrimoniales dans la France rurale du XIXᵉ siècle', *Études Rurales*, **46**, pp. 23–33.

Jollivet, M. (1965) 'L'utilisation des lieux de naissance pour l'analyse de l'espace social d'un village', *Revue Française de Sociologie*, **6**, pp. 74–95.

Jones, H. R. (1965) 'A study of rural migration in central Wales', *Transactions, Institute of British Geographers*, **37**, pp. 31–45.

Jörberg, L. (1973) 'The industrial revolution in the Nordic countries', in Cipolla, C. M. (ed.), *The Fontana Economic History of Europe: The Emergence of Industrial Societies*, Part Two, pp. 375–487 (London: Collins/Fontana).

Joyce, F. (ed.) (1977) *Metropolitan Development and Change: The West Midlands: A Policy Review* (Farnborough: Teakfield).

Kamen, H. (1971) *The Iron Century: Social Change in Europe, 1550–1660* (London: Weidenfeld and Nicolson).

Kay, G. (1967) *Social Geography of Zambia* (London: London U.P.).

Kellett, J.R. (1969) *The Impact of Railways in Victorian Cities* (London: Routledge and Kegan Paul).

Kennedy, R. E. (1973) *The Irish: Emigration, Marriage and Fertility* (Berkeley: California U.P.).

Kervasdoué, J. de *et al.* (1976) 'La loi et le changement social: un diagnostic. La loi du 16 juillet 1971 sur les fusions et regroupements de communes', *Revue Française de Sociologie*, **17**, pp. 423–50.

Keyfitz, N. (1971) 'Migration as a means of population control'. *Population Studies*, **25**, pp. 63–72.

Kindelberger, C. P. (1965) 'Mass migration, then and now', *Foreign Affairs*, **43**, pp. 647–58.

King, R. L. (1978) 'Return migration: a neglected aspect of population geography', *Area*, **10**, pp. 175–82.

Klaassen, L. H. and **Drewe, P.** (1973) *Migration Policy in Europe* (Farnborough: Saxon House).

Klein, H. S. (1978) *The Middle Passage: Comparative Studies in the Atlantic Slave Trade* (Princeton, N.J.: Princeton U.P.).

Koebner, R. (1966) 'The settlement and colonization of Europe', in Postan, M. M. (ed.), *The Cambridge Economic History of Europe*, Vol. 1: *The Agrarian Life of the Middle Ages*, pp. 1–91 (Cambridge: Cambridge U.P.).

Köllman, W. (1969) 'The process of urbanization in Germany at the height of the industrialization period', *Journal of Contemporary History*, **4**, pp. 59–76.

Kosiński, L. and **Prothero, R. M.** (1970) 'Migrations and population pressures on resources', in Zelinsky, W., Kosiński, L. and Prothero, R. M. (eds), *Geography and a Crowding World*, pp. 251–8 (New York: Oxford U.P.).

Kosiński, L. A. and **Prothero, R. M.** (eds) (1975) *People on the Move: Studies in Internal Migration* (London: Methuen).

Kossman, E. H. (1970) 'The Low Countries', in Cooper, J. P. (ed.), *The New Cambridge Modern History*, Vol. 4: *The Decline of Spain and the Thirty Years War, 1609–48/59*, pp. 359–84 (Cambridge: Cambridge U.P.).

Krause, J. T. (1958) 'Changes in English fertility and mortality, 1781–1850', *Economic History Review*, 2nd Series, **11**, pp. 52–70.

Küchemann, C. F., **Boyce, A. J**, and **Harrison, G. A.** (1967) 'A demographic and genetic study of a group of Oxfordshire villages', *Human Biology*, **39**, pp. 251–76.

Kühne, I. (1974) *Die Gebirgsentvölkerung im Nördlichen und Mittleren Appenin in der Zeit nach dem Zweiten Weltkrieg*, Erlanger Geographische Arbeiten No. 1, Fränkischen Geographischen Gesellschaft.

Kulldorff, G. (1955) *Migration Probabilities*, Lund Studies in Geography, 14B (Lund: Gleerup).

Lambert, J. *et al.* (1978) *Housing Policy and the State: Allocation, Access and Control* (London: Macmillan).

Lane, A. (1974) *The Union Makes Us Strong* (London: Arrow).

Langer, W. (1975) 'American foods and Europe's population growth, 1750–1850', *Journal of Social History*, **8**, pp. 51–66.

Larivière, J. P. (1971) 'L'émigration des ruraux corréziens: intensité et courants de destination', *Norois*, **18**, pp. 601–13.

Laserwitz, B. (1971) 'Sampling theory and procedures', in Blalock, H. M. and Blalock, A. (eds), *Methodology in Social Research*, pp. 278–328 (New York: McGraw-Hill).

Laslett, P. and **Harrison, J.** (1964) 'Clayworth and Cogenhoe', in Bell, H. E. and Ollard, R. L. (eds), *Historical Essays, 1600–1750 Presented to David Ogg*, pp. 157–84 (London: Black).

Law, C. M. (1967) 'The growth of urban population in England and Wales, 1801–1911', *Transactions,*

Institute of British Geographers, **41**, pp. 125–44.
Lawton, R. (1953) 'Genesis of population', in Smith, W. *et al.*, (eds), *A Scientific Survey of Merseyside*, pp. 120–31 (Liverpool: Liverpool U.P.).
Lawton, R. (1972) 'An age of great cities', *Town Planning Review*, **43**, pp. 199–224.
Lawton, R. (ed.) (1978) *The Census and Social Structure: An Interpretive Guide to Nineteenth Century Censuses for England and Wales* (London: Cass).
Lee, E. S. (1966) 'A theory of migration', *Demography*, **3**, pp. 47–57.
Leloup, Y. (1972) 'L'émigration portugaise dans le monde et ses conséquences pour le Portugal', *Revue de Géographie de Lyon*, **47**, pp. 59–76.
Leonard, O. E. and **Hannon, J. H.** (1977) 'Those left behind: recent social changes in a heavy emigration area of North Central New Mexico', *Human Organization*, **36**, pp. 384–94.
Le Roy Ladurie, E., Jacquart, J. and **Neveux, H.** (1975) *Histoire de la France Rurale.* Tome 2, *L'Âge Classique des Paysans, de 1340 à 1789* (Paris: Seuil).
Leslie, G. R. and **Richardson, A. H.** (1961) 'Life-cycle, career pattern, and the decision to move', *American Sociological Review*, **26**, pp. 894–902.
Levine, N. (1973) 'Old culture – new culture: a study of migrants in Ankara', *Social Forces*, **51**, pp. 355–68.
Lieber, S. R. (1978) 'Place utility and migration', *Geografiska Annaler* **60B**, pp. 16–27.
Lindberg, J. S. (1930) *The Background of Swedish Emigration to the United States* (Minneapolis: Minnesota U.P.).
Locoh, T. (1970) 'La population des ménages agricoles. Emigration et vieillissement. Résultats depuis 1962 et perspectives jusqu'en 1975', *Population*, **25**, pp. 497–516.
Lowenthal, D. and **Comitas, L.** (1962) 'Emigration and depopulation: some neglected aspects of population geography', *Geographical Review*, **52**, pp. 195–210.
Mabogunje, A. (1970) 'Systems approach to a theory of rural–urban migration', *Geographical Analysis*, **2**, pp. 1–18.
McDonald, J. R. (1969) 'Labor immigration in France, 1946–1965', *Annals, Association of American Geographers*, **59**, pp. 116–34.
McGee, T. G. (1971) *The Urbanization Process in the Third World: Explorations in Search of a Theory* (London: Bell).
McKenzie, D. F. (1958) 'Apprenticeship in the Stationers Company, 1550–1640', *The Library*, **13**, pp. 292–8.
Malthus, T. R. (1798) *An Essay on the Principle of Population*, reprinted for the Royal Economic Society, 1926 (London: Macmillan).
Mannucci, C. (1970) 'Emigrants in the Upper Milanese area', in Jansen, C. J. (ed.) *Readings in the Sociology of Migration*, pp. 257–67 (Oxford: Pergamon).
Marble, D. F. and **Nystuen, J. D.** (1963) 'An approach to the direct measurement of community mean information fields', *Papers and Proceedings, Regional Science Association*, **11**, pp. 99–109.
Martine, G. (1975) 'Volume, characteristics and consequences of internal migration in Colombia', *Demography*, **12**, pp. 193–208.
Masser, I. and **Gould, W. T. S.** (1975) *Inter-Regional Migration in Tropical Africa*, Special Publication No. 8, Institute of British Geographers.
Mathieu, N. (1974) 'Quelques aspects principaux des transformations récentes de la structure sociale dans les campagnes françaises', *Geographia Polonica*, **29**, pp. 169–80.
Mathur, A. (1964) 'The anatomy of disguised unemployment', *Oxford Economic Papers*, **16**, pp. 161–93.
Meinig, D. W. (1965) 'The Mormon culture region: strategies and patterns in the geography of the American West, 1847–1964', *Annals, Association of American Geographers*, **55**, pp. 191–220.
Mendras, H. (1958) *Les Paysans et la Modernisation de l'Agriculture* (Paris: Centre National de la Recherche Scientifique).
Mendras, H. (1967) *La Fin des Paysans: Innovation et Changement dans l'Agriculture Française* (Paris: Sédéis).
Merlin, P. (1971) *L'Exode Rural*, Cahier de l'I.N.E.D. No. 59 (Paris: P.U.F.).
Michelson, W. (1977) *Environmental Choice, Human Behavior, and Residential Satisfaction* (New York: Oxford U.P.).
Middleton, J. F. M. (1960) 'The Lugbara', in Richards, A. I. (ed.), *East African Chiefs*, pp. 326–43 (London: Faber).
Miller, E. (1972) 'A note on the role of distance in migration: costs of mobility versus intervening opportunity', *Journal of Regional Science*, **12**, pp. 475–8.
Miller, E. E. (1964) 'The English economy in the thirteenth century: implications of recent research', *Past and Present*, **28**, pp. 21–40.
Milward, A. S. and **Saul, S. B.** (1973) *The Economic Development of Continental Europe, 1780–1870* (London: Allen and Unwin).
Minami, R. (1961) 'An analysis of Malthus' population theory', *Journal of Economic Behaviour*, **1**, pp. 53–63.
Miracle, M. P. and **Berry, S. A.** (1970) 'Migrant labour and economic development', *Oxford Economic Papers*, **22**, pp. 86–109.
Mitchell, J. C. (1956) 'Urbanisation, detribalisation and stabilisation in Southern Africa: a problem

of definition and measurement', in Forde, D. (ed.), *Social Implications of Industralisation and Urbanisation in Africa South of the Sahara*, pp. 693–711 (Paris: UNESCO).

Mitchell, J. C. (1961) 'Wage labour and African population movements in Central Africa', in Barbour, K. M. and Prothero, R. M. (eds), *Essays on Africa Populations*, pp. 193–248 (London: Routledge and Kegan Paul).

Mitchell, J. C. (1969) 'Tribe and social change in South Central Africa: a situational approach', *Journal of Asian and African Studies*, 5, pp. 83–125.

Moes, J. E. (1958) 'A dynamic interpretation of Malthus' principle of population', *Kyklos*, 11, pp. 58–83.

Moir, H. (1976) 'Relationships between urbanization levels and the industrial structure of the labour force', *Economic Development and Cultural Change*, 25, pp. 123–35.

Molohan, M. J. B. (1957) *Detribalisation* (Dar es Salaam: Government Printer).

Morel, A. (1972) 'L'espace social d'un village picard', *Études Rurales*, 45, pp. 62–80.

Morrill, R. L. (1963) 'The distribution of migration distances', *Papers and Proceedings, Regional Science Association*, 11, pp. 75–84.

Morrill, R. L. (1965) *Migration and the Spread and Growth of Urban Settlement*, Lund Studies in Geography, 26B (Lund: Gleerup).

Morrill, R. L. and Pitts, F. R. (1967) 'Marriage, migration and the mean information field: a study in uniqueness and generality', *Annals, Association of American Geographers*, 57, pp. 401–22.

Murton, B. J. (1972) 'Some aspects of the cognitive–behavioural approach to environments: a review', *New Zealand Journal of Geography*, 53, pp. 1–8.

Ng, R. C. Y. (1975) 'Internal migration in south east Asian countries', in Kosiński, L. and Prothero, R. M. (eds), *People on the Move*, pp. 181–92 (London: Methuen).

North, D. C. and Thomas, R. P. (1973) *The Rise of the Western World: A New Economic History* (Cambridge: Cambridge U.P.).

Nystuen, J. D. and Dacey, M. F. (1961) 'A graph theory interpretation of nodal regions', *Papers and Proceedings, Regional Science Association*, 7, pp. 30–42.

Odell, P. R. and Preston, D. A. (1973) *Economies and Societies in Latin America: A Geographical Interpretation* (London: Wiley).

Ogden, P. E. (1973) *Marriage Patterns and Population Mobility: A Study in Rural France*, Research Paper No. 7, School of Geography, University of Oxford.

Ogden, P. E. (1974) 'Expression spatiale des contacts humains et changement de la société: l'exemple de l'Ardèche, 1860–1970', *Revue de Géographie de Lyon*, 49, pp. 191–209.

Ogden, P. E. (1975a) 'France from Waterloo to World War II. 2: Empty France', *Geographical Magazine*, 48, pp. 94–7.

Ogden, P. E. (1975b) *Demographic Change and Population Mobility in the Eastern Massif Central, 1861–1971*, Unpublished D. Phil. thesis, University of Oxford.

Ogden, P. E. and Winchester, S. W. C. (1975) 'The residential segregation of provincial migrants in Paris in 1911', *Transactions, Institute of British Geographers*, 65, pp. 29–44.

Oliver, F. R. (1964) 'Inter-regional migration and unemployment, 1951–61', *Journal, Royal Statistical Society*, 127A, pp. 42–75.

Olsson, G. (1965) 'Distance and human interaction: a migration study', *Geografiska Annaler*, 47B, pp. 3–43.

Olsson, G. (1970) 'Explanation, prediction and meaning variance: an assessment of distance interaction models', *Economic Geography*, 46, pp. 223–33.

Ominde, S. H. (1968) *Land and Population Movements in Kenya* (London: Heinemann).

Osborne, H. (1964) *Bolivia: A Land Divided*, (Oxford: Oxford U.P.).

Pahl, R. E. (1965) *Urbs in Rure: The Metropolitan Fringe in Hertfordshire*, Geographical Papers No. 2, London School of Economics.

Pahl, R. E. (1966) 'The rural–urban continuum', *Sociologia Ruralis*, 6, pp. 299–329.

Pahl, R. E. (1970a) *Whose City?* (London: Longman).

Pahl, R. E. (1970b) 'Introduction: minorities in European cities', *New Atlantis*, 2, pp. 5–11.

Paillat, P. (1976) 'Le vieillissement de la France rurale. Intensité, évolution, diffusion et typologie', *Population*, 31, pp. 1147–88.

Paine, S. (1974) *Exporting Workers: The Turkish Case* (Cambridge: Cambridge U.P.).

Patten, J. (1973) *Rural–Urban Migration in Pre-Industrial England*, Research Paper No. 6, School of Geography, University of Oxford.

Peach, G. C. K. (1968) *West Indian Migration to Britain* (Oxford: Oxford U.P.).

Peach, G. C. K. (ed.) (1975) *Urban Social Segregation* (London: Longman).

Peláes, C. and Martine, G. (1974) 'Population trends in the 1960's: some implications for development', *Economic Bulletin for Latin America*, 19, pp. 95–126.

Pérez-Díaz, V. M. (1973) 'Processus de changement dans les communautés rurales de Castille', *Études Rurales*, 51, pp. 7–26.

Pérez-Díaz, V. M. (1974) *Pueblos y Clases Sociales en el Campo Español* (Madrid: Siglo XXI De España).

Perry, P. J. (1969) 'Working class isolation and mobility in rural Dorset, 1837–1936. A study of marriage distances', *Transactions, Institute of British Geographers*, 46, pp. 121–41.

Peters, G. L. (1976) 'The sex selectivity of out-migration: an Appalachian example', *Yearbook, Association of Pacific Coast Geographers*, **38**, pp. 99–109.

Petersen, W. (1958) 'A general typology of migration', *American Sociological Review*, **23**, pp. 256–66.

Peterson, G. L. (1967) 'A model of preference: quantitative analysis of the perception of the visual appearance of residential neighbourhoods', *Journal of Regional Science*, **7**, pp. 19–31.

Pinchemel, P. (1957) *Structures Sociales et Dépopulation Rurale de la Plaine Picarde de 1836 à 1936* (Paris: A. Colin).

Pitié, J. (1971) *Exode Rural et Migrations Intérieures en France: l'Exemple de la Vienne et du Poitou-Charentes* (Poitiers: Éditions Norois).

Pollard, S. (1959) *A History of Labour in Sheffield* (Liverpool: Liverpool U.P.).

Pollock, N. C. and **Agnew, S.** (1963) *An Historical Geography of South Africa* (London: Longman).

Pooley, C. G. (1977) 'The residential segregation of migrant communities in mid-Victorian Liverpool', *Transactions, Institute of British Geographers*, New Series, **2**, pp. 364–82.

Porter, R. (1956) 'An approach to migration through its mechanism', *Geografiska Annaler*, **38**, pp. 317–43.

Potrykowska, A. (1975) 'Morocco', in Jones, R. (ed.), *Essays in World Urbanization*, pp. 324–30 (London: Philip).

Pounds, N. J. G. (1973) *An Historical Geography of Europe, 450 B.C. –A.D. 1330* (Cambridge: Cambridge U.P.).

Pounds, N. J. G. (1974) *An Economic History of Medieval Europe* (London: Longman).

Pourcher, G. (1964) *Le Peuplement de Paris. Origine Régionale. Composition Sociale. Attitudes et Motivations*, Cahier de l'I.N.E.D. No. 43 (Paris: P.U.F.).

Preston, D. A. (1969) 'Rural emigration in Andean America', *Human Organization*, **28**, pp. 279–87.

Prothero, R. M. (1964) 'Continuity and change in African population mobility', in Steel, R. W. and Prothero, R. M. (eds), *Geographers and the Tropics: Liverpool Essays*, pp. 189–214 (London: Longman).

Prothero, R. M. (1968) 'Migration in tropical Africa', in Caldwell, J. C. and Okonjo, C. (eds), *The Population of Tropical Africa*, pp. 250–63 (London: Longman).

Pryor, R. J. (1969) '"Laws of Migration"? – the experience of Malaysia and other countries', *Geographica* (Kuala Lumpur), **5**, pp. 65–76.

Puls, W. W. (1975) 'Gastarbeiter oder Einwanderer?', *Geographische Rundschau*, **2**, pp. 49–60.

Rabut, O. (1973) 'Les étrangers en France', *Population*, **28**, pp. 620–49.

Rambaud, P. (1962) *Économie et Sociologie de la Montagne, Albiez-le-Vieux en Maurienne* (Paris: A. Colin).

Rambaud, P. (1969) *Société Rurale et Urbanisation* (Paris: Seuil).

Ramsøy, N. R. (1966) 'Assortive mating and the structure of cities', *American Sociological Review*, **31**, pp. 773–86.

Ravenstein, E. G. (1876) 'Census of the British Isles, 1871: birthplaces and migration', *Geographical Magazine*, **3**, pp. 173–7, 201–6, 229–33.

Ravenstein, E. G. (1885) 'The laws of migration', *Journal, Statistical Society*, **48**, pp. 167–235.

Ravenstein, E. G. (1889) 'The laws of migration', *Journal, Statistical Society*, **52**, pp. 214–301.

Redford, A. (1926) *Labour Migration in England, 1800–1850*, 3rd edition revised by Chaloner, W. H., published 1976 (Manchester: Manchester U.P.).

Rees, P. H. and **Wilson, A. G.** (1973) 'Accounts and models for spatial demographic analysis. 1: aggregate population', *Environment and Planning*, **5**, pp. 61–90.

Rees, P. H. and **Wilson, A. G.** (1975) 'Accounts and models for spatial demographic analysis. 2: rates and life tables', *Environment and Planning*, **7**, pp. 199–231.

Reiter, R. R. (1972) 'Modernization in the south of France: the village and beyond', *Anthropological Quarterly*, **45**, pp. 35–53.

Reynier, E. (1934) *Le Pays de Vivarais* (Valence: Impr. de Charpin et Reyne).

Richards, A. I. (ed.) (1954) *Economic Development and Tribal Change: A Study of Immigrant Labour in Buganda* (Cambridge: Heffer).

Richards, A. I. (1969) *The Multicultural States of East Africa* (Montreal: McGill-Queen's U.P.).

Richmond, A. H. (1968) 'Return migration from Canada to Britain', *Population Studies*, **22**, pp. 263–71.

Riddell, J. B. (1970a) 'On structuring a migration model', *Geographical Analysis*, **2**, pp. 403–9.

Riddell, J. B. (1970b) *The Spatial Dynamics of Modernisation in Sierra Leone: Structure, Diffusion and Response* (Evanston: Northwestern U.P.).

Rieger, J. H. (1972) 'Geographic mobility and the occupational attainment of rural youth: a longitudinal evaluation', *Rural Sociology*, **37**, pp. 189–207.

Riemann, F. (1975) 'Konsequenzen für den ländlichen Raum aus der rückläufigen Bevölkerungszahl', *Raumforschung und Raumordnung*, **33**, pp. 163–8.

Rizvi, S. M. H. (1973) 'Disguised unemployment – an over-all view', *International Journal of Agrarian Affairs*, **5**, pp. 430–57.

Robertson, W. C. (1939) 'Population and agriculture with special reference to agricultural overpopulation', in International Institute of Agriculture, *Documentation for the European Conference on Rural Life*, pp. 11–70 (Rome: League of Nations).

Robinson, W. C. (1964) 'The development of modern population theory', *American Journal of Economics and Sociology*, **23**, pp. 375–92.

Robinson, W. C. (1969) 'Types of disguised rural unemployment and some policy implications', *Oxford Economic Papers*. **21**, pp. 373–86.

Robson, B. T. (1973) 'A view on the urban scene', in Chisholm, M. and Rodgers, H. B. (eds), *Studies in Human Geography*, pp. 203–41 (London: Heinemann).

Rochas, J. (1977) 'Aménager le territoire – avec quels hommes? Richesses et contraintes démographiques', *Economie Rurale*, **118**, pp. 14–22.

Roseman, C. C. (1971) 'Migration as a spatial and temporal process', *Annals, Association of American Geographers*, **61**, pp. 589–98.

Rossi, P. H. (1955) *Why Families Move: A Study of the Social Psychology of Urban Residential Mobility* (New York: Free Press).

Rougier, H. (1977) 'Les migrations des Valser au Moyen-Age et leurs effets sur le paysage (Grisons, Suisse)', *Bulletin de l'Association de Géographes Français*, **439–40**, pp. 33–42.

Roussel, L. (1970) 'Measuring rural–urban drift in developing countries: a suggested method', *International Labour Review*, **101**, pp. 229–46.

Royle, S. A. (1977) 'Social stratification from early census returns: a new approach', *Area*, **9**, pp. 215–19.

Rudé, G. (1978) *Protest and Punishment: The Story of the Social and Political Protesters Transported to Australia, 1788–1868* (Oxford: Clarendon Press).

Ruiz, P. M. (1972) 'Notas sobre el éxodo rural y la evolución de la población en una comarca de Tierra de Campos', *Revista de Estudios Agro-Sociales,* **21**, pp. 23–60.

Russell, J. C. (1959) 'Medieval midland and northern migration to London', *Speculum*, **34**, pp. 641–5.

Russell, J. C. (1972) 'Population in Europe, 500–1500', in Cipolla, C. M. (ed.), *The Fontana Economic History of Europe: The Middle Ages*, pp. 25–70 (London: Collins/Fontana).

Saarinen, T. F. (1966) *Perception of the Drought Hazard on the Great Plains*, Research Paper No. 106, Department of Geography, University of Chicago.

Salt, J. and **Clout, H. D.** (eds) (1976) *Migration in Post-War Europe: Geographical Essays* (Oxford: Oxford U.P.).

Samuel, R. (1977) 'The workshop of the world: steam power and hand technology in mid-Victorian Britain', *History Workshop*, **3**, pp. 6–72.

Sauvy, A. (1969) *General Theory of Population* (London: Weidenfeld and Nicolson).

Saville, J. (1957) *Rural Depopulation in England and Wales, 1851–1951* (London: Routledge and Kegan Paul).

Schenk, W. (1975) 'Ausländer, insbesonders ausländiche Arbeitsnehmer, in der Altstadt von Nürnberg', *Nürnberger Wirtschafts- und Sozialgeographische Arbeiten*, **24**, pp. 221–34.

Schnapper, D. (1976) 'Tradition culturelle et appartenance sociale: émigrés italiens et migrants français dans la région parisienne', *Revue Française de Sociologie*, **17**, pp. 485–98.

Schnore, L. F. (1964) 'Urban structure and suburban selectivity', *Demography*, **1**, pp. 164–76.

Schofield, R. S. (1970) 'Age-specific mobility in an eighteenth century rural English parish', *Annales de Démographie Historique*, **6**, pp. 261–74.

Schofield, R. S. (1972) 'Sampling in historical research', in Wrigley, E. A. (ed.), *Nineteenth Century Society*, pp. 146–90 (Cambridge: Cambridge U.P.).

Schultz, T. P. (1971) 'Rural–urban migration in Colombia', *Review of Economics and Statistics*, **53**, pp. 157–63.

Schulze, R., Artis, J. and **Beegle, J. A.** (1963) 'The measurement of community satisfaction and the decision to migrate', *Rural Sociology*, **28**, pp. 279–83.

Schwind, P. J. (1971) *Migration and Regional Development in the United States, 1950–1960*, Research Paper No. 133, Department of Geography, University of Chicago.

Selke, W. (1974) 'Regionale Prognosen der Ausländerwanderung in der Bundesrepublik Deutschland und Möglichkeiten ihrer Steuerung', *Informationen zur Raumentwicklung*, **2**, pp. 39–48.

Semmings, I. (1960) 'Norwegian emigration in the nineteenth century', *Scandinavian Economic History Review*, **8**, pp. 150–74.

Sen, S. (1974) *A Richer Harvest: New Horizons for Developing Countries* (New Delhi: Tata McGraw-Hill).

Sen Gupta, P. (1970) 'Population and resource development in India', in Zelinsky, W., Kosiński, L. and Prothero, R. M. (eds), *Geography and a Crowding World*, pp. 424–41 (New York: Oxford U.P.).

Shanin, T. (ed.) (1971) *Peasants and Peasant Societies* (Harmondsworth: Penguin).

Shannon, H. A. and **Grebenik, E.** (1943) *The Population of Bristol*, Occasional Paper No. 11, National Institute of Economic and Social Research, Cambridge.

Shaw, M. (1977) 'The ecology of social change: Wolverhampton, 1851–1871', *Transactions, Institute of British Geographers*, New Series, **2**, pp. 332–48.

Shryock, H. S. and **Larmon, E. A.** (1965) 'Some longitudinal data on internal migration', *Demography*, **2**, pp. 579–92.

Siegel, S. (1956) *Non-Parametric Statistics for the Behavioural Sciences* (New York: McGraw-Hill).

Siegfried, A. (1949) *Géographie Électorale de l'Ardèche sous la IIIe République*, Cahier de la F.N.S.P. No. 9 (Paris: A. Colin).

Simkins, P. D. (1970) 'Migration as a response to population pressure: the case of the Philippines', in Zelinsky, W., Kosiński, L. and Prothero, R. M. (eds), *Geography and a Crowding World*, pp. 259–68 (New York: Oxford U.P.).

Simmons, J. W. (1968) 'Changing residence in the city: a review of intra-urban mobility', *Geographical Review*, **58**, pp. 622–51.

Sinha, J. A. (1976) 'Population and agriculture', in Tabah, I. L. (ed.), *Population Growth and Economic Development in the Third World*, Vol. 1, pp. 251–305 (Dolhain: Ordina Editions).

Sjaastad, L. A. (1962) 'The costs and returns of human migration', *Journal of Political Economy*, **70**, pp. 80–93.

Smith, C. T. (1971) 'The Central Andes', in Blakemore, H. and Smith, C. T. (eds), *Latin America: Geographical Perspectives*, pp. 263–334 (London: Methuen).

Smout, T. C. (1974) 'The lessons of Norwegian agrarian history: a review article', *Scottish Historical Review*, **53**, pp. 69–76.

Sonnenfeld, J. (1967) 'Environmental perception and adaptation level in the Arctic', in Lowenthal, D. (ed.), *Environmental Perception and Behavior*, pp. 42–59, Research Paper No. 109, Department of Geography, University of Chicago.

Southall, A. W. (1954) 'Alur migrants', in Richards, A. I. (ed.), *Economic Development and Tribal Change: A Study of Immigrant Labour in Buganda*, pp. 141–60 (Cambridge: Heffer).

Southall, A. W. (1961) 'Population movements in East Africa', in Barbour, K. M. and Prothero, R. M. (eds), *Essays on African Populations*, pp. 157–92 (Oxford: Oxford U.P.).

Southall, A. W. (1967) 'The demographic and social effects of migration on the populations of East Africa', *Proceedings of the World Population Conference, Belgrade, 30 August–10 September 1965*, Vol. 4, pp. 235–8 (New York: United Nations).

Southall, A. W. (ed.) (1971) *Social Change in Modern Africa* (Oxford: Oxford U.P.).

Speare, A. (1970) 'Home ownership, life cycle stage, and residential mobility', *Demography*, **7**, pp. 449–58.

Speare, A. (1971) 'A cost–benefit model of rural to urban migration in Taiwan', *Population Studies*, **25**, pp. 117–30.

Speare, A. (1974) 'Urbanization and migration in Taiwan', *Economic Development and Cultural Change*, **22**, pp. 302–19.

Speare, A., Goldstein, S. and Frey, W. H. (1974) *Residential Mobility, Migration and Metropolitan Growth* (Cambridge, Mass.: Bellinger Publishing).

Spencer, J. E. and Thomas, W. L. (1978) *Introducing Cultural Geography*, 2nd edition (New York: Wiley).

Stedman Jones, G. (1971) *Outcast London* (Oxford: Oxford U.P.).

Stoltman, J. P. and Ball, J. M. (1970) 'Migration and the local economic factor in rural Mexico', *Human Organization*, **30**, pp. 47–56.

Stouffer, S. A. (1940) 'Intervening opportunities: a theory relating mobility and distance', *American Sociological Review*, **5**, pp. 845–67.

Stouffer, S. A. (1960) 'Intervening opportunities and competing migrants', *Journal of Regional Science*, **2**, pp. 1–26.

Sutcliffe, A. and Smith, R. (1974) *History of Birmingham*, Vol. 3: *Birmingham, 1939–1970* (Oxford: Oxford U.P.).

Sutter, J. (1958) 'Évolution de la distance séparant les domiciles des futurs époux (Loir-et-Cher 1870–1954, Finistère 1911–1953)', *Population*, **13**, pp. 227–58.

Sutter, J. and Goux, J. M. (1962) 'Évolution de la consanguinité en France de 1926 à 1958 avec des données récentes détaillées', *Population*, **17**, pp. 683–702.

Taeuber, K. E. (1961) 'Duration of residence analysis of internal migration in the United States', *Milbank Memorial Fund Quarterly*, **34**, pp. 116–31.

Taeuber, K. E. (1966) 'Cohort migration', *Demography*, **3**, pp. 416–22.

Taeuber, K. E., Haenszel, W. and Sirken, M. G. (1961) 'Residence histories and exposure residences for the United States population', *Journal, American Statistical Association*, **56**, pp. 824–34.

Taeuber, K. E. and Taeuber, A. F. (1964) 'White migration and socio-economic differences between cities and suburbs', *American Sociological Review*, **29**, pp. 718–29.

Tannous, A. I. (1942) 'Emigration, a force of social change in an Arab village', *Rural Sociology*, **7**, pp. 62–74.

Taylor, P. J. (1971) 'Distance transformation and distance decay functions', *Geographical Analysis*, **3**, pp. 221–38.

Taylor, P. J. (1975) *Distance Decay in Spatial Interactions*, Concepts and Techniques in Modern Geography No. 2 (Norwich: GeoAbstracts).

Teitelbaum, M. (1974) 'Population and development: is a concensus possible?', *Foreign Affairs*, **52**, pp. 742–60.

Thomas, B. (1954) *Migration and Economic Growth: A Study of Great Britain and the Atlantic Economy* (Cambridge: Cambridge U.P.).

Thomas, B. (1962) 'Wales and the Atlantic economy', in Thomas, B. (ed.), *The Welsh Economy: Studies in Expansion*, pp. 1–29 (Cardiff: University of Wales Press).

Thomas, B. (1972) *Migration and Urban Development* (London: Methuen).

Thomas, D. S. (1941) *Social and Economic Aspects of Swedish Population Movements, 1750–1933* (New York: Macmillan).

Thomas, J. G. (1972) 'Population changes and the provision of services', in Ashton, J. and Long, W. H. (eds), *The Remoter Rural Areas of Britain*, pp. 91–106 (Edinburgh: Oliver and Boyd).

Thomas, R. N. (1971) 'Internal migration in Latin America: an analysis of recent literature', in Lentnek, B., Carmin, R. L. and Martinson, T. L. (eds), *Geographic Research on Latin America: Benchmark 1970*, pp. 104–18. (Muncie, Indiana: Ball State University).

Thompson, E. P. (1968) *The Making of the English Working Class* (Harmondsworth: Penguin).

Tillott, P. M. (1972) 'Sources of inaccuracy in the 1851 and 1861 censuses', in Wrigley, E. A. (ed.), *Nineteenth Century Society*, pp. 82–133 (Cambridge: Cambridge U.P.).

Tinkler, K. J. (1970) 'Perception and prejudice: student preferences for employment and residence in Uganda', in Tinkler, K. J. and Funnell, D. C. (eds), *Perception and Nodality in Uganda*, pp. 1–25, Occasional Paper No. 15, Department of Geography, Makerere University.

Toney, M. B. (1973) 'Religious preference and migration', *International Migration Review*, **7**, pp. 281–8.

Tranter, N. (1973) *Population Since the Industrial Revolution: The Case of England and Wales* (London: Croom Helm).

Tugault, Y. (1973) *La Mesure de la Mobilité. Cinq Études sur les Migrations Internes*, Cahier de l'I.N.E.D. No. 67 (Paris: P.U.F.).

United Nations (1954) *Progress in Land Reform* (New York: United Nations, Department of Economic Affairs).

United Nations (1968) *Urbanization: Development Policies and Planning* (New York: United Nations).

United Nations (1971) *Monthly Bulletin of Statistics*, November.

United Nations (1973) *The Determinants and Consequences of Population Trends: New Summary of Findings on Interaction of Demographic, Economic and Social Factors*, Population Studies No. 50 (New York: United Nations, Department of Economic and Social Affairs).

United Nations (1974) *Demographic Yearbook, 1973* (New York: United Nations).

Vries, J. de (1974) *The Dutch Rural Economy in the Golden Age, 1500–1700* (New Haven: Yale U.P.).

Vries, J. de (1976) *The Economy of Europe in an Age of Crisis, 1600–1750* (Cambridge: Cambridge U.P.).

Walle, E. van de (1972) 'Implications of increases in rural density', in Ominde, S. H. and Ejiogu, C. N. (eds), *Population Growth and Economic Development in Africa*, pp. 117–22 (London: Heinemann).

Weber, A. F. (1963) *The Growth of Cities in the Nineteenth Century: A Study in Statistics*, (Ithaca, N.Y.: Cornell U.P.).

Weber, E. (1977) *Peasants into Frenchmen: The Modernization of Rural France, 1870–1914* (London: Chatto and Windus).

West Midlands Regional Study (1971) *A Developing Strategy for the West Midlands* (Birmingham).

White, P. E. (1974) *The Social Impact of Tourism on Host Communities: A Study of Language Change in Switzerland*, Research Paper No. 9, School of Geography, University of Oxford.

Willis, K. G. (1974) *Problems in Migration Analysis* (Farnborough: Saxon House).

Willis, K. G. (1975) 'Regression models of migration: an econometric reappraisal of some techniques', *Geografiska Annaler*, **57B**, pp. 42–54.

Wilson, A. G. (1970) *Entropy in Urban and Regional Modelling* (London: Pion).

Wolpert, J. (1965) 'Behavioral aspects of the decision to migrate', *Papers and Proceedings, Regional Science Association*, **15**, pp. 159–69.

Wolpert, J. (1966) 'Migration as an adjustment to environmental stress', *Journal of Social Issues*, **22**, pp. 92–102.

Wolpert, J. (1967) 'Distance and directional bias in inter-urban migratory streams', *Annals, Association of American Geographers*, **57**, pp. 605–16.

Wood, L. J. (1970) 'Perception studies in geography', *Transactions, Institute of British Geographers*, **50**, pp. 129–42.

Woodham-Smith, C. (1962) *The Great Hunger, Ireland 1845–49* (London: Hamilton).

Woods, R. I. (1967) 'Aspects of the scale problem in the calculation of segregation indices: London and Birmingham, 1961 and 1971', *Tijdschrift voor Economische en Sociale Geografie*, **67**, pp. 169–74.

Woods, R. I. (1979) *Population Analysis in Geography* (London: Longman).

Wright, G. (1964) *Rural Revolution in France. The Peasantry in the Twentieth Century* (Stanford, California: Stanford U.P.).

Wrigley, E. A. (1966) 'Family limitation in pre-industrial England', *Economic History Review*, 2nd Series, **19**, pp. 82–109.

Wrigley, E. A. (1967) 'A simple model of London's importance in changing English society and economy, 1650–1750', *Past and Present*, **37**, pp. 44–70.

Wylie, L. (1957) *Village in the Vaucluse* (Cambridge, Mass.: Harvard U.P.).

Wylie, L. (ed.) (1966) *Chanzeaux. A Village in Anjou* (Cambridge, Mass.: Harvard U.P.).

Wylie, L. *et al.* (1968) 'Habitat et migrations à Chanzeaux (Maine et Loir)', *Études Rurales*, **29**, pp. 62–102.

Yannopoulos, G. N. (1971) 'Economic integration and labour movements with reference to the EEC countries', in Denton, G. R. (ed.), *Economic Integration in Europe*, 2nd edition, pp. 220–45 (London: Weidenfeld and Nicolson).

Zaidan, G. C. (1969) 'Population growth and economic development', *Finance and Development*, **1**, pp. 2–8.

Zeldin, T. (1973) *France, 1848–1945*, Vol. 1: *Love, Ambition and Politics* (Oxford: Oxford U.P.).

Zeldin, T. (1977) *France, 1848–1945*. Vol. 2: *Intellect, Taste and Anxiety*, (Oxford: Oxford U.P.).

Zelinsky, W. (1971) 'The hypothesis of the mobility transition', *Geographical Review*, **61**, pp. 219–49.

Zondag, C. H. (1966) *The Bolivian Economy, 1952–65: The Revolution and Its Aftermath* (New York: Praeger).

Index